THE CIVIL RIGHTS READER

The Civil Rights Reader

BASIC DOCUMENTS OF THE
CIVIL RIGHTS MOVEMENT

EDITED BY *Leon Friedman*

FOREWORD BY *Martin Duberman*

WALKER AND COMPANY NEW YORK

Revised 1968 Edition

Foreword, Introduction, compilation, bibliography, editorial
commentary Copyright © 1967, 1968 by Leon Friedman.

CONTENTS

Foreword

The documents in this collection are a reflection of the Second Reconstruction in American history. They record a constructive and hopeful period. For a brief time it looked as if white America was about to face up to the hollowness of its official morality, was ready at last to convert the ringing expressions of equality in our historic state papers into reality. We now know that such hopes were excessive. A history of the movement can now be charted because the movement itself is played out. The civil rights coalition is in disarray, the mood of the country has turned conservative, and the energies of the federal government have been diminished by its uncertain mandate and its own divided will. The accurate words *are* "played out," not "completed." Like the First Reconstruction of the 1860s, the second one of the 1960s has stopped tragically short of the hopes once held out for it.

I do not mean that nothing has been accomplished. Something has been, and those who deny any advance, falsify the evidence almost as much as those who claim we are already standing on Mt. Pisgah and in sight of the Promised Land. Still, the record of achievement, on balance, is depressingly slight.

First, there is the matter of public schools. It took ten years, following the Supreme Court decision of 1954, to place 2.5% of Negro children in the deep South in previously all-white schools. Then, from 1964-65, the figure shot up to about 12%. Recent gains are largely due to Title VI of the 1964 Civil Rights Act, which gave the federal government a new weapon to use against segregation: it allowed federal funds to be cut off from any program in which discrimination was found to exist.

But although the Department of Health, Education and Welfare has begun to employ Title VI against recalcitrant school boards, it has still not used it widely in other areas where segregation exists—hospitals, for example. David Sanford has pointed out (in the *New Republic* of August 27, 1966) that since 94.6% of all hospitals have been approved to participate in Medicare programs, the assumption is that they no longer discriminate, for in order to qualify they have had to file with HEW "assurances of compliance" with Title VI; in fact, Sanford argues, these "compliances" have thus far been "full of tokenism and gradualism."

Even in regard to the schools, the utilization of Title VI, while producing comparatively rapid progress in the last two years, has still not radically altered the existing pattern of segregation. A survey released by the Office of Education in July, 1966, shows that 80% of white children in first grade attend schools that are 90% or more white, while 65% of all Negro first-graders attend schools that are 90% Negro. And in five deep South states—Georgia, Alabama, South Carolina, Mississippi and Louisiana—resistance to desegregation is almost as strong as ever. In Mississippi, for example, as of December, 1966, there were still only 6,200 of the state's 312,000 Negro pupils attending integrated classes. Moreover, the quality of education in all-Negro schools everywhere remains inferior to that in white schools; the Office of Education survey reports that in the metropolitan Northeast, for example, the Negro student has (on the basis of standard achievement tests) by 12th grade fallen 3.3 years behind his white counterpart.

Even if the federal government *was* to combat school segregation to the full extent of its powers, the battle could not easily be won. In most urban centers it will be maintained simply because it is a direct reflection of residential segregation, which is itself on the increase. In 40 of the 45 largest Southern cities, the index of residential segregation has shown a net gain since 1940. In the North, as a Lou Harris poll released in *Newsweek* in August, 1966, reveals, 46% of the white population still objects to having a Negro family live next door (as do 69% of Southern whites). Moreover, touted urban renewal programs have done almost nothing to create racially integrated areas—the Negro ghetto has simply been removed to a new location. Only widespread busing can break the pattern of segregated schools, and resistance to that expedient is fierce.

Another obstacle to integration is a new phenomenon known as "segregation by flight"; that is, in order to avoid sending their children to desegregated schools, whites will either flee the city for a suburb or, alternatively, will enroll their children in parochial and private schools. The most notorious example is Washington, D.C., where 85% of public school students are now Negro. But the pattern is widespread in the North. In Philadelphia, to give another example, 57% of public school pupils (as of April, 1966) are now nonwhite in a city that is 70% white; indeed white enrollment is greater in Philadelphia's private schools than in the city's entire public school system.

The deep South continues to rely on the more traditional devices of economic and physical retaliation. Where public facilities have been formally desegregated, pressure has been exerted to prevent Negroes from utilizing those facilities. Usually the pressure is indirect: a hint is given to a Negro employee that his job depends on "keeping his place," or, as in Mississippi, a law is passed requiring that the names

x

of all applicants for voter registration be published in the local newspaper. Sometimes, of course, direct violence is used. In the deep South, "uppity" Negroes continue to be murdered—and under "mysterious circumstances" that defy investigation.

* * *

Turning from social to economic matters, the picture is even less reassuring. In June, 1966, the National Industrial Conference Board released a two-volume study of hiring attitudes and practices. It reveals that for the last decade the nonwhite unemployment rate has been more than double that of white workers. In 1955, it was 3.6% for whites, 7.9% for nonwhites; in 1964, it was 4.6% against 9.8%. Similar disparities show up in wage patterns. More than 50% of nonwhite males earn less than $3,000 a year, with the average Negro earning about half as much as the average white worker. It is true that opportunities have expanded for the small number of Negroes qualified for white collar employment, but the great mass of Negro workers holds unskilled or semi-skilled positions, and for these people, future prospects are dim. By 1970 our labor force will have been further swelled by the babies of the post-war "boom" who are now reaching employment age; at the same time, automation and technological advances will further shrink the number of available unskilled jobs. Thus while the tiny Negro middle class will continue to find unprecedented opportunities, the vast majority of Negro workers will find its economic position increasingly in jeopardy. As Daniel Moynihan has put it, "in terms of employment and income and occupational status, it is quite possible the Negro community is moving in two directions, or rather that two Negro communities are moving in opposite directions."

* * *

In the area of political rights there have been undeniable gains, though the Voting Rights Act of 1965 has not yet been used to its full potential. The provision that federal examiners can be sent into locales to accept applications to register where less than 50% of the qualified population was voting, has been used sparingly. Examiners have gone into a total of only 42 counties, though in many areas the registration figures are far below the designated 50%. Where examiners have been sent—mostly to Alabama, Mississippi and Louisiana—the increase in Negro voter registration has been impressive, demonstrating once again that limited progress in civil rights can be as much ascribed to a lack of implementation as to a lack of legislation.

As the number of Negro voters has increased, so, ironically, has the realization that the vote, once thought a panacea, in fact provides only limited leverage with which to exert pressure for change. It should be remembered that even if Negroes should some day vote in proportion to their numbers, their power will be small. Out of 1,139 Southern counties, for example, only 85 have Negro voting-age majorities—and not a single Congressional district has one. Even in those 85 counties a majority need not guarantee the success of Negro candidates at the polls—as the defeat of the Black Panther party in Lowndes County, Alabama, demonstrated in the election of November, 1966. Moreover, many of the basic ills from which the Negro suffers—inadequate housing, lack of job opportunities, inferior education—cannot be solved on the county level. These are national phenomena requiring national resources for their solution. Whether these resources will be allocated in sufficient amounts in turn depends on the strength of the civil rights coalition.

Yet here the prospects are unpromising. No new "populist" coalition of the underclasses and their sympathizers seems likely. Civil rights organizations are themselves divided and feuding, with SNCC and CORE increasingly committed to black nationalism and separatism. This development, in turn (along with riots like Watts and the feeling that the two recent civil rights bills have "solved the problem"), has led to a decline in white sympathy. Finally, those groups thought to be the likeliest candidates for a reform coalition are either politically impotent (like the campus activists of SDS—Students for a Democratic Society) or (like the organized labor movement) increasingly identified with the establishment. The defeat in Congress of the 1966 civil rights bill is only the most dramatic example of this loss of a national consensus over civil rights. The Lou Harris poll of August, 1966, shows that 63% of whites (as compared with 50% in 1963) now oppose even peaceful Negro demonstrations, while no less than 70% think the Negro "is trying to move too fast." The effect on the Negro community of this shift in white attitudes is to convince many that integration is either impossible or undesirable, to increase the apathy or anger which alternately displays itself in "dropping out" or in turning to the slogans of Black Power.

All of this is gloomy enough. Yet it is possible to hold to some measure of optimism, if only of the most cautious kind. It is at least true, for example, that the South is no longer a unit behind the doctrine of white supremacy. In a few states—notably Mississippi, Alabama, Georgia and Louisiana—the white majority remains overwhelmingly racist, but in others, like North Carolina and Tennessee, a pattern of real change can be detected. It is not change sufficiently great to allow for large-scale optimism; equality is hardly making giant strides.

Nor is it the stuff, God knows, of which moral revolutions are made—and ultimately nothing less than that is required. Yet if it turns out that we have *time* to await slow, piecemeal advances, they may yet, in their cumulative effect, produce that revolution.

A second cause for mild comfort is the Negro's own determination. Though the disappointments of the past few years have undoubtedly fostered additional cynicism and fear in the Negro community, much faith, remarkably, does seem to remain. Two out of three Negroes questioned by Lou Harris in his August, 1966, poll felt that life had improved for them since 1963, and the blandishments of Black Power, separatism, nationalism and violence continue to have only marginal appeal.

Finally, it is possible to argue that Northern whites have a deeper commitment to equality than they had during the First Reconstruction. This argument, to be sure, is highly vulnerable—as the figures in Lou Harris' poll make clear. Moreover, to the extent Northerners *have* been converted to egalitarianism, the conversion may be more rational and willed than emotional and felt. I am not sneering at this; if everyone in the country had arrived at at least an intellectual commitment to equality, we would be far better off than we are. But I do think it is important to keep in mind that on a visceral level, even many "liberals" are uncertain of their feelings and, because of that, cannot be excessively relied upon. Intellectually they may have outgrown the racist assumptions of their culture, may have become aware of the falsity and cruelty of those assumptions and disciplined themselves into acting accordingly. Yet—chiefly at an unconscious level—they cannot wholly root out some lingering anti-Negro sentiment. After all, in our racist culture, such feelings were ingested with our pablum and cannot be entirely exorcised simply by wishing to do so.

And we would be foolish to expect that they can be. This is a point worth stressing. We must not hold out the unrealistic hope that this generation can achieve true *feelings* of brotherhood; we will do well if we can bring it to *act* according to the principles of brotherhood. Perhaps some future generation, brought up in a more truthful and humane spirit will move beyond outward conformity to inner conviction. But the myths and assumptions of white supremacy are too central a part of our heritage to expect that, on a deep emotional level, we can wholly uproot them in a single generation.

To achieve even the limited goal of equality before the law, we must be prepared to exercise force. We must also be prepared, as a result, for a fair amount of social upheaval. Despite the powerful elements working against legal equality, there are grounds, as I have argued, for qualified optimism. But if racism is to be overcome, we must have not only additional legislation, but legislation actually enforced—unlike the record compiled with the acts of 1964 and 1965.

It is often argued that egalitarian legislation cannot be imposed upon an unwilling people. We can agree, of course, that it would be better if change came voluntarily; enforced legislation is not the ideal way. But given the lateness of the hour and the intransigence of the opposition, it is apparently the only way. It will be said in answer to this, that if change is imposed, it cannot produce lasting results; one cannot legislate against prejudice; stateways cannot change folkways. But this argument mistakes the primary intention of egalitarian legislation, which is aimed not at eradicating prejudice but at curtailing its outward expression. And this much legislation *can* do effectively (if enforced); it can insist that people obey the law, regardless of their feelings about that law. There is even evidence that in the long run legislation can affect the prejudice itself. As the psychologist Gordon Allport has argued, when you force a man to change his outward pattern of behavior, you may eventually change his inner attitudes and feelings. This is probably not true of what Allport calls "compulsive bigots." Such people must simply be forced to obey the law, we cannot hold out the hope that by so doing they will undergo an inner conversion as well.

I do not believe, however, that most white Americans are confirmed bigots—except in a few and increasingly isolated areas. Or perhaps it might be better put this way: I believe that the racial bigotry of most Americans is counterbalanced by their belief in Christian and democratic ethics, and the resulting tension between their prejudices and their values produces the guilt which can creatively respond to egalitarian legislation. For these Americans, their private consciences are at least partly in line with the legal prods being exerted upon them. Most Americans, after all, *have* been weaned on the precepts—or at least the slogans—of Christianity and democracy; that is, the idea that all men are brothers, that we should love one another, that every life has unique value and every man the natural right to make of his life what he can. These ideas conflict basically, disastrously, with racial intolerance. And somewhere most Americans know it. They try to bury the conflict between their practices and their values, but the conflict will not stay buried. When legislation is passed which forces them to honor their own democratic and Christian assumptions, to conform, as it were, to their better selves, they often greet the legislation with something like relief—that is, after an initial display of fury which is in part real, in part a concession to what they take to be local mores.

Much of what I have said about the prospects of achieving justice for Negro-Americans is highly problematical; speculations about the future always are. My own feelings waver very much between doubt and hope, sometimes coming down on the latter side, more often in recent months, on the former. It is true that there are signs of progress all around us, slow, agonizing progress. But progress—though American mythology dislikes dealing with this fact—is reversible (as the First Reconstruction proves). History is not the story of inevitable and continuing improvement, though Americans have a special fondness for that assumption because it helps to excuse them from active exertion in behalf of change.

We must be alert to the fact that the reform impulse can spend itself before reaching its goals, that a reverse trend can set in and erase previous gains. In 1967, as in 1877, there are again clear signs that such a trend has in fact begun. If it is not resisted, it may well accelerate. In short, we can hardly afford to rest on our laurels—pitiful as they are. If further gains toward racial equality are to come, they will result from hard work, not from reliance on the assumed benevolence of time and the Deity.

Martin Duberman
February 1, 1967

Introduction

The most important social upheaval in the United States during the past twenty years has been the civil rights movement. In terms of the magnitude and extent of the evils to be corrected, the number of persons directly affected, the courage of the leaders and participants, the concern felt by a national audience, and the corrective steps proposed or taken by both state and federal government, the effort to gain for the Negro the rights and benefits to which he is so clearly entitled has engaged the nation more than any other issue of our times.

Of course the evils have been with us for over a century. That serious action to correct them took place only after World War II is a result of the curious blend of conscience and politics that has governed much of the American experience. Negro groups, organized after the war by able and politically-aware leaders, claimed what was promised and due them under the Constitution. Their substantial contribution to the war gave the claim a moral justification that was all but impossible to ignore. C. Vann Woodward, in his perceptive book "The Strange Career of Jim Crow," points out that the fight against Hitler's racist ideology brought about a disaffection with the creed of white supremacy in force in the United States. American society, stirred at last by an awareness of what extreme racial feeling could lead to, began to take a fresh look at the state of its Negro population. At the same time, a great migration of Negroes from the South to the northern urban centers was taking place. The increased Negro population in the cities gave the Negro a political power which both major parties had to contend with.

These developments continued to be the most significant elements in the civil rights movement. In their southern campaigns, Negro leaders developed a political sophistication and a strategic brilliance that would be difficult to find duplicated in modern American politics. Time and time again they set goals that were so minimal, the right to them so well established, and the means of obtaining them so reasonable, that any refusal to grant them could not possibly be justified. When southern racists reacted as they did in Birmingham, St. Augustine, or Selma, the conscience of America was thoroughly aroused. Few were not affected in some way by the pictures of snarling dogs and firehoses in Birmingham, the beatings on the beach at St. Augustine, and the murders in Neshoba

County and Selma. Congressmen and Senators, no less than the man in the street, felt something had to be done.

The civil rights movement had two main thrusts from the beginning: a drive for liberty and a drive for equality. The division between the two was primarily geographic. In most northern areas Negroes could vote, their right to demonstrate or to assemble was unquestioned, and they enjoyed relative freedom from official interference with their rights. Injustices did exist, and a Negro's liberties in the North were not on the same level as those of a white man. But the distance between Negro and white in the North—at least in the area of rights—was far less than the distance between them in the southern states.

Thus the main force of the civil rights movement in the South was to win the basic rights of citizenship. The civil rights movement in the North, however, focused on the drive for equality: an effort was made to make available to Negroes what Daniel Moynihan has called "the full range of American economic, social and political life and . . . a fully comparable share of the successes, no less than . . . of the small winners and of the outright failures." That drive aimed at the Negro being given not merely an equal opportunity, but actually obtaining an equal social and economic status with his white brothers. Thus, the fight in the South was primarily a fight by the politically and legally enslaved; the fight in the North was (and is) by the poor.

The nature of each drive was also quite different. In the South the goals were specific, quantitative and personalized. It was possible to start a campaign to register a definite number of voters in one particular county within a limited time period, or to remove a notoriously bad sheriff or police chief. But— aside from problems of union discrimination —where or how or against whom does one begin a campaign to increase Negro employment? How does one measure whether a Negro child in Harlem has received the quality of education that is due him? Who is the enemy when a Negro family is evicted from its home in a city to make way for new luxury apartments? The problems are too diffuse to be encompassed in single campaigns and the evil is too institutionalized to be susceptible of swift and definite defeat. The problems in the North are built into the very structure of society and cannot be dealt with by single blows.

The division between the two drives has also been one of time. At first the South occupied almost the entire stage. Only in 1965 did Martin Luther King begin to spend more of his time in Chicago or Cleveland than in Selma or Hattiesburg. Many of the other civil rights leaders concerned themselves increasingly with the situation in northern cities.

xviii

Congress also shifted its attention from the southern Negro's rights to the northern Negro's economic status.

The shift was inevitable, but it did not mean that the fight for liberty in the South had been won. As late as November, 1966 a Negro arrested for drunkenness in a small Alabama town could still be beaten to death in jail. When the television cameras and newsmen departed from St. Augustine, Florida in 1964, and from Selma in 1965, the pattern of life returned very much to what it had always been. In many—but not all—rural counties in Mississippi, Alabama and Georgia where no significant civil rights movement had ever taken place, the day-to-day existence of the Negro continued as in the past. The 1966 Civil Rights Bill contained important provisions to improve the southern jury system and thus to insure more equal justice for the Negro. Unfortunately, because it was coupled with a drive for open housing provisions in the North, the provision was not enacted into law.

Both drives are equally important and progress in the first area, though by no means complete, has not been matched in the other. Rashi Fein writes that things look different depending not only upon where you stand but also upon where you look. Bayard Rustin, looking to the North, has recently pointed out that: "The day-to-day lot of the ghetto has not been improved by the various judicial and legislative measures of the past decade." Rustin notes that more Negroes are unemployed today than in 1954; the gap between the wages of the Negro worker and the white worker is wider; and while the unemployment rate among white youths is decreasing, the rate among Negro youths has increased. In 1966, 65% of first grade Negro students in the country as a whole attended schools that were from 90% to 100% black. Obviously there was still much to do in all areas.

The triumphs and courage, the drama and emotion, as well as the deaths and defeats in the movement have been captured in the documents collected in these pages. Many of the basic documents of the movement have already become world famous: Martin Luther King's "I Have a Dream" speech delivered during the march on Washington on August 28, 1963; James Baldwin's "The Fire Next Time;" President Kennedy's speech after the Birmingham crisis, and President Johnson's speech after Selma are part of the great literature of our time.

There are also many lesser known writings and statements which show the valor and feeling of the participants in the movement: Elizabeth Eckford's description of her entry into Little Rock High School; Hartman Turnbow's account of an attempt to vote in Mississippi, and Charles Morgan's moving speech after the killing of four Negro teenagers in Birmingham in 1963. Writings by some of the important leaders of the movement—Martin Luther King, James Farmer, Roy Wilkins,

Malcolm X and others—have a power which is still extraordinarily compelling.

The documents also show how the government responded to the Negro's claim for his rightful place in American society. The recommendations of the President's Committee in 1947 set minimum goals for governmental action which—twenty years later—have still not been achieved. However, some progress was made in the four Civil Rights Acts of 1957, 1960, 1964 and 1965, which are set out or described in these pages. The important role played by the Supreme Court and the federal courts in the Negro revolution are also shown here. The Supreme Court, not paralyzed by Senatorial filibuster and the seniority system in Congress, helped to break the political ice jam in many instances when it appeared the movement had no place to go. Its landmark decision in *Brown* v. *Board of Education* is included in the collection.

Because of the relative newness of the northern civil rights drive, and the difference in its scope and direction, the documents relating to the North are fewer and of a different type. They include, primarily, studies such as the famous Moynihan report on the Negro family, and economic analyses of the failings of our industrial society. There are, of course, many individual injustices in the North against the Negro (as shown by the decision in *Lankford* v. *Gelston*), but the chief focus in the North is on the structural defects that keep the Negro poor and isolated.

The documents have been organized to tell the history of the movement, to show who the leaders and participants were, and what has been accomplished in the past twenty years. They also try to recreate the exhilaration of the times. For many—as the selections from "Letters from Mississippi" show—the summer of 1964 was the Spanish Civil War of this generation. The enthusiasm for the justness of the fight is something all America shared for a moment.

The recent fight over "black power" indicates that the new fight for equality and the continuation of the fight for liberty will be by organizations and through tactics completely directed by Negro leaders and not by sympathetic white liberals. Certainly, American society should have no concern over this kind of "black power." Oscar Handlin has stated:

> As long as common memories, experience and interests make the Negroes a group, they will find it advantageous to organize and act as such, and the society will better be able to accommodate them as equals on those terms than it could under the pretense that integration could wipe out the past.

In this new phase, the Negro groups will still need their white allies. Stokely Carmichael says:

This does not mean we don't welcome help, or friends. But we want the right to decide whether anyone is, in fact, our friend . . . Most liberal whites react to "black power" with the question, what about me?, rather than saying: Tell me what you want me to do and I'll see if I can do it.

The civil rights movement is not merely a Negro fight. It may be, as many of the Negro writers have said, that no white man knows what it is to be a Negro, and that white efforts to fuse the Negro into middle class American society are futile and undesired. But many of the white soldiers in the civil rights movement joined it not because they are capable of any immediate empathy with the Negro, or because they wish to make him into their own image. Their reasons were much more selfish than that. Any society which permits 10 per cent of its people to suffer continuous injustice and deprivation is repugnant to them. The existence of racial bigotry that permits the killing of a Negro by a Southern sheriff, the slums of Harlem, or the racial obscenities of the white mobs outside of Chicago, is a continuous slur on the values of American society.

Thus, both societies must make the effort, each for its own sake, to break the legacy of prejudice and injustice handed down to us for so many years. Only at that point can every American be, in the words of an old Negro spiritual: "Free at last, free at last, thank God almighty, free at last."

I

The Starting Point

On December 5, 1946, President Harry S. Truman appointed a distinguished group of Americans as members of the President's Committee on Civil Rights. Charles E. Wilson, President of General Electric was the Chairman. The Committee held a series of public hearings, ordered a number of staff studies made, and received hundreds of communications from interested private citizens and organizations. Almost a year after its appointment it submitted a written report to the President. The report, published under the title "To Secure These Rights," outlined "wherein and to what extent we are presently failing to live up to the American ideal." It described what it felt was the Government's responsibility to safeguard the civil rights of all Americans and recommended a complete program of action to remedy the shortcomings described.

Although the report tried to accentuate the progress that was being made, the precise description of lynchings, police brutality, restrictions on suffrage, and economic and educational inequities to which the Negro community was subject made a great impact. The fact that the Government lent its full support to the report and that important representatives of the business and labor community were represented on the Committee helped create strong political pressures to enact new civil rights legislation. However, principally because of the Senate filibuster, it was years before any significant civil rights legislation was passed. Indeed, of the many proposals made by the 1946 Committee, perhaps half have never been put into effect—including establishment of regional offices of the Civil Rights Division of the Justice Department, the training of a special F.B.I. unit for civil rights work, the creation of a Joint Standing Committee on Civil Rights in Congress, new legislation to supplement Sections

241 and 242 of Title 18 of the United States Code,* increase of the maximum penalty under Section 242, and the enactment of an anti-lynching law. Many of the laws which were in fact passed since 1947 have their genesis in the President's Committee recommendations. Other proposals, such as more expanded definition and application of Sections 241 and 242 of Title 18 of the United States Code have been put into effect by the Supreme Court rather than Congress.

The description of the condition of the Negro community in 1947 given in the report serves as a useful starting point in any account of the civil rights movement. The selections which follow show that lynching and police brutality were still a matter of course after World War II; that voting rights were practically nonexistent for the southern Negro community and that educational opportunities for the Negro were seriously restricted. The report serves as a useful guide on how much progress has been made in the past twenty years.

To Secure These Rights: The Report of the President's Committee on Civil Rights (1947)

*   *   *   *

The Ideal of Freedom and Equality

The central theme in our American heritage is the importance of the individual person. From the earliest moment of our history we have believed that every human being has an essential dignity and integrity which must be respected and safeguarded. Moreover, we believe that the welfare of the individual is the final goal of group life. Our American heritage further teaches that to be secure in the rights he wishes for himself, each man must be willing to respect the rights of other men. This is the conscious recognition of a basic moral principle: all men are created equal as well as free. Stemming from this principle is the obligation to build social institutions that will guarantee equality of opportunity to all men. Without this equality freedom becomes an illusion. Thus the only aristocracy that is consistent with the free way of life is an aristocracy of talent and achievement. The grounds on which

---

* Sections 241 and 242 of Title 18 of the United States Code are the principal federal criminal laws in the civil rights field. Section 241 punishes any conspiracy to injure or intimidate a person in the exercise of a constitutional right. Section 242 punishes deprivation of any federal right "under color of law," that is by or through any state official. The maximum penalty under Section 241 is ten years and under 242 is one year.

our society accords respect, influence or reward to each of its citizens must be limited to the quality of his personal character and of his social contribution.

This concept of equality which is so vital a part of the American heritage knows no kinship with notions of human uniformity or regimentation. We abhor the totalitarian arrogance which makes one man say that he will respect another man as his equal only if he has "*my* race, *my* religion, *my* political views, *my* social position." In our land men are equal, but they are free to be different. From these very differences among our people has come the great human and national strength of America.

Thus, the aspirations and achievements of each member of our society are to be limited only by the skills and energies he brings to the opportunities equally offered to all Americans. We can tolerate no restrictions upon the individual which depend upon irrelevant factors such as his race, his color, his religion or the social position to which he is born.

The rights essential to the citizen in a free society can be described in different words and in varying orders. The three great rights of the Declaration of Independence have just been mentioned. Another noble statement is made in the Bill of Rights of our Constitution. A more recent formulation is found in the Four Freedoms.

Four basic rights have seemed important to this Committee and have influenced its labors. We believe that each of these rights is essential to the well-being of the individual and to the progress of society.

1. *The Right to Safety and Security of the Person*

Freedom can exist only where the citizen is assured that his person is secure against bondage, lawless violence, and arbitrary arrest and punishment. Freedom from slavery in all its forms is clearly necessary if all men are to have equal opportunity to use their talents and to lead worthwhile lives. Moreover, to be free, men must be subject to discipline by society only for commission of offenses clearly defined by law and only after trial by due process of law. Where the administration of justice is discriminatory, no man can be sure of security. Where the threat of violence by private persons or mobs exists, a cruel inhibition of the sense of freedom of activity and security of the person inevitably results. Where a society permits private and arbitrary violence to be done to its members, its own integrity is inevitably corrupted. It cannot permit human beings to be imprisoned or killed in the absence of due process of law without degrading its entire fabric.

2. The Right to Citizenship and its Privileges

Since it is a purpose of government in a democracy to regulate the activity of each man in the interest of all men, it follows that every mature and responsible person must be able to enjoy full citizenship and have an equal voice in his government. Because the right to participate in the political process is customarily limited to citizens there can be no denial of access to citizenship based upon race, color, creed, or national origin. Denial of citizenship for these reasons cheapens the personality of those who are confined to this inferior status and endangers the whole concept of a democratic society.

To deny qualified citizens the right to vote while others exercise it is to do violence to the principle of freedom and equality. Without the right to vote, the individual loses his voice in the group effort and is subjected to rule by a body from which he has been excluded. Likewise, the right of the individual to vote is important to the group itself. Democracy assumes that the majority is more likely as a general rule to make decisions which are wise and desirable from the point of view of the interests of the whole society than is any minority. Every time a qualified person is denied a voice in public affairs, one of the components of a potential majority is lost, and the formation of a sound public policy is endangered.

*   *   *   *

3. The Right to Freedom of Conscience and Expression

In a free society there is faith in the ability of the people to make sound, rational judgments. But such judgments are possible only where the people have access to all relevant facts and to all prevailing interpretations of the facts. How can such judgments be formed on a sound basis if arguments, viewpoints, or opinions are arbitrarily suppressed? How can the concept of the marketplace of thought in which truth ultimately prevails retain its validity if the thought of certain individuals is denied the right of circulation? The Committee reaffirms our tradition that freedom of expression may be curbed by law only where the danger to the well-being of society is clear and present.

*   *   *   *

4. The Right to Equality of Opportunity

It is not enough that full and equal membership in society entitles the individual to an equal voice in the control of his government; it must also give him the right to enjoy the benefits of society and to contribute to its progress. The opportunity of each individual to obtain useful employment, and to have access to services in the fields of education, housing, health, recreation and transportation, whether available free or at a price, must be provided with complete disregard for race, color, creed, and national origin. Without this equality of opportunity the individual is deprived of the chance to develop his potentialities and to share the fruits of society. The group also suffers through the loss of the contributions which might have been made by persons excluded from the main channels of social and economic activity.

* * * *

The Condition of Our Rights

1. The Right to Safety and Security of the Person

Vital to the integrity of the individual and to the stability of a democratic society is the right of each individual to physical freedom, to security against illegal violence, and to fair, orderly legal process. Most Americans enjoy this right, but it is not yet secure for all. Too many of our people still live under the harrowing fear of violence or death at the hands of a mob or of brutal treatment by police officers. Many fear entanglement with the law because of the knowledge that the justice rendered in some courts is not equal for all persons. In a few areas the freedom to move about and choose one's job is endangered by attempts to hold workers in peonage or other forms of involuntary servitude.

THE CRIME OF LYNCHING

In 1946 at least six persons in the United States were lynched by mobs. Three of them had not been charged, either by the police or anyone else, with an offense. Of the three that had been charged, one had been accused of stealing a saddle. (The real thieves were discovered after the lynching.) Another was said to have broken into a house. A third was charged with stabbing a man. All were Negroes. During the same year, mobs were prevented from lynching 22 persons, of whom 21 were Negroes, 1 white.

On July 20, 1946, a white farmer, Loy Harrison, posted bond for the release of Roger Malcolm from the jail at Monroe, Georgia. Malcolm, a young Negro, had been involved in a fight with his white employer during the course of which the latter had been stabbed. It is reported that there was talk of lynching Malcolm at the time of the incident and while he was in jail. Upon Malcolm's release, Harrison started to drive Malcolm, Malcolm's wife, and a Negro overseas veteran, George Dorsey, and his wife, out of Monroe. At a bridge along the way a large group of unmasked white men, armed with pistols and shotguns, was waiting. They stopped Harrison's car and removed Malcolm and Dorsey. As they were leading the two men away, Harrison later stated, one of the women called out the name of a member of the mob. Thereupon the lynchers returned and removed the two women from the car. Three volleys of shots were fired as if by a squad of professional executioners. The coroner's report said that at least 60 bullets were found in the scarcely recognizable bodies. Harrison consistently denied that he could identify any of the unmasked murderers. State and federal grand juries reviewed the evidence in the case, but no person has yet been indicted for the crime.

Later that summer, in Minden, Louisiana, a young Negro named John Jones was arrested on suspicion of housebreaking. Another Negro youth, Albert Harris, was arrested at about the same time, and beaten in a effort to implicate Jones. He was then released, only to be rearrested after a few days. On August 6th, early in the evening, and before there had been any trial of the charges against them, Jones and Harris were released by a deputy sheriff. Waiting in the jail yard was a group of white men. There was evidence that, with the aid of the deputy sheriff, the young men were put into a car. They were then driven into the country. Jones was beaten to death. Harris, left for dead, revived and escaped. Five persons, including two deputy sheriffs, were indicted and brought to trial in a federal court for this crime. All were acquitted.

These are two of the less brutal lynchings of the past years. The victims in these cases were not mutilated or burned.

The record for 1947 is incomplete. There has been one lynching, one case in which the victim escaped, and other instances where mobs have been unable to accomplish their purpose. On February 17, 1947, a Negro youth named Willie Earle, accused of fatally stabbing a taxi driver in the small city of Greenville, South Carolina, was removed from jail by a mob, viciously beaten and finally shot to death. In an unusual and impressive instance of state prosecution, 31 men were tried for this crime. All were acquitted on the evening of May 21, 1947. Early the next morning, in Jackson, North Carolina, another Negro youth, Godwin Bush, arrested on a charge of approaching a white woman, was removed from a local jail by a mob, after having been exhibited through the town by the sheriff. Bush succeeded in escaping from his abductors, and, after hiding for two days in nearby woods, was able to surrender himself safely into the custody of FBI agents and officers of the state. The Committee finds it encouraging to note that the Governor of North Carolina has made vigorous efforts to bring to justice those responsible for this attempted lynching.

While available statistics show that, decade by decade, lynchings have decreased, this Committee has found that in the year 1947 lynching remains one of the most serious threats to the civil rights of Americans. It is still possible for a mob to abduct and murder a person in some sections of the country with almost certain assurance of escaping punishment for the crime. The decade from 1936 through 1946 saw at least 43 lynchings. No person received the death penalty, and the majority of the guilty persons were not even prosecuted.

The communities in which lynchings occur tend to condone the crime. Punishment of lynchers is not accepted as the responsibility of state or local governments in these communities. Frequently, state officials participate in the crime, actively or passively. Federal efforts to punish the crime are resisted. Condonation of lynching is indicated by the failure of some local law enforcement officials to make adequate efforts to break up a mob. It is further shown by failure in most cases to make any real effort to apprehend or try those guilty. If the federal government enters a case, local officials sometimes actively resist the federal investigation. Local citizens often combine to impede the effort to apprehend the criminals by convenient "loss of memory"; grand juries refuse to indict; trial juries acquit in the face of overwhelming proof of guilt.

The large number of attempted lynchings highlights, even more than those which have succeeded, the widespread readiness of many communities to resort to mob violence. Thus, for seven of the years from 1937 to 1946 for which statistics are reported, the conservative estimates of the Tuskegee Institute show that 226 persons were rescued from threatened lynching. Over 200 of these were Negroes.

Most rescues from lynchings are made by local officials. There is heartening evidence that an ever-increasing number of these officers have the will and the courage to defend their prisoners against mob action. But this reflects only partial progress toward adequate law enforcement. In some instances lynchers are dissuaded by promises that the desired result will be accomplished "legally" and the machinery of justice is sometimes sensitive to the demands of such implied bargains. In some communities there is more official zeal to avoid mob violence which will injure the reputation of the community than there is to protect innocent persons.

The devastating consequences of lynchings go far beyond what is shown by counting the victims. When a person is lynched and the lynchers go unpunished, thousands wonder where the evil will appear again and what mischance may produce another victim. And every time lynchers go unpunished, Negroes have learned to expect other forms of violence at the hands of private citizens or public officials. In describing the thwarted efforts of the Department of Justice to identify those responsible for one lynching, J. Edgar Hoover stated to the Committee: "The arrogance of most of the white population of that county was unbelievable, and the fear of the Negroes was almost unbelievable."

The almost complete immunity from punishment enjoyed by lynchers is merely a striking form of the broad and general immunity from punishment enjoyed by whites in many communities for less extreme offenses against Negroes. Moreover, lynching is the ultimate threat by which his inferior status is driven home to the Negro. As a terrorist device, it reinforces all the other disabilities placed upon him. The threat of lynching always hangs over the head of the southern Negro; the knowledge that a misinterpreted word or action can lead to his death is a dreadful burden.

POLICE BRUTALITY

We have reported the failure of some public officials to fulfill their most elementary duty—the protection of persons against mob violence. We must also report more widespread and varied forms of official misconduct. These include physical attacks by police officers on members of minority groups, the use of third degree methods to extort confessions, and brutality against prisoners. Civil rights violations of this kind are by no means universal and many law enforcement agencies have gone far in recent years toward stamping out these evils.

In various localities, scattered throughout the country, unprofessional or undisciplined police, while avoiding brutality, fail to recognize and to safeguard the civil rights of the citizenry. Insensitive to the necessary limits of police authority, untrained officers frequently overstep the bounds of their proper duties. At times this appears in unwarranted arrests, unduly prolonged detention before arraignment, and abuse of the search and seizure power. Cases involving these breaches of civil rights constantly come before the courts. The frequency with which such cases arise is proof that improper police conduct is still widespread, for it must be assumed that there are many instances of the abuse of police power which do not reach the courts. Most of the victims of such abuses are ignorant, friendless persons, unaware of their rights, and without the means of challenging those who have violated those rights.

Where lawless police forces exist, their activities may impair the civil rights of any citizen. In one place the brunt of illegal police activity may fall on suspected vagrants, in another on union organizers, and in another on unpopular racial or religious minorities, such as Negroes, Mexicans, or Jehovah's Witnesses. But wherever unfettered police lawlessness exists, civil rights may be vulnerable to the prejudices of the region or of dominant local groups, and to the caprice of individual policemen. Unpopular, weak, or defenseless groups are most apt to suffer.

Considerable evidence in the files of the Department of Justice supports this assertion. For example, in one case in 1945 a group of white juvenile offenders made an abortive effort to escape from a midwestern prison. The attempt was quickly and fairly easily subdued. In the course of the attempt a trusty was injured. The prison officials, after rounding up the boys, allowed other trusties to vent their anger at the injury to their comrade by physically attacking the defenseless prisoners. After this had occurred the boys were then severely beaten, one by one, by the prison officials.

Much of the illegal official action which has been brought to the attention of the Committee is centered in the South. There is evidence of lawless police action against whites and Negroes alike, but the dominant pattern is that of race prejudice. J. Edgar Hoover referred, in his testimony before the Committee, to a particular jail where "it was seldom that a Negro man or women was incarcerated who was not given a severe beating, which started off with a pistol whipping and ended with a rubber hose."

The files of the Department abound with evidence of illegal official action in southern states. In one case, the victim was arrested on a charge of stealing a tire, taken to the courthouse, beaten by three officers with a blackjack until his head was a bloody pulp, and then dragged unconscious through the streets to the jail where he was thrown, dying, onto the floor. In another case, a constable arrested a Negro, against whom he bore a personal grudge, beat him brutally with a bullwhip and then forced his victim, in spite of his protestations of being unable to swim, to jump into a river where he drowned. In a third case, there was evidence that officers arrested a Negro maid on a charge of stealing jewelry from her employer, took her to jail and severely beat and whipped her in an unsuccessful effort to extort a confession. All of these cases occurred within the last five years.

There are other cases in the files of the Department of Justice of officers who seem to be "trigger-happy" where weak or poor persons are concerned. In a number of instances, Negroes have been shot, supposedly in self-defense, under circumstances indicating, at best, unsatisfactory police work in the handling of criminals, and, at worst, a callous willingness to kill.

Toward the end of the work of this Committee a particularly shocking instance of this occurred. On July 11, 1947, eight Negro prisoners in the State highway prison camp in Glynn County, Georgia, were killed by their white guards as they allegedly attempted to escape.

The Glynn County grand jury exonerated the warden of the camp and four guards of all charges. At later hearings on the highway prison camp system held by the State Board of Corrections, conflicting evidence was presented. But one witness testified that there was no evidence that the prisoners were trying to escape. In any case, he said it was not necessary to use guns on them in the circumstances. "There was no justification for the killing. I saw the Negroes where they fell. Two were killed where they crawled under the bunkhouse and two others as they ran under their cells. The only thing they were trying to escape was death. Only one tried to get over the fence." The warden and four guards were indicted by a federal grand jury on October 1, 1947.

It is difficult to accept at face value police claims in cases of this type that action has been taken against prisoners in "self defense" or to "prevent escape." Even if these protestations are accepted, the incidence of shooting in the ordinary course of law enforcement in some sections of the country is a serious reflection on these police forces. Other officers in other places seem able to enforce the law and to guard prisoners without resort to violent means.

The total picture—adding the connivance of some police officials in lynchings to their record of brutality against Negroes in other situations—is, in the opinion of this Committee, a serious reflection on American justice. We know that Americans everywhere deplore this violence. We recognize further that there are many law enforcement officers in the South and the North who do not commit violent acts against Negroes or other friendless culprits. We are convinced, however, that the incidence of police brutality against Negroes is disturbingly high.

ADMINISTRATION OF JUSTICE

In addition to the treatment experienced by the weak and friendless person at the hands of police officers, he sometimes finds that the judicial process itself does not give him full and equal justice. This may appear in unfair and perfunctory trials, or in fines and prison sentences that are heavier than those imposed on other members of the community guilty of the same offenses.

In part, the inability of the Negro, Mexican, or Indian to obtain equal justice may be attributed to extrajudicial factors. The low income of a member of any one of these minorities may prevent him from securing competent counsel to defend his rights. It may prevent him from posting bail or bond to secure his release from jail during trial. It may predetermine his choice, upon conviction, of paying a fine or going to jail. But these facts should not obscure or condone the extent to which

the judicial system itself is responsible for the less-than-equal justice
meted out to members of certain minority groups.

*   *   *   *

THE RIGHT TO VOTE

The right of all qualified citizens to vote is today considered axio-
matic by most Americans. To achieve universal adult suffrage we have
carried on vigorous political crusades since the earliest days of the Republic. In theory the aim has been achieved, but in fact there are many
backwaters in our political life where the right to vote is not assured
to every qualified citizen. The franchise is barred to some citizens because of race; to others by institutions or procedures which impede free
access to the polls. Still other Americans are in substance disfranchised
whenever electoral irregularities or corrupt practices dissipate their votes
or distort their intended purpose. Some citizens—permanent residents
of the District of Columbia—are excluded from political representation
and the right to vote as a result of outmoded national traditions. As a
result of such restrictions, all of these citizens are limited, in varying
degrees, in their opportunities to seek office and to influence the conduct
of government on an equal plane with other American citizens.

The denial of the suffrage on account of race is the most serious present
interference with the right to vote. Until very recently, American Negro
citizens in most southern states found it difficult to vote. Some Negroes
have voted in parts of the upper South for the last twenty years. In recent
years the situation in the deep South has changed to the point where
it can be said that Negroes are beginning to exercise the political rights
of free Americans. In the light of history, this represents progress,
limited and precarious, but nevertheless progress.

This report cannot adequately describe the history of Negro disfranchisement. At different times, different methods have been employed.
As legal devices for disfranchising the Negro have been held unconstitutional, new methods have been improvised to take their places. Intimidation and the threat of intimidation have always loomed behind these
legal devices to make sure that the desired result is achieved.

Until 1944, the white primary, by which participation in the Democratic primary is limited to white citizens, was used in Texas, Alabama,
Arkansas, Georgia, Louisiana, and Mississippi as the most effective modern "legal" device for disfranchising Negroes. While some southern
Negroes succeeded in spite of various obstacles in voting in general elections, almost none voted in the Democratic primaries. Since the Democratic primary is the only election of any significance, the device of the
white primary resulted in exclusion of Negroes from government in these

states. Over a period of time, advocates of white supremacy had refined this device to the point where it seemed to be constitutionally foolproof. The command of the Fifteenth Amendment, prohibiting states from abridging suffrage because of race or color, was circumvented by purporting to vest the power to exclude Negroes in the political party rather than in the state.

But in 1944, the United States Supreme Court in the case of *Smith* v. *Allwright* overruled an earlier decision and held the Texas white primary illegal. It declared that the exclusion rules of the Texas Democratic Party were in effect the rules of the state and were therefore forbidden by the Fifteenth Amendment.

Some states adapted their primary laws to the Supreme Court ruling, others resisted, first, by refusing to open white primaries to Negroes until further litigation made the Texas ruling applicable to them, then, by devising other methods of depriving Negroes of the ballot. Today the effort to preserve the pure white electoral system in these states is continuing.

Two states, Louisiana and Texas, repealed white primary provisions immediately after the Supreme Court decision; Florida, Alabama, and Georgia were forced to do so by further court rulings. South Carolina called a special session of the state legislature at which all state laws in any way regulating primaries were repealed. The theory governing this action was that by placing the primaries entirely outside the law and the structure of government the ruling in *Smith* v. *Allwright* would be rendered inapplicable.

*   *   *   *

In addition to formal, legal methods of disfranchisement, there are the long-standing techniques of terror and intimidation, in the face of which great courage is required of the Negro who tries to vote. In the regions most characterized by generalized violence against Negroes, little more than "advice" is often necessary to frighten them away from the polls. They have learned, through the years, to discover threats in mood and atmosphere. In one case in a deep southern state, a middle-class Negro who had courageously attempted to vote and to complain to the Department of Justice when he was refused access to the polls, subsequently became so afraid of reprisal that he indicated uncertainty whether he would be willing to testify in court. He asked, if he should decide to testify, to be given ample notice of the date so that he could first move his family out of the region.

*   *   *   *

THE RIGHT TO EDUCATION

The United States has made remarkable progress toward the goal of universal education for its people. The number and variety of its schools and colleges are greater than ever before. Student bodies have become increasingly representative of all the different peoples who make up our population. Yet we have not finally eliminated prejudice and discrimination from the operation of either our public or our private schools and colleges. Two inadequacies are extremely serious. We have failed to provide Negroes and, to a lesser extent, other minority group members with equality of educational opportunities in our public institutions, particularly at the elementary and secondary school levels. We have allowed discrimination in the operation of many of our private institutions of higher education, particularly in the North with respect to Jewish students.

Discrimination in public schools.—The failure to give Negroes equal educational opportunities is naturally most acute in the South, where approximately 10 million Negroes live. The South is one of the poorer sections of the country and has at best only limited funds to spend on its schools. With 34.5 percent of the country's population, 17 southern states and the District of Columbia have 39.4 percent of our school children. Yet the South has only one-fifth of the taxpaying wealth of the nation. Actually, on a percentage basis, the South spends a greater share of its income on education than do the wealthier states in other parts of the country. For example, Mississippi, which has the lowest expenditure per school child of any state, is ninth in percentage of income devoted to education. A recent study showed Mississippi spending 3.41 percent of its income for education as against New York's figure of only 2.61 percent. But this meant $400 per classroom unit in Mississippi, and $4,100 in New York. Negro and white school children both suffer because of the South's basic inability to match the level of educational opportunity provided in other sections of the nation.

But it is the South's segregated school system which most directly discriminates against the Negro. This segregation is found today in 17 southern states and the District of Columbia. Poverty-stricken though it was after the close of the Civil War, the South chose to maintain two sets of public schools, one for whites and one for Negroes. With respect to education, as well as to other public services, the Committee believes that the "separate but equal" rule has not been obeyed in practice. There is a marked difference in quality between the educational opportunities offered white children and Negro children in the separate schools. Whatever test is used—expenditure per pupil, teachers' salaries, the number of pupils per teacher, transportation of students, adequacy of school buildings and educational equipment, length of school term, extent of curriculum—Negro students are invariably at a disadvantage. Opportunities for Negroes in public institutions of higher education in the South—particularly at the professional graduate school level—are severely limited.

*   *   *   *

Discrimination in places of public accommodation.—When we turn from public services supplied by government to those supplied by private enterprise, discrimination against minorities becomes more pronounced. Our social conscience has brought about an elimination of some of the most flagrant inequalities in the distribution of government services. But it is often blind to the serious effect upon the individual which results from the discriminatory rendering of service by private agencies.

Most Americans patronize restaurants, theaters, shops, and other places offering service to the public according to their individual preferences and their ability to pay. They take their right to enter such places and to be served for granted. This is not the case with other Americans. Because of their race or their color or their creed, they are barred from access to some places and given unequal service in others. In many sections of this country, some people must pause and give thought before they enter places serving the public if they wish to avoid embarrassment, arrest, or even possible violence.

As interpreted by the Supreme Court the Constitution does not guarantee equal access to places of public accommodation and amusement. A Civil Rights Act was passed by Congress in 1875 which declared that no distinction should be made because of race or color in the accommodations offered by inns, public conveyances, theaters, and similar places. This act was declared unconstitutional by the Supreme Court in 1883, in the *Civil Rights Cases.* Thereafter legislation on the matter was left entirely to the states. They may, and do, either compel segregation, or outlaw it, or they may leave it to the managers of private establishments to make whatever distinction they wish in selecting their patrons.

Eighteen states have statutes prohibiting discrimination in places of public accommodation. These states prohibit discrimination in restaurants, and usually in other eating places. Most of them prohibit discrimination in public conveyances of all types, and over half of them, in theaters and barber shops. All include some general phrase, such as "and all other places of public accommodation." The courts, however, have tended to limit this general phrasing by the list of specific places. The statutes can be enforced by criminal action or by a civil suit for damages.

At the other extreme, 20 states by law compel segregation in one way or another. The remaining 10 states have no laws on the subject. In the states with compulsory segregation laws Negroes are usually separated from whites in all forms of public transportation, and in hotels, restaurants, and places of amusement. Fourteen states require railroads to separate the races, and two authorize railroads to provide such separation. Train conductors are given power to enforce these laws. Under the Supreme Court decision in *Morgan* v. *Virginia,* such laws do not apply to passengers in interstate transportation. However, this decision does not prevent carriers from voluntarily enforcing segregation. Eight states require separate waiting rooms, 11 require separation in buses, 10 in street cars and three in steamships and ferries. In instances where completely separate facilities are provided, as in railroad coaches and waiting rooms, those set aside for the Negro are usually inferior in quality.

In the states which do legally secure the right of access, practice does not necessarily conform to the law. One prominent Negro has stated that it is difficult to find a meal or a hotel room in the downtown areas of most northern cities. The display of "whites only" signs may sometimes go unchallenged. When laws guaranteeing equal access to places of public accommodation are enforced, the penalty is usually small and the chance of being prosecuted or sued a second time is slight.

Devices to get around the law are more common than direct violation of the law. Unwanted customers are discouraged from patronizing places by letting them wait indefinitely for service, charging higher prices, giving poor service, and publicly embarrassing them in various ways. In a recent campaign to compel enforcement of a civil rights statute in Cincinnati, many restaurants closed their doors to make repairs. Nevertheless, these campaigns are often successful, and without the statutes would be impossible. In Chicago in 1946, the Mayor's Commission on Human Relations invoked the State Civil Rights Statute to break down the bars against Negroes in the roller-skating rinks of the city.

Sometimes the pattern of segregation in public-service facilities spreads from the states having compulsory separation of the races to states which are free from such laws. For example, the Pennsylvania Railroad in its terminal in New York City segregates Negroes in coaches on through trains bound for the South, even though it does not do so on its own trains operating as far as Washington.

*   *   *   *

Segregation Reconsidered

The "Separate But Equal" Failure

Mention has already been made of the "separate but equal" policy of the southern states by which Negroes are said to be entitled to the same public service as whites but on a strictly segregated basis. The theory behind this policy is complex. On one hand, it recognizes Negroes as citizens and as intelligent human beings entitled to enjoy the status accorded the individual in our American heritage of freedom. It theoretically gives them access to all the rights, privileges, and services of a civilized, democratic society. On the other hand, it brands the Negro with the mark of inferiority and asserts that he is not fit to associate with white people.

Legally enforced segregation has been followed throughout the South since the close of the Reconstruction era. In these states it is generally illegal for Negroes to attend the same schools as whites; attend theaters patronized by whites; visit parks where whites relax; eat, sleep or meet in hotels, restaurants, or public halls frequented by whites. This is only a partial enumeration—legally imposed separation of races has become highly refined. In the eyes of the law, it is also an offense for whites to attend "Negro" schools, theaters and similar places. The result has been the familiar system of racial segregation in both public and private institutions which cuts across the daily lives of southern citizens from the cradle to the grave.

Legally-enforced segregation has been largely limited to the South. But segregation is also widely prevalent in the North, particularly in housing, and in hotel and restaurant accommodations. Segregation has not been enforced by states alone. The federal government has tolerated it even where it has full authority to eliminate it.

*   *   *   *

The Supreme Court and Segregation

The Fourteenth Amendment forbids a state to deny "to any person within its jurisdiction the equal protection of the laws." Moreover, the general spirit of the three Civil War Amendments seems to guarantee to all persons a full and equal status in American society.

Yet the Supreme Court, beginning with its decision in *Plessy* v. *Ferguson*, in 1896, has approved state legislation requiring segregation between Negroes and whites on the theory that segregation, as such, is not discriminatory. The Court dismissed the contention that "the enforced separation of the two races stamps the colored race with a badge of inferiority," and observed, "if this be so, it is not by reason of anything found in the act, but solely because the colored race chooses to put that construction upon it." So long as laws requiring segregation do not establish unequal facilities, the legal doctrine holds, there is no unreasonable discrimination and therefore no denial of equal protection under the law.

This judicial legalization of segregation was not accomplished without protest. Justice Harlan, a Kentuckian, in one of the most vigorous and forthright dissenting opinions in Supreme Court history, denounced his colleagues for the manner in which they interpreted away the substance of the Thirteenth and Fourteenth Amendments. In his dissent in the *Plessy* case, he said:

> Our Constitution is color blind, and neither knows nor tolerates classes among citizens. * * *
> We boast of the freedom enjoyed by our people above all other peoples. But it is difficult to reconcile that boast with a state of the law which, practically, puts the brand of servitude and degradation upon a large class of our fellow citizens, our equals before the law. The thin disguise of "equal" accommodations * * * will not mislead anyone, or atone for the wrong this day done.

If evidence beyond that of dispassionate reason was needed to justify Justice Harlan's statement, history has provided it. Segregation has become the cornerstone of the elaborate structure of discrimination against some American citizens. Theoretically this system simply duplicates educational, recreational and other public services, according facilities to the two races which are "separate but equal." In the Committee's opinion this is one of the outstanding myths of American history for it is almost always true that while indeed separate, these facilities are far from equal. Throughout the segregated public institutions, Negroes have been denied an equal share of tax-supported services and facilties. So far as private institutions are concerned, there is no specific legal disability on the right of Negroes to develop equal institutions of their own. However, the economic, social, and indirect legal obstacles to this course are staggering.

Following the *Plessy* decision, the Supreme Court for many years enforced with a degree of leniency the rule that segregated facilities must be equal. Gradually, however, the Court became stricter about requiring a showing of equality. During the last decade, in line with its vigorous defense of civil rights generally, the Court has been particularly insistent upon adherence to the "equal" part of the separate but equal rule. In 1938, in *Missouri ex rel. Gaines v. Canada,* it held that Missouri might not fulfill its obligation under the rule by offering to pay the tuition of a

Negro resident of Missouri at an out-of-state law school in lieu of permitting him to attend the law school at the University of Missouri. The Court laid down the plain rule that if a state chooses to provide within its borders specialized educational facilities for citizens of one race, it must make similar provision, also within its borders, for citizens of other races.

This insistence upon equal facilities is encouraging. Experience requires the prediction, however, that the degree of equality will never be complete, and never certain. In any event we believe that not even the most mathematically precise equality of segregated institutions can properly be considered equality under the law. No argument or rationalization can alter this basic fact: a law which forbids a group of American citizens to associate with other citizens in the ordinary course of daily living creates inequality by imposing a caste status on the minority group.

*   *   *   *

The Committee's Recommendations

I. *To strengthen the machinery for the protection of civil rights, the President's Committee recommends:*
1. The reorganization of the Civil Rights Section of the Department of Justice to provide for:
    The establishment of regional offices;
    A substantial increase in its appropriation and staff to enable it to engage in more extensive research and to act more effectively to prevent civil rights violations;
    An increase in investigative action in the absence of complaints;
    The greater use of civil sanctions;
    Its elevation to the status of a full division in the Department of Justice.
    The creation of regional offices would enable the Civil Rights Section to provide more complete protection to civil rights in all sections of the country. It would lessen its present complete dependence upon United States Attorneys and local FBI agents for its work in the field. Such regional offices should be established in eight or nine key cities throughout the country, and be staffed with skilled personnel drawn from the local areas. These offices should serve as receiving points for complaints arising in the areas, and as local centers or research, investigation, and preventive action. Close cooperation should be maintained between these offices, local FBI agents, and the United States Attorneys.
    The Department of Justice has suggested that heads of these regional offices should have the status of Assistant United States Attorneys, thereby preserving the centralization of federal criminal law enforcement.

The President's Committee is fearful that under this plan the goal of effective, courageous, and nonpolitical civil rights protection in the field will not be reached unless satisfactory measures are taken to prevent these assistants from becoming mere political subordinates within the offices of the United States Attorneys.

Additional funds and personnel for research and preventive work would free the Civil Rights Section from its present narrow status as a prosecutive agency. Through the use of properly developed techniques and by the maintenance of continuous checks on racial and other group tensions, much could be done by the Section to reduce the number of lynchings, race riots, election irregularities, and other civil rights violations. Troublesome areas, and the activities of organizations and individuals who foment race tensions could be kept under constant scrutiny.

A larger staff and field-office facilties would also make it possible for the Section to undertake investigations of suspected civil rights violations, without waiting for the receipt of complaints. There are many problems, such as the possible infringement of civil rights resulting from practices used in committing persons to mental institutions, which might be so studied. These investigations in the absence of complaints could also be combined with educational and mediation efforts to check chronic incidents of police brutality or persistent interferences with the right to vote.

The difficulty of winning convictions in many types of criminal civil rights cases is often great. The Committee believes that the Civil Rights Section should be granted increased authority, by Congress if necessary, to make appropriate use of civil sanctions, such as suits for damages or injunctive relief, suits under the Declaratory Judgment Act, and the right of intervention by means of briefs amicus curiae in private litigation where important issues of civil rights law are being determined.

Finally, the Committee urges congressional action raising the Civil Rights Section to full divisional status in the Department of Justice under the supervision of an Assistant Attorney General. We believe this step would give the federal civil rights enforcement program prestige, power, and efficiency that it now lacks. Moreover, acceptance of the above recommendations looking toward increased activity by the Civil Rights Section and the passage by Congress of additional civil rights legislation would give this change added meaning and necessity.

2. The establishment within the FBI of a special unit of investigators trained in civil rights work.

The creation of such a unit of skilled investigators would enable the FBI to render more effective service in the civil rights field than is now possible. At the present time, its investigators are concerned with enforcement of all federal criminal statutes. In some instances, its agents have seemingly lacked the special skills and knowledge necessary to effective handling of civil rights cases, or have not been readily available for work in this area.

These special agents should work in close harmony with the Civil Rights Section and its regional offices.

*   *   *   *

4. The establishment of a permanent Commission on Civil Rights in the Executive Office of the President, preferably by Act of Congress;
   And the simultaneous creation of a Joint Standing Committee on Civil Rights in Congress.

In a democratic society, the systematic, critical review of social needs and public policy is a fundamental necessity. This is especially true of a field like civil rights, where the problems are enduring, and range widely. From our own effort, we have learned that a temporary, sporadic approach can never finally solve these problems.

Nowhere in the federal government is there an agency charged with the continuous appraisal of the status of civil rights, and the efficiency of the machinery with which we hope to improve that status. There are huge gaps in the available information about the field. A permanent Commission could perform an invaluable function by collecting data. It could also carry on technical research to improve the fact-gathering methods now in use. Ultimately, this would make possible a periodic audit of the extent to which our civil rights are secure. If it did this and served as a clearing house and focus of coordination for the many private, state, and local agencies working in the civil rights field, it would be invaluable to them and to the federal government.

A permanent Commission on Civil Rights should point all of its work towards regular reports which would include recommendations for action in the ensuing periods. It should lay plans for dealing with broad civil rights problems, such as those arising from the technological displacement and probable migration of southern Negroes to cities throughout the land. It should also investigate and make recommendations with respect to special civil rights problems, such as the status of Indians and their relationship to the federal government.

The Commission should have effective authority to call upon any agency of the executive branch for assistance. Its members should be appointed by the President with the approval of the Senate. They should hold a specified number of regular meetings. A full-time director should be provided with an adequate appropriation and staff.

Congress, too, can be aided in its difficult task of providing the legislative ground work for fuller civil rights. A standing committee, established jointly by the House and the Senate, would provide a central place for the consideration of proposed legislation. It would enable Congress to maintain continuous liaison with the permanent Commission. A group of men in each chamber would be able to give prolonged study to this complex area and would become expert in its legislative needs.

*   *   *   *

6. The increased professionalization of state and local police forces.

The Committee believes that there is a great need at the state and local level for the improvement of civil rights protection by more aggressive and efficient enforcement techniques. Police training programs, patterned after the FBI agents' school and the Chicago Park District Program, should be instituted. They should be oriented so as to indoctrinate officers with an awareness of civil rights problems. Proper treatment by the police of those who are arrested and incarcerated in local jails should be stressed. Supplemented by salaries that will attract and hold competent personnel, this sort of training should do much to make police forces genuinely professional.

II. *To strengthen the right to safety and security of the person, the President's Committee recommends:*

1. The enactment by Congress of new legislation to supplement Section 51 [§241] of Title 18 of the United States Code which would impose the same liability on one person as is now imposed by that statute on two or more conspirators.

The Committee believes that Section 51 [§241] has in the past been a useful law to protect federal rights against encroachment by both private individuals and public officers. It believes the Act has great potential usefulness today. Greater efforts should be made through court tests to extend and make more complete the list of rights safeguarded by this law.

2. The amendment of Section 51 [§241] to remove the penalty provision which disqualifies persons convicted under the Act from holding public office.

There is general agreement that this particular penalty creates an unnecessary obstacle to the obtaining of convictions under the Act and that it should be dropped.

3. The amendment of Section 52 [§242] to increase the maximum penalties that may be imposed under it from a $1,000 fine and a one-year prison term to a $5,000 fine and a ten-year prison term, thus bringing its penalty provisions into line with those in Section 51 [§241].

At the present time the Act's penalties are so light that it is technically a misdemeanor law. In view of the extremely serious offenses that have been and are being successfully prosecuted under Section 52, [§242] it seems clear that the penalties should be increased.

4. The enactment by Congress of a new statute, to supplement Section 52 [§242], specifically directed against police brutality and related crimes.

This Act should enumerate such rights as the right not to be deprived of property by a public officer except by due process of law; the right to be free from personal injury inflicted by a public officer; the right to engage in a lawful activity without interference by a public officer; and the right to be free from discriminatory law enforcement resulting from either active or passive conduct by a public officer.

This statute would meet in part the handicap in the use of Section 52 [§242] imposed by the Supreme Court in *Screws* v. *United States*. This was the case in which the Court required prosecutors to establish that defendants had willfully deprived victims of a "specific constitutional right." In later prosecutions, the Civil Rights Section has found it very difficult to prove that the accused acted in a "willful" manner. By spelling out some of the federal rights which run against public officers, the supplementary statute would relieve the Civil Rights Section of this extraordinary requirement.

The Committee considered and rejected a proposal to recommend the enactment of a supplementary statute in which an attempt would be made to include a specific enumeration of all federal rights running against public officers. Such an enumeration would inevitably prove incomplete with the passage of time and might prejudice the protection of omitted rights. However, the committee believes that a new statute, such as the one here recommended, enumerating the rights for the protection of which Section 52 [§242] is now most commonly employed, is desirable.

5. The enactment by Congress of an antilynching act.

The Committee believes that to be effective such a law must contain four essential elements. First, it should define lynching broadly. Second, the federal offense ought to cover participation of public officers in a lynching, or failure by them to use proper measures to protect a person accused of a crime against mob violence. The failure or refusal of public officers to make proper efforts to arrest members of lynch mobs and to bring them to justice should also be specified as an offense.

Action by private persons taking the law into their own hands to mete out summary punishment and private vengeance upon an accused person; action by either public offices or private persons meting out summary punishment and private vengeance upon a person because of his race, color, creed or religion—these too must be made crimes.

Third, the statute should authorize immediate federal investigation in lynching cases to discover whether a federal offense has been committed. Fourth, adequate and flexible penalties ranging up to a $10,000 fine and a 20-year prison term should be provided.

The constitutionality of some parts of such a statute, particularly those providing for the prosecution of private persons, has been questioned. The Committee believes that there are several constitutional bases upon which such a law might be passed and that these are sufficiently strong to justify prompt action by Congress.

*   *   *   *

III. *To strengthen the right to citizenship and its privileges, the President's Committee recommends:*

1. Action by the states or Congress to end poll taxes as a voting prerequisite.

Considerable debate has arisen as to the constitutionality of a federal statute abolishing the poll tax. In four times passing an anti-poll tax bill, the House of Representatives has indicated its view that there is a reasonable chance that it will survive a court attack on constitutional grounds. We are convinced that the elimination of this obstacle to the right of suffrage must not be further delayed. It would be appropriate and encouraging for the remaining poll tax states voluntarily to take this step. Failing such prompt state action, we believe that the nation, either by act of Congress, or by constitutional amendment, should remove this final barrier to universal suffrage.

2. The enactment by Congress of a statute protecting the right of qualified persons to participate in federal primaries and elections against interference by public officers and private persons.

This statute would apply only to federal elections. There is no doubt that such a law can be applied to primaries which are an integral part of the federal electoral process or which affect or determine the result of a federal election. It can also protect participation in federal election campaigns and discussions of matters relating to national political issues. This statute should authorize the Department of Justice to use both civil and criminal sanctions. Civil remedies should be used wherever possible to test the legality of threatened interferences with the suffrage before voting rights have been lost.

3. The enactment by Congress of a statute protecting the right to qualify for, or participate in, federal or state primaries or elections against discriminatory action by state officers based on race or color, or depending on any other unreasonable classification of persons for voting purposes.

This statute would apply to both federal and state elections, but it would be limited to the protection of the right to vote against discriminatory interferences based on race, color, or other unreasonable classification. Its constitutionality is clearly indicated by the Fourteenth and Fifteenth Amendments. Like the legislation suggested under (2) it should authorize the use of civil and criminal sanctions by the Department of Justice.

*   *   *   *

V. *To strengthen the right to equality of opportunity, the President's Committee recommends:*
1. In general:
   The elimination of segregation, based on race, color, creed, or national origin, from American life.

The separate but equal doctrine has failed in three important respects. First, it is inconsistent with the fundamental equalitarianism of the American way of life in that it marks groups with the brand of inferior status. Secondly, where it has been followed, the results have been separate and unequal facilities for minority peoples. Finally, it has kept people apart despite incontrovertible evidence that an environment favorable to civil rights is fostered whenever groups are permitted to live and work together. There is no adequate defense of segregation.

   The conditioning by Congress of all federal grants-in-aid and other forms of federal assistance to public or private agencies for any purpose on the absence of discrimination and segregation based on race, color, creed, or national origin.

We believe that federal funds, supplied by taxpayers all over the nation, must not be used to support or perpetuate the pattern of segregation in education, public housing, public health services, or other public services and facilities generally. We recognize that these services are indispensable to individuals in modern society and to further social progress. It would be regrettable if federal aid, conditioned on nonsegregated services, should be rejected by sections most in need of such aid. The Committee believes that a reasonable interval of time may be allowed for adjustment to such a policy. But in the end it believes that segregation is wrong morally and practically and must not receive financial support by the whole people.

A minority of the Committee favors the elimination of segregation as an ultimate goal but opposes the imposition of a federal sanction. It believes that federal aid to the states for education, health, research and other public benefits should be granted provided that the states do not discriminate in the distribution of the funds. It dissents, however, from the majority's recommendation that the abolition of segregation be made a requirement, until the people of the states involved have themselves abolished the provisions in their state constitutions and laws which now require segregation. Some members are against the nonsegregation requirement in educational grants on the ground that it represents federal control over education. They feel, moreover, that the best way ultimately to end segregation is to raise the educational level of the people in the states affected; and to inculcate both the teachings of religion regarding human brotherhood and the ideals of our democracy regarding freedom and equality as a more solid basis for genuine and lasting acceptance by the peoples of the states.

2. For employment:

> The enactment of a federal Fair Employment Practice Act prohibiting all forms of discrimination in private employment, based on race, color, creed, or national origin.

A federal Fair Employment Practice Act prohibiting discrimination in private employment should provide both educational machinery and legal sanctions for enforcement purposes. The administration of the act should be placed in the hands of a commission with power to receive complaints, hold hearings, issue cease-and-desist orders and seek court aid in enforcing these orders. The Act should contain definite fines for the violation of its procedural provisions. In order to allow time for voluntary adjustment of employment practices to the new law, and to permit the establishment of effective enforcement machinery, it is recommended that the sanction provisions of the law not become operative until one year after the enactment of the law.

The federal act should apply to labor unions and trade and professional associations, as well as to employers, insofar as the policies and practices of these organizations affect the employment status of workers.

*   *   *   *

3. For education:

> Enactment by the state legislatures of fair educational practice laws for public and private educational institutions, prohibiting discrimination in the admission and treatment of students based on race, color, creed, or national origin.

These laws should be enforced by independent administrative commissions. These commissions should consider complaints and hold hearings to review them. Where they are found to be valid, direct negotiations with the offending institution should be undertaken to secure compliance with the law. Wide publicity for the commission's findings would influence many schools and colleges sensitive to public opinion to abandon discrimination. The final sanction for such a body would be the cease-and-desist order enforceable by court action. The Committee believes that educational institutions supported by churches and definitely identified as denominational should be exempted.

There is a substantial division within the Committee on this recommendation. A majority favors it.

*   *   *   *

6. For public services:

    The enactment by Congress of a law stating that discrimination and segregation, based on race, color, creed, or national origin, in the rendering of all public services by the national government is contrary to public policy;

    The enactment by the states of similar laws;

The elimination of discrimination and segregation depends largely on the leadership of the federal and state governments. They can make a great contribution toward accomplishing this end by affirming in law the principle of equality for all, and declaring that public funds, which belong to the whole people, will be used for the benefit of the entire population.

    The establishment by act of Congress or executive order of a unit in the federal Bureau of the Budget to review the execution of all government programs, and the expenditures of all government funds, for compliance with the policy of nondiscrimination;

Continual surveillance is necessary to insure the nondiscriminatory execution of federal programs involving use of government funds. The responsibility for this task should be located in the Bureau of the Budget which has the duty of formulating the executive budget and supervising the execution of appropriation acts. The Bureau already checks the various departments and agencies for compliance with announced policy. Administratively, this additional function is consistent with its present duties and commensurate with its present powers.

*   *   *   *

    The enactment by the states of laws guaranteeing equal access to places of public accommodation, broadly defined, for persons of all races, colors, creeds, and national origins.

Since the Constitution does not guarantee equal access to places of public accommodation, it is left to the states to secure that right. In the 18 states that have already enacted statutes, we hope that enforcement will make practice more compatible with theory. The civil suit for damages and the misdemeanor penalty have proved to be inadequate sanctions to secure the observance of these laws. Additional means, such as the revocation of licenses, and the issuance of cease-and-desist orders by administrative agencies are needed to bring about wider compliance. We think that all of the states should enact such legislation, using the broadest possible definition of public accommodation.

*   *   *   *

VI. *To rally the American people to the support of a continuing program to strengthen civil rights, the President's Committee recommends:* A long term campaign of public education to inform the people of the civil rights to which they are entitled and which they owe to one another.

The most important educational task in this field is to give the public living examples of civil rights in operation. This is the purpose of our recommendations which have gone before. But there still remains the job of driving home to the public the nature of our heritage, the justification of civil rights and the need to end prejudice. This is a task which will require the cooperation of the federal, state, and local governments and of private agencies. We believe that the permanent Commission on Civil Rights should take the leadership in serving as the coordinating body. The activities of the permanent Commission in this field should be expressly authorized by Congress and funds specifically appropriated for them.

*   *   *   *

II

Milestones of the Movement

THE SCHOOL SEGREGATION CASES (1954)

Little if any progress was made between the President's Committee Report in 1947 and the school segregation cases decided in 1954. Chief Justice Warren's unanimous opinion in Brown v. Board of Education, set out below, gave the civil rights movement a new start. In clear non-legalistic language, Chief Justice Warren declared that the separate but equal doctrine laid down by the Supreme Court sixty years before had no basis in the Constitution. The fact that he relied upon a series of psychological and sociological studies to support his conclusion (one is reproduced in this book's section on Education) showed the judicial realism which has governed many of the decisions of the Warren Court and has led to a series of important rulings in support of the civil rights movement.

Brown v. Board of Education of Topeka (1954)

MR. CHIEF JUSTICE WARREN delivered the opinion of the Court.

These cases come to us from the States of Kansas, South Carolina, Virginia, and Delaware. They are premised on different facts and different local conditions, but a common legal question justifies their consideration together in this consolidated opinion.

In each of the cases, minors of the Negro race, through their legal representatives, seek the aid of the courts in obtaining admission to the public schools of their community on a nonsegregated basis. In each instance, they had been denied admission to schools attended by white children under laws requiring or permitting segregation according to race. This segregation was alleged to deprive the plaintiffs of the equal protection of the laws under the Fourteenth Amendment. In each of the cases other than the Delaware case, a three-judge federal district court denied relief to the plaintiffs on the so-called "separate but equal" doctrine announced by this Court in *Plessy* v. *Ferguson,* 163 U.S. 537. Under that doctrine, equality of treatment is accorded when the races are provided substantially equal facilities, even though these facilities be separate. In the Delaware case, the Supreme Court of Delaware adhered to that doctrine, but ordered that the plaintiffs be admitted to the white schools because of their superiority to the Negro schools.

The plaintiffs contend that segregated public schools are not "equal" and cannot be made "equal," and that hence they are deprived of the equal protection of the laws. Because of the obvious importance of the question presented, the Court took jurisdiction. Argument was heard in the 1952 Term, and reargument was heard this Term on certain questions propounded by the Court.

Reargument was largely devoted to the circumstances surrounding the adoption of the Fourteenth Amendment in 1868. It covered exhaustively consideration of the Amendment in Congress, ratification by the states, then existing practices in racial segregation, and the views of proponents and opponents of the Amendment. This discussion and our own investigation convince us that, although these sources cast some light, it is not enough to resolve the problem with which we are faced. At best, they are inconclusive. The most avid proponents of the post-War Amendments undoubtedly intended them to remove all legal distinctions among "all persons born or naturalized in the United States." Their opponents, just as certainly, were antagonistic to both the letter and the spirit of the Amendments and wished them to have the most limited effect. What others in Congress and the state legislature had in mind cannot be determined with any degree of certainty.

An additional reason for the inconclusive nature of the Amendment's history, with respect to segregated schools, is the status of public education at that time. In the South, the movement toward free common schools, supported by general taxation, had not yet taken hold. Education of white children was largely in the hands of private groups. Education of Negroes was almost non-existent, and practically all of the race were illiterate. In fact, any education of Negroes was forbidden by law in some states. Today, in contrast, many Negroes have achieved outstanding success in the arts and sciences as well as in the business and professional world. It is true that public school education at the time of the Amendment had advanced further in the North, but the effect of the Amendment on Northern States was generally ignored in the congressional debates. Even in the North, the conditions of public education did not approximate those existing today. The curriculum was usually rudimentary; ungraded schools were common in rural areas; the school term was but three months a year in many states; and compulsory school attendance was virtually unknown. As a consequence, it is not surprising that there should be so little in the history of the Fourteenth Amendment relating to its intended effect on public education.

In the first cases in this Court construing the Fourteenth Amendment, decided shortly after its adoption, the Court interpreted it as proscribing all state-imposed discriminations against the Negro race. The doctrine of "separate but equal" did not make its appearance in this Court until 1896 in the case of *Plessy* v. *Ferguson, supra,* involving not education but transportation. American courts have since labored with the doctrine for over half a century. In this Court, there have been six cases involving the "separate but equal" doctrine in the field of public education. In *Cumming* v. *County Board of Education,* 175 U. S. 528, and *Gong Lum* v. *Rice,* 275 U. S. 78, the validity of the doctrine itself was not challenged. In more recent cases, all on the graduate school level, inequality was found in that specific benefits enjoyed by white students were denied to Negro students of the same educational qualifications. *Missouri ex rel. Gaines* v. *Canada,* 305 U. S. 337; *Sipuel* v. *Oklahoma,* 332 U. S. 631; *Sweatt* v. *Painter,* 339 U. S. 629; *McLaurin* v. *Oklahoma State Regents,* 339 U. S. 637. In none of these cases was it necessary to re-examine the doctrine to grant relief to the Negro plaintiff. And in *Sweatt* v. *Painter, supra,* the Court expressly reserved decision on the question whether *Plessy* v. *Ferguson* should be held inapplicable to public education.

In the instant cases, that question is directly presented. Here, unlike *Sweatt* v. *Painter,* there are findings below that the Negro and white schools involved have been equalized, or are being equalized, with respect to buildings, curricula, qualifications and salaries of teachers, and other "tangible" factors. Our decision, therefore, cannot turn on merely a comparison of these tangible factors in the Negro and white schools involved in each of the cases. We must look instead to the effect of segregation itself on public education.

In approaching this problem, we cannot turn the clock back to 1868 when the Amendment was adopted, or even to 1896 when *Plessy* v. *Ferguson* was written. We must consider public education in the light of its full development and its present place in American life throughout the Nation. Only in this way can it be determined if segregation in public schools deprives these plaintiffs of the equal protection of the laws.

Today, education is perhaps the most important function of state and local governments. Compulsory school attendance laws and the great expenditures for education both demonstrate our recognition of the importance of education to our democratic society. It is required in the performance of our most basic public responsibilities, even service in the armed forces. It is the very foundation of good citizenship. Today it is a principal instrument in awakening the child to cultural values, in preparing him for later professional training, and in helping him to adjust normally to his environment. In these days, it is doubtful that any child may reasonably be expected to succeed in life if he is denied the opportunity of an education. Such an opportunity, where the state has undertaken to provide it, is a right which must be made available to all on equal terms.

We come then to the question presented: Does segregation of children in public schools solely on the basis of race, even though the physical facilities and other "tangible" factors may be equal, deprive the children of the minority group of equal educational opportunities? We believe that it does.

In *Sweatt* v. *Painter, supra,* in finding that a segregated law school for Negroes could not provide them equal educational opportunities, this Court relied in large part on "those qualities which are incapable of objective measurement but which make for greatness in a law school." In *McLaurin* v. *Oklahoma State Regents, supra,* the Court, in requiring that a Negro admitted to a white graduate school be treated like all other students, again resorted to intangible considerations: ". . . . his ability to study, to engage in discussions and exchange views with other students, and, in general, to learn his profession." Such considerations apply with added force to children in grade and high schools. To separate them from others of similar age and qualifications solely because of their race generates a feeling of inferiority as to their status in the community that may affect their hearts and minds in a way unlikely ever to be undone. The effect of this separation on their educational opportunities was well stated by a finding in the Kansas case by a court which nevertheless felt compelled to rule against the Negro plaintiffs:

"Segregation of white and colored children in public schools has a detrimental effect upon the colored children. The impact is greater when it has the sanction of the law; for the policy of separating the races is usually interpreted as denoting the inferiority of the negro group. A sense of inferiority affects the motivation of a child to learn. Segregation with the sanction of law, therefore, has a tendency to [retard] the educational and mental development of negro children and to deprive them of some of the benefits they would receive in a racial[ly] integrated school system."

Whatever may have been the extent of psychological knowledge at the time of *Plessy* v. *Ferguson,* this finding is amply supported by modern authority.* Any language in *Plessy* v. *Ferguson* contrary to this finding is rejected.

We conclude that in the field of public education the doctrine of "separate but equal" has no place. Separate educational facilities are inherently unequal. Therefore, we hold that the plaintiffs and others similarly situated for whom the actions have been brought are, by reason of the segregation complained of, deprived of the equal protection of the laws guaranteed by the Fourteenth Amendment. This disposition makes unnecessary any discussion whether such segregation also violates the Due Process Clause of the Fourteenth Amendment.

Because these are class actions, because of the wide applicability of this decision, and because of the great variety of local conditions, the formulation of decrees in these cases presents problems of considerable complexity. On reargument, the consideration of appropriate relief was necessarily subordinated to the primary question—the constitutionality of segregation in public education. We have now announced that such segregation is a denial of the equal protection of the laws. In order that we may have the full assistance of the parties in formulating decrees, the cases will be restored to the docket, and the parties are requested to present further argument on Questions 4 and 5 previously propounded by the Court for the reargument this Term. The Attorney General of the United States is again invited to participate. The Attorneys General of the states requiring or permitting segregation in public education will also be permitted to appear as *amici curiae* upon request to do so by September 15, 1954, and submission of briefs by October 1, 1954.

It is so ordered.

THE MONTGOMERY BUS BOYCOTT (1955)

A year after the Brown decision, came what Louis E. Lomax called "the birth of the Negro revolt." On December 1, 1955, Mrs. Rosa Parks,

---

* K.B. Clark, Effect of Prejudice and Discrimination on Personality Development (Midcentury White House Conference on Children and Youth, 1950); Witmer and Kotinsky, Personality in the Making (1952), c. VI; Deutscher and Chein, The Psychological Effects of Enforced Segregation: A Survey of Social Science Opinion, 26 J. Psychol. 259 (1948); Chein, What are the Psychological Effects of Segregation Under Conditions of Equal Facilities?, 3 Int. J. Opinion and Attitude Res. 229 (1949); Brameld, Educational Costs, in Discrimination and National Welfare (MacIver, ed., 1949), 44-48; Frazier, The Negro in the United States (1949), 674-681. And see generally Myrdal, An American Dilemma (1944).

was arrested on the Cleveland Avenue bus in Montgomery, Alabama. The arrest gave rise to the first organized drive by Negroes in defense of their rights. Led by Martin Luther King, at the time a twenty-seven-year-old Doctor of Divinity, the Negroes of Montgomery refused to ride the Montgomery buses until they were desegregated. Reverend King's forceful description of the boycott in his book, "Stride Toward Freedom," selections of which appear below, shows what well-organized, united activity can do.

Stride Toward Freedom, MARTIN LUTHER KING, JR. (1958)

*   *   *   *

Chapter 3. The Decisive Arrest

On December 1, 1955, an attractive Negro seamstress, Mrs. Rosa Parks, boarded the Cleveland Avenue bus in downtown Montgomery. She was returning home after her regular day's work in the Montgomery Fair—a leading department store. Tired from long hours on her feet, Mrs. Parks sat down in the first seat behind the section reserved for whites. Not long after she took her seat, the bus operator ordered her, along with three other Negro passengers, to move back in order to accommodate boarding white passengers. By this time every seat in the bus was taken. This meant that if Mrs. Parks followed the driver's command she would have to stand while a white male passenger, who had just boarded the bus, would sit. The other three Negro passengers immediately complied with the driver's request. But Mrs. Parks quietly refused. The result was her arrest.

There was to be much speculation about why Mrs. Parks did not obey the driver. Many people in the white community argued that she had been "planted" by the NAACP in order to lay the groundwork for a test case, and at first glance that explanation seemed plausible, since she was a former secretary of the local branch of the NAACP. So persistent and persuasive was this argument that it convinced many reporters from all over the country. Later on, when I was having press conferences three times a week—in order to accommodate the reporters and journalists who came to Montgomery from all over the world—the invariable first question was: "Did the NAACP start the bus boycott?"

But the accusation was totally unwarranted, as the testimony of both Mrs. Parks and the officials of the NAACP revealed. Actually, no one can understand the action of Mrs. Parks unless he realizes that eventually the cup of endurance runs over, and the human personality cries out, "I can take it no longer." Mrs. Parks's refusal to move back was her intrepid affirmation that she had had enough. It was an individual expression of a timeless longing for human dignity and freedom. She was not "planted" there by the NAACP, or any other organization; she was planted there by her personal sense of dignity and self-respect. She was anchored to that seat by the accumulated indignities of days gone by and the boundless aspirations of generations yet unborn. She was a victim of both the forces of history and the forces of destiny. She had been tracked down by the *Zeitgeist*—the spirit of the time.

Fortunately, Mrs. Parks was ideal for the role assigned to her by history. She was a charming person with a radiant personality, soft spoken and calm in all situations. Her character was impeccable and her dedication deep-rooted. All of these traits together made her one of the most respected people in the Negro community.

Only E. D. Nixon—the signer of Mrs. Parks's bond—and one or two other persons were aware of the arrest when it occurred early Thursday evening. Later in the evening the word got around to a few influential women of the community, mostly members of the Women's Political Council. After a series of telephone calls back and forth they agreed that the Negroes should boycott the buses. They immediately suggested the idea to Nixon, and he readily concurred. In his usual courageous manner he agreed to spearhead the idea.

Early Friday morning, December 2, Nixon called me. He was so caught up in what he was about to say that he forgot to greet me with the usual "hello" but plunged immediately into the story of what had happened to Mrs. Parks the night before. I listened, deeply shocked, as he described the humiliating incident. "We have taken this type of thing too long already," Nixon concluded, his voice trembling. "I feel that the time has come to boycott the buses. Only through a boycott can we make it clear to the white folks that we will not accept this type of treatment any longer."

I agreed at once that some protest was necessary, and that the boycott method would be an effective one.

Just before calling me Nixon had discussed the idea with Rev. Ralph Abernathy, the young minister of Montgomery's First Baptist Church, who was to become one of the central figures in the protest, and one of my closest associates. Abernathy also felt a bus boycott was our best course of action. So for thirty or forty minutes the three of us telephoned back and forth concerning plans and strategy. Nixon suggested that we call a meeting of all the ministers and civic leaders the same evening in order to get their thinking on the proposal, and I offered my church as the meeting place. The three of us got busy immediately. With the sanction of Rev. H. H. Hubbard—president of the Baptist Ministerial Alliance—Abernathy and I began calling all of the Baptist ministers. Since most of the Methodist ministers were attending a denominational meeting in one of the local churches that afternoon, it was possible for Abernathy to get the announcement to all of them simultaneously. Nixon reached Mrs. A. W. West—the widow of a prominent dentist—and enlisted her assistance in getting word to the civic leaders.

By early afternoon the arrest of Mrs. Parks was becoming public knowledge. Word of it spread around the community like uncontrolled fire. Telephones began to ring in almost rhythmic succession. By two o'clock an enthusiastic group had mimeographed leaflets concerning the arrest and the proposed boycott, and by evening these had been widely circulated.

As the hour for the evening meeting arrived, I approached the doors of the church with some apprehension, wondering how many of the leaders would respond to our call. Fortunately, it was one of those pleasant winter nights of unseasonable warmth, and to our relief, almost everybody who had been invited was on hand. More than forty people, from every segment of Negro life, were crowded into the large church meeting room. I saw physicians, schoolteachers, lawyers, businessmen, postal workers, union leaders, and clergymen. Virtually every organization of the Negro community was represented.

The largest number there was from the Christian ministry. Having left so many civic meetings in the past sadly disappointed by the dearth of ministers participating, I was filled with joy when I entered the church and found so many of them there; for then I knew that something unusual was about to happen.

Had E. D. Nixon been present, he would probably have been automatically selected to preside, but he had had to leave town earlier in the afternoon for his regular run on the railroad. In his absence, we concluded that Rev. L. Roy Bennett—as president of the Interdenominational Ministerial Alliance—was the logical person to take the chair. He agreed and was seated, his tall, erect figure dominating the room.

The meeting opened around seven-thirty with H. H. Hubbard leading a brief devotional period. Then Bennett moved into action, explaining the purpose of the gathering. With excited gestures he reported on Mrs. Parks's resistance and her arrest. He presented the proposal that the Negro citizens of Montgomery should boycott the buses on Monday in protest. "Now is the time to move," he concluded. "This is no time to talk; it is time to act."

So seriously did Bennett take his "no time to talk" admonition that for quite a while he refused to allow anyone to make a suggestion or even raise a question, insisting that we should move on and appoint committees to implement the proposal. This approach aroused the opposition of most of those present, and created a temporary uproar. For almost forty-five minutes the confusion persisted. Voices rose high, and many people threatened to leave if they could not raise questions and offer suggestions. It looked for a time as though the movement had come to an end before it began. But finally, in the face of this blistering protest, Bennett agreed to open the meeting to discussion.

Immediately questions began to spring up from the floor. Several people wanted further clarification of Mrs. Parks's actions and arrest. Then came the more practical questions. How long would the protest last? How would the idea be further disseminated throughout the community? How would the people be transported to and from their jobs?

As we listened to the lively discussion, we were heartened to notice that, despite the lack of coherence in the meeting, not once did anyone question the validity or desirability of the boycott itself. It seemed to be the unanimous sense of the group that the boycott should take place.

The ministers endorsed the plan with enthusiasm, and promised to go to their congregations on Sunday morning and drive home their approval of the projected one-day protest. Their coöperation was significant, since virtually all of the influential Negro ministers of the city were present. It was decided that we should hold a city-wide mass meeting on Monday night, December 5, to determine how long we would abstain from riding the buses. Rev. A. W. Wilson—minister of the Holt Street Baptist Church—offered his church, which was ideal as a meeting place because of its size and central location. The group agreed that additional leaflets should be distributed on Saturday, and the chairman appointed a committee, including myself, to prepare the statement.

Our committee went to work while the meeting was still in progress. The final message was shorter than the one that had appeared on the first leaflets, but the substance was the same. It read as follows:

> Don't ride the bus to work, to town, to school, or any place Monday, December 5.
> Another Negro woman has been arrested and put in jail because she refused to give up her bus seat.
> Don't ride the buses to work, to town, to school, or anywhere on Monday. If you work, take a cab, or share a ride, or walk.
> Come to a mass meeting, Monday at 7:00 P.M., at the Holt Street Baptist Church for further instruction.

After finishing the statement the committee began to mimeograph it on the church machine; but since it was late, I volunteered to have the job completed early Saturday morning.

The final question before the meeting concerned transportation. It was agreed that we should try to get the Negro taxi companies of the city—eighteen in number, with approximately 210 taxis—to transport the people for the same price that they were currently paying on the bus. A committee was appointed to make this contact, with Rev. W. J. Powell, minister of the Old Ship A.M.E. Zion Church, as chairman.

With these responsibilities before us the meeting closed. We left with our hearts caught up in a great idea. The hours were moving fast. The clock on the wall read almost midnight, but the clock in our souls revealed that it was daybreak.

I was so excited that I slept very little that night, and early the next morning I was on my way to the church to get the leaflets out. By nine o'clock the church secretary had finished mimeographing the 7000 leaflets and by eleven o'clock an army of women and young people had taken them off to distribute by hand.

Those on the committee that was to contact the taxi companies got to work early Saturday afternoon. They worked assiduously, and by evening they had reached practically all of the companies, and triumphantly reported that every one of them so far had agreed to coöperate with the proposed boycott by transporting the passengers to and from work for the regular ten-cent bus fare.

Meanwhile our efforts to get the word across to the Negro community were abetted in an unexpected way. A maid who could not read very well came into possession of one of the unsigned appeals that had been distributed Friday afternoon. Apparently not knowing what the leaflet said, she gave it to her white employer. As soon as the employer received the notice she turned it over to the local newspaper, and the *Montgomery Advertiser* made the contents of the leaflet a front-page story on Saturday morning. It appears that the *Advertiser* printed the story in order to let the white community know what the Negroes were up to; but the whole thing turned out to the Negroes' advantage, since it served to bring the information to hundreds who had not previously heard of the plan. By Sunday afternoon word had spread to practically every Negro citizen of Montgomery. Only a few people who lived in remote areas had not heard of it.

*   *   *   *

Chapter 4.   The Day of Days, December 5

My wife and I awoke earlier than usual on Monday morning. We were up and fully dressed by five-thirty. The day for the protest had arrived, and we were determined to see the first act of this unfolding drama. I was still saying that if we could get 60 per cent coöperation the venture would be a success.

Fortunately, a bus stop was just five feet from our house. This meant that we could observe the opening stages from our front window. The first bus was to pass around six o'clock. And so we waited through an interminable half hour. I was in the kitchen drinking my coffee when I heard Coretta cry, "Martin, Martin, come quickly!" I put down my cup and ran toward the living room. As I approached the front window Coretta pointed joyfully to a slowly moving bus: "Darling, it's empty!" I could hardly believe what I saw. I knew that the South Jackson line, which ran past our house, carried more Negro passengers than any other line in Montgomery, and that this first bus was usually filled with domestic workers going to their jobs. Would all of the other buses follow the pattern that had been set by the first? Eagerly we waited for the next bus. In fifteen minutes it rolled down the street, and like the first, it was empty. A third bus appeared, and it too was empty of all but two white passengers.

I jumped in my car and for almost an hour I cruised down every major street and examined every passing bus. During this hour, at the peak of the morning traffic, I saw no more than eight Negro passengers riding the buses. By this time I was jubilant. Instead of the 60 per cent coöperation we had hoped for, it was becoming apparent that we had reached almost 100 per cent. A miracle had taken place. The once dormant and quiescent Negro community was now fully awake.

All day long it continued. At the afternoon peak the buses were still as empty of Negro passengers as they had been in the morning. Students of Alabama State College, who usually kept the South Jackson bus crowded, were cheerfully walking or thumbing rides. Job holders had either found other means of transportation or made their way on foot. While some rode in cabs or private cars, others used less conventional means. Men were seen riding mules to work, and more than one horse-drawn buggy drove the streets of Montgomery that day.

During the rush hours the sidewalks were crowded with laborers and domestic workers, many of them well past middle age, trudging patiently to their jobs and home again, sometimes as much as twelve miles. They knew why they walked, and the knowledge was evident in the way they carried themselves. And as I watched them I knew that there is nothing more majestic than the determined courage of individuals willing to suffer and sacrifice for their freedom and dignity.

Many spectators had gathered at the bus stops to watch what was happening. At first they stood quietly, but as the day progressed they began to cheer the empty buses and laugh and make jokes. Noisy young-sters could be heard singing out, "No riders today." Trailing each bus through the Negro section were two policemen on motorcycles, assigned by the city commissioners, who claimed that Negro "goon squads" had been organized to keep other Negroes from riding the buses. In the course of the day the police succeeded in making one arrest. A college student who was helping an elderly woman across the street was charged with "intimidating passengers." But the "goon squads" existed only in the commission's imagination. No one was threatened or intimidated for riding the buses; the only harassment anyone faced was that of his own conscience.

Around nine-thirty in the morning I tore myself from the action of the city streets and headed for the crowded police court. Here Mrs. Parks was being tried for disobeying the city segregation ordinance. Her attorney, Fred D. Gray—the brilliant young Negro who later be-came the chief counsel for the protest movement—was on hand to defend her. After the judge heard the arguments, he found Mrs. Parks guilty and fined her ten dollars and court costs (a total of fourteen dollars). She appealed the case. This was one of the first clear-cut instances in which a Negro had been convicted for disobeying the segregation law. In the past, either cases like this had been dismissed or the pople involved had been charged with disorderly conduct. So in a real sense the arrest and conviction of Mrs. Parks had a twofold impact: it was a precipita-ing factor to arouse the Negroes to positive action; and it was a test of the validity of the segregation law itself. I am sure that supporters of such prosecutions would have acted otherwise if they had had the prescience to look beyond the moment.

*　*　*　*

Within five blocks of the church I noticed a traffic jam. Cars were lined up as far as I could see on both sides of the street. It was a moment before it occurred to me that all of these cars were headed for the mass meeting. I had to park at least four blocks from the church, and as I started walking I noticed that hundreds of people were standing outside. In the dark night, police cars circled slowly around the area, surveying the orderly, patient, and good-humored crowd. The three or four thousand people who could not get into the church were to stand cheerfully throughout the evening listening to the proceedings on the loudspeakers that had been set up outside for their benefit. And when, near the end of the meeting, these speakers were silenced at the request of the white people in surrounding neighborhoods, the crowd would still remain quietly, content simply to be present.

It took fully fifteen minutes to push my way through to the pastor's study, where Dr. Wilson told me that the church had been packed since five o'clock. By now my doubts concerning the continued success of our venture were dispelled. The question of calling off the protest was now academic. The enthusiasm of these thousands of people swept everything along like an onrushing tidal wave.

It was some time before the remaining speakers could push their way to the rostrum through the tightly packed church. When the meeting began it was almost half an hour late. The opening hymn was the old familiar "Onward, Christian Soldiers," and when that mammoth audience stood to sing, the voices outside swelling the chorus in the church, there was a mighty ring like the glad echo of heaven itself.

Rev. W. F. Alford, minister of the Beulah Baptist Church, led the congregation in prayer, followed by a reading of the Scripture by Rev. U. J. Fields, minister of the Bell Street Baptist Church. Then the chairman introduced me. As the audience applauded, I rose and stood before the pulpit. Television cameras began to shoot from all sides. The crowd grew quiet.

Without manuscript or notes, I told the story of what had happened to Mrs. Parks. Then I reviewed the long history of abuses and insults that Negro citizens had experienced on the city buses. "But there comes a time," I said, "when people get tired. We are here this evening to say to those who have mistreated us so long that we are tired—tired of being segregated and humiliated; tired of being kicked about by the brutal feet of oppression." The congregation met this statement with fervent applause. "We had no alternative but to protest," I continued. "For many years, we have shown amazing patience. We have sometimes given our white brothers the feeling that we liked the way we were being treated. But we come here tonight to be saved from that patience that makes us patient with anything less than freedom and justice." Again the audience interrupted with applause.

Briefly I justified our actions, both morally and legally. "One of the great glories of democracy is the right to protest for right." Comparing our methods with those of the White Citizens Councils and the Ku Klux Klan, I pointed out that while "these organizations are protesting for the perpetuation of injustice in the community, we are protesting for the birth of justice in the community. Their methods lead to violence and lawlessness. But in our protest there will be no cross burnings. No white person will be taken from his home by a hooded Negro mob and brutally murdered. There will be no threats and intimidations. We will be guided by the highest principles of law and order."

With this groundwork for militant action, I moved on to words of caution. I urged the people not to force anybody to refrain from riding the buses. "Our method will be that of persuasion, not coercion. We will only say to the people, 'Let your conscience be your guide.' " Emphasizing the Christian doctrine of love, "our actions must be guided by the deepest principles of our Christian faith. Love must be our regulating ideal. Once again we must hear the words of Jesus echoing across the centuries: 'Love your enemies, bless them that curse you, and pray for them that despitefully use you.' If we fail to do this our protest will end up as a meaningless drama on the stage of history, and its memory will be shrouded with the ugly garments of shame. In spite of the mistreatment that we have confronted we must not become bitter, and end up by hating our white brothers. As Booker T. Washington said, 'Let no man pull you so low as to make you hate him.' " Once more the audience responded enthusiastically.

Then came my closing statement. "If you will protest courageously, and yet with dignity and Christian love, when the history books are written in future generations, the historians will have to pause and say, 'There lived a great people—a black people—who injected new meaning and dignity into the veins of civilization.' This is our challenge and our overwhelming responsibility." As I took my seat the people rose to their feet and applauded. I was thankful to God that the message had gotten over and that the task of combining the militant and the moderate had been at least partially accomplished. The people had been as enthusiastic when I urged them to love as they were when I urged them to protest.

*   *   *   *

Many will inevitably raise the question, why did this event take place in Montgomery, Alabama, in 1955? Some have suggested that the Supreme Court decision on school desegregation, handed down less than two years before, had given new hope of eventual justice to Negroes everywhere, and fired them with the necessary spark of encouragement to rise against their oppression. But although this might help to explain why the protest occurred when it did, it cannot explain why it happened in Montgomery.

Certainly, there is a partial explanation in the long history of injustice on the buses of Montgomery. The bus protest did not spring into being full grown as Athena sprang from the head of Zeus; it was the culmination of a slowly developing process. Mrs. Parks's arrest was the precipitating factor rather than the cause of the protest. The cause lay deep in the record of similar injustices. Almost everybody could point to an unfortunate episode that he himself had experienced or seen.

But there comes a time when people get tired of being trampled by oppression. There comes a time when people get tired of being plunged into the abyss of exploitation and nagging injustice. The story of Montgomery is the story of 50,000 such Negroes who were willing to substitute tired feet for tired souls, and walk the streets of Montgomery until the walls of segregation were finally battered by the forces of justice.

But neither is this the whole explanation. Negroes in other communities confronted conditions equally as bad, and often worse. So we cannot explain the Montgomery story merely in terms of the abuses that Negroes suffered there. Moreover, it cannot be explained by a preëxistent unity among the leaders, since we have seen that the Montgomery Negro community prior to the protest was marked by divided leadership, indifference, and complacency. Nor can it be explained by the appearance upon the scene of new leadership. The Montgomery story would have taken place if the leaders of the protest had never been born.

So every rational explanation breaks down at some point. There is something about the protest that is suprarational; it cannot be explained without a divine dimension. Some may call it a principle of concretion, with Alfred N. Whitehead; or a process of integration, with Henry N. Wieman; or Being-itself, with Paul Tillich; or a personal God. Whatever the name, some extra-human force labors to create a harmony out of the discords of the universe. There is a creative power that works to pull down mountains of evil and level hilltops of injustice. God still works through history His wonders to perform. It seems as though God had decided to use Montgomery as the proving ground for the struggle and triumph of freedom and justice in America. And what better place for it than the leading symbol of the Old South? It is one of the splendid ironies of our day that Montgomery, the Cradle of the Confederacy, is being transformed into Montgomery, the cradle of freedom and justice.

The day of days, Monday, December 5, 1955, was drawing to a close. We all prepared to go to our homes, not yet fully aware of what had happened. The deliberations of that brisk, cool night in December will not be forgotten. That night we were starting a movement that would gain national recognition; whose echoes would ring in the ears of people of every nation; a movement that would astound the oppressor, and

bring new hope to the oppressed. That night was Montgomery's moment
in history.

*   *   *   *

THE SIT-IN CAMPAIGN (1960)

*For the next four years after the Montgomery bus boycott, the main
action of the civil rights movement took place in the courts, primarily
in school desegregation cases. The Little Rock crisis of 1957 showed
the extent to which Southern racists—both in government and without
—were prepared to fight. (Elizabeth Eckford's moving description of her
attempt to enter Little Rock High School is reproduced in the section
on Education.)*

*In 1960 the movement gathered force in the development of the
"sit-in" campaign. Montgomery had shown what nonviolent direct
action could do in the way of securing to the Negro his legal rights.
When Joseph McNeill, Ezelle Blair, Jr., Franklin McCain and David
Richmond, freshmen at A. & T. College in Greensboro, North Carolina,
sat for hours at the Woolworth lunch counter without being served,
they set into motion what Howard Zinn calls "a movement that would
soon take on the proportions of a revolution." The following selection
from his "SNCC: The New Abolitionists," shows the great impact that
the Greensboro sit-in was to have upon the participants, and upon the
young Negroes of the South who became the leaders of the direct
action phase of the revolution.*

SNCC: The New Abolitionists, HOWARD ZINN (1964)

*   *   *   *

Chapter 2.   Out of the Sit-ins

"My stomach always hurt a little on the way to a sit-in. . . . I guess
it's the unexpected." Candie Anderson, a white girl attending Fisk University as an exchange student from Pomona College in California, had
joined her Negro classmates to demonstrate against segregation in Nashville, Tennesseee. It was the explosion of sit-ins throughout the South
in early 1960 that led to the formation of the Student Nonviolent Coordinating Committee.

On February 1, 1960, four freshmen at A & T College in Greensboro,
North Carolina, took seats at a lunch counter downtown, not knowing
they were starting a movement that would soon take on the proportions
of a revolution. "For about a week," David Richmond recalled later,
"we four fellows sat around the A & T campus, talking about the inte-

gration movement. And we decided we ought to go down to Woolworth's and see what would happen." They spent an hour sitting at the Woolworth's counter, with no service. Then the counter was closed for the day, and they went home.

In a matter of days, the idea leaped to other cities in North Carolina. During the next two weeks, sit-ins spread to fifteen cities in five Southern states. Within the following year, over 50,000 people—most were Negroes, some were white—had participated in one kind of demonstration or another in a hundred cities, and over 3600 demonstrators spent time in jail. But there were results to show: by the end of 1961, several hundred lunch counters had been desegregated in scores of cities —in Texas, Oklahoma, the border states of the South, and even as far as Atlanta, Georgia. A wall of resistance, however, apparently impenetrable, faced the student in the rest of Georgia, South Carolina, Alabama, Mississippi, Louisiana—the hard-core Deep South.

It is hard to overestimate the electrical effect of that first sit-in in Greensboro, as the news reached the nation on television screens, over radios, in newspapers. In his Harlem apartment in New York City, Bob Moses, a former Harvard graduate student and mathematics teacher, saw a picture of the Greensboro sit-inners. "The students in that picture had a certain look on their faces," he later told writer Ben Bagdikian, "sort of sullen, angry, determined. Before, the Negro in the South had always looked on the defensive, cringing. This time they were taking the initiative. They were kids my age, and I knew this had something to do with my own life. . . ."

In Atlanta, Morehouse College student Julian Bond, who wrote poetry and thought about being a journalist, reacted quickly to the Greensboro sit-in. He and another student, discussing it in the Yates & Milton drug store across the street from the campus, decided to summon Morehouse men to a meeting. Out of that grew the Atlanta student movement, which six weeks later erupted in one of the largest and best organized sit-in demonstrations of all.

Also in Atlanta, seventeen-year-old Ruby Doris Smith, a sophomore at Spelman College, heard about the Greensboro sit-in and ran home that evening to see it on television:

> I began to think right away about it happening in Atlanta, but I wasn't ready to act on my own. When the student committee was formed in the Atlanta University Center, I told my older sister, who was on the Student Council at Morris Brown College, to put me on the list. And when two hundred students were selected for the first demonstration, I was among them. I went through the food line in the restaurant at the State Capitol with six

other students, but when we got to the cashier, she wouldn't take our money. She ran upstairs to get the Governor. The Lieutenant-Governor came down and told us to leave. We didn't, and went to the county jail.

Charles ("Chuck") McDew, a husky former athlete from Massilon, Ohio, was studying at South Carolina State College in Orangeburg. McDew had never adjusted to South Carolina; he had been arrested three times in his first three months there, and was struck by a policeman for trying to enter the main YMCA. When, during Religious Emphasis Week at the College, some visiting white Protestant ministers had responded negatively to his question about attending their churches, and a rabbi invited him to the temple, he converted to Judaism. With the news of Greensboro being discussed all around him, McDew read in the Talmud: "If I am not for myself, then who is for me? If I am for myself alone, then what am I? If not now, when?" He became a leader of the local sit-in movement.

To these young people, the Supreme Court decision of 1954 was a childhood memory. The Montgomery bus boycott of 1955, the first mass action by Southern Negroes, though also dimly remembered, was an inspiration. The trouble at Little Rock in 1957 was more vivid, with the unforgettable photos of the young Negro girl walking past screaming crowds towards Central High School. The Greensboro sit-ins struck a special chord of repressed emotion, and excitement raced across the Negro college campuses of the South.

Bob Moses, Julian Bond, Ruby Doris Smith, Chuck McDew: all were to become stalwarts in the Student Nonviolent Coordinating Committee. And for so many others in SNCC, the Greensboro sit-in—more than the Supreme Court decision, more than the Little Rock crisis, more than the Montgomery bus boycott, more than the recent declarations of independence by a host of African nations, and yet, perhaps, owing its galvanic force to the accumulation of all these events—was a turning point in their lives. James Forman, studying French in graduate school in the North, began turning his thoughts southward. Exactly what was going on in the minds of so many other students, soon to leave school for "The Movement," remains unknown.

Out of the Nashville, Tennessee, sit-ins, a battalion of future SNCC people took shape. Tall, quiet, Marion Barry, a graduate student in chemistry at Fisk University, who would later become the first chairman of SNCC, took a leading part in the Nashville sit-ins from the beginning. His father, a Mississippi farmer, migrated to Memphis, Tennessee, and Barry went to school there. As an undergraduate at LeMoyne College in Memphis, he publicly protested an anti-Negro remark made by a prominent white trustee of the college, created an uproar in the city, and barely avoided being expelled.

> I came to Fisk . . . inquired about forming a college chapter of the NAACP . . . . But we didn't do much. . . . We had not at any time thought of direct action. . . . In the meantime in Greensboro, N.C., the student movement began February 1, 1960. So we in Nashville decided we wanted to do something about it. . . . I remember the first time I was arrested, about February 27. . . . I took a chance on losing a scholarship or not receiving my Master's degree. But to me, if I had received my scholarship and Master's degree, and still was not a free man, I was not a man at all.

John Lewis, short, fiery, from a small town in Alabama, was also in Nashville as a seminary student when the sit-ins began. He immediately became involved and went to jail four times. "My mother wrote me a letter and said 'Get out of the movement,' but I couldn't. . . . I wrote her and said, 'I have acted according to my convictions and according to my Christian conscience. . . . My soul will not be satisfied until freedom, justice, and fair play become a reality for all people.' " Lewis later followed Marion Barry and Chuck McDew to become Chairman of SNCC.

"Do show yourself friendly on the counter at all times. Do sit straight and always face the counter. Don't strike back, or curse back if attacked. Don't laugh out. Don't hold conversations. Don't block entrances." These were the instructions to sit-in demonstrators in Nashville. They demanded a careful balance of quiet non-resistance and a determined militancy, and perhaps no one better expressed this than Diane Nash, a tiny, slender, campus beauty queen at Fisk, one of the pillars of the Nashville student movement and later a founder of SNCC. When students were being cross-examined at the trials that followed the Nashville demonstrations, one of the standard questions was: "Do you know Diane Nash?" Friendship with her was apparently full of perils.

Twelve days after the Greensboro incident, forty students sat in at Woolworth's in Nashville. There was at first some discussion about whether the white exchange students should go along, but finally the prevailing opinion was in favor. Candie Anderson recalls:

> That first sit-in was easy. . . . It was a Thursday afternoon and it was snowing. There were not many people downtown. Store personnel ran around nervously. . . . My friends were determined to be courteous and well-behaved . . . . Most of them read or studied while they sat at the counters, for three or four hours. I heard them remind each other not to leave cigarette ashes on the counter, to take off their hats, etc. . . . When the sit-in was over

we all met in church. There must have been five hundred kids there, and we all sang together. . . .

By the fourth sit-in, tension was mounting rapidly. There was violence that day. Lighted cigarettes were pushed against the backs of girls sitting at the counter. A white sit-inner, on a stool beside a Negro girl, became a special object of attention by the crowd nearby. Someone kept calling him a "nigger-lover." When he didn't respond he was pulled off the stool, thrown to the floor, and kicked. At McClellan's variety store, a white man kept blowing cigar smoke into the face of a Negro sitting at the counter, a Fisk University student named Paul LePrad, who made no move. This infuriated the man. He pulled the student from his stool and hit him. LePrad got back on the stool. He was pulled off again and hit. The police came and arrested LePrad and the seventeen students sitting in with him.

The group at Woolworth's, where Candie Anderson was, heard about this incident. They decided to go to McClellan's to protest.

> There was a rope around the stools, showing that the counter was closed. We climbed over the rope. A policeman stood there and said quite clearly, "Do not sit down," and we sat down . . . I became suddenly aware of the crowd of people standing behind us. . . . Young kids threw french fried potatoes at us, and gum, and cigarette butts. I looked down the counter at Barbara Crosby in a straight pink skirt and nice white blouse, and at Stephen in a dark suit, with a calculus book. . . . The policemen simply lined up behind us and peeled us two by two off the stools. . . . The crowd in the store . . . shouted out approval. They said about Barbara and me. . . . Oh, white . . . WHITE, WHITE, WHITE! Three paddy wagons were blinking at us from the street. Once more we had to walk through those crowds. Some one spit right in front of me. . . . The TV cameras took lots of pictures and we drove off to the Nashville city jail.

With seventy-six students in jail, a group of NAACP people in Nashville met the next day and pledged support. Fisk University President Stephen Wright said: "Students have been exposed all their lives to the teachings of the great American scriptures of democracy, freedom, and equality, and no literate person should be surprised that they reflect these teachings in their conduct."

But at white Vanderbilt University in Nashville, where a thirty-one-year-old Negro named James Lawson was enrolled in the Divinity School, it was different. Lawson, a conscientious objector and a pacifist, believed in nonviolent resistance. When the first mass arrests took place, news-papermen quoted him as saying he would advise students to violate the law. The *Nashville Banner* immediately called this "incitation to anarchy" and added: "There is no place in Nashville for flannel-mouthed agitators, white or colored—under whatever sponsorship, imported for preachment of mass disorder; self-supported vagrants, or paid agents of strife-breeding organizations." The Vanderbilt trustees, one of whom was the publisher of the *Nashville Banner,* another of whom was president of one of the large department stores where sit-ins had taken place, voted the next day to give Lawson the choice of withdrawing from the movement or dismissal from the University.

Charging the press with distorting his statements, Lawson refused to leave the movement, and in early March he was expelled, three months before his scheduled graduation. Most of the sixteen faculty members of the divinity school, all white, protested. By May, eleven of them, as well as Dean J. Robert Nelson, had resigned over the refusal of the school to re-admit Lawson, leaving four persons on the divinity school faculty. The *Richmond News Leader* commented: "Good riddance . . . Vanderbilt University will be better off. . . ."

The Nashville sit-ins continued, with arrests, trials, and students deciding to stay in jail in protest rather than pay fines or put up bond. Chief defense lawyer for the students was sixty-two-year-old Z. Alexander Looby, a distinguished Negro attorney, born in Trinidad, and a member of the Nashville City Council.

On April 19, at five o'clock in the morning, while Looby and his wife were asleep in the backroom of their home, one block away from Fisk University's campus, a bomb exploded on his porch. In her dormitory room, Candie Anderson was awakened by the noise. "Only one time in my life have I heard a sound worse than the one when Mr. Looby's house was bombed," she wrote later. "That was when a girl fainted and I heard her head hit the floor. That's the kind of feeling it left when we heard the explosion. . . . It would have seemed unreal, I think, if the sirens had not kept insistently coming. . . ."

One hundred and forty-seven windows were blown out in Meharry Medical School across the street, and the front part of the Looby's house was demolished, but the attorney and his wife were not hurt. Perhaps, as James Bevel (who married Diane Nash) said, "The Devil has got to come out of these people." For after the bombing, and after a protest march of 2000 Negroes on City Hall, negotiations for desegregation got under way in earnest. In early May, four theaters and six lunch counters downtown declared an end to the color line. In the meantime, the sit-ins had spread to Chattanooga, Knoxville, Memphis, and Oak Ridge. By late spring, seven Tennessee cities had desegregated some of their lunch counters.

CORE, with its long emphasis on nonviolent direct action, played an important part, once the sit-ins began, as an educational and organizing agent. Tom Gaither, of Claflin College in Orangeburg, South Carolina, tells of CORE classes which started there, inspired by the Rock Hill sit-ins. (Those, the first in South Carolina, took place even before the first Nashville sit-ins, with one hundred students from two Negro junior colleges sitting in.)

The Orangeburg students held classes in nonviolence over a period of three or four days for students from Claflin College and South Carolina State, both Negro colleges, and then picked forty students who felt confident in the use of nonviolent techniques. Here is a sample of the instructions to people being schooled in nonviolence:

> You may choose to face physical assault without protecting yourself, hands at the sides, unclenched; or you may choose to protect yourself, making plain you do not intend to hit back. If you choose to protect yourself, you practice positions such as these:
>
> To protect the skull, fold the hands over the head.
>
> To prevent disfigurement of the face, bring the elbows together in front of the eyes.
>
> For girls, to prevent internal injury from kicks, lie on the side and bring the knees upward to the chin; for boys, kneel down and arch over, with skull and face protected.

The Kress five and dime store in Orangeburg became the object of careful plans. Students checked the store entrances, counted the number of stools at the lunch counter, calculated exactly the number of minutes it took to walk from a central point on campus to the Kress store. On February 25, the sit-ins began, and lunch counters closed in downtown Orangeburg. A thousand students were being trained meanwhile, and a mass march through the streets of the city took place, with no violence, no arrests.

When lunch counters reopened on March 14, followed by another great march designed to support a new wave of sit-ins, the police moved in with tear gas bombs and water hoses. The weather was sub-freezing. Students were drenched and knocked off their feet by the water pressure. One of these was a blind girl. Over five hundred were arrested and, with the jails full, three hundred and fifty were jammed into a chicken coop and enclosed by a seven-foot wire fence. There was no shelter against the bitter cold.

Meanwhile, students jammed into the basement of the city jail were sweating in 90-degree temperatures from the nearby boiler room. One student, drenched from head to toe, was locked in solitary confinement with water three inches deep covering the cell floor. Requests for dry clothing were denied. A Claflin College nurse came to give first aid, and had to force her way inside. Two hundred students marched around the courthouse in protest. Tom Gaither, the movement's leader (and today a professional civil rights worker with CORE), was marching with them when he was seized and put into jail.

The sit-ins were spreading southward now. They were also becoming larger and better organized. In Atlanta, where they were preceded by many meetings and by a sensational full-page ad of eloquent protest in the *Atlanta Constitution* addressed to a startled white community, the sit-ins were planned like a military operation. On March 15, at exactly 11:00 A.M., two hundred students moved into ten downtown restaurants which had been carefully selected because they were connected with city or county or federal government, and were therefore subject to the Fourteenth Amendment's requirement that *public* places may not discriminate. Seventy-six students were arrested, and the city of Atlanta was never the same again.

There was some violence in those first months of the sit-ins. In Jacksonville, Florida, the city was in turmoil for three days: a white sit-in student was attacked in jail and his jaw was broken; a sixteen-year-old Negro boy was pistol-whipped by the Ku Klux Klan; a Negro man unconnected with the demonstrations who went through a police roadblock was shot to death by a white service station attendant. In Atlanta, acid was thrown at sit-in leader Lonnie King. In Frankfort, Kentucky, the gymnasium of a Negro college was set afire. In Columbia, South Carolina, a Negro sit-in student was stabbed. In Houston, Texas, a twenty-seven-year-old Negro was kidnaped and flogged with a chain, and the symbol KKK was carved on his chest.

Mississippi responded with a special savagery. When students marched down the street in Jackson, police used clubs, tear gas, and police dogs. Women, children, and a photographer were beaten by police and bystanders, and some demonstrators were bitten by dogs. In Biloxi, Mississippi, Negroes trying to use a public beach were attacked with clubs and chains by crowds of whites, and ten were wounded by gunfire.

Yet, considering the number of people involved in demonstrations and the intense psychological tremors accompanying this sudden attack by long-quiescent Negroes on the old way of life, violence was minimal. The restraint of the demonstrators themselves was one factor; they gave the least possible excuse for club-happy and trigger-happy policemen, and the most the police could justify, in most cases, was carting them off to jail. The ratio of social change, both immediate and long term, to the resulting violence, was extremely high.

The sit-ins marked a turning point for the Negro American, subordinate for three hundred years. He was rebelling now, not with the blind, terrible, understandable hatred of the slave revolts, but with skill in organization, sophistication in tactics, and an unassailable moral position. With these went a ferocious refusal to retreat. What had been an orderly, inch-by-inch advance via legal processes now became a revolution in which unarmed regiments marched from one objective to another with bewildering speed.

The idea so long cherished by Southern whites—and by many Northerners too—that the Southern Negro (whether through ignorance or intimidation or a shrewd recognition of reality) was content with the way things were, that only a handful of agitators opposed the system of segregation, was swept aside by the mass marches, demonstrations, meetings. Montgomery had been the first sign of this, and now it was made clear beyond argument that Negroes all across the South had only been waiting for an opportunity to end their long silence.

*   *   *   *

THE FREEDOM RIDES (1961)

A year later another direct mass action campaign was organized: The Freedom Rides. Led primarily by James Farmer of CORE, a group of freedom riders left Washington, D.C. en route to New Orleans to enforce their rights as interstate travelers. The violence they met, described in Louis E. Lomax's "The Negro Revolt," underscored how far apart was the law as declared by the Supreme Court, and its enforcement in the Deep South.

The Negro Revolt, LOUIS E. LOMAX (1962)

*   *   *   *

Chapter 11. The Freedom Rides

. . . On February 1, 1961, forty-year-old James Farmer became national director of the Congress of Racial Equality. On March 13, CORE announced that it would conduct freedom rides through the South to test racial discrimination in interstate travel terminals. On April 28, CORE wrote President Kennedy and advised him that the rides would soon be under way and asked for federal protection. On May 4, after three days of training and indoctrination, the freedom rides began their journey from Washington, D.C.

It had taken James Farmer exactly three months to get the freedom rides on the road.

The freedom rides were born in James Farmer's anxious mind and spirit. Even as he was packing his bags and moving from the NAACP office along New York's West Fortieth Street to CORE's Spartan quarters down on Park Row, Farmer was planning what he would do and how he would do it.

Farmer, a former Methodist clergyman, has always been an "action man." He was among the concerned group of Negroes and whites who formed CORE in 1942 because they felt legalism was not sufficient to win the battle against segregation. He served as CORE's first national chairman, but divided his time among CORE and several other organizations in the field of civil liberties and world peace. Five years later, James Farmer was among those who took a freedom ride under the sponsorship of the Fellowship of Reconciliation. The main objective of this 1947 freedom ride was to test discrimination on trains engaged in interstate travel, and to discover to what extent the states of the upper South had complied with a decision rendered by the Supreme Court in 1946 when it declared that different racial regulations by various states imposed an undue hardship on interstate travel facilities.

As he assumed his duties as national director of CORE, Farmer remembered another Court decision that had not been implemented. In 1958 Bruce Boyington was refused service in a bus station in Richmond, Virginia. When Boyington refused to leave the lunchroom, he was arrested and charged with trespassing. The Court disregarded the constitutional arguments advanced by Boyington and NAACP lawyers and ruled that, under the Interstate Commerce Act, segregation in terminal stations was illegal whether the terminal was owned by the bus company or not. The ruling turned on that section of the statute which forbids busses to "subject any particular person to any unjust discrimination or any unjust or unreasonable prejudice."

The Boyington decision had been a paper decision. Practically every bus terminal in the South maintained segregated facilities. Everybody knew it, but Jim Farmer decided to do something about it.

After talking the plan over with his own staff, particularly with Marvin Rich, the executive secretary of CORE, Farmer sought the counsel and aid of Roy Wilkins, his former boss at the NAACP. Wilkins listened sympathetically and promised Farmer aid from local NAACP branches along the way. Wilkins wrote various branch heads along the route Farmer planned to take and asked them to give aid and comfort. Most branches responded favorably, but some did not. The Jackson, Mississippi, branch, for example, wrote Farmer that whereas they wished him God's blessings they could be of little aid on the day the freedom riders were scheduled to arrive in Jackson. Not that the Jackson NAACP

leaders feared white reprisals; their inability to help the proposed freedom riders stemmed rather from the fact that the local NAACP would be
having its annual Freedom Fund drive at the time and could not afford
to divide its energies.

On May 4, the biracial group of freedom riders left Washington, D.C.,
en route to New Orleans. There were thirteen participants, six whites
and seven Negroes, including James Farmer. The riders ranged in age
from eighteen to sixty-one, and their number fluctuated during the course
of the ride. The Southern Regional Council has compiled a chronology
of the ride; it reads like an American nightmare:

May   4   Ride begins from Washington; arrives in Richmond.
May   7   Arrival in Danville (Va.); dispute over restaurant service
          settled quietly at Trailways terminal.
May   8   Arrival in Charlotte (N.C.); arrest of one Rider for trespass
          while demanding shoeshine at Union bus terminal.
May   9   Arrival in Rock Hill (S.C.) and attack in Greyhound terminal;
          white waiting room at Trailways terminal is closed when bus
          pulls in.
May 10   Defendant in Charlotte trespass case acquitted. Two Riders
          arrested in Winnsboro (S.C.) and released after several hours;
          charges dropped.
May 12   Arrival in Augusta (Ga.); all facilities used.
May 13   Traveling through Athens (Ga.), where all facilities are used,
          and arrival in Atlanta; restaurant closed at Greyhound station.
          The Court of Appeals of the Fifth Circuit directs a lower
          court to "obliterate" the distinction between interstate and
          intrastate passengers at the train terminal in Birmingham. This
          is one of the many stations in the South with one waiting
          room for white and Negro interstate passengers, and a second
          for Negro intrastate passengers.

While in Atlanta, James Farmer received word of his father's death
in Washington, D.C. Farmer temporarily left the ride and flew to Washington for his father's funeral.

May 14   Some Riders are served at Trailways terminal in Atlanta.
          Entire group leaves for Birmingham, riding in Trailways and
          Greyhound busses.
          Department of Justice advises Birmingham police it has re-
          ceived warnings of planned violence when busses reach their
          city. Greyhound bus met by mob in Anniston; passengers

prevented from getting off. Tires slit and go flat six miles out of Anniston. Men following in automobiles attempt to board but are prevented by a state law enforcement officer who has been riding bus. An incendiary device thrown through a window sets fire to the bus, which is completely destroyed. All passengers are removed, and 12 admitted to hospital, mostly for smoke inhalation; they later resume their ride to Birmingham. The Trailways bus also encounters the mob in Anniston, and faced by it the driver orders Negroes to the rear. One Negro and two white Riders beaten. Bus continues on to Birmingham, where Riders are attacked when they get off; one of them requires over 50 head stitches. At neither Anniston nor Birmingham is anyone arrested. Despite warnings of probable trouble, no police are on hand at Birmingham, and none arrive until ten minutes after fighting begins.

May 15   Greyhound bus drivers refuse to drive group on to Montgomery. Riders take plane for New Orleans, arriving there late at night. Governor Patterson issues his first statement, advising Riders to "get out of Alabama as quickly as possible."
Attorney General Kennedy asks the state to provide police protection; the Governor first agrees and then changes his position.

May 16   Riders stay in seclusion in New Orleans. In Birmingham, three men are arrested for taking part in the attack of the 14th.

May 17   Riders meet at church in New Orleans and then disband. This ends the original CORE-planned ride.

The freedom ride had caught national attention, however, and several groups began to send riders of their own into the Alabama trouble spots. Although the original CORE-planned ride disbanded on May 17, several members of CORE's ride remained in Montgomery; James Farmer rejoined the ride there and they, along with other groups, carried the ride to its dramatic climax in Jackson, Mississippi. From May 17 on there were four organizations involved in the ride: CORE, the Nashville Student Movement, the Student Non Violent Coordinating Committee and Martin Luther King's Southern Christian Leadership Conference. Several concerned individuals—rabbis from Chicago, white college professors from Eastern universities and a Negro-white lawyer team from New York—also joined the ride at this point.

May 17   A bus arrives in Birmingham from Nashville, carrying new contingent of Freedom Riders. This is a group of college students affiliated with Southern Christian Leadership Conference. Two white students are in the group. Police meet bus on outskirts of city, arrest 2 Riders who refuse to change seats. Two policemen ride bus into Birmingham, where a crowd is waiting at the terminal. Drivers refuse to carry group on to Montgomery, and 10 Riders (8 Negro and 2 white) plus 5 sympathizers taken into protective custody.

May 18   Riders stay in jail; one of the white students released in custody of her father. The 5 Birmingham Negroes released. Attorney General Kennedy tries unsuccessfully to reach Governor Patterson by telephone.

May 19   Two of the jailed students (1 white, 1 Negro) receive suspended fines and are released. The remaining 7 are carried by Police Commissioner Connor in the early morning 120 miles to the Tennessee line and are put out of the car. They are back in Birmingham in the afternoon, where, joined by 10 or so others, including 3 whites, they unsuccessfully seek bus service to Montgomery. Spend the night in waiting room. An Alabama court enjoins CORE and its followers from further "freedom rides." Patrolmen read order on incoming busses. Both President Kennedy and the Attorney General try unsuccessfully to reach the Governor by telephone; the President talks with the Lieutenant Governor.

John Seigenthaler, administrative assistant to the Attorney General, confers in Montgomery with the Governor.

May 20   The Governor says: "We are going to do all we can to enforce the laws of the state on the highways and everywhere else, but we are not going to escort these agitators. We stand firm on that position."

At 8:30 A.M., after 18 hours of waiting, the Riders are taken on a Greyhound bus for Montgomery. The F.B.I. advises local police in Montgomery of probability of violence; are assured that local authority sufficient. On arrival, a "race riot involving hundreds broke out." At least 6 Riders are beaten, 3 severely. The mob attacks Negroes who have no connection with the Riders, and whites who appear sympathetic. News photographers are attacked. John Seigenthaler is knocked unconscious and left on a sidewalk for more than 20 minutes. Police arrive about 10 minutes after fighting begins, and do not for some time succeed in dispersing the mob, which continues its attacks. The police arrest at least 8 "integrationists." After again trying to reach the Governor, the Attorney General orders federal marshals to Montgomery, and also obtains in Federal District Court an injunction against the Ku-Klux-Klan, the National States Rights party, and other individuals interfering with "peaceful interstate travel by bus." President Kennedy appeals to state and local officials of Alabama for order.

May 21   Federal marshals continue to pour in.

The Reverend Martin Luther King, Jr., president of the Southern Christian Leadership Conference, cuts short a speaking tour and flies to Montgomery from Chicago, to address a Negro mass meeting at a church. A mob, composed largely of white youths, forms outside. It is dispersed after bitter rioting by the federal marshals and state patrolmen, with some aid from the local police. The Negroes are penned in the church until early the next morning. Governor Patterson proclaims martial law in Montgomery, and National Guardsmen appear. Deputy Attorney General Byron White comes to Montgomery to take charge of federal activities; the Governor angrily denounces federal intervention during a conference with Mr. White. The American Nazi party announces plans to send a "hate bus" from Washington to New Orleans.

Alabama Associated Press Association condemns "the breakdown of civilized rule" in Alabama. It singles out Alabama Public Safety Director Floyd Mann as "the one notable example" of an officer carrying out his duties. Negro leaders at the mass meeting also praise Mr. Mann.

Governor Barnett of Mississippi wires an offer of support to Governor Patterson.

May 22   Eight hundred National Guardsmen on duty. More federal marshals ordered in. The Attorney General says that they will stay until the situation is brought under control by the state. He says further that Public Safety Director Mann is acting with vigor and skill, but that the Governor is not cooperating.

The Montgomery Ministerial Association calls for all "necessary steps" to prevent further mob action and violence.

The "hate bus" leaves Washington.

Federal agents arrest 4 men on charge of firing the bus at Anniston.

Additional students begin arriving in Montgomery, from Nashville, New Orleans and New York.

Deputy Attorney General White says that arrests of Freedom Riders for violating the state injunction against them will not cause federal intervention.

Eighteen hundred pupils evacuated from two white junior high schools after phoned bombing threats.

May 23   "Hate bus" passes through Montgomery, escorted through the town by federal officers. Reaches New Orleans, where passengers have difficult time finding lodging.

Montgomery is quiet; National Guardsmen patrol city. One person arrested in connection with riots.

In reply to a protest from Alabama Congressmen, the Attorney General calls for action on the part of the Governor and local police, "not merely words of intention."

The Governor at a press conference blames the Sunday night riot on the federal marshals.

Justice Department officials are in continuing telephone discussions with Mississippi officials.

A press conference is held by M. L. King, Jr., CORE Director James Farmer, Montgomery minister Ralph Abernathy, and students Diane Nash and John Lewis. They announce that the Ride will continue at no matter what cost. A few more students arrive in Montgomery.

The Rotary Club of Montgomery demands withdrawal of federal marshals. The Board of Directors of the Chamber of Commerce calls on local law enforcement agencies to "maintain and preserve" law and order. The Junior Chamber of Commerce condemns agitators and regrets failure of local police. The Louisiana legislature commends Governor Patterson.

Governor Barnett has Mississippi National Guard on stand-by alert.

May 24   Heavily protected and escorted by National Guardsmen, some of the Riders leave Montgomery on a Trailways bus about 7:00 A.M. Before leaving they eat at the bus terminal, thus achieving an objective. Later in the morning a second bus carries the rest. The escorts convoy the busses to the Mississippi line, where patrol cars of that state take over. On arrival in Jackson, 27 Riders, including James Farmer, are arrested when they seek service at the white lunch counters and use of the white rest rooms of the terminal, on charges of breach of peace and refusal to obey an officer. There are no disturbances otherwise. In Montgomery, additional Riders show up, the small group including professors and students from the North. The Department of Justice asks in Federal District Court for an injunction to prohibit the heads of the Birmingham and Montgomery police departments from interfering with interstate travel. The complaint asserts that all have been derelict in performing their duties.

The Attorney General also issues a statement appealing for a "cooling-off period." Southern Christian Leadership Conference executive Martin King promptly says "no."

The Greyhound Corporation orders disciplinary action against its employees in Montgomery who refused food service to Negroes.

In New Orleans, the "hate bus" passengers are jailed for "unreasonably" alarming the public.

In La Grange (Ga.), 5 men attempting to organize an obstruction to the bus carrying the latest group of Riders to Montgomery are arrested.

May 25   The Reverend S. D. Seay, Sr., Negro leader, is shot in the wrist in Montgomery by a bullet from a passing car.

The latest group of Riders is arrested while eating at the Trailways terminal in Montgomery, along with Wyatt T. Walker, executive director of the Southern Christian Leadership Conference, and two Negro ministers: the Reverends Abernathy and Shuttlesworth. Charge: breach of peace.

The Reverend Abernathy and 6 Riders file suit in Federal District Court asking invalidation of Alabama's bus terminal segregation laws. The Department of Justice promptly agrees to the judge's request that it enter the case as a friend of the court; the Department also asks for a speedy hearing.

The New Orleans city council urges police to escort Riders, if they come, through city non-stop.

May 26   Meeting in Atlanta with a few others, M. L. King, Jr. announces that there will be a "temporary lull but no cooling off" in the Rides.

Police heads in Birmingham and Montgomery are under subpoena to produce records of their activities. The Northern professors and students post bail and are released from Montgomery jail.

In Jackson the 27 are convicted, fined $200 each, and given 60-day suspended jail sentence. Stringent measures are enforced during the trial, including use of police dogs to drive persons away from the front of the courthouse.

Alabama and Georgia authorities arrest a man in Rome (Ga.) for attack on Birmingham TV reporter during riots there.

The executive secretary of the NAACP dissents from the plea for a "cooling off."

May 27   Six white teen-agers, arrested in Montgomery for wounding of the Reverend S. D. Seay, Sr., released in parents' custody.

The vice-chairman of Americans for Democratic Action urges Freedom Riders to disregard the Attorney General's plea for a "cooling off."

A Freedom Riders Coordinating Committee is formed in Atlanta, composed of representatives of SCLC, CORE, the Nashville Student Movement, and the Student Non Violent Coordinating Committee; M. L. King, Jr. explains the non-representation of the NAACP on the grounds that it is primarily a "legalistic body." Both the Negroes in jail in Montgomery and the Nazis in jail in New Orleans are fasting. Five of the 27 in Jackson are released on bond; 4 accept bail so that they can stand trial in New Orleans on earlier charges growing out of the picketing of downtown stores.

May 28   Seventeen Riders, coming from Montgomery and Memphis, are arrested in Jackson when they attempt to desegregate the waiting room. The contingent coming from Montgomery were escorted to the bus terminal by Guardsmen, where they found facilities closed.

May 29   Trial begins in federal court in Montgomery on the government's complaint against Montgomery and Birmingham police heads; C. V. Henley, a former Montgomery reserve policeman, has been brought into the suit. At issue also is the continuation of the restraining order against the Klan leaders.

Martial law is ended in Montgomery.

In Jackson, 19 of the first group of Riders are put to work at a prison farm; 3 others are released on appeal bond. The 17 who arrived May 28 are convicted on breach of peace charges, and sentenced to 60 days or $200; they choose jail.

In La Grange (Ga.), 3 of those arrested on May 24 are convicted and 2 bound over to a higher court.

Attorney General Kennedy requests the Interstate Commerce Commission to ban by regulations segregation in interstate bus terminals.

Sept. 22   The Interstate Commerce Commission issues an order banning segregation in interstate terminal facilities.

Nov. 1   The ICC order banning segregation in terminal facilities becomes effective.

On final count the freedom rides (actually, there were at least a dozen of them) involved over a thousand persons representing four major organizations. The rides themselves cost an estimated twenty thousand dollars and the legal expenses that grew out of them exceeded three hundred thousand dollars. The rides did the job, however, and, as of this writing, interstate terminal segregation is all but a thing of the past. Some cities in the deep, deep South are still holding out, but the issue is about settled.

The rides complete the emergence of CORE as, without question, the boldest and most imaginative organization in the civil rights field. Since its organization in 1942 CORE had achieved a number of quiet, though very real, gains but was not thought of as among the top Negro leadership organizations. Even the sit-ins were not CORE's work; the students launched the movement and then CORE came in to help them along the way. The freedom rides were something else, however; the original ride was planned and financed by CORE, and its national director, James Farmer, was among those who were beaten and jailed. True, other organizations moved onto the freedom ride trail and SCLC's executive director, Wyatt Walker, and his wife joined the rides and were both jailed. But, without question, the glory and the victory of the freedom rides belongs to CORE and to James Farmer.

*　　*　　*　　*

THE UNIVERSITY OF MISSISSIPPI RIOT (1962)

Violence erupted again a year later when James Meredith enrolled at the University of Mississippi as its first Negro student. Meredith, born in Attala County in Mississippi, served in the Air Force from 1953 to 1960, rising to the rank of Staff Sergeant. In January 1961, he made his first attempt to register at the University of Mississippi. For the next 18 months Mississippi fought a losing battle in the courts to keep its University all white. Despite a series of curious judicial rulings by two federal judges (Sidney Mize and Ben F. Cameron) the Fifth Circuit Court of Appeals and Justice Hugo L. Black declared that Mississippi must accept Meredith. Governor Ross Barnett, playing an elaborate political charade, told his followers that he would never yield on the issue. At the same time he was talking frequently over the phone to Robert F. Kennedy to work out some compromise. On Sunday, September 30, 1962 Meredith was finally flown to Oxford, Mississippi in a federal plane and driven to the campus. President Kennedy, who had thought for many years that Eisenhower's use of federal troops at Little Rock had been a mistake (he thought federal marshals could have done the job as well), was extremely reluctant to commit federal troops unless absolutely necessary. Largely because of Barnett's last-minute treachery in withdrawing state troopers he had promised the Kennedys he would use to maintain law and order, an angry mob of whites, some coming from many miles away, attacked the federal marshals on the University of Mississippi campus. In order to forestall a full scale riot, President Kennedy addressed the nation on that night and urged the Mississippians to live up to their honor and to obey the law. The speech set out below had little effect. For fifteen hours open warfare reigned on the campus. Federal troops, arriving late, finally cleared the campus on Monday morning, but only after two individuals, including a French correspondent, had been killed during the riot.

Report to the Nation on the Situation at the University of Mississippi, PRESIDENT JOHN F. KENNEDY (September 30, 1962)

Report to the Nation on the Situation

Good evening, my fellow citizens:

The orders of the court in the case of Meredith versus Fair are beginning to be carried out. Mr. James Meredith is now in residence on the campus of the University of Mississippi.

This has been accomplished thus far without the use of National Guard or other troops. And it is to be hoped that the law enforcement officers of the State of Mississippi and the Federal marshals will continue to be sufficient in the future.

All students, members of the faculty, and public officials in both Mississippi and the Nation will be able, it is hoped, to return to their normal activities with full confidence in the integrity of American law.

This is as it should be, for our Nation is founded on the principle that observance of the law is the eternal safeguard of liberty and defiance of the law is the surest road to tyranny. The law which we obey includes the final ruling of the courts, as well as the enactments of our legislative bodies. Even among law-abiding men few laws are universally loved, but they are uniformly respected and not resisted.

Americans are free, in short, to disagree with the law but not to disobey it. For in a government of laws and not of men, no man, however prominent or powerful, and no mob, however unruly or boisterous, is entitled to defy a court of law. If this country should ever reach the point where any man or group of men by force or threat of force could long defy the commands of our court and our Constitution, then no law would stand free from doubt, no judge would be sure of his writ, and no citizen would be safe from his neighbors.

In this case in which the United States Government was not until recently involved, Mr. Meredith brought a private suit in Federal court against those who were excluding him from the University. A series of Federal courts all the way to the Supreme Court repeatedly ordered Mr. Meredith's admission to the University. When those orders were defied, and those who sought to implement them threatened with arrest and violence, the United States Court of Appeals consisting of Chief Judge Tuttle of Georgia, Judge Hutcheson of Texas, Judge Rives of Alabama, Judge Jones of Florida, Judge Brown of Texas, Judge Wisdom of Louisiana, Judge Gewin of Alabama, and Judge Bell of Georgia, made clear the fact that the enforcement of its order had become an obligation of the United States Government. Even though this Government had not originally been a party to the case, my responsibility as President was therefore inescapable. I accept it. My obligation under the Constitution and the statutes of the United States was and is to implement the orders of the court with whatever means are necessary, and with as little force and civil disorder as the circumstances permit.

It was for this reason that I federalized the Mississippi National Guard as the most appropriate instrument, should any be needed, to preserve law and order while United States marshals carried out the orders of the court and prepared to back them up with whatever other civil or military enforcement might have been required.

I deeply regret the fact that any action by the executive branch was necessary in this case, but all other avenues and alternatives, including persuasion and conciliation, had been tried and exhausted. Had the police powers of Mississippi been used to support the orders of the court, instead of deliberately and unlawfully blocking them, had the University of Mississippi fulfilled its standard of excellence by quietly admitting this applicant in conformity with what so many other southern State universities have done for so many years, a peaceable and sensible solution would have been possible without any Federal intervention.

This Nation is proud of the many instances in which Governors, educators, and everyday citizens from the South have shown to the world the gains that can be made by persuasion and good will in a society ruled by law. Specifically, I would like to take this occasion to express the thanks of this Nation to those southerners who have contributed to the progress of our democratic development in the entrance of students regardless of race to such great institutions as the State-supported universities of Virginia, North Carolina, Georgia, Florida, Texas, Louisiana, Tennessee, Arkansas, and Kentucky.

I recognize that the present period of transition and adjustment in our Nation's Southland is a hard one for many people. Neither Mississippi nor any other southern State deserves to be charged with all the accumulated wrongs of the last 100 years of race relations. To the extent that there has been failure, the responsibility for that failure must be shared by us all, by every State, by every citizen.

Mississippi and her University, moreover, are noted for their courage, for their contribution of talent and thought to the affairs of this Nation. This is the State of Lucius Lamar and many others who have placed the national good ahead of sectional interest. This is the State which had four Medal of Honor winners in the Korean war alone. In fact, the Guard unit federalized this morning, early, is part of the 155th Infantry, one of the 10 oldest regiments in the Union and one of the most decorated for sacrifice and bravery in 6 wars.

In 1945 a Mississippi sergeant, Jake Lindsey, was honored by an unusual joint session of the Congress. I close therefore with this appeal to the students of the University, the people who are most concerned.

You have a great tradition to uphold, a tradition of honor and courage won on the field of battle and on the gridiron as well as the University campus. You have a new opportunity to show that you are men of patriotism and integrity. For the most effective means of upholding the law is not the State policeman or the marshals or the National Guard. It is you. It lies in your courage to accept those laws with which you disagree as well as those with which you agree. The eyes of the Nation and of all the world are upon you and upon all of us, and the honor of your University and State are in the balance. I am certain that the great majority of the students will uphold that honor.

There is in short no reason why the books on this case cannot now be quickly and quietly closed in the manner directed by the court. Let us preserve both the law and the peace and then healing those wounds that are within we can turn to the greater crises that are without and stand united as one people in our pledge to man's freedom.

Thank you and good night.

BIRMINGHAM (1963)

In the following months the center of activity shifted from Mississippi to Alabama. In April, 1963, led by the Reverends Fred Shuttlesworth, Martin Luther King, and Ralph D. Abernathy, Birmingham Negroes staged a campaign of sit-ins and demonstrations. On Good Friday, April 12, 1963, a protest march led by King, Abernathy, and Shuttlesworth was met by policemen led by Eugene "Bull" Connor, the Birmingham police commissioner, and aided by a number of snarling police dogs. In May protest marchers, including many school children, faced both police dogs and fire hoses powerful enough to rip bark from nearby elm trees. News pictures of the fire hoses knocking Negroes to the ground, and of police dogs attacking the demonstrators were flashed around the world. A temporary accord was reached in late May, but it was broken by the bombing of the A. G. Gaston Motel (the headquarters for the movement) and the home of the Reverend A. D. King (the younger brother of Martin Luther King).

In the meantime, Governor George C. Wallace of Alabama threatened to block the entry of two Negro applicants to the summer session of the University of Alabama. In response, President Kennedy wired the Governor that he would use all necessary force to make sure that federal court orders providing for admission of the Negro students would be obeyed. On June 11, 1963, President Kennedy made a nationwide television broadcast (the speech is reproduced below) which Anthony Lewis of the New York Times called "one of the great speeches in the history of the American Presidency."

But the fight was not over in Birmingham. On September 10, 1963, twenty Negro children were admitted to previously all white public schools in Alabama. Only five days later the peace was again broken. While a children's Bible class was being conducted at the 16th Street Baptist Church, one of the starting points for many of the spring marches, a dynamite blast virtually destroyed the school, injured 14 Negro children and killed four Negro teenage girls. The next day Charles Morgan, Jr., a young white lawyer, spoke before the Birmingham Young Mens' Business Club. His moving and forceful speech, which was to lead to his exile from Birmingham, attracted national attention.

Address to the Nation on Civil Rights, PRESIDENT JOHN F. KENNEDY (June 11, 1963)

*   *   *   *

I hope that every American, regardless of where he lives, will stop and examine his conscience about this and other related incidents. This nation was founded by men of many nations and backgrounds. It was founded on the principle that all men are created equal, and that the rights of every man are diminished when the rights of one man are threatened.

Today we are committed to a worldwide struggle to promote and protect the rights of all who wish to be free. And when Americans are sent to Vietnam or West Berlin we do not ask for whites only.

It ought to be possible, therefore, for American students of any color to attend any public institution they select without having to be backed up by troops. It ought to be possible for American consumers of any color to receive equal service in places of public accommodation, such as hotels and restaurants, and theatres and retail stores, without being forced to resort to demonstrations in the street.

And it ought to be possible for American citizens of any color to register and to vote in a free election without interference or fear of reprisal. It ought to be possible, in short, for every American to enjoy the privileges of being American without regard to his race or his color.

In short, every American ought to have the right to be treated as he would wish to be treated, as one would wish his children to be treated. But this is not the case.

The Negro baby born in America today, regardless of the section or the state in which he is born, has about one-half as much chance of completing a high school as a white baby, born in the same place, on the same day; one-third as much chance of completing college; one-third as much chance of becoming a professional man; twice as much chance of becoming unemployed; about one-seventh as much chance of earning ten thousand dollars a year; a life expectancy which is seven years shorter and the prospects of earning only half as much.

This is not a sectional issue. Difficulties over segregation and discrimination exist in every city, in every state of the Union, producing in many cities a rising tide of discontent that threatens the public safety. Nor is this a partisan issue. In time of domestic crisis, men of good will and generosity should be able to unite regardless of party or politics. This is not a legal or legislative issue alone. It is better to settle these matters in the courts than on the streets, and new laws are needed at every level. But law alone cannot make men see right.

We are confronted primarily with a moral issue. It is as old as the Scriptures and is as clear as the American Constitution. The heart of the question is whether all Americans are to be afforded equal rights and equal opportunities; whether we are going to treat our fellow Americans as we want to be treated.

If an American, because his skin is dark, cannot eat lunch in a restaurant open to the public; if he cannot send his children to the best public school available; if he cannot vote for the public officials who represent him; if, in short, he cannot enjoy the full and free life which all of us want, then who among us would be content to have the color of his skin changed and stand in his place?

Who among us would then be content with the counsels of patience and delay? One hundred years of delay have passed since President Lincoln freed the slaves, yet their heirs, their grandsons, are not fully free. They are not yet freed from the bonds of injustice; they are not yet freed from the social and economic oppression. And this nation, for all its hopes and all its boasts, will not be fully free until all its citizens are free.

We preach freedom around the world, and we mean it. And we cherish our freedom here at home. But are we to say to the world— and much more importantly to each other—that this is the land of the free, except for the Negroes; that we have no second-class citizens, except Negroes; that we have no class or caste system, no ghettos, no master race, except with respect to Negroes.

Now the time has come for this nation to fulfill its promise. The events in Birmingham and elsewhere have so increased the cries for equality that no city or state or legislative body can prudently choose to ignore them. The fires of frustration and discord are burning in every city, North and South. Where legal remedies are not at hand, redress is sought in the streets in demonstrations, parades and protests, which create tensions and threaten violence—and threaten lives.

We face, therefore, a moral crisis as a country and a people. It cannot be met by repressive police action. It cannot be left to increased demonstrations in the streets. It cannot be quieted by token moves or talk. It is a time to act in the Congress, in your state and local legislative body, and, above all, in all of our daily lives.

It is not enough to pin the blame on others, to say this is a problem of one section of the country or another, or deplore the facts that we face. A great change is at hand, and our task, our obligation, is to make that revolution, that change peaceful and constructive for all. Those who do nothing are inviting shame as well as violence. Those who act boldly are recognizing right as well as reality. . . .

In this respect, I want to pay tribute to those citizens, North and South, who've been working in their communities to make life better for all. They are acting not out of a sense of legal duty but out of a sense of human decency. Like our soldiers and sailors in all parts of the world, they are meeting freedom's challenge on the firing line and I salute them for their honor—their courage.

My fellow Americans, this is a problem which faces us all, in every city of the North as well as the South. Today there are Negroes unemployed—two or three times as many as whites; there is inadequate education; Negroes are moving into the large cities, unable to find work, young people particularly are out of work; they are without hope, denied equal rights, denied the opportunity to eat at a restaurant or a lunch counter or go to a movie theatre, denied the right to a decent education, denied almost today the right to attend a state university even though qualified.

It seems to me that these are matters which concern us all—not merely Presidents, or congressman, or governors, but every citizen of the United States. This is one country. It has become one country because all of us and all the people who came here had an equal chance to develop their talents.

We cannot say to ten per cent of the population that "you can't have that right. Your children can't have the chance to develop whatever talents they have; the only way that they're going to get their rights is to go in the street and demonstrate."

I think we owe them and we owe ourselves a better country than that. Therefore, I'm asking for your help in making it easier for us to move ahead and provide the kind of equality of treatment which we would want ourselves—to give a chance for every child to be educated to the limit of his talent.

As I've said before, not every child has an equal talent or an equal ability or equal motivation. But they should have the equal right to develop their talent and their ability and their motivation to make something of themselves. We have a right to expect that the Negro community will be responsible, will uphold the law. But they have a right to expect the law will be fair, that the Constitution will be color blind, as Justice Harlan said at the turn of the century.

This is what we're talking about. This is a matter which concerns this country and what it stands for, and in meeting it I ask the support of all our citizens.

Thank you very much.

Speech Before Birmingham Young Men's Business Club, CHARLES MORGAN (September 16, 1963)

Four little girls were killed in Birmingham Sunday. A mad, remorseful, worried community asks "Who did it? Who threw that bomb? Was it a Negro or a white?"

The answer should be "We all did it." Every last one of us is condemned for that crime and the bombing before it and the ones last month, last year, a decade ago. We all did it.

A short time later, white policemen kill a Negro and wound another. A few hours later two young men on a motor bike shoot and kill a

Negro child. Fires break out and, in Montgomery, white youths assault Negroes. And all across Alabama, an angry, guilty people cry out their mocking shouts of indignity and say they wonder, "Why?" "Who?" Everyone then "deplores" the "dastardly" act.

But, you know the "who" of "who did it?" is really rather simple. The "who" is every individual who talks about the "niggers" and spreads the seeds of his hate to his neighbor and his son. The jokester, the crude oaf whose racial jokes rock the party with laughter. The "who" is every governor who ever shouted for lawlessness and became a law violator.

It is every senator and every representative who in the halls of Congress stands and with mock humility tells the world that things back home aren't really like they are. It is courts that move ever so slowly and newspapers that timorously defend the law. It is all the Christians and all the ministers who spoke too late in anguished cries against violence.

It is the coward in each of us who clucks admonitions. We are ten years of lawless preachments, ten years of criticism of law, of courts, of our fellow man, a decade of telling school children the opposite of what the civics books say. We are a mass of intolerance and bigotry and stand indicted before our young. We are cursed by the failure of each of us to accept responsibility, by our defense of an already dead institution.

Sunday, while Birmingham, which prides itself on the number of its churches, was attending worship service, a bomb went off and an all-white police force moved into action, a police force which has been praised by city officials and others at least once a day for a month or so. A police force which has solved no bombings. A police force which many Negroes feel is perpetrating the very evils we decry. And why would Negroes think this?

There are no Negro policemen; there are no Negro sheriff's deputies. Few Negroes have served on juries. Few have been allowed to vote, few have been allowed to accept responsibility, or granted even a simple part to play in the administration of justice. Do not misunderstand me. It is not that I think that white policemen had anything whatsoever to do with the killing of these children or previous bombings. It's just that Negroes who see an all-white police force must think in terms of its failure to prevent or solve the bombings and think perhaps Negroes would have worked a little bit harder. They throw rocks and bottles and bullets. And we whites don't seem to know why the Negroes are lawless. So, we lecture them.

Birmingham is the only city in America where police chief and sheriff in the school crisis had to call our local ministers together to tell them to do their duty. The ministers of Birmingham who have done so little for Christianity call for prayer at high noon in a city of lawlessness and, in the same breath, speak of our city's "image." Did those ministers visit the families of the Negroes in their hour of travail? Did any of them go to the homes of their brothers and express their regret in person or pray with the crying relatives? Do they admit Negroes into their ranks at the church?

Who is guilty? A moderate mayor elected to change things in Birmingham and who moves so slowly and looks elsewhere for leadership? A business community which shrugs its shoulders and looks to the police or perhaps somewhere else for leadership? A newspaper which has tried so hard of late, yet finds it necessary to lecture Negroes every time a Negro home is bombed? A Governor who offers a reward but mentions not his own failure to preserve either segregation or law and order? And what of those lawyers and politicians who counsel people as to what the law is not when they know full well what the law is?

Those four little Negro girls were human beings. They have lived their fourteen years in a leaderless city; a city where no one accepts responsibility; where everybody wants to blame somebody else. A city with a reward fund which grew like Topsy as a sort of sacrificial offering, a balm for the conscience of the "good people." The "good people" whose ready answer is for those "right-wing extremists" to shut up. People who absolve themselves of guilt. The liberal lawyer who told me this morning, "Me? I'm not guilty," then proceeded to discuss the guilt of the other lawyers, the ones who told the people that the Supreme Court did not properly interpret the law. And that's the way it is with the southern liberals. They condemn those with whom they disagree for speaking while they sigh in fearful silence.

Birmingham is a city in which the major industry, operated from Pittsburgh, never tried to solve the problem. It is a city where four little Negro girls can be born into a second-class school system, live a segregated life, ghettoed into their own little neighborhoods, restricted to Negro churches, destined to ride in Negro ambulances, to Negro wards of hospitals or to a Negro cemetery. Local papers, on their front and editorial pages, call for order and then exclude their names from obituary columns.

And who is really guilty? Each of us. Each citizen who has not consciously attempted to bring about peaceful compliance with the decisions of the Supreme Court of the United States, each citizen who has ever said "they ought to kill that nigger," every citizen who votes for the candidate with the bloody flag; every citizen and every school-board member and school teacher and principal and businessman and judge and lawyer who has corrupted the minds of our youth; every person in this community who has in any way contributed during the past several years to the popularity of hatred, is at least as guilty, or more so, than the demented fool who threw that bomb.

What's it like living in Birmingham? No one ever really has and no one will until this city becomes part of the United States.

Birmingham is not a dying city; it is dead.

FREEDOM SUMMER (1964)

Birmingham was in a sense the last of the great defensive battles. From that point on Negroes moved to the offensive, direct action groups spreading through many sections of the South. In the spring of 1964, St. Augustine, Florida, was the scene of a series of demonstrations, in one of which Massachusetts Governor Endicott Peabody's mother was arrested. The young leaders of the direct action organizations pressed a series of voting registration drives. In the summer of 1964, "Freedom Summer" attracted white allies from all over the country, many of whom were to risk their lives, particularly in Mississippi, to help the movement. The selection of letters from "Letters from Mississippi" shows the enthusiasm and sincerity of those who participated in the Mississippi summer project. The fact that Andrew Goodman and Michael Schwerner (both white) were murdered alongside James Chaney during that Mississippi summer showed that the movement had become a fight by a large portion of white America for a just society.

Letters From Mississippi (1964)

Gulfport, July 8

Canvassing, the main technique in voter registration, is an art, and like an art, it is not a scheduled thing. You don't work from 9 to 5. There is no such thing as a completed job until *everyone* is registered. When you cheat and take a lunch hour (and it feels like cheating) you suddenly find yourself reviewing a failure or a success to discover the whys: maybe I should have bullied him slightly, or maybe I should have talked less—and relied on silences. Did I rush him? Should I never have mentioned registering at all, and just tried to make friends and set him at ease? It goes on and on. . . .

Techniques and approaches vary. Mine is often like this:

Hi. My name is Steve M. (shake hands, having gotten name, address, from a mailbox). I'm with COFO. There are a lot of us working in this area, going from house to house trying to encourage people to go down and register to vote. (Pause). Are you a registered voter? (This is the direct technique. Often people, being afraid, will lie and say yes, but you can usually tell, because they will be very proud.) Are you planning on going down soon? (This makes them declare themselves. Usually they say "yes" or "I hadn't thought about it much." The other answer is "No, I ain't going down at all." "Well, I have a sample of the registration form." (Take it out and hand it to them.) "You know, some people are a little afraid to go down because they don't quite know what they're getting into. It's something new and different, and they're not sure about it."

Then I go on, "You know, it is so important that everyone get the vote. As it stands now, that man downtown in charge of roads doesn't have to listen to the Negroes. They can't put him out of office. He should be working *for* you." (Much gossip, chatter, mutual questions through all this).

Then pull out the Freedom Democratic Party application.

"This is a protest party. Anyone can join to protest the laws about voter registration and the way elections are carried out."

You get the picture. It goes on, 10 hours a day, 6 days a week. On Sundays we rest by working at other things. We go to church. Since all visitors are allotted time to speak, I relate voter registration to God. I have become a pretty good preacher. . . .

Dear folks,   Mileston, August 18

One can't move onto a plantation cold; or canvas a plantation in the same manner as the Negro ghetto in town. It's far too dangerous. Many plantations—homes included—are posted, meaning that no trespassing is permitted, and the owner feels that he has the prerogative to shoot us on sight when we are in the house of one of *his* Negroes.

Before we canvas a plantation, our preparation includes finding out whether the houses are posted, driving through or around the plantation without stopping, meanwhile making a detailed map of the plantation.

We're especially concerned with the number of roads in and out of the plantation. For instance, some houses could be too dangerous to canvas because of their location near the boss man's house and on a dead end road.

In addition to mapping, we attempt to talk to some of the tenants when they are off the plantation, and ask them about conditions. The kids often have contacts, and can get on the plantation unnoticed by the boss man, with the pretense of just visiting friends.

Our canvassing includes not only voter registration, but also extensive reports on conditions—wages, treatment by the boss man, condition of the houses, number of acres of cotton, etc. Much more such work needs to be done. The plantation system is crucial in Delta politics and economics, and the plantation system must be brought to an end if democracy is to be brought to the Delta. . . .

Love,
Joel

July 18

. . . Four of us went to distribute flyers announcing the meeting. I talked to a woman who had been down to register a week before. She was afraid. Her husband had lost his job. Even before we got there a couple of her sons had been man-handled by the police. She was now full of wild rumors about shootings and beatings, etc. I checked out two of them later. They were groundless. This sort of rumor-spreading is quite prevalent when people get really scared. . . .

At 6 P.M. we returned to Drew for the meeting, to be held in front of a church (they wouldn't let us meet inside, but hadn't told us not to meet outside). A number of kids collected and stood around in a circle with about 15 of us to sing freedom songs. Across the street perhaps 100 adults stood watching. Since this was the first meeting in town, we passed out mimeoed song sheets. Fred Miller, Negro from Mobile, stepped out to the edge of the street to give somebody a sheet. The cops nabbed him. I was about to follow suit so he wouldn't be alone, but Mac's policy [Charles McLaurin, SNCC project director] was to ignore the arrest. We sang on mightily "Ain't going to let no jailing turn me around." A group of girls was sort of leaning against the cars on the periphery of the meeting. Mac went over to encourage them to join us. I gave a couple of song sheets to the girls. A cop rushed across the street and told me to come along. I guess I was sort of aware that my actions would get me arrested, but felt that we had to show these girls that we were not afraid. I was also concerned with what might happen to Fred if he was the only one.

. . . The cop at the station was quite scrupulous about letting me make a phone call. I was then driven to a little concrete structure which looked like a power house. I could hear Fred's courageous, off-key rendition of a freedom song from inside and joined him as we approached. He was very happy to see me. Not long thereafter, four more of our group were driven up to make their calls . . .

The Drew jail consists of three small cells off a wide hall. It was filthy, hot and stuffy. A cop came back to give us some toilet paper.

We sang songs for a while, and yelled greetings to Negroes who drove by curiously. One of the staff workers had been in jail 106 times. I asked the cop if he could open another cell as there were not enough beds accessible to us. He mumbled something about how that would be impossible and left. They hadn't confiscated anything and one of the guys had a battered copy of *The Other America,* so we divided up the chapters. I got the dismal one on the problems of the aged . . . To be old and forgotten is certainly a worse sentence than mine (I wouldn't recommend that book for those planning to do time) . . .

Well, the night was spent swatting mosquitoes. An old Negro couple walked by in front of the jail and asked how we were doing. They said they supported us and the old lady said, "God bless you all." This, in the context of a tense town with a pretty constant stream of whites in cars driving by. . . .

Dear Mom and Dad: Holly Spring

The atmosphere in class is unbelievable. It is what every teacher dreams about—real, honest enthusiasm and desire to learn anything and everything. The girls come to class of their own free will. They respond to everything that is said. They are excited about learning. They drain me of everything that I have to offer so that I go home at night completely exhausted but very happy. . . .

I start out at 10:30 teaching what we call the Core Curriculum, which is Negro History and the History and Philosophy of the Movement, to about fifteen girls ranging from 15 to 25 years of age. I have one girl who is married with four children, another who is 23 and a graduate from a white college in Tennessee, also very poorly educated. The majority go to a Roman Catholic High School in Holly Springs and have therefore received a fairly decent education by Mississippi standards. They can, for the most part, express themselves on paper but their skills in no way compare to juniors and seniors in northern suburban schools.

In one of my first classes, I gave a talk on Haiti and the slave revolt which took place there at the end of the eighteenth century. I told them how the French government (during the French Revolution) abolished slavery all over the French Empire. And then I told them that the English decided to invade the island and take it over for a colony of their own. I watched faces fall all around me. They knew that a small island, run by former slaves, could not defeat England. And then I told them that the people of Haiti succeeded in keeping the English out. I watched a smile spread slowly over a girl's face. And I felt girls sit up and look at me intently. Then I told them that Napoleon came to power, reinstated slavery, and sent an expedition to reconquer Haiti.

Their faces began to fall again. They waited for me to tell them that France defeated the former slaves, hoping against hope that I would say that they didn't. But when I told them that the French generals tricked the Haitian leader Toussaint to come aboard their ship, captured him and sent him back to France to die, they knew that there was no hope. They waited for me to spell out the defeat. And when I told them that Haiti did succeed in keeping out the European powers and was recognized finally as an independent republic, they just looked at me and smiled. The room stirred with a gladness and a pride that this could have happened. And I felt so happy and so humble that I could have told them this little story and it could have meant so much.

We have also talked about what it means to be a Southern white who wants to stand up but who is alone, rejected by other whites and not fully accepted by the Negroes. We have talked about their feelings about Southern whites. One day three little white girls came to our school and I asked them to understand how the three girls felt by remembering how it feels when they are around a lot of whites. We agreed that we would not stare at the girls but try to make them feel as normal as possible.

Along with my Core class I teach a religion class at one every afternoon and a class on non-violence at four-fifteen. All my classes are approximately an hour. Both these classes are made up of four to six girls from my morning class and about four boys of the same age group. In religion they are being confronted for the first time with people whom they respect who do not believe in God and with people who believe in God but do not take the Bible literally. It's a challenging class because I have no desire to destroy their belief, whether Roman Catholic or Baptist, but I want them to learn to look at all things critically and to learn to separate fact from interpretation and myth in all areas, not just religion.

Every class is beautiful. The girls respond, respond, respond. And they disagree among themselves. I have no doubt that soon they will be disagreeing with me. At least this is one thing that I am working towards. They are a sharp group. But they are under-educated and starved for knowledge. They know that they have been cheated and they want anything and everything that we can give them.

I have a great deal of faith in these students. They are very mature and very concerned about other people. I really think that they will be able to carry on without us. At least this is my dream . . .

Love,

Pam

Indianola, August 17

I can see the change. The 16-year-old's discovery of poetry, of Whitman and Cummings and above all, the struggle to express thoughts in words, to translate ideas into concrete written words. After two weeks a child finally looks me in the eye, unafraid, acknowledging a bond of trust which 300 years of Mississippians said should never, could never exist. I can feel the growth of self-confidence . . .

Biloxi, Aug. 16

In the Freedom School one day during poetry writing, a 12-year-old girl handed in this poem to her teacher:

What Is Wrong?

What is wrong with me everywhere I go
No one seems to look at me.
Sometimes I cry.

I walk through woods and sit on a stone.
I look at the stars and I sometimes wish.

Probably if my wish ever comes true,
Everyone will look at me.

Then she broke down crying in her sister's arms. The Freedom School here had given this girl the opportunity of meeting someone she felt she could express her problems to . . .

To my brother,   Ruleville

Last night, I was a long time before sleeping, although I was extremely tired. Every shadow, every noise—the bark of a dog, the sound of a car—in my fear and exhaustion was turned into a terrorist's approach. And I believed that I heard the back door open and a Klansman walk in, until he was close by the bed. Almost paralyzed by the fear, silent, I finally shone my flashlight on the spot where I thought he was standing . . . I tried consciously to overcome this fear. To relax, I began to breathe deep, think the words of a song, pull the sheet up close to my neck . . . still the tension. Then I rethought why I was here, rethought what could be gained in view of what could be lost. All this was in rather personal terms, and then in larger scope of the whole Project. I remembered Bob Moses saying he had felt justified in asking hundreds of students to go to Mississippi because he was not asking anyone to do something that he would not do . . . I became aware of the uselessness of fear that immobilizes an individual. Then I began to relax.

"We are not afraid. Oh Lord, deep in my heart, I do believe, We Shall Overcome Someday" and then I think I began to truly understand what the words meant. Anyone who comes down here and is not afraid I think must be crazy as well as dangerous to this project where security is quite important. But the type of fear that they mean when they, when we, sing "we are not afraid" is the type that immobilizes. . . . The songs help to dissipate the fear. Some of the words in the songs do not hold real meaning on their own, others become rather monotonous—but when they are sung in unison, or sung silently by oneself, they take on new meaning beyond words or rhythm . . . There is almost a religious quality about some of these songs, having little to do with the usual concept of a god. It has to do with the miracle that youth has organized to fight hatred and ignorance. It has to do with the holiness of the dignity of man. The god that makes such miracles is the god I do believe in when we sing "God is on our side." I know I am on that god's side. And I do hope he is on ours.

Jon, please be considerate to Mom and Dad. The fear I just expressed, I am sure they feel much more intensely without the relief of being here to know exactly how things are. Please don't go defending me or attacking them if they are critical of the Project. . . .

They said over the phone "Did you know how much it takes to make a child?" and I thought of how much it took to make a Herbert Lee (or many others whose names I do not know) . . . I thought of how much it took to be a Negro in Mississippi twelve months a year for a lifetime. How can such a thing as a life be weighed? . . .

> With constant love,
> Heather

Dear Folks,   Laurel, August, 11

. . . The memorial service began around 7:30 with over 120 people filling the small, wooden-pew lined church. David Dennis of CORE, the Assistant Director for the Mississippi Summer Project, spoke for COFO. He talked to the Negro people of Meridian—it was a speech to move people, to end the lethargy, to make people stand up. It went something like this:

"I am not here to memorialize James Chaney, I am not here to pay tribute—I am too sick and tired. Do YOU hear me, I am S-I-C-K and T-I-R-E-D. I have attended too many memorials, too many funerals. This has got to stop. Mack Parker, Medgar Evers, Herbert Lee, Lewis Allen, Emmett Till, four little girls in Birmingham, a 13-year-old boy in Birmingham, and the list goes on and on. I have attended these funerals and memorials and I am SICK and TIRED. But the trouble is that

YOU are NOT sick and tired and for that reason YOU, yes YOU, are to blame, Everyone of your damn souls. And if you are going to let this continue now then you are to blame, yes YOU. Just as much as the monsters of hate who pulled the trigger or brought down the club; just as much to blame as the sheriff and the chief of police, as the governor in Jackson who said that he 'did not have time' for Mrs. Schwerner when she went to see him, and just as much to blame as the President and Attorney General in Washington who wouldn't provide protection for Chaney, Goodman and Schwerner when we told them that protection was necessary in Neshoba County . . . Yes, I am angry, I AM. And it's high time that you got angry too, angry enough to go up to the courthouse Monday and register—everyone of you. Angry enough to take five and ten other people with you. Then and only then can these brutal killings be stopped. Remember it is your sons and your daughters who have been killed all these years and you have done nothing about it, and if you don't do nothing NOW baby, I say God Damn Your Souls. . . ."

Dear Blake,   Mileston, August 9

. . . Dave finally broke down and couldn't finish and the Chaney family was moaning and much of the audience and I were also crying. It's such an impossible thing to describe but suddenly again, as I'd first realized when I heard the three men were missing when we were still training up at Oxford, I felt the sacrifice the Negroes have been making for so long. How the Negro people are able to accept all the abuses of the whites—all the insults and injustices which make me ashamed to be white—and then turn around and say they want to love us, is beyond me. There are Negroes who want to kill whites and many Negroes have much bitterness but still the majority seem to have the quality of being able to look for a future in which whites will love the Negroes. Our kids talk very critically of all the whites around here and still they have a dream of freedom in which both races understand and accept each other. There is such an overpowering task ahead of these kids that sometimes I can't do anything but cry for them. I hope they are up to the task, I'm not sure I would be if I were a Mississippi Negro. As a white northerner I can get involved whenever I feel like it and run home whenever I get bored or frustrated or scared. I hate the attitude and position of the Northern whites and despise myself when I think that way. Lately I've been feeling homesick and longing for pleasant old Westport and sailing and swimming and my friends. I don't quite know what to do because I can't ignore my desire to go home and yet I feel I am a much weaker person than I like to think I am because I do have these emotions. I've always tried to avoid situations which aren't so nice, like arguments and dirty houses and now maybe Mississippi. I asked my father if I could stay down here for a whole year and I was almost glad when he said "no" that we couldn't afford it because it would mean supporting me this year in addition to three more years of college. I have a desire to go home and to read a lot and go to Quaker meetings and be by myself so I can think about all this rather than being in the middle of it all the time. But I know if my emotions run like they have in the past, that I can only take that pacific sort of life for a little while and then I get the desire to be active again and get involved with knowing other people. I guess this all sounds crazy and I seem to always think out my problems as I write to you. I am angry because I have a choice as to whether or not to work in the Movement and I am playing upon that choice and leaving here. I wish I could talk with you 'cause I'd like to know if you ever felt this way about anything. I mean have you ever despised yourself for your weak conviction or something. And what is making it worse is that all those damn northerners are thinking of me as a brave hero . . .

Martha

Dear Friends,   En route back to Meridian, September
    Many people, including those who supported my going to Mississippi as part of the Summer Project, and those who believe that the Summer Project has been an important thing, have expressed shock and disapproval at my decision to go back to Mississippi, and have attempted to dissuade me from returning. I have been amazed at this response.

    There is a certainty, when you are working in Mississippi, that it is important for you to be alive and to be alive doing just what you are doing. And whatever small bit we did for Mississippi this summer, Mississippi did ten times as much for us. Working there has given me clarity about what I want to be learning in college that three years in Widener Library could not give. Now that I have taught, I know what I want to learn about teaching. Now that I have helped people understand what it means to be a citizen in a democracy, I know things that I still have to understand. Now that I have worked with people to change the society in which they live, I know what I want to learn about societies and how other people have changed theirs. . . .

    I guess the thing that pulls me back most are the people who made us a part of their community. People I knew in Mississippi could honestly and unselfconsciously express affection in a way that few people I know in the North are able to do. They did not have to be "cool" or "one up" or "careful" . . . In Mississippi I have felt more love, more sympathy and warmth, more community than I have known in my life. And especially the children pull me back. . . .

I should tell you that it is not as easy to go back to Mississippi as it may sound from this letter. I am frightened by the probability of much greater violence . . . I will be working a lot more on my own, and it will probably be much lonelier. . . .

Gail

SELMA (1965)

Although it had now become clear that every act of violence against the Negro for asserting his rights in the South was a shock to the national conscience and could only lead to strong federal countermeasures, the southern racist continued to be a prisoner of the blind, destructive forces which could only alienate the rest of the country and drag him to defeat. The events of Birmingham had unquestionably led to the Civil Rights Act of 1964. In March, 1965, the intransigence of Governor George Wallace of Alabama, Albert J. Lingo, the Director of Public Safety, and James Clark, the Sheriff of Selma, was to lead to the Voting Rights Act of 1965. The efforts of Negroes to register and vote in Dallas County, Alabama, had been blocked by intimidation and coercion by Selma officials. In protest, a group of Negroes attempted to march from Selma to Montgomery, setting out on Sunday, March 7, 1965. They were met by a force of Alabama state troopers under Colonel Lingo and a detachment of Selma deputies under Sheriff Clark. The beatings and tear gas which the Negro demonstrators were subjected to led to an influx of sympathetic members of the movement—doctors, lawyers, priests, nuns—from all over the country, who demanded the right to demonstrate. Luckily Selma was under the jurisdiction of one of the strong federal judges in the South, Frank Johnson. Judge Johnson, outlining in a brilliant opinion the long history of harassment and intimidation in Selma, permitted a protest march to go forward and ordered Governor Wallace to supply necessary protection. The demonstrations and the killings of Jimmy Lee Jackson, the Reverend James J. Reeb, and Mrs. Viola Liuzzo during this period led directly to the passage of the 1965 Voting Rights Act.

Judge Johnson's Opinion in *Williams v. Wallace* (March 17, 1965)

Hosea WILLIAMS, John Lewis and Amelia Boynton, on behalf of

themselves and others similarly situated, Plaintiffs,
United States of America, Plaintiff-Intervenor,

v.

Honorable George C. WALLACE, as Governor of the State of Alabama,
Al Lingo, as Director of Public Safety for the State of Alabama, and
James G. Clark, as Sheriff of Dallas County, Alabama, Defendants.
March 17, 1965.

JOHNSON, District Judge.

The plaintiffs as Negro citizens and the members of the class they
represent filed with this Court on March 8, 1965, their complaint, motion for temporary restraining order and motion for a preliminary injunction. . . .

The defendant George C. Wallace is the Governor and chief executive officer of the State of Alabama. The defendant Albert J. Lingo is
the Director of Public Safety of the State of Alabama, and the defendant
James G. Clark, Jr., is the Sheriff of Dallas County, Alabama. The Governor as the chief executive officer of the State of Alabama is charged
with the faithful execution of the laws of the State of Alabama and of
the United States of America; in such capacity, the Governor controls
and supervises the defendant Albert J. Lingo, and through the defendant
Lingo the Governor controls and directs the activities of the Alabama
Highway Patrol, also known as the Alabama State Troopers. The defendant Lingo as director is in the active control of the Alabama Highway Patrol.

The plaintiffs seek to have this Court guarantee their right to assemble
and demonstrate peaceably for the purpose of redressing their grievances
concerning the right to register to vote in the State of Alabama without
unlawful interference. Included in the rights plaintiffs seek and ask this
Court to adjudicate is that of walking peaceably along the public highway in the State of Alabama between Selma and Montgomery. Plaintiffs also ask this Court to enjoin and restrain the defendants and all
persons acting in concert with them from arresting, harassing, threatening, or in any way interfering with their peaceful, nonviolent march
from Selma, Alabama, to Montgomery, Alabama, for the purpose of
protesting injustices and petitioning their State government, particularly
the chief executive officer—the Governor—for redress of grievances.

*   *   *   *

Under Alabama law, registration is prerequisite to voting in any election. In several counties in central Alabama, including Dallas County
wherein Selma, Alabama, is located, fewer than 10% of the Negroes
of voting age are registered to vote. For the purpose of obtaining better

political representation for Negro citizens in these counties, the Negro communities, through local and national organizations, have conducted voter registration drives in recent years. These voter registration drives in Dallas and other central Alabama counties have been intensified since September, 1964. Public demonstrations have been held in these several counties, particularly in Dallas County, for the purpose of encouraging Negroes to attempt to register to vote and also for the purpose of protesting discriminatory voter registration practices in Alabama. The demonstrations have been peaceful. At the same time, cases have been filed in the United States District Courts in this district and also in the Southern District of Alabama; these cases are designed to secure to Negro citizens their right to register to vote in several central Alabama counties. . . .

The efforts of these Negro citizens to secure this right to register to vote in some of these counties, have accomplished very little. For instance, in Dallas County, as of November, 1964, where Negro citizens of voting age outnumber white citizens of voting age, only 2.2% of the Negroes were registered to vote. In Perry County as of August, 1964, where the Negro citizens of voting age outnumber white citizens, only 7% of the Negroes were registered to vote. In Wilcox County as of December, 1963, where the Negro citizens of voting age outnumber white citizens over two to one, 0% of the Negro citizens were registered to vote as contrasted with the registration of 100% of the white citizens of voting age in this county. In Hale County, where Negro citizens of voting age outnumber white citizens, only 3.6% of these Negro citizens have been registered to vote. The evidence in this case reflects that, particularly as to Selma, Dallas County, Alabama, an almost continuous pattern of conduct has existed on the part of defendant Sheriff Clark, his deputies, and his auxiliary deputies known as "possemen" of harassment, intimidation, coercion, threatening conduct, and, sometimes, brutal mistreatment toward these plaintiffs and other members of their class who were engaged in their demonstrations for the purpose of encouraging Negroes to attempt to register to vote and to protest discriminatory voter registration practices in Alabama. This harassment, intimidation and brutal treatment has ranged from mass arrests without just cause to forced marches for several miles into the countryside, with the sheriff's deputies and members of his posse herding the Negro demonstrators at a rapid pace through the use of electrical shocking devices (designed for use on cattle) and night sticks to prod them along. The Alabama State Troopers, under the command of the defendant Lingo, have, upon several occasions, assisted the defendant Sheriff Clark in these activities, and the State troopers, along with Sheriff Clark as an "invited guest," have extended the harassment and intimidating activities into Perry County, where, on February 18, 1965, when approximately 300 Negroes were engaged in a peaceful demonstration by marching from a Negro church to the Perry County Courthouse for the purpose of publicly protesting racially discriminatory voter registration practices in Perry County, Alabama, the Negro demonstrators were stopped by the State troopers under the command of the defendant Lingo, and the Negro demonstrators were at that time pushed, prodded, struck, beaten and knocked down. This action resulted in the injury of several Negroes, one of whom was shot by an Alabama State Trooper and subsequently died.

In Dallas County, Alabama, the harassment and brutal treatment on the part of defendants Lingo and Clark, together with their troopers, deputies and "possemen," and while acting under instructions from Governor Wallace, reached a climax on Sunday, March 7, 1965. Upon this occasion approximately 650 Negroes left the church in Selma, Alabama, for the purpose of walking to Montgomery, Alabama, to present to the defendant Governor Wallace their grievances concerning the voter registration processes in these central Alabama counties and concerning the restrictions and the manner in which these restrictions had been imposed upon their public demonstrations. These Negroes proceeded in an orderly and peaceful manner to a bridge near the south edge of the City of Selma on U.S. Highway 80 that leads to Montgomery, Alabama, which is located approximately 45 miles east of Selma. They proceeded on a sidewalk across the bridge and then continued walking on the grassy portion of the highway toward Montgomery until confronted by a detachment of between 60 to 70 State troopers headed by the defendant Colonel Lingo, by a detachment of several Dallas County deputy sheriffs, and numerous Dallas County "possemen" on horses, who were headed by Sheriff Clark. Up to this point the Negroes had observed all traffic laws and regulations, had not interfered with traffic in any manner, and had proceeded in an orderly and peaceful manner to the point of confrontation. They were ordered to disperse and were given two minutes to do so by Major Cloud, who was in active command of the troopers and who was acting upon specific instructions from his superior officers. The Negroes failed to disperse, and within approximately one minute (one minute of the allotted time not having passed), the State troopers and the members of the Dallas County sheriff's office and "possemen" moved against the Negroes. The general plan as followed by the State troopers in this instance had been discussed with and was known to Governor Wallace. The tactics employed by the State troopers, the deputies and "possemen" against these Negro demonstrators were similar to those recommended for use by the United

States Army to quell armed rioters in occupied countries. The troopers, equipped with tear gas, nausea gas and canisters of smoke, as well as billy clubs, advanced on the Negroes. Approximately 20 canisters of tear gas, nausea gas, and canisters of smoke were rolled into the Negroes by these State officers. The Negroes were then prodded, struck, beaten and knocked down by members of the Alabama State Troopers. The mounted "possemen," supposedly acting as an auxiliary law enforcement unit of the Dallas County sheriff's office, then, on their horses, moved in and chased and beat the fleeing Negroes. Approximately 75 to 80 of the Negroes were injured, with a large number being hospitalized.

The acts and conduct of these defendants, together with the members of their respective enforcement agencies, as outlined above, have not been directed toward enforcing any valid law of the State of Alabama or furthering any legitimate policy of the State of Alabama, but have been for the purpose and have had the effect of preventing and discouraging Negro citizens from exercising their rights of citizenship, particularly the right to register to vote and the right to demonstrate peaceably for the purpose of protesting discriminatory practices in this area. By these actions and by this conduct, the defendants, together with other members of their enforcement agencies, have intimidated, threatened and coerced Negro citizens in this section of Alabama for the purpose of interfering with citizens and preventing them from exercising certain of their basic constitutional rights—i. e., the right to register to vote, peaceably assemble, remonstrate with governmental authorities and petition for redress of grievances. The attempted march alongside U. S. Highway 80 from Selma, Alabama, to Montgomery, Alabama, on March 7, 1965, involved nothing more than a peaceful effort on the part of Negro citizens to exercise a classic constitutional right; that is, the right to assemble peaceably and to petition one's government for the redress of grievances.

*   *   *   *

The law is clear that the right to petition one's government for the redress of grievances may be exercised in large groups. Indeed, where, as here, minorities have been harassed, coerced and intimidated, group association may be the only realistic way of exercising such rights. . . .

This Court recognizes, of course, that government authorities have the duty and responsibility of keeping their streets and highways open and available for their regular uses. Government authorities are authorized to impose regulations in order to assure the safety and convenience of the people in the use of public streets and highways provided these regulations are reasonable and designed to accomplish that end. . . . As has been demonstrated above, the law in this country constitutionally guarantees that a citizen or group of citizens may assemble and petition their government, or their governmental authorities, for redress of their grievances even by mass demonstrations as long as the exercise of these rights is peaceful. These rights may also be exercised by marching, even along public highways, as long as it is done in an orderly and peaceful manner; and these rights to assemble, demonstrate and march are not to be abridged by arrest or other interference so long as the rights are asserted within the limits of not unreasonably interfering with the exercise of the rights by other citizens to use the sidewalks, streets and highways, and where the protestors and demonstrators are conducting their activities in such a manner as not to deprive the other citizenry of their police protection. As was stated in Kelly v. Page, supra, there must be in cases like the one now presented, a "constitutional boundary line" drawn between the competing interests of society. This Court has the duty and responsibility in this case of drawing the "constitutional boundary line." In doing so, it seems basic to our constitutional principles that the extent of the right to assemble, demonstrate and march peaceably along the highways and streets in an orderly manner should be commensurate with the enormity of the wrongs that are being protested and petitioned against. In this case, the wrongs are enormous. The extent of the right to demonstrate against these wrongs should be determined accordingly.

*   *   *   *

This Court finds the plaintiffs' proposed plan to the extent that it relates to a march along U. S. Highway 80 from Selma to Montgomery, Alabama, to be a reasonable one to be used and followed in the exercise of a constitutional right of assembly and free movement within the State of Alabama for the purpose of petitioning their State government for redress of their grievances. It is recognized that the plan as proposed and as allowed reaches, under the particular circumstances of this case, to the outer limits of what is constitutionally allowed. However, the wrongs and injustices inflicted upon these plaintiffs and the members of their class (part of which have been herein documented) have clearly exceeded—and continue to exceed—the outer limits of what is constitutionally permissible. As stated earlier in this opinion, the extent of a group's constitutional right to protest peaceably and petition one's government for redress of grievances must be, if our American Constitution is to be a flexible and "living" document, found and held to be commensurate with the enormity of the wrongs being protested and petitioned against. This is particularly true when the usual, basic and constitutionally-provided means of protesting in our American way—voting—have been deprived. It must never be forgotten that our Constitution is "intended to endure for ages to come, and consequently to be adapted to the various crises of human affairs." With an application of these principles to the facts of this case, plaintiffs' proposed plan of march from Selma to Montgomery, Alabama, for its intended purposes, is clearly a reasonable exercise of a right guaranteed by the Constitution of the United States . . .

THE WATTS RIOT (1965)

The riots in various northern cities during the summers of 1964, 1965 and 1966 were certainly not the result of strategic plans made by civil rights leaders. They were spontaneous outbursts bred by long periods of resentment, aggravated by the Negro's dashed hopes for the freedom and equality he had begun to think were his. Nevertheless, the riots are a milestone in the movement because they showed how deep the Negro's anger was, and because they undoubtedly had an effect on white America's attitude toward the civil rights struggle. They resulted in the first step away from the movement by large groups of white allies. The Watts riot in Los Angeles, undoubtedly the most severe of the episodes, was examined by a special commission appointed by Governor Brown and headed by John McCone.

The McCone Report on the Watts Riot (1965)

*   *   *   *

144 Hours in August 1965

The Frye Arrests   •

On August 11, 1965, California Highway Patrolman Lee W. Minikus, a Caucasian, was riding his motorcycle along 122nd street, just south of the Los Angeles City boundary, when a passing Negro motorist told him he had just seen a car that was being driven recklessly. Minikus gave chase and pulled the car over at 116th and Avalon, in a predominantly Negro neighborhood, near but not in Watts. It was 7:00 p.m.

The driver was Marquette Frye, a 21-year-old Negro, and his older brother, Ronald, 22, was a passenger. Minikus asked Marquette to get out and take the standard Highway Patrol sobriety test. Frye failed the test, and at 7:05 p.m., Minikus told him he was under arrest. He radioed for his motorcycle partner, for a car to take Marquette to jail, and a tow truck to take the car away.

They were two blocks from the Frye home, in an area of two-story apartment buildings and numerous small family residences. Because it was a very warm evening, many of the residents were outside.

Ronald Frye, having been told he could not take the car when Marquette was taken to jail, went to get their mother so that she could claim the car. They returned to the scene about 7:15 p.m. as the second motorcycle patrolman, the patrol car, and tow truck arrived. The original group of 25 to 50 curious spectators had grown to 250 to 300 persons.

Mrs. Frye approached Marquette and scolded him for drinking. Marquette, who until then had been peaceful and cooperative, pushed her away and moved toward the crowd, cursing and shouting at the officers that they would have to kill him to take him to jail. The patrolmen pursued Marquette and he resisted.

The watching crowd became hostile, and one of the patrolmen radioed for more help. Within minutes, three more highway patrolmen arrived. Minikus and his partner were now struggling with both Frye brothers. Mrs. Frye, now belligerent, jumped on the back of one of the officers and ripped his shirt. In an attempt to subdue Marquette, one officer swung at his shoulder with a night stick, missed, and struck him on the forehead, inflicting a minor cut. By 7:23 p.m., all three of the Fryes were under arrest, and other California Highway Patrolmen and, for the first time, Los Angeles police officers had arrived in response to the call for help.

Officers on the scene said there were now more than 1,000 persons in the crowd. About 7:25 p.m., the patrol car with the prisoners, and the tow truck pulling the Frye car, left the scene. At 7:31 p.m., the Fryes arrived at a nearby sheriff's substation.

Undoubtedly the situation at the scene of the arrest was tense. Belligerence and resistance to arrest called for forceful action by the officers. This brought on hostility from Mrs. Frye and some of the bystanders, which, in turn, caused increased actions by the police. Anger at the scene escalated and, as in all such situations, bitter recriminations from both sides followed.

Considering the undisputed facts, the Commission finds that the arrest of the Fryes was handled efficiently and expeditiously. The sobriety test administered by the California Highway Patrol and its use of a transportation vehicle for the prisoner and a tow truck to remove his car are in accordance with the practices of other law enforcement agencies, including the Los Angeles Police Department.

The Spitting Incident

As the officers were leaving the scene, someone in the crowd spat on one of them. They stopped withdrawing and two highway patrolmen went into the crowd and arrested a young Negro woman and a man who was said to have been inciting the crowd to violence when the officers were arresting her. Although the wisdom of stopping the withdrawal to make these arrests has been questioned, the Commission finds no basis for criticizing the judgment of the officers on the scene.

Following these arrests, all officers withdrew at 7:40 p.m. As the last police car left the scene, it was stoned by the now irate mob.

As has happened so frequently in riots in other cities, inflated and distorted rumors concerning the arrests spread quickly to adjacent areas. The young woman arrested for spitting was wearing a barber's smock, and the false rumor spread throughout the area that she was pregnant and had been abused by police. Erroneous reports were also circulated concerning the treatment of the Fryes at the arrest scene.

The crowd did not disperse, but ranged in small groups up and down the street, although never more than a few blocks from the arrest scene. Between 8:15 p.m. and midnight, the mob stoned automobiles, pulled Caucasian motorists out of their cars and beat them, and menaced a police field command post which had been set up in the area. By 1:00 a.m., the outbreak seemed to be under control but, until early morning hours, there were sporadic reports of unruly mobs, vandalism, and rock throwing. Twenty-nine persons were arrested.

A Meeting Misfires

On Thursday morning, there was an uneasy calm, but it was obvious that tensions were still high. A strong expectancy of further trouble kept the atmosphere tense in the judgment of both police and Negro leaders. The actions by many individuals, both Negro and white, during Thursday, as well as at other times, to attempt to control the riots are commendable. We have heard many vivid and impressive accounts of the work of Negro leaders, social workers, probation officers, churchmen, teachers, and businessmen in their attempts to persuade the people to desist from their illegal activities, to stay in their houses and off the street, and to restore order.

However, the meeting called by the Los Angeles County Human Relations Commission, at the request of county officials, for the purpose of lowering the temperature misfired. That meeting was held beginning about 2:00 p.m. in an auditorium at Athens Park, eleven blocks from the scene of the arrest. It brought together every available representative of neighborhood groups and Negro leaders to discuss the problem. Members of the press, television, and radio covered the meeting. Various elected officials participated and members of the Los Angeles Police Department, Sheriff's Office and District Attorney's Office were in attendance as observers.

Several community leaders asked members of the audience to use their influence to persuade area residents to stay home Thursday evening. Even Mrs. Frye spoke and asked the crowd to "help me and others calm this situation down so that we will not have a riot tonight." But one Negro high school youth ran to the microphones and said the rioters would attack adjacent white areas that evening. This inflammatory remark was widely reported on television and radio, and it was seldom balanced by reporting of the many responsible statements made at the meeting. Moreover, it appears that the tone and conduct of the meeting shifted, as the meeting was in progress, from attempted persuasion with regard to the maintenance of law and order to a discussion of the grievances felt by the Negro.

Following the main meeting, certain leaders adjourned to a small meeting where they had discussions with individuals representing youth gangs and decided upon a course of action. They decided to propose that Caucasian officers be withdrawn from the troubled area, and that Negro officers in civilian clothes and unmarked cars be substituted. Members of this small group then went to see Deputy Chief of Police Roger Murdock at the 77th Street Station, where the proposals were rejected by him at about 7:00 p.m. They envisaged an untested method of handling a serious situation that was rapidly developing. Furthermore, the proposal to use only Negro officers ran counter to the policy of the Police Department, adopted over a period of time at the urging of Negro leaders, to deploy Negro officers throughout the city and not concentrate them in the Negro area. Indeed, when the proposal came the police had no immediate means of determining where the Negro officers on the forces were stationed. At this moment, rioting was breaking out again, and the police felt that their established procedures were the only way to handle what was .developing as another night of rioting. Following those procedures, the police decided to set up a perimeter around the center of trouble and keep all crowd activity within that area.

An Alert Is Sounded

About 5:00 p.m. Thursday, after receiving a report on the Athens Park meeting, Police Chief William H. Parker called Lt. Gen. Roderic Hill, the Adjutant General of the California National Guard in Sacramento, and told him that the Guard might be needed. This step was taken pursuant to a procedure instituted by Governor Brown and agreed upon in 1963 and 1964 between the Los Angeles Police Department, the Governor and the Guard. It was an alert that the Guard might be needed.

Pursuant to the agreed-upon procedure, General Hill sent Colonel Robert Quick to Los Angeles to work as liaison officer. He also alerted the commanders of the 40th Armored Division located in Southern California to the possibility of being called. In addition, in the absence of Governor Brown who was in Greece, he called the acting Governor,

Lieutenant Governor Glenn Anderson, in Santa Barbara, and informed him of the Los Angeles situation.

The Emergency Control Center at Police Headquarters—a specially outfitted command post—was opened at 7:30 p.m. on Thursday. That day, one hundred and ninety deputy sheriffs were asked for and assigned. Between 6:45 and 7:15 p.m., crowds at the scene of the trouble of the night before had grown to more than 1,000. Firemen who came into the area to fight fires in three overturned automobiles were shot at and bombarded with rocks. The first fire in a commercial establishment was set only one block from the location of the Frye arrests, and police had to hold back rioters as firemen fought the blaze.

Shortly before midnight, rock-throwing and looting crowds for the first time ranged outside the perimeter. Five hundred police officers, deputy sheriffs and highway patrolmen used various techniques, including fender-to-fender sweeps by police cars, in seeking to disperse the mob. By 4:00 a.m. Friday, the police department felt that the situation was at least for the moment under control. At 5:09 a.m., officers were withdrawn from emergency perimeter control.

During the evening on Thursday, Lt. Gov. Anderson had come to his home in suburban Los Angeles from Santa Barbara. While at his residence, he was informed that there were as many as 8,000 rioters in the streets. About 1:00 a.m. Friday, he talked by phone to John Billett of his staff and with General Hill, and both advised him that police officials felt the situation was nearing control. About 6:45 a.m., at Lt. Gov. Anderson's request, Billet called the Emergency Control Center and was told by Sergeant Jack Eberhardt, the intelligence officer on duty, that "the situation was rather well in hand," and this information was promptly passed on to Anderson. Anderson instructed Billett to keep in touch with him and left Los Angeles at 7:25 a.m. for a morning meeting of the Finance Committee of the Board of Regents of the University of California in Berkeley, and an afternoon meeting of the full Board.

Friday, the 13th

Around 8:00 a.m., crowds formed again in the vicinity of the Frye arrests and in the adjacent Watts business area, and looting resumed. Before 9:00 a.m., Colonel Quick called General Hill in Sacramento from the Emergency Control Center and told him riot activity was intensifying.

At approximately 9:15 a.m., Mayor Sam Yorty and Chief Parker talked on the telephone, and they decided, at that time, to call the Guard. Following this conversation, Mayor Yorty went to the airport and boarded a 10:05 flight to keep a speaking engagement at the Commonwealth Club in San Francisco. Mayor Yorty told our Commission that "by about

10:00 or so, I have to decide whether I am going to disappoint that audience in San Francisco and maybe make my city look rather ridiculous if the rioting doesn't start again, and the mayor has disappointed that crowd." The Mayor returned to the City at 3:35 p.m.

The riot situation was canvassed in a Los Angeles Police Department staff meeting held at 9:45 a.m. where Colonel Quick, of the California National Guard, was in attendance, along with police officials. At 10:00 a.m., according to Colonel Quick, Chief Parker said, "It looks like we are going to have to call the troops. We will need a thousand men." Colonel Quick has said that Chief Parker did not specifically ask him to get the National Guard. On the other hand, Chief Parker has stated that he told Colonel Quick that he wanted the National Guard and that Quick indicated that he would handle the request.

In any event, at 10:15 a.m., Colonel Quick informed General Hill by telephone that Chief Parker would probably request 1,000 national guardsmen. General Hill advised Colonel Quick to have Chief Parker call the Governor's office in Sacramento. At 10:50 a.m., Parker made the formal request for the National Guard to Winslow Christian, Governor Brown's executive secretary, who was then in Sacramento, and Christian accepted the request.

By mid-morning, a crowd of 3,000 had gathered in the commercial section of Watts and there was general looting in that district as well as in adjacent business areas. By the time the formal request for the Guard had been made, ambulance drivers and firemen were refusing to go into the riot area without an armed escort.

Calling the Guard

At approximately 11:00 a.m., Christian reached Lt. Gov. Anderson by telephone in Berkeley and relayed Chief Parker's request. Lt. Gov. Anderson did not act on the request at that time. We believe that this request from the chief law enforcement officer of the stricken city for the National Guard should have been honored without delay. If the Lieutenant Governor was in doubt about conditions in Los Angeles, he should, in our view, have confirmed Chief Parker's estimate by telephoning National Guard officers in Los Angeles. Although we are mindful that it was natural and prudent for the Lieutenant Governor to be cautious in acting in the absence of Governor Brown, we feel that, in this instance, he hesitated when he should have acted.

Feeling that he wished to consider the matter further, Lt. Gov. Anderson returned to Los Angeles by way of Sacramento. A propeller-driven National Guard plane picked him up at Oakland at 12:20 p.m., and reached McClellan Air Force Base, near Sacramento, at 1:00 p.m. Anderson met with National Guard officers and civilian staff members and received various suggestions, ranging from advice from Guard officers that he commit the Guard immediately to counsel from some civilian staff members that he examine the situation in Los Angeles and meet with Chief Parker before acting. Although Anderson still did not reach a decision to commit the Guard, he agreed with Guard officers that the troops should be assembled in the Armories at 5 p.m., which he had been told by General Hill was the earliest hour that it was feasible to do so. Hill then ordered 2,000 men to be at the armories by that hour. Anderson's plane left Sacramento for Los Angeles at 1:35 p.m. and arrived at 3:35 p.m.

At the time Lt. Gov. Anderson and General Hill were talking in Sacramento, approximately 856 Guardsmen in the 3rd Brigade were in the Long Beach area 12 miles to the south, while enroute from San Diego, outfitted with weapons, to summer camp at Camp Roberts. We feel it reasonable to conclude, especially since this unit was subsequently used in the curfew area, that further escalation of the riots might have been averted if these Guardsmen had been diverted promptly and deployed on station throughout the riot area by early or mid-afternoon Friday.

Friday afternoon, Hale Champion, State Director of Finance, who was in the Governor's office in Los Angeles, reached Governor Brown in Athens.. He briefed the Governor on the current riot situation, and Brown said he felt the Guard should be called immediately, that the possibility of a curfew should be explored, and that he was heading home as fast as possible.

Early Friday afternoon, rioters jammed the streets, began systematically to burn two blocks of 103rd Street in Watts, and drove off firemen by sniper fire and by throwing missiles. By late afternoon, gang activity began to spread the disturbances as far as fifty and sixty blocks to the north.

Lieutenant Governor Anderson arrived at the Van Nuys Air National Guard Base at 3:35 p.m. After talking with Hale Champion who urged him to call the Guard, Anderson ordered General Hill to commit the troops. At 4:00 p.m., he announced this decision to the press. At 5:00 p.m., in the Governor's office downtown, he signed the proclamation officially calling the Guard.

By 6.00 p.m., 1,336 National Guard troops were assembled in the armories. These troops were enroute to two staging areas in the rioting area by 7:00 p.m. However, neither the officials of the Los Angeles Police Department nor officers of the Guard deployed any of the troops until shortly after 10:00 p.m. Having in mind these delays, we believe that law enforcement agencies and the National Guard should develop contingency plans so that in future situations of emergency, there will be a better method at hand to assure the early commitment of the National Guard and the rapid deployment of the troops.

The first death occurred between 6:00 and 7:00 p.m. Friday, when a Negro bystander, trapped on the street between police and rioters, was shot and killed during an exchange of gunfire.

The Worst Night

Friday was the worst night. The riot moved out of the Watts area and burning and looting spread over wide areas of Southeast Los Angeles several miles apart. At 1:00 a.m. Saturday, there were 100 engine companies fighting fires in the area. Snipers shot at firemen as they fought new fires. That night, a fireman was crushed and killed on the fire line by a falling wall, and a deputy sheriff was killed when another sheriff's shotgun was discharged in a struggle with rioters.

Friday night, the law enforcement officials tried a different tactic. Police officers made sweeps on foot, moving en masse along streets to control activity and enable firemen to fight fires. By midnight, Friday, another 1,000 National Guard troops were marching shoulder to shoulder clearing the streets. By 3:00 a.m. Saturday, 3,356 guardsmen were on the streets, and the number continued to increase until the full commitment of 13,900 guardsmen was reached by midnight on Saturday. The maximum commitment of the Los Angeles Police Department during the riot period was 934 officers; the maximum for the Sheriff's Office was 719 officers.

Despite the new tactics and added personnel, the area was not under control at any time on Friday night, as major calls of looting, burning, and shooting were reported every two to three minutes. On throughout the morning hours of Saturday and during the long day, the crowds of looters and patterns of burning spread out and increased still further until it became necessary to impose a curfew on the 46.5 square-mile area on Saturday. Lieutenant Governor Anderson appeared on television early Saturday evening to explain the curfew, which made it a crime for any unauthorized persons to be on the streets in the curfew area after 8:00 p.m.

The Beginning of Control

Much of the Saturday burning had been along Central Avenue. Again using sweep tactics, the guardsmen and police were able to clear this area by 3:30 p.m. Guardsmen rode "shotgun" on the fire engines and effectively stopped the sniping and rock throwing at firemen. Saturday evening, road blocks were set up in anticipation of the curfew. The massive show of force was having some effect although there was still riot activity and rumors spread regarding proposed activity in the south central area.

When the curfew started at 8:00 p.m., police and guardsmen were able to deal with the riot area as a whole. Compared with the holocaust of Friday evening, the streets were relatively quiet. The only major exception was the burning of a block of stores on Broadway between 46th and 48th Streets. Snipers again prevented firemen from entering the area, and while the buildings burned, a gun battle ensued between law enforcement officers, the Guard, and the snipers.

During the day Sunday, the curfew area was relatively quiet. Because many markets had been destroyed, food distribution was started by churches, community groups, and government agencies. Governor Brown, who had returned Saturday night, personally toured the area, talking to residents. Major fires were under control but there were new fires and some rekindling of old ones. By Tuesday, Governor Brown was able to lift the curfew and by the following Sunday, only 252 guardsmen remained.

Coordination between the several law enforcement agencies during the period of the riot was commendable. When the California Highway Patrol called for help on Wednesday evening, the Los Angeles Police Department responded immediately. When the situation grew critical Thursday evening, the Los Angeles Sheriff's Office committed substantial forces without hesitation. Indeed, the members of all law enforcement agencies—policemen, sheriff's officers, Highway Patrolmen, city Marshalls —and the Fire Departments as well—worked long hours, in harmony and with conspicuous bravery, to quell the disorder. However, the depth and the seriousness of the situation were not accurately appraised in the early stages, and the law enforcement forces committed and engaged in the several efforts to bring the riots under control on Thursday night and all day Friday proved to be inadequate. It required massive force to subdue the riot, as demonstrated by the effectiveness of the Guard when it moved into position late Friday night and worked in coordination with the local law enforcement units.

Other Areas Affected

As the word of the South Los Angeles violence was flashed almost continuously by all news media, the unrest spread. Although outbreaks in other areas were minor by comparison with those in South Central Los Angeles, each one held dangerous potential. San Diego, 102 miles away, had three days of rioting and 81 people were arrested. On Friday night, there was rioting in Pasadena, 12 miles from the curfew zone.

There, liquor and gun stores were looted and Molotov cocktails and fire bombs were thrown at police cars. Only prompt and skillful handling by the police prevented this situation from getting out of control.

Pacoima, 20 miles north, had scattered rioting, looting, and burning. There was burning in Monrovia, 25 miles east. On Sunday night, after the curfew area was quiet, there was an incident in Long Beach, 12 miles south. About 200 guardsmen and Los Angeles police assisted Long Beach police in containing a dangerous situation which exploded when a policeman was shot when another officer's gun discharged as he was being attacked by rioters. Several fires were set Sunday night in the San Pedro-Wilmington area, 12 miles south.

Was There a Pre-established Plan?

After a thorough examination, the Commission has concluded that there is no reliable evidence of outside leadership or pre-established plans for the rioting. The testimony of law enforcement agencies and their respective intelligence officers supports this conclusion. The Attorney General, the District Attorney, and the Los Angeles police have all reached the conclusion that there is no evidence of a pre-plan or a pre-established central direction of the rioting activities. This finding was submitted to the Grand Jury by the District Attorney.

This is not to say that there was *no* agitation or promotion of the rioting by local groups or gangs which exist in pockets throughout the south central area. The sudden appearance of Molotov cocktails in quantity and the unexplained movement of men in cars through the areas of great destruction support the conclusion that there was organization and planning after the riots commenced. In addition, on that tense Thursday, inflammatory handbills suddenly appeared in Watts. But this cannot be identified as a master plan by one group; rather it appears to have been the work of several gangs, with membership of young men ranging in age from 14 to 35 years. All of these activities intensified the rioting and caused it to spread with increased violence from one district to another in the curfew area.

The Grim Statistics

The final statistics are staggering. There were 34 persons killed and 1,032 reported injuries, including 90 Los Angeles police officers, 136 firemen, 10 national guardsmen, 23 persons from other governmental agencies, and 773 civilians. 118 of the injuries resulted from gunshot wounds. Of the 34 killed, one was a fireman, one was a deputy sheriff, and one a Long Beach policeman.

In the weeks following the riots, Coroner's Inquests were held regarding thirty-two of the deaths.* The Coroner's jury ruled that twenty-six of the deaths were justifiable homicide, five were homicidal, and one was accidental. Of those ruled justifiable homicide, the jury found that death was caused in sixteen instances by officers of the Los Angeles Police Department and in seven instances by the National Guard.

It has been estimated that the loss of property attributable to the riots was over $40 million. More than 600 buildings were damaged by burning and looting. Of this number, more than 200 were totally destroyed by fire. The rioters concentrated primarily on food markets, liquor stores, furniture stores, clothing stores, department stores, and pawn shops. Arson arrests numbered 27 and 10 arson complaints were filed, a relatively small number considering that fire department officials say that all of the fires were incendiary in origin. Between 2,000 and 3,000 fire alarms were recorded during the riot, 1,000 of these between 7:00 a.m. on Friday and 7:00 a.m. on Saturday. We note with interest that no residences were deliberately burned, that damage to schools, libraries, churches and public buildings was minimal, and that certain types of business establishments, notably service stations and automobile dealers, were for the most part unharmed.

There were 3,438 adults arrested, 71% for burglary and theft. The number of juveniles arrested was 514, 81% for burglary and theft. Of the adults arrested, 1,232 had never been arrested before; 1,164 had a "minor" criminal record (arrest only or convictions with sentence of 90 days or less); 1,042 with "major" criminal record (convictions with sentence of more than 90 days). Of the juveniles arrested, 257 had never been arrested before; 212 had a "minor" criminal record; 43 had a "major" criminal record. Of the adults arrested, 2,057 were born in 16 southern states whereas the comparable figure for juveniles was 131. Some of the juveniles arrested extensively damaged the top two floors of an auxiliary jail which had been opened on the Saturday of the riots.

Those involved in the administration of justice—judges, prosecutors, defense counsel, and others—merit commendation for the steps they took to cope with the extraordinary responsibility thrust on the judicial system by the riots. By reorganizing calendars and making special assignments, the Los Angeles Superior and Municipal Courts have been able to meet the statutory deadlines for processing the cases of those arrested. Court statistics indicate that by November 26, the following dispositions had been made of the 2,278 felony cases filed against adults: 856 were found guilty; 155 were acquitted; 641 were disposed of prior to trial, primarily

---

* The Coroner's Inquest into one of the deaths was cancelled at the request of the deceased's family. There was no inquest into the death of the deputy sheriff because of pending criminal proceedings.

by dismissal; 626 are awaiting trial. Of the 1,133 misdeameanor cases filed, 733 were found guilty, 81 were acquitted, 184 dismissed and 135 are awaiting trial.

The police and Sheriff's Department have long known that many members of gangs, as well as others, in the south central area possessed weapons and knew how to use them. However, the extent to which pawn shops, each one of which possessed an inventory of weapons, were the immediate target of looters, leads to the conclusion that a substantial number of the weapons used were stolen from these shops. During the riots, law enforcement officers recovered 851 weapons. There is no evidence that the rioters made any attempt to steal narcotics from pharmacies in the riot area even though some pharmacies were looted and burned.

Overwhelming as are the grim statistics, the impact of the August rioting on the Los Angeles community has been even greater. The first weeks after the disorders brought a flood tide of charges and recriminations. Although this has now ebbed, the feeling of fear and tension persists, largely unabated, throughout the community. A certain slowness in the rebuilding of the fired structures has symbolized the difficulty in mending relationships in our community which were so severely fractured by the August nightmare.

*   *   *   *

THE MEREDITH MISSISSIPPI MARCH (1966)

Although by 1966 much progress had been made, in many places in the deep South the Negro was still not secure in the rights guaranteed under the Constitution and might still be the victim of violence. When James Meredith attempted to walk from the Mississippi border to Jackson he was shot by a roadside sniper. Another protest march in the summer of 1966, described below by Renata Adler, brought new slogans and leaders to the national scene. Stokely Carmichael's call for "Black Power," introduced a new element into the complex, unresolved movement for Negro rights.

Mississippi, RENATA ADLER (1966)

For three weeks in June, a civil-rights demonstration, under black leadership, and with local Negroes in the overwhelming majority, passed successfully from the northern border of Mississippi to the state capital, crossing several counties whose most distinguished citizens had been Negroes who died for civil rights. One of the triumphs of that demonstration—the James Meredith March Against Fear—was that none of the marchers were murdered. They were not, like the Selma marchers, protected by the federal government. They demanded protection from the state, and, with certain lapses along the way, they got it. For those weeks in June, white Mississippians and black saw state troopers surrounding Negroes not to oppress but to shield them, not to give them orders but to come to terms with their demands. With the support of federal law, and the authority of their own courage and intelligence, the Negro leaders required the government of Mississippi to deal with them—for the first time—as men. For this reason, if for no other, the march marked a turning point in the Negro's relationship to the white community, North and South.

From its beginnings, ever since Abolition, the civil-rights movement has been the child of Northern white liberalism. In a different sense, the Southern segregationist has regarded the Negro as his child. With the march, the movement proved that as long as the law prevents acts of violence against it from going unpunished, it can assume its own adult leadership—including responsibility for its own radical children. On this occasion, the children were the workers of S.N.C.C. (the Student Nonviolent Coördinating Committee), and the worried parents were the workers of S.C.L.C. (the Southern Christian Leadership Conference). Other members of the family were the understanding older relative, CORE (the Congress of Racial Equality); two rich, conservative older relatives, the N.A.A.C.P. (the National Association for the Advancement of Colored People) and the National Urban League; and two industrious cousins, M.C.H.R. (the Medical Committee for Human Rights) and the Delta Ministry of the N.C.C. (the National Council of Churches). The issues, but for their repercussions outside the state of Mississippi, would not have been issues at all. All branches of the movement were united in trying to develop political assertiveness where the need is great— among the Negro masses, too poor to afford the restaurants integrated by sit-ins, too ignorant to attend the colleges now open to them, too heavily oppressed to vote. The leaders, by marching in a state where they are hated by violent men, hoped to dramatize personal courage, and to inspire local Negroes to take the physical and economic risks that still accompany a Negro's registering to vote in Mississippi. For every large minority, the vote is the key to political power, and that S.N.C.C.'s rallying cry of "Black Power!" should have proved divisive—and even dangerous—is only the latest in a series of ironies that have beset that organization from the beginning.

A campus offshoot of Dr. Martin Luther King's S.C.L.C., S.N.C.C. always comes to the national attention when it is on the brink of going out of existence. S.N.C.C. workers—young intellectuals who have tried valiantly to "speak to the needs" of a poor black community—drew the movement to the rural South, only to be outdone by better-organized and better-financed civil-rights groups and by the federal government. S.N.C.C. leaders were subject to grinding pressures—personal danger, responsibility for lives, internal dissension—which seemed to wear them down. And it was S.N.C.C. leaders—whose awareness of the complexity of moral and social issues had always, characteristically, involved them in agonized conferences lasting several weeks—who came up with the simplistic "Black Power!" slogan. To the marchers, the meaning of the chant was clear: it was a rallying cry for Negroes to vote as a bloc, to take over communities in which they constitute a majority, and to exercise some political leverage in communities in which they constitute a large minority. The local black audience—full of affection for the young radicals but all too conscious of what the power realities in Mississippi are—virtually ignored the chant as bravado. White Southerners heard the challenge to white supremacy and braced themselves. And Northern liberals, already bored or disaffected by tensions in the movement, heard only the overtones; a mob chanting *anything,* and particularly a spondee followed by an unaccented syllable, seemed distressingly reminiscent of pre-war German rhetoric, and alienated white sympathies—which the movement will need as long as the need for a movement exists—still further. (What black extremists in the Northern ghettos heard remains to be seen.) "Black Power!" turned out to be, at best, an expression of political naïveté; at worst, it could be misconstrued as a call to violence, which would bring on retaliatory violence to oppress the Negro more heavily than ever, and cause the country to cheat itself once again of the equal participation of its black minority.

Another irony, which almost obscured the purpose of the march, was that violence should appear to be a major issue in the movement. The only marcher who seriously advocated "violent revolution" was a white college graduate, unemployed, wearing a baseball cap and a few days' growth of beard. He became known to reporters as the House Marxist, and he provoked from Negro marchers such comments as "I don't know what to say to you," "The first thing you whites want to do when you come to the movement is make policy," "Everyone has a right to his opinion until he hurts someone else," and "We gonna have a non-violent march no matter who here." The House Marxist joined the march at Batesville and left it at Grenada—muttering that the march itself was "only a tool of the power structure in Washington." It is true that the marchers were often kept awake for much of the night by discussions of the Negro's right to bear arms in his own defense. But the issue was always just that—self-defense—and discussions of it were largely academic. Even S.C.L.C. workers have tacitly acknowledged that the strategy of non-violence, so effective in integrating lunch counters, is simply pointless when it comes to facing armed night riders on a Southern highway. Negro communities have for years afforded their civil-rights workers what protection they could, and not even the Mississippi government has made an issue of it. The march's ideologues—mostly Northern pacifists and hipsters, who kept insisting that the argument lay "between a Selma and a Watts"—brought the question unnecessarily into the open and managed to produce what eventually became a split in the movement. (The mere fact that Medgar Evers, James Chaney, Andrew Goodman, and Michael Schwerner, among so many, are dead while Byron de La Beckwith, Sheriff Lawrence Rainey, and Deputy Sheriff Cecil Price, among so many others, are still alive should be testimony enough to the movement's commitment to non-violence. There have been no white-supremacist martyrs yet.) Marchers who, giving way under the strain, exchanged threats and insults with bystanders were quickly surrounded by other marchers and roundly scolded; but when a memorial service in Philadelphia, Mississippi, was engulfed by a white mob armed with hoes and axe handles, the marchers fought back with their fists, and no one—not even the vocal pacifists—protested.

Perhaps the reason for the disproportionate emphasis on divisive issues during the march was that civil-rights news—like news of any unified, protracted struggle against injustice—becomes boring. One march, except to the marchers is very like another. Tents, hot days, worried nights, songs, rallies, heroes, villains, even tear gas and clubbings—the props are becoming stereotyped. Radicals and moderate observers alike long for a breakthrough into something fresh. The institution of the civil-rights march, however, is likely to occupy a long moment in American history, and the country might as well become familiar with the cast.

The Drones: In every march, there seem to be a number of white participants from out of the state who come with only the fuzziest comprehension of the issues but with a strong conviction that civil rights is a good thing to walk for. The last to be informed of events and decisions—after the police, the press, the nation as a whole—the drones trudge wearily along. They become objects of hostility when Negro marchers—forgetting that the only whites within scorning distance are likely to be friendly whites—mistake who their enemies are. In the March Against Fear, the drones turned out to be the only continuous marchers. Leaders dropped out repeatedly—Martin Luther King (S.C.L.C.) to attend to affairs in Chicago, Floyd McKissick (CORE) for a speaking engagement in New York, Stokely Carmichael (S.N.C.C.) for a television appearance in Washington—and most of the local Negroes could march only part of the way. But the drones stuck it out. Some were thrust into action, and reacted in various ways to dangers of which they had not been fully aware. A mustachioed anthropologist from a Northern university, for example, volunteered for a voter-registration task force in Charleston, Mississippi. When the white population proved hostile, he simply drove back to the march, leaving the rest of the task force to fend for itself. After two more incidents of this kind, he was punched in the jaw by another marcher, and wisely went home. Two drones from the North arrived in a station wagon, bringing their three-year-old son with them. The child, whom they left alone for naps in their car by the side of the road, became covered with mosquito bites, and was twice found wandering by himself, screaming in terror at the sight of a large, barking dog. On the night of the tent-pitching in Canton, Mississippi, the child was rendered unconscious by tear gas, but his parents were preoccupied with what they thought was the need to precipitate another episode. "We've got to pitch those tents again," they insisted, on the second night in Canton. "By backing down, we're only deceiving the local people." (The drones were the last to learn it was the local Negroes who decided that they had proved their point and that another act of civil disobedience would be unnecessarily dangerous.)

The Press: Reporters (on this occasion, we were among them) have become, despite their neutrality as observers, an integral part of the movement as they cover one of the last of the just wars. Some of the time, the television networks alone had more than a hundred men accompanying the march, with planes and helicopters overhead, couriers cruising along the line of march in cars, a press truck, and walkie-talkies adding to the din of the already crowded airwaves. (The night security guard, the Deacons for Defense and Justice, and even passing Klansmen were all equipped with citizens'-band radios. The police and the F.B.I., of course, had radios of their own.) At times when the marchers were silent, the only sounds along the route were disembodied voices. The press was jeered by roadside segregationists, threatened by troopers during the tear-gassing in Canton, harassed by a water moccasin planted aboard the press truck in Yalobusha County, and attacked outright by the mob in Philadelphia, but all this did not make the civil-rights workers any the less unhappy with what they came to regard as their unfavorable reviews. Marchers accused the reporters of exaggerating dissension in the movement (when there was a brief argument aboard the press truck, marchers gleefully cried, "Dissension in the press! A split! A split!" Reporters responded with cries of "Press Power!"), and even of generating some dissension by distorted reporting of events. As far as the wire services were concerned, the marchers had a point. The Associated Press, in particular, made almost daily errors in its coverage—errors that seemed to reflect a less than sympathetic view. The A.P. quoted Stokely Carmichael's cry, in the face of the tear gas, "Now is the time to separate the men from the mice!" as "Now is the time to separate the men from the whites!"—implying racism in what had been only a call for courage. It repeatedly identified Willie Ricks, a demagogue affiliated with S.N.C.C., as an aide to Dr. King, of S.C.L.C.— implying that the organization most deeply committed to non-violence was severely compromised. The sort of story that A.P. was determined to listen for and report is suggested by a question that an A.P. correspondent asked some civil-rights workers who were arming themselves to repel a second attack on their headquarters in Philadelphia; he wondered whether the incident would "encourage Negroes in the promiscuous killing of whites." In a sense, of course, the A.P.'s mistaken report of James Meredith's death was what brought the civil-rights leaders and the press to Memphis in the first place; but there were signs each day that subscribers to the wire service, North and South, were getting a distorted version of what was going on in Mississippi. Other members of the press were more than competent. Their mere presence contributed substantially to the safety of the marchers, and they have proved to be an important factor in the pacification of the South.

The White Supremacists: Stock characters out of the Southern bestiary, they line the route of every march. Shouting epithets, waving flags, wielding hoses, throwing objects, or just gazing in malevolent silence, they congregate most often at gas stations and grocery stores—a grotesque parody of small-town America. In conversation, they invariably protest that "our niggers are happy," express earnest worry about "niggers raping our women," and show their only traces of real animation when they contemplate disposing of the problem. "I'd spray the whole bunch with sulfuric acid," said a Navy recruiter in Greenwood. "What I'd do," said a tourist from Arab, Alabama, sputtering over his grits, "I'd get me some dynamite, and run me a line to the side of the road . . ."

The more cultivated elements of the segregationist community have evolved their own schizophrenic logic. "Negroes have always been able to vote here," the Greenwood newspaper proudly editorialized, and added, "This county was one of the first in the country to receive federal registrars." "You better get out of here before you need an undertaker," a sheriff said to a voter-registration task force. Then he muttered to himself, "They just came in here, mouthin'."

But there are signs of progress, or at least of resignation. "We didn't want this to happen, but what the hell!" said Joseph Lee, the editor of the newspaper in Grenada—a town that had twice run out a team of COFO (Council of Federated Organizations) workers, but in which the marchers registered more than twelve hundred voters. "There are things we used to do that we don't know now why we did them. We didn't know why we did them *then*. There are still some people who hang back and look sore. And a man who's a little weak in the head can make as much trouble as a Rhodes Scholar. But these days I tell my own Negroes to get their fanny on over and register." The Grenada city manager, however, was reconciled in his own way. "Most of your Negroes registering are either very old or young," he said. "Your old ones—well, the vote isn't till 1967. And the young ones—a lot of them will be going to Vietnam. And some of them won't be coming back."

There are advances in law enforcement. Despite the fact that several marchers were kicked and beaten by troopers during the tear-gas episode (a medical worker suffered three broken ribs and a collapsed lung), the troopers were not—by the standards of Watts, for example—especially brutal; they exercised what might be termed self-restraint. The sheriff of Sunflower County, where the White Citizens Councils were born, is a graduate of the F.B.I. school and, like many other local officials whom the Justice Department has quietly encouraged to attend federal schools, coöperates in seeing to it that federal law is observed. Charles Snodgrass, in charge of the march for the Mississippi Highway Patrol, won the marchers' respect for his integrity; and he worked closely with John Doar—an assistant Attorney General so respected by Negroes and whites alike that, in the words of one marcher, "He seems to be the only one left in the Justice Department who knows what's going on. Without John Doar, there'd be a lot more dead in Mississippi." Even the most extreme elements are, almost unconsciously, changing. The mob in Philadelphia, shouting, surging forward, throwing eggs and Coke bottles, listened to every phrase spoken by Dr. King long enough to scream an ugly answer to it. (Sometimes they listened and screamed so carefully that Dr. King appeared to be leading them in a responsive reading.) And a waitress in Jackson readily conceded, "Your whites in Neshoba County, they're the meanest people in the state." (Then she added, as if overcome by her own liberalism, "They got Indian blood in them.") And there are some real liberals. "It takes about ten drinks for me to say what I really think," a lady in Jackson said. "Why, we've never done anything that's right for the Negro. All we did was starve him, and work him, and shoot him in the back. I don't see how they could run their counties any worse than the whites have been running them."

The Local Negroes: Strong leadership is developing in the small communities, and the march left little registration teams everywhere in its wake. Canton alone already had Annie Devine, of the Mississippi Freedom Democratic Party, who, with mud still on her dress and with her eyes still red from the tear gas, rose to announce, simply, "We are not going to stay ignorant, and backward, and scared;" and young Flonzie Goodlow, of the N.A.A.C.P., who, despite white intimidation and jealous opposition from misguided workers for S.N.C.C. in the past, brought so many Negroes to vote that she could announce her own intention of running for registrar in 1967; and George Raymond, of CORE, who was a voice of gentle moderation throughout the march, and diverted the marchers at moments of crisis with singing. Then, there are the local non-leaders, like the delegation from Holmes County that came to offer the marchers lodging, and, upon learning that the march was skirting Holmes, acknowledged, "There are other places in badder shape. Whichever way they go, we're going to support it." And like Hura Montgomery, a Negro farmer in Louise, who permitted the marchers to pitch their tents on his land. "I was possibly hoping they wouldn't ask," he said, "but somebody had to let them in."

The March Leaders: Robert Green, of S.C.L.C., a tall young professor of psychology at Michigan State, was liaison man for the march. Addressing the local police with quiet authority, planting an American flag on the statue of Jefferson Davis in Grenada ("The South you led will never stand again. Mississippi must become part of the Union"), leaping over the cowcatcher to board a locomotive moving toward the line of march in Jackson (he commanded the engineer to stop, and persuaded the angry marchers to keep marching), reassuring a troubled white worker for the Urban League ("We need the conservative groups, too. We need to engage the problem at every level"), and reasoning quietly with the few advocates of arms among the marchers ("The whites will simply seal you off and crush you, as they did in Watts. Our only course is to confront them again and again with the force of non-violence. It's the glory of the movement"), Green played a part in the march which itself changed the face of Mississippi. The police respected his fearlessness and his dignity. The towns were so shaken by his treatment of the monument in Grenada that several other monuments along the route were guarded by six Negro trusties from the state penitentiary, to prevent a recurrence of the desecration. And the marchers were sufficiently impressed by his courage and intelligence to respond consistently to his leadership.

Floyd McKissick, the national director of CORE, was always called upon to lead the marchers on days when they had to start promptly and walk fast, and to make practical announcements concerning strategy and finances. McKissick, an attorney from Durham, North Carolina, marched for the most part with patience and good humor. When a lady from Charleston, Mississippi, a Negro, came to the campsite at Enid Dam in the night to wish him well, and to tell him that "there are [liberal] whites in Charleston who are just as scared as we are," he discussed with her for an hour the question of whether it was time for the movement to make contact with white liberals in Mississippi. It was McKissick who served the marchers their lunch on days when he led them, and who, after many nights disrupted by the arguments of ideologues, the buzzing of transistor radios, and the nervous jokes of the night security guard, announced that "anyone who disturbs the marchers' sleep tonight will be hauled out and sent home." It was McKissick who mediated between S.N.C.C. and S.C.L.C. But on the night of the tear gas in Canton McKissick's patience simply broke. The contrast between police treatment of peaceful Negro trespassers on the grounds of an illegally segregated school and the reluctance of the police in Philadelphia to intervene against an armed white mob seemed to overwhelm the lawyer in him. He was almost incoherent with rage, and close to tears. "I'm tired of having to *negotiate* for our constitutional *rights*," he said. "Some people said we ought to confront President Johnson. I say the hell with it. When the tear gas came, I fell off that truck like a scrambled egg. You didn't *want* that school, but they made it yours. They don't call it *white* power. They just call it *power*. I'm committed to non-violence, but I say what we need is to get us some *black* power."

Stokely Carmichael, the young chairman of S.N.C.C., argued most persuasively for black political power, and when, as he saw it, he was continuously misrepresented by the press, he became obdurate and began to make himself eminently misrepresentable. What he had in mind throughout the march was a Populist movement in the South: White S.N.C.C. workers would address themselves to the white poor, black S.N.C.C. workers would address themselves to the black poor, and since the blacks would outnumber the whites, the new Populists would naturally be under Negro leadership, and would present an encouraging example of Negro effectiveness to Negroes throughout the country. Tall, lean, and intellectual, Carmichael spoke to the crowds at night, punctuating his words with a finger pointed at the ground, enunciating a phrase slowly and then repeating it rapidly, bending his knees to add emphasis to his soft, tense voice. It was Carmichael who said, "It is time to stop being ashamed of being black. It is time to stop trying to be white. When you see your daughter playing in the fields, with her nappy hair, and her wide nose, and her thick lips, tell her she is beautiful. *Tell your daughter she is beautiful.*" It was Carmichael who, wherever he went, picked up children and carried them, and who, when the marchers swarmed into a Negro lady's house for a drink of water, reprimanded them by saying, "None of you asked where that lady got the water. None of you bothered to find out that she has to carry that water in buckets a mile and a half. These are things we ought to be talking about." (Carmichael himself hauled water for the lady.) It was also Carmichael who, having lived for six summers under the fear and strain that assail a S.N.C.C. worker in the South, became hysterical for several minutes after the tear-gas episode in Canton. "Don't make your stand here," said Carmichael, the militant, sobbing and wandering about in circles. "I just can't stand to see any more people get shot." The following evening, it was Carmichael who wanted the marchers to risk putting up the tents again in the schoolyard, and who, overruled by Dr. King and the local people, sulked. (When James Lawson, a member of S.C.L.C., and a founder of S.N.C.C., told him later that he had been wrong, he accepted the criticism and agreed.) Although on the night of the Philadelphia riot Carmichael said, "This is S.N.C.C.'s night, man. This is our suit," he never forced an issue, never exhorted the marchers to violence, never, in spite of his militancy, put people in unnecessary danger. And it was Carmichael, the militant, who, in the words of one reporter, "came all over shy" when fifteen thousand people, assembled in Tougaloo, sang "Happy Birthday" to him (twenty-five) and James Meredith (thirty-three); and the night itself seemed to break out in smiles. (As for Meredith, who had been such an enigma throughout his personal ordeal, he simply melted before this friendly, sentimental face of America. "This is the happiest birthday I've ever had," he said.) In later interviews, Carmichael (like Meredith) was as uncompromising in not urging non-violence—and in not urging violence, either—as he had ever been.

Dr. Martin Luther King, of S.C.L.C., proved on the march that he is still *the* leader of the movement, and perhaps the most forceful voice of conscience in the country. People came from all over Mississippi to see him, and responded to the measured, rational cadences of his voice. Time after time, he averted a crisis among the marchers, and his aides— Hosea Williams, leading gentle hymns and silent night marches, and Andy Young, making soft, persuasive speeches, called forth the same extraordinary discipline with which he is able to inspire the movement. Turning to Sheriff Rainey, in Philadelphia, and saying, "I believe in my heart that the murderers are somewhere around me at this moment," and turning back to the marchers, under attack from a far larger crowd, to say, "I am not afraid of any man," Dr. King set an example of pure courage. Exhorting the marchers in Canton to remain calm under the tear gas, or addressing a church full of Negroes in Cleveland, Mississippi, so movingly that a five-year-old girl began to sob and say over and over again, "I want to go with him," Dr. King was a superb spiritual leader. Bringing a busload of juvenile-gang leaders from Chicago to Mississippi, in the hope of diverting their energies to the non-violent cause of civil rights, Dr. King proved himself again an incomparable strategist and pedagogue. And a few phrases like "America, land of the free and home of the brave. Land of free white men, and home of brave Negroes" proved that Dr. King's rhetoric has not lost its cutting edge.

The march was led by complicated men with divergent ideologies, just as the movement is, and their differences are the same ones that divide the nation at large. The response of the white community—alarm and hurt among liberals, and, among reactionaries, alarm and threats to use the white man's undeniably superior force—conceals a failure to hear what the movement is saying. For too long, civil rights has been treated as though it were only the Negro's struggle, with some benevolent white liberal support to help it along; what the movement seeks now is not benevolence but a recognition of reality: the Negro's rights are *law*— and for the white community to resist or ignore the law implies the collapse of an entire legal and moral system. It has become intolerable to the Negro to win so slowly what is his by right, and it has become too costly, in every possible sense, to go on denying him his just place in this society.

CHICAGO (1966)

The Meredith March was not the only civil rights activity during the summer of 1966. In Chicago, the Rev. Martin Luther King directed a campaign against discrimination in the sale and rental to Negroes of homes in the white suburbs of that city. The campaign was met by white crowds as hostile and unruly as those in Mississippi. The following account from The New York Times *describes what happened during one of these marches during August 1966:*

Dr. King and 400 Jeered in Chicago Housing March,
DONALD JANSON (1966)

Chicago, Aug. 21—The Rev. Dr. Martin Luther King Jr. led 400 civil rights workers through an all-white neighborhood of southeastern Chicago late today in support of his campaign for open housing. He was greeted by hoots and scornful shouts by many of the whites who lined the route.

As the march began, a downpour drenched marchers and hecklers alike.

"White power!" yelled the whites, many of them youths, some from other neighborhoods.

[In the Marquette Park area of Chicago, white youths, spurred by speeches of American Nazis and Ku Klux Klansmen, attacked a Negro and his white woman companion in an automobile, United Press International reported. Policemen fired into the air to drive off a mob of several hundred white youths, the news service said.]

Dr. King's demonstration was delayed until 5:30 P.M. because he had a broadcast to make in midafternoon.

Some of the crowd of about 1,000 lining the streets had been waiting all afternoon to see the march.

Four hundred policemen protected the marchers from harm. The East Side community is between the Indiana line and South Deering, scene of a major racial explosion last decade.

Youths raced cars with "white power" lettered on the sides through the neighborhood today. Others carried signs saying "George Lincoln Rockwell [the American Nazi party head] for President."

One carried a sign saying "kill 'em" on the back of a cardboard box that said "Merry Christmas" on the other side.

When the rains came, the marchers burst into freedom songs. Someone held an umbrella over Dr. King, but his black suit was quickly soaked anyway.

Dr. King issued a statement saying that South Deering was represented in the State Legislature by Nick Svalina and Henry Leonard, "the only two Democratic Representatives to vote against an open occupancy bill in the 1953 session of the Legislature." The bill failed by two votes.

The South Deering neighborhood was the scene of great racial tension in 1953 when a few Negro families moved into its Trumbull Park housing project.

Angry white mobs often numbered in the thousands. Some 1,200 policemen were needed to control them during disturbances that continued as long as the Negroes remained in the project.

A special detail of the Police Department was quartered in an apartment in the project for five years to handle repeated bombings and other incidents. Before the turmoil subsided, property had been damaged extensively and 280 white persons had been arrested.

The community is one of inexpensive homes of blue-collar wage earners, many of Polish, Slavic and Russian extraction. Many contend that they fear a sale of homes in their neighborhood to Negroes would hurt the value of their property.

Dr. King, however, said on the "Meet the Press" television program this afternoon that anti-Negro hatred that has existed for a long time was at the base of the trouble.

He attributed it, especially in "lower income enclaves," to unfounded fears that Negroes create slums and constitute a threat to jobs held by others.

He denied that civil rights demonstrations create this hatred. Rather, he said, they merely "arouse" latent hostility. The demonstrations are needed, he said, to call attention to the underlying social ills.

In Chicago, Dr. King noted, the marches have led to top-level conferences with city and realty officials to seek solutions to the social "evil" of housing discrimination.

Dr. King participated in the program by special hookup from a studio in Chicago.

Dr. King's Southern Christian Leadership Conference and associated Chicago civil rights groups have been demonstrating for open housing in all-white Chicago neighborhoods for more than a month.

Today they also sent demonstrators into the suburbs. Real estate offices that allegedly discriminate against Negroes in the sale and rental of homes were picketed in Evergreen Park, west of Chicago, and Chicago Heights, south of the city.

Next Sunday, Dr. King has announced, his followers will march in suburban Cicero. The last time a Negro family tried to move into a flat in Cicero, in 1951, the unsuccessful effort touched off a race riot. A mob of 5,000 whites burned the family's belongings and heavily damaged the apartment building.

The rioting was halted only by calling up the National Guard. The Cook County Sheriff, Richard B. Ogilvie, says the guard will be needed again if Dr. King carries out his intentions.

Dr. King explained the expansion of the marches to the suburbs by saying the suburbs were part of the metropolitan area and that the goal of the federated Chicago Freedom Movement was to make the entire metropolis an open city for Negro residence.

Dr. King held today's march within the maximum of 500 persons decreed by an injunction obtained by the city Friday. But he threatened yesterday to resort to civil disobedience in violation of the court order unless the city indicates willingness this week to strengthen enforcement of its ordinance or pass a more effective one.

In the month of demonstrations here so far, scores of marchers have been injured by rocks and bottles tossed by white rioters.

III
The Leaders

MARTIN LUTHER KING, JR.

The selections that follow are a representative group of the writings and speeches of a number—but not all—of the leaders of the civil rights movement.

Martin Luther King's "I Have a Dream" speech which he delivered from the steps of the Lincoln Memorial during the March on Washington on August 28, 1963, has already become world famous. A New York Times correspondent reported: "he ignited the crowd with words that might have been written by the sad, brooding man enshrined within the memorial."

"I Have A Dream" Speech, MARTIN LUTHER KING, JR. (August 28, 1963)

Five score years ago, a great American, in whose symbolic shadow we stand, signed the Emancipation Proclamation. This momentous decree came as a great beacon light of hope to millions of Negro slaves who had been seared in the flames of withering injustice. It came as a joyous daybreak to end the long night of captivity.

But one hundred years later, we must face the tragic fact that the Negro is still not free. One hundred years later, the life of the Negro is still sadly crippled by the manacles of segregation and the chains of discrimination. One hundred years later, the Negro lives on a lonely island of poverty in the midst of a vast ocean of material prosperity. One hundred years later, the Negro is still languished in the corners of American society and finds himself an exile in his own land. So we have come here today to dramatize an appalling condition.

In a sense we have come to our nation's Capitol to cash a check. When the architects of our republic wrote the magnificent words of the Constitution and the Declaration of Independence, they were signing a promissory note to which every American was to fall heir. This note was a promise that all men would be guaranteed the unalienable rights of life, liberty, and the pursuit of happiness.

It is obvious today that America has defaulted on this promissory note insofar as her citizens of color are concerned. Instead of honoring this sacred obligation, America has given the Negro people a bad check; a check which has come back marked "insufficient funds." But we refuse to believe that the bank of justice is bankrupt. We refuse to believe that there are insufficient funds in the great vaults of opportunity of this nation. So we have come to cash this check—a check that will give us upon demand the riches of freedom and the security of justice. We have also come to this hallowed spot to remind America of the fierce urgency of *now*. This is no time to engage in the luxury of cooling off or to take the tranquilizing drug of gradualism. *Now* is the time to make real the promises of Democracy. *Now* is the time to rise from the dark and desolate valley of segregation to the sunlit path of racial justice. *Now* is the time to open the doors of opportunity to all of God's children. *Now* is the time to lift our nation from the quicksands of racial injustice to the solid rock of brotherhood.

It would be fatal for the nation to overlook the urgency of the moment and to underestimate the determination of the Negro. This sweltering summer of the Negro's legitimate discontent will not pass until there is an invigorating autumn of freedom and equality. 1963 is not an end, but a beginning. Those who hope that the Negro needed to blow off steam and will now be content will have a rude awakening if the Nation returns to business as usual. There will be neither rest nor tranquility in America until the Negro is granted his citizenship rights. The whirlwinds of revolt will continue to shake the foundations of our Nation until the bright day of justice emerges.

But there is something that I must say to my people who stand on the warm threshold which leads into the palace of justice. In the process of gaining our rightful place we must not be guilty of wrongful deeds. Let us not seek to satisfy our thirst for freedom by drinking from the cup of bitterness and hatred.

We must forever conduct our struggle on the high plane of dignity and discipline. We must not allow our creative protest to degenerate into physical violence. Again and again we must rise to the majestic heights of meeting physical force with soul force. The marvelous new militancy which has engulfed the Negro community must not lead us to a distrust of all white people, for many of our white brothers, as evidenced by their presence here today, have come to realize that their destiny is tied up with our destiny and their freedom is inextricably bound to our freedom. We cannot walk alone.

And as we walk, we must make the pledge that we shall march ahead. We cannot turn back. There are those who are asking the devotees of civil rights, "when will you be satisfied?" We can never be satisfied as long as the Negro is the victim of the unspeakable horrors of police brutality. We can never be satisfied as long as our bodies, heavy with the fatigue of travel, cannot gain lodging in the motels of the highways and the hotels of the cities. We cannot be satisfied as long as the Negro's basic mobility is from a smaller ghetto to a larger one. We can never be satisfied as long as a Negro in Mississippi cannot vote and a Negro in New York believes he has nothing for which to vote. No, no we are not satisfied, and we will not be satisfied until justice rolls down like waters and righteousness like a mighty stream.

I am not unmindful that some of you have come here out of great trials and tribulations. Some of you have come fresh from narrow jail cells. Some of you have come from areas where your quest for freedom left you battered by the storms of persecution and staggered by the winds of police brutality. You have been the veterans of creative suffering. Continue to work with the faith that unearned suffering is redemptive.

Go back to Mississippi, go back to Alabama, go back to South Carolina, go back to Georgia, go back to Louisiana, go back to the slums and ghettos of our northern cities, knowing that somehow this situation can and will be changed. Let us not wallow in the valley of despair.

I say to you today, my friends, that in spite of the difficulties and frustrations of the moment I still have a dream. It is a dream deeply rooted in the American dream.

I have a dream that one day this nation will rise up and live out the true meaning of its creed: "We hold these truths to be self-evident; that all men are created equal."

I have a dream that one day on the red hills of Georgia the sons of former slaves and the sons of former slaveowners will be able to sit down together at the table of brotherhood.

I have a dream that one day even the state of Mississippi, a desert state sweltering with the heat of injustice and oppression, will be transformed into an oasis of freedom and justice.

I have a dream that my four little children will one day live in a nation where they will not be judged by the color of their skin but by the content of their character.

I have a dream today.

I have a dream that one day the state of Alabama, whose governor's lips are presently dripping with the words of interposition and nullification, will be transformed into a situation where little black boys and black girls will be able to join hands with little white boys and white girls and walk together as sisters and brothers.

I have a dream today.

I have a dream that one day every valley shall be exalted, every hill and mountain shall be made low, the rough places will be made plains, and the crooked places will be made straight, and the glory of the Lord shall be revealed, and all flesh shall see it together.

This is our hope. This is the faith with which I return to the South. With this faith we will be able to hew out of the mountain of despair a stone of hope. With this faith we will be able to transform the jangling discords of our nation into a beautiful symphony of brotherhood. With this faith we will be able to work together, to pray together, to struggle together, to go to jail together, to stand up for freedom together, knowing that we will be free one day.

This will be the day when all of God's children will be able to sing with new meaning "My country 'tis of thee, sweet land of liberty, of thee I sing. Land where my fathers died, land of the pilgrim's pride, from every mountainside, let freedom ring."

And if America is to be a great nation this must become true. So let freedom ring from the prodigious hilltops of New Hampshire. Let freedom ring from the mighty mountains of New York. Let freedom ring from the heightening Alleghenies of Pennsylvania!

Let freedom ring from the snowcapped Rockies of Colorado!

Let freedom ring from the curvaceous peaks of California!

But not only that; let freedom ring from Stone Mountain of Georgia!

Let freedom ring from Lookout Mountain of Tennessee!

Let freedom ring from every hill and mole hill of Mississippi. From every mountainside, let freedom ring.

When we let freedom ring, when we let it ring from every village and every hamlet, from every state and every city, we will be able to speed up that day when all of God's children, black men and white men, Jews and Gentiles, Protestants and Catholics, will be able to join hands and sing in the words of the old Negro spiritual, "Free at last! free at last! thank God almighty, we are free at last!"

MALCOLM X

At the other end of the political spectrum from Reverend King was Malcolm X, whose meteoric career as chief lieutenant of the Black

Muslim movement was ended by an assassin's bullet on February 21, 1965. These selections from his autobiography include two speeches typical of Malcolm X, one to a group of his followers, the other to a college audience. His analysis of how the Negro could use his political power is also presented.

The Autobiography of Malcolm X, MALCOLM X (1965)

*   *   *   *

(i)

"My black brothers and sisters—of all religious beliefs, or of no religious beliefs—we all have in common the greatest binding tie we could have . . . we all are *black* people!

"I'm not going to take all day telling you some of the greatnesses of The Honorable Elijah Muhammad. I'm just going to tell you now his *greatest* greatness! He is the *first,* the *only* black leader to identify, to you and me, *who* is our enemy!

"The Honorable Elijah Muhammad is the first black leader among us with the *courage* to tell us—out here in public—something which when you begin to think of it back in your homes, you will realize we black people have been *living* with, we have been *seeing,* we have been *suffering,* all of our lives!

"Our *enemy* is the *white man!*

"And why is Mr. Muhammad's teaching us this such a great thing? Because when you know *who* your enemy is, he can no longer keep you divided, and fighting, one brother against the other! Because when you *recognize* who your enemy is, he can no longer use trickery, promises, lies, hypocrisy, and his evil acts to keep you deaf, dumb, and blinded!

"When you recognize *who* your enemy is, he can no longer brainwash you, he can no longer pull wool over your eyes so that you never stop to see that you are living in pure *hell* on this earth, while *he* lives in pure *heaven* right on this same earth!—This enemy who tells you that you are both supposed to be worshipping the same white Christian God that—you are told—stands for the *same* things for *all* men!

"Oh, *yes,* that devil is our enemy. I'll *prove* it! Pick up any daily newspaper! Read the false charges leveled against our beloved religious leader. It only points up the fact that the Caucasian race never wants any black man who is not their puppet or parrot to speak for our people. This Caucasian devil slavemaster does not want or trust us to leave him —yet when we stay here among him, he continues to keep us at the very *lowest level* of his society!

"The white man has always *loved* it when he could keep us black men tucked away somewhere, always out of sight, around the corner! The white man has always *loved* the kind of black leaders whom he could ask, 'Well, how's things with your people up there?' But because Mr. Elijah Muhammad takes an uncompromising stand with the white man, the white man *hates* him! When you hear the *white man* hate him, you, too, because you don't understand Biblical prophecy, wrongly label Mr. Muhammad—as a racist, a hate-teacher, or of being anti-white and teaching black supremacy—"

*   *   *   *

"My black brothers and sisters—*no* one will know *who* we are . . . until *we* know who we are! We never will be able to *go* anywhere until we know *where* we are! The Honorable Elijah Muhammad is giving us a true identity, and a true position—the first time they have ever been *known* to the American black man!

"You can be around this man and never *dream* from his actions the power and the authority he has—" (Behind me, believe me when I tell you, I could *feel* Mr. Muhammad's *power.*)

"He does not *display*, and *parade*, his *power!* But no other black leader in America has followers who will lay down their lives if he says so! And I don't mean all of this non-violent, begging-the-white-man kind of dying . . . all of this sitting-in, sliding-in, wading-in, eating-in, diving-in, and all the rest—

"My black brothers and sisters, you have come from your homes to hear—now you are *going* to hear—America's *wisest* black man! America's *boldest* black man! America's most *fearless* black man! This wilderness of North America's most *powerful* black man!"

*   *   *   *

(ii)

"Time and time again, the black, the brown, the red, and the yellow races have witnessed and suffered the white man's small ability to understand the simple notes of the spirit. The white man seems tone deaf to the total orchestration of humanity. Every day, his newspapers' front pages show us the world that he has created.

"God's wrathful judgment is close upon this white man stumbling and groping blindly in wickedness and evil and spiritual darkness.

"Look—remaining today are only two giant white nations, America and Russia, each of them with mistrustful, nervous satellites. America is propping up most of the remaining white world. The French, the Belgians, the Dutch, the Portuguese, the Spanish and other white nations have weakened steadily as non-white Asians and Africans have recovered their lands.

"America is subsidizing what is left of the prestige and strength of the once mighty Britain. The sun has set forever on that monocled, pith-helmeted resident colonialist, sipping tea with his delicate lady in the non-white colonies being systematically robbed of every valuable resource. Britain's superfluous royalty and nobility now exist by charging tourists to inspect the once baronial castles, and by selling memoirs, perfumes, autographs, titles, and even themselves.

"The whole world knows that the white man cannot survive another war. If either of the two giant white nations pushes the button, white civilization will die!

"And we see again that not ideologies, but race, and color, is what binds human beings. Is it accidental that as Red Chinese visit African and Asian countries, Russia and America draw steadily closer to each other?

"The collective white man's history has left the non-white peoples no alternative, either, but to draw closer to each other. Characteristically, as always, the devilish white man lacks the moral strength and courage to cast off his arrogance. He wants, today, to 'buy' friends among the non-whites. He tries, characteristically, to cover up his past record. He does not possess the humility to admit his guilt, to try and atone for his crimes. The white man has perverted the simple message of love that the Prophet Jesus lived and taught when He walked upon this earth."

*　　*　　*　　*

(iii)

The black man in North America was mentally sick in his cooperative, sheeplike acceptance of the white man's culture.

The black man in North America was spiritually sick because for centuries he had accepted the white man's Christianty—which asked the black so-called Christian to expect no true Brotherhood of Man, but to endure the cruelties of the white so-called Christians. Christianity had made black men fuzzy, nebulous, confused in their thinking. It had taught the black man to think if he had no shoes, and was hungry, "we gonna get shoes and milk and honey and fish fries in Heaven."

The black man in North America was economically sick and that was evident in one simple fact: as a consumer, he got less than his share, and as a producer gave *least*. The black American today shows us the perfect parasite image—the black tick under the delusion that he is progressing because he rides on the udder of the fat, three-stomached cow that is white America. For instance, annually, the black man spends over $3 billion for automobiles, but America contains hardly any franchised black automobile dealers. For instance, forty per cent of the expensive imported Scotch whisky consumed in America goes down the throats of the status-sick black man; but the only black-owned distilleries are in bathtubs, or in the woods somewhere. Or for instance—a scandalous shame—in New York City, with over a million Negroes, there aren't twenty black-owned businesses employing over ten people. It's because black men don't own and control their own community's retail establishments that they can't stabilize their own community.

The black man in North America was sickest of all politically. He let the white man divide him into such foolishness as considering himself a black "Democrat," a black "Republican," a black "Conservative," or a black "Liberal" . . . when a ten-million black vote bloc could be the deciding balance of power in American politics, because the white man's vote is almost always evenly divided. The polls are one place where every black man could fight the black man's cause with dignity, and with the power and the tools that the white man understands, and respects, and fears, and cooperates with. Listen, let me tell you something! If a black bloc committee told Washington's worst "nigger-hater," "We represent ten million votes," why, that "nigger-hater" would leap up: 'Well, how *are* you? Come on *in* here!" Why, if the Mississippi black man voted in a bloc, Eastland would pretend to be more liberal than Jacob Javits—or Eastland would not survive in his office. Why else is it that racist politicians fight to keep black men from the polls?

Whenever any group can vote in a bloc, and decide the outcome of elections, and it *fails* to do this, then that group is politically sick. Immigrants once made Tammany Hall the most powerful single force in American politics. In 1880, New York City's first Irish Catholic Mayor was elected and by 1960 America had its first Irish Catholic President. America's black man, voting as a bloc, could wield an even more powerful force.

U.S. politics is ruled by special-interest blocs and lobbies. What group has a more urgent special interest, what group needs a bloc, a lobby, more than the black man? Labor owns one of Washington's largest non-government buildings—situated where they can literally watch the White House—and no political move is made that doesn't involve how Labor feels about it. A lobby got Big Oil its depletion allowance. The farmer, through his lobby, is the most government-subsidized special-interest group in America today, because a million farmers vote, not as Democrats, or Republicans, liberals, conservatives, but as farmers.

Doctors have the best lobby in Washington. Their special-interest influence successfully fights the Medicare program that's wanted, and needed, by millions of other people. Why, there's a Beet Growers' Lobby! A Wheat Lobby! A Cattle Lobby! A China Lobby! Little countries no one ever heard of have their Washington lobbies, representing their special interests.

The government has departments to deal with the special-interest groups that make themselves heard and felt. A Department of Agriculture cares for the farmers' needs. There is a Department of Health, Education and Welfare. There is a Department of the Interior—in which the Indians are included. Is the farmer, the doctor, the Indian, the greatest problem in America today? No—it is the black man! There ought to be a Pentagon-sized Washington department dealing with every segment of the black man's problems.

Twenty-two million black men! They have given America four hundred years of toil; they have bled and died in every battle since the Revolution; they were in America before the Pilgrims, and long before the mass immigrations—and they are still today at the bottom of everything!

Why, twenty-two million black people should tomorrow give a dollar apiece to build a skyscraper lobby building in Washington, D.C. Every morning, every legislator should receive a communication about what the black man in America expects and wants and needs. The demanding voice of the black lobby should be in the ears of every legislator who votes on any issue.

The cornerstones of this country's operation are economic and political strength and power. The black man doesn't have the economic strength—and it will take time for him to build it. But right now the American black man has the political strength and power to change his destiny overnight.

JAMES BALDWIN

James Baldwin, though not an administrator or political figure, was thrust into a position of leadership as a brilliant and eminent writer and one of the most articulate of the spokesmen for civil rights. The following selection from his book The Fire Next Time *is an important statement about the direction and goals of the movement.*

The Fire Next Time, JAMES BALDWIN (1963)
* * * *

White Americans find it as difficult as white people elsewhere do to divest themselves of the notion that they are in possession of some intrinsic value that black people need, or want. And this assumption—

which, for example, makes the solution to the Negro problem depend on the speed with which Negroes accept and adopt white standards—is revealed in all kinds of striking ways, from Bobby Kennedy's assurance that a Negro can become President in forty years to the unfortunate tone of warm congratulation with which so many liberals address their Negro equals. It is the Negro, of course, who is presumed to have become equal—an achievement that not only proves the comforting fact that perseverance has no color but also overwhelmingly corroborates the white man's sense of his own value. Alas, the value can scarcely be corroborated in any other way; there is certainly little enough in the white man's public or private life that one should desire to imitate. White men, at the bottom of their hearts, know this. Therefore, a vast amount of the energy that goes into what we call the Negro problem is produced by the white man's profound desire not to be judged by those who are not white, not to be seen as he is, and at the same time a vast amount of the white anguish is rooted in the white man's equally profound need to be seen as he is, to be released from the tyranny of his mirror. All of us know, whether or not we are able to admit it, that mirrors can only lie, that death by drowning is all that awaits one there. It is for this reason that love is so desperately sought and so cunningly avoided. Love takes off the masks that we fear we cannot live without and know we cannot live within. I use the word "love" here not merely in the personal sense but as a state of being, or a state of grace—not in the infantile American sense of being made happy but in the tough and universal sense of quest and daring and growth. And I submit, then, that the racial tensions that menace Americans today have little to do with real antipathy—on the contrary, indeed—and are involved only symbolically with color. These tensions are rooted in the very same depths as those from which love springs, or murder. The white man's unadmitted—and apparently, to him, unspeakable—private fears and longings are projected onto the Negro. The only way he can be released from the Negro's tyrannical power over him is to consent, in effect, to become black himself, to become a part of that suffering and dancing country that he now watches wistfully from the heights of his lonely power and, armed with spiritual traveller's checks, visits surreptitiously after dark. How can one respect, let alone adopt, the values of a people who do not, on any level whatever, live the way they say they do, or 'the way they say they should? I cannot accept the proposition that the four-hundred-year travail of the American Negro should result merely in his attainment of the present level of the American civilization. I am far from convinced that being released from the African witch doctor was worthwhile if I am now—

in order to support the moral contradictions and the spiritual aridity of my life—expected to become dependent on the American psychiatrist. It is a bargain I refuse. The only thing white people have that black people need, or should want, is power—and no one holds power forever. White people cannot, in the generality, be taken as models of how to live. Rather, the white man is himself in sore need of new standards, which will release him from his confusion and place him once again in fruitful communion with the depths of his own being. And I repeat: The price of the liberation of the white people is the liberation of the blacks—the total liberation, in the cities, in the towns, before the law, and in the mind. Why, for example—especially knowing the family as I do—I should *want* to marry your sister is a great mystery to me. But your sister and I have every right to marry if we wish to, and no one has the right to stop us. If she cannot raise me to her level, perhaps I can raise her to mine.

In short, we, the black and the white, deeply need each other here if we are really to become a nation—if we are really, that is, to achieve our identity, our maturity, as men and women. To create one nation has proved to be a hideously difficult task; there is certainly no need now to create two, one black and one white. But white men with far more political power than that possessed by the Nation of Islam movement have been advocating exactly this, in effect, for generations. If this sentiment is honored when it falls from the lips of Senator Byrd, then there is no reason it should not be honored when it falls from the lips of Malcolm X. And any Congressional committee wishing to investigate the latter must also be willing to investigate the former. They are expressing exactly the same sentiments and represent exactly the same danger. There is absolutely no reason to suppose that white people are better equipped to frame the laws by which I am to be governed than I am. It is entirely unacceptable that I should have no voice in the political affairs of my own country, for I am not a ward of America; I am one of the first Americans to arrive on these shores.

This past, the Negro's past, of rope, fire, torture, castration, infanticide, rape; death and humiliation; fear by day and night, fear as deep as the marrow of the bone; doubt that he was worthy of life, since everyone around him denied it; sorrow for his women, for his kinfolk, for his children, who needed his protection, and whom he could not protect; rage, hatred, and murder, hatred for white men so deep that it often turned against him and his own, and made all love, all trust, all joy impossible—this past, this endless struggle to achieve and reveal and confirm a human identity, human authority, yet contains, for all its horror, something very beautiful. I do not mean to be sentimental about

suffering—enough is certainly as good as a feast—but people who cannot suffer can never grow up, can never discover who they are. That
man who is forced each day to snatch his manhood, his identity, out of
the fire of human cruelty that rages to destroy it knows, if he survives
his effort, and even if he does not survive it, something about himself
and human life that no school on earth—and, indeed, no church—can
teach. He achieves his own authority, and that is unshakable. This is
because, in order to save his life, he is forced to look beneath appear-
ances, to take nothing for granted, to hear the meaning behind the words.
If one is continually surviving the worst that life can bring, one eventually ceases to be controlled by a fear of what life can bring; whatever
it brings must be borne. And at this level of experience one's bitterness
begins to be palatable, and hatred becomes too heavy a sack to carry.
The apprehension of life here so briefly and inadequately sketched has
been the experience of generations of Negroes, and it helps to explain
how they have endured and how they have been able to produce children of kindergarten age who can walk through mobs to get to school.
It demands great force and great cunning continually to assault the
mighty and indifferent fortress of white supremacy, as Negroes in this
country have done so long. It demands great spiritual resilience not to
hate the hater whose foot is on your neck, and an even greater miracle
of perception and charity not to teach your child to hate. The Negro
boys and girls who are facing mobs today come out of a long line of
improbable aristocrats—the only genuine aristocrats this country has
produced. I say "this country" because their frame of reference was
totally American. They were hewing out of the mountain of white supremacy the stone of their individuality. I have great respect for that
unsung army of black men and women who trudged down back lanes
and entered back doors, saying "Yes, sir" and "No, Ma'am" in order to
acquire a new roof for the schoolhouse, new books, a new chemistry lab,
more beds for the dormitories, more dormitories. They did not like
saying "Yes, sir" and "No, Ma'am," but the country was in no hurry to
educate Negroes, these black men and women knew that the job had to
be done, and they put their pride in their pockets in order to do it. It
is very hard to believe that they were in any way inferior to the white
men and women who opened those back doors. It is very hard to believe that those men and women, raising their children, eating their
greens, crying their curses, weeping their tears, singing their songs, making their love, as the sun rose, as the sun set, were in any way inferior
to the white men and women who crept over to share these splendors
after the sun went down. But we must avoid the European error; we must
not suppose that, because the situation, the ways, the perceptions of black

people so radically differed from those of whites, they were racially superior. I am proud of these people not because of their color but because of their intelligence and their spiritual force and their beauty. The country should be proud of them, too, but, alas, not many people in this country even know of their existence. And the reason for this ignorance is that a knowledge of the role these people played—and play—in American life would reveal more about America to Americans than Americans wish to know.

The American Negro has the great advantage of having never believed that collection of myths to which white Americans cling: that their ancestors were all freedom-loving heroes, that they were born in the greatest country the world has ever seen, or that Americans are invincible in battle and wise in peace, that Americans have always dealt honorably with Mexicans and Indians and all other neighbors or inferiors, that American men are the world's most direct and virile, that American women are pure. Negroes know far more about white Americans than that; it can almost be said, in fact, that they know about white Americans what parents—or, anyway, mothers—know about their children, and that they very often regard white Americans that way. And perhaps this attitude, held in spite of what they know and have endured, helps to explain why Negroes, on the whole, and until lately, have allowed themselves to feel so little hatred. The tendency has really been, insofar as this was possible, to dismiss white people as the slightly mad victims of their own brainwashing. One watched the lives they led. One could not be fooled about that; one watched the things they did and the excuses that they gave themselves, and if a white man was really in trouble, deep trouble, it was to the Negro's door that he came. And one felt that if one had had that white man's worldly advantages, one would never have become as bewildered and as joyless and as thoughtlessly cruel as he. The Negro came to the white man for a roof or for five dollars or for a letter to the judge; the white man came to the Negro for love. But he was not often able to give what he came seeking. The price was too high; he had too much to lose. And the Negro knew this, too. When one knows this about a man, it is impossible for one to hate him, but unless he becomes a man—becomes equal—it is also impossible for one to love him. Ultimately, one tends to avoid him, for the universal characteristic of children is to assume that they have a monopoly on trouble, and therefore a monopoly on *you*. (Ask any Negro what he knows about the white people with whom he works. And then ask the white people with whom he works what they know about *him*.)

How can the American Negro past be used? It is entirely possible that this dishonored past will rise up soon to smite all of us. There are some wars, for example (if anyone on the globe is still mad enough to go to war) that the American Negro will not support, however many of his people may be coerced—and there is a limit to the number of people any government can put in prison, and a rigid limit indeed to the practicality of such a course. A bill is coming in that I fear America is not prepared to pay. "The problem of the twentieth century," wrote W. E. B. Du Bois around sixty years ago, "is the problem of the color line." A fearful and delicate problem, which compromises, when it does not corrupt, all the American efforts to build a better world— here, there, or anywhere. It is for this reason that everything white Americans think they believe in must now be reëxamined. What one would not like to see again is the consolidation of peoples on the basis of their color. But as long as we in the West place on color the value that we do, we make it impossible for the great unwashed to consolidate themselves according to any other principle. Color is not a human or a personal reality; it is a political reality. But this is a distinction so extremely hard to make that the West has not been able to make it yet. And at the center of this dreadful storm, this vast confusion, stand the black people of this nation, who must now share the fate of a nation that has never accepted them, to which they were brought in chains. Well, if this is so, one has no choice but to do all in one's power to change that fate, and at no matter what risk —eviction, imprisonment, torture, death. For the sake of one's children, in order to minimize the bill that *they* must pay, one must be careful not to take refuge in any delusion—and the value placed on the color of the skin is always and everywhere and forever a delusion. I know that what I am asking is impossible. But in our time, as in every time, the impossible is the least that one can demand— and one is, after all, emboldened by the spectacle of human history in general, and American Negro history in particular, for it testifies to nothing less than the perpetual achievement of the impossible.

When I was very young, and was dealing with my buddies in those wine- and urine-stained hallways, something in me wondered, *What will happen to all that beauty?* For black people, though I am aware that some of us, black and white, do not know it yet, are very beautiful. And when I sat at Elijah's table and watched the baby, the women, and the men, and we talked about God's—or Allah's—vengeance, I wondered, when that vengeance was achieved, *What will happen to all that beauty then?* I could also see that the intransigence and ignorance of the white world might make that vengeance inevitable—a vengeance that does not really depend on, and cannot really be executed by, any person or organization, and that cannot be prevented by any police force or army: historical vengeance, a cosmic vengeance, based on the law that we recognize when we say, "Whatever goes up must come down." And here we are, at the center of the arc, trapped in the gaudiest, most valuable, and most improbable water wheel the world has ever seen. Everything now, we must assume, is in our hands; we have no right to assume otherwise. If we—and now I mean the relatively conscious whites and the relatively conscious blacks, who must, like lovers, insist on, or create, the consciousness of the others—do not falter in our duty now, we may be able, handful that we are, to end the racial nightmare, and achieve our country, and change the history of the world. If we do not now dare everything, the fulfillment of that prophecy, recreated from the Bible in song by a slave, is upon us: *God gave Noah the rainbow sign, No more water, the fire next time!*

JAMES FARMER, ROY WILKINS, STOKELY CARMICHAEL, WHITNEY YOUNG

Among the established leaders of the movement were James Farmer of CORE; Roy Wilkins of the NAACP, Stokely Carmichael of SNCC and Whitney Young of the National Urban League. Their writings and statements show some of the differences which have recently emerged in the ideology of the movement.

Freedom — When?, JAMES FARMER (1965)

*   *   *   *

No word has served to epitomize the movement's goals for these last ten years as well as "integration." We would be integrated into America and destroy "segregation," the hated opposite of this new concept. So we demanded integrated schools and housing and employment, and integrated commercial messages on television, and integrated casts on opera and dramatic stages, and integrated movies, and mayors' committees, and civic-planning boards, etc. The value of integration took on the status of a self-evident truth.

Today, however, many Negroes, gripped by a new wave of self-pride and group-pride, are beginning to ask critical questions of the integrationist creed: How can we be prideful without advocating an inverted form of "separate but equal"? Is self-pride another term for self-segregation? Must we renounce ourselves and our community for the sake of integration?

Let me say immediately that much of "integration" remains valid for us and, in our view, for America, but with somewhat altered emphasis and meaning.

What do we mean by "integration"? For some the term means complete assimilation, a kind of random dispersal of Negroes throughout the society and the economy. There would be no Negro neighborhoods, no Negro schools, no jobs reserved for Negroes. America would be a land of individuals who were American and nothing else, and Negro individuals would differ from their fellow Americans only in their skin color— that most insignificant of human differences. Some of us even dreamed that differences of color too would soon melt away when love and color-blindness permeated the land. As I have said, no one can question the ultimate goodness of this ideal. The question is: Is it too good to be true?

Integration has been the nation's implicit ideal since America was a glint in Jefferson's eye. It is nothing but Jeffersonian individualism extended to all people. But it did not become a practical political goal until quite recently, and the reasons for this make an important story. Like most Americans, Negroes were still accepting "separate but equal" as the law of the land as late as the mid-forties, and our major efforts were expended in making the "equal" of "separate but equal" a reality. In the decades before the 1954 Supreme Court decision desegregating schools the NAACP brought to the court cases treating discrimination in education, voting, interstate and intrastate travel, public facilities, and selection of juries. The court in those years invariably found that Negro facilities were palpably unequal and ruled that segregation was constitutional only if facilities and accommodations were truly equal. In other words, the whole burden of the civil rights movement's case then was: If facilities are going to be separate, at least make them equal. Separate but equal was reaffirmed.

Toward the end of the forties NAACP lawyers and strategists began to argue that in certain respects separate facilities could never be equal. For example, a Negro relegated to a Negro law school could not hope to make professional contacts that would enable him to swim in the main stream of the profession as readily as someone at a white law school— and this was true no matter how beautiful the buildings and how well-stocked the library at the Negro law school was. A Pullman seat in a car reserved for Negroes could not be the equal of a seat in the white car because the manifest intention of "for Negroes only" was to convey inferiority. By a natural process of evolution the demand for what we might term equal-if-separate turned into a demand for desegregation.

To argue that a beautiful Negro law school or a plush seat in a Negro Pullman was inferior to its white counterpart demanded some subtlety. To argue that the segregated public school system treated

Negroes as second-class citizens demanded no subtlety at all. Comparison of expenditures per student, school plant, teachers' salaries, experience and training of teachers, books and supplies, and other measurable factors, made it clear that throughout the country, and in the South particularly, the Negro, forced by law and fact into segregated schools, was being deprived of equality under law. The 1954 Supreme Court decision attempted to correct this intolerable inequity in the only way practical and intelligent men could—by eliminating the dual school systems.

But the court added a theoretical dimension to its factual and practical findings: "Separate educational facilities," it said, "are *inherently unequal*" [emphasis added] and it cited as evidence certain psychological data—principally those of Professor Kenneth Clark—which document the serious psychological damage race separation causes in Negro youngsters. Now, I am not certain what "inherently unequal" or even "separate educational facilities" mean in this context, and I will want to return to these phrases shortly; but first I would like to explain how we interpreted the court's decision. For us it was a recognition of what every Negro knows: that the system of segregation was mounted and perpetuated for the purpose of keeping the black man down; that it was and is a conspiracy to instill in the Negro *and the white* a sense of Negro inferiority. Segregation is slavery made legal. Segregation *means* inferiority, as indelibly as the scarlet letter meant adulteress to the New England Puritans. The Negro knows this; it was intended that he know this, and so too must any American with the most rudimentary sense of history know it. And now the court was saying that this country would segregate no more. So we began to protest against segregated schools of all kinds, *de facto* and *de jure,* demanding quality integrated education, knowing all the time that we were combating and helping eliminate the hated *meaning* which had been assigned to our lives.

As separate schools were inferior, so too were separate neighborhoods (quite obviously the *meaning* of segregated neighborhoods is simply that the great white world doesn't want black folk living next to it; anyone who doubts this need only observe the hysteria and violence which ensue when a Negro family moves into a white neighborhood). The effect of living in an enforced ghetto is conveyed graphically in the desolation and wreckage, human and material, in which most Negroes live today. So we moved to desegregate housing and some aimed at dismantling the ghetto.

Indeed, every instance and symbol of segregation and every invidious discrimination could now be legitimately challenged. There are millions, and we took them on one by one, case by case. At lunch counters, restaurants, rest rooms, swimming pools, amusement parks, beaches, labor unions, banks, factories, offices, department stores, professional societies, churches, colleges. To the most rabid integrationists even the institutions of Negro communal life were implicated. They saw no reason for a Negro Medical Society; all energies must be directed to breaking down the AMA. Negro colleges, Negro churches, Negro newspapers were at best tolerated as unnecessary anachronisms.

Integration was a white man's cause as well as a black man's, and the literally thousands of interracial organizations which came into being to fight the good fight became themselves temporary models of integrated living. CORE was one, and remains one. Many whites recognize the superiority complex demanded of the white man in a segregated system to be as harmful in its way as the inferiority complex demanded of Negroes. Many quite sincerely set about curing themselves and their neighborhoods and schools of this affliction.

The rabid integrationist aims at mixing every unit of society in "ideal" proportions. In middle-class neighborhoods housing committees were formed to persuade reluctant white homeowners to accept respectable Negroes, and courageous and well-to-do Negroes were sought who would brave white wrath. And when one or two Negroes had entered a neighborhood, the same committees, now with the eager help of the Negroes, organized to keep other Negroes out. We mustn't let the neighborhood tip, they said. Housing developments adopted informal quotas to help engineer integrated living. Dedicated builders, like Morris Milgrim of Philadelphia, began to persuade investors that quality housing projects, open to all, could return a modest profit, and integrated oases soon sprang up in several previously all-white deserts. Many liberals grew uncomfortable with the irony that in order to achieve integration they had to adopt racial quotas of various sorts, designating Negroes in order to eliminate racial designations, as it were, and some became discouraged at the solemn spectacle of Negroes chasing whites from suburb to suburb—in quest of integration. But among white liberals and some black liberals the dream of complete integration persisted.

Almost imperceptibly the demand for desegregation had shaded into a demand for black dispersal and assimilation. We were told, and for a while told ourselves, that *all* Negro separation was inherently inferior, and some folk began to think that Negroes couldn't be fully human in the presence of other Negroes. But what of Africa? Was separation inferior there too? And what of the *de facto* separation of other minority groups, the Jews and Chinese, for example. Was separation so self-evidently inferior for them as it was for us?

I am not a lawyer, but I think that the phrase "separate educational facilities are inherently unequal," which supports the philosophy of total integration, invites some misinterpretation. Separation need not be inferior in all cases and all places. What is crucial is the *meaning* the culture places upon the separation. Separation, in other words, is not necessarily segregation, *though in America, Negro separation in fact and in law means segregation.* This is the crucial insight. The separation of Negroes in America *means* segregation—slavery. In its decision the Supreme Court was offering a particular and indisputable reading of the meaning of American history. In the context of our civilization with its history of racism, the court said, separate educational institutions are inherently inferior.

When a Negro child goes through the doors of a segregated school, he knows implicitly that his culture is telling him to go there because he is not fit to be with others, and every time a Negro child hears of a white parent who becomes hysterical at the thought that his child will have to endure the likes of him, he feels the pressure of his inferiority a little more firmly. As a result he is damaged. And this too the Supreme Court saw. As long as the ideology of racial inferiority and superiority persists, segregation will be an insult and blackness a stigma.

One does not undo the accumulated meanings of centuries by waving a magic wand: *"Abracadabra! Once you were segregation. Now you are separation."* This is tokenism: the belief that by one gesture, one concession, yes, even one sincere cry of the heart, one moment of honest compassion, the country will transform the manifest meaning of historic life-ways. The desegregation fight is crucial to all Americans. What we are attempting is nothing less than to reverse the latent *meaning* of our lives and practices. For a civilization to do this takes remarkable strength of purpose, time, persistence, and most of all honesty. Because the foot is on his neck, Negroes have been much more honest about America than the whites. We know this civilization is still segregated in its heart of hearts. We test the spirit of its ways, and white Americans who would be honest about America listen attentively when we tell them about their country.

Now, this distinction between separation and segregation was often made by Malcolm X. Time and again, he denied that the Black Muslims were segregationists. We are separationists, he said, not segregationists. Without qualification all American Negroes hate segregation. Some Negroes, however, would *choose* to live separately, and Malcolm saw this and tried to make it a *legitimate* desire. But in one very essential respect I differ strongly with Malcolm. He believed that Negroes can change the manifest meaning of their separated existence solely by the force of their own wills. I believe that there is much Negroes can do for themselves, but I do not believe they can separate truly if the nation does not simultaneously desegregate.

Culturally we are Americans, and like all men we know ourselves, in part, by what our culture tells us about ourselves. The fact is that American segregationists take delight in the Black Muslims' program. I do not believe the rumor that the Ku Klux Klan and some Texas millionaires support the Muslims, but I do know that they take no small comfort from Muslim activities. Even CORE's decision to emphasize self-help in the Negro community succeeds in making Parents and Taxpayers Associations breathe easier. And Negroes know this. In other words, there is a certain validity to the integrationist insight that separate Negro efforts and institutions simply perpetuate segregation. If, in his heart of hearts, the Negro believes that self-separation is only a rationalization for cowardly acceptance of segregation, then separation will fail.

The only way Negro separation would not mean segregation is if the Negro has the sense that he chooses to live separately, and this will happen only when total freedom of choice is a reality in America. Desegregation and the development of Negro self-pride work side by side. Desegregation makes separation possible. *

What we wish is the freedom of choice which will cause any choice we make to seem truly our own. That freedom of choice must apply throughout American society and American life. A person should be able to choose where he wants to live and live there. If he chooses to live in Lovely Lane in Orchard Gardens, he should be able to, if he has the money to swing it. He should be able to work at any job for which he is qualified and equipped, regardless of his color. Jim Brown, a thoughtful man and pretty good fullback, offended some people when he said that he personally wouldn't want to live with whites but that he damned well wanted to know that he could if he did want to. I think he represents the thinking of many Negroes.

But many other Negroes will choose to integrate; they should be permitted to. James Baldwin asks whether it is worth integrating into a sinking ship. Many middle-class Negroes, whose spines are straighter than Baldwin and others suppose, would answer, "You're damned right it is." Many will buy their twenty- or thirty-thousand-dollar homes and move into neighborhoods which suit them culturally and financially. Indeed, most Negroes integrating such a neighborhood will probably have a higher educational level than their white neighbors, prejudice being what it is. It is easy to scoff at the spectacle of a middle-class Negro shoving his way into a white enclave. Some say, "Does white approval

---

* Of course, Negroes do not have the right to exclude whites who choose to live among them.

mean that much? Why go where you're not wanted?" But I have known many of these men. They brave abuse nobly and stand tough witness to noble ideals. Their acts shake the system of segregation and for that reason their efforts are more closely connected to efforts to eliminate the psychological ghetto than is commonly granted.

We must not forget that there are solid, perhaps incomparable, values in truly integrated living. W. E. B. Du Bois, a proud black man, once said that the real tragedy in our world today is not that men are poor; all men know something of poverty. Nor that men are ignorant; what is truth? Nor that men are wicked; who is good? But that men know so little of men.

It is important for Negroes to know white men and for white men to know Negroes. I might add that white men should insist that we live among them for their own sakes. And if some Negroes resist white blandishments, they will be fuller men for having resisted a valuable temptation.

Those who glibly abuse "middle-class" Negroes often commit the racist fallacy of demanding that black men behave according to their definition of him. If a black man wants to skip five thousand lunches, as Dick Gregory says, in order to buy a Cadillac, then he should. At CORE we have come to believe that in a free society many Negroes will choose to live and work separately, *although not in total isolation.* They will cultivate the pride in themselves which comes in part from their efforts to make this a free land. Even those living and working in "racially balanced" situations will value their Negro identity more than before. In helping themselves, they will come to love themselves. From loving themselves, they will determine to help themselves. They will be Americans and Negroes. They will be free to pick and choose from several rich traditions. They may thrill to the example of modern Africa and search out the richness of Africa's past as Du Bois did. Or they may as Americans and Westerners seize as models such great American cultural heroes as Lincoln or Hemingway or Duke Ellington. They will be as American as St. Patrick's Day and Columbus Day and Rosh Hashanah.

We are beginning now to see a more ideal division of effort within CORE and among the groups comprising the entire civil rights movement. Clearly the desegregation movement must continue unabated. We must demand that segregation end. Tokenism of all kinds must be rejected. We shall demand quality integrated education, now definitely adding to it the demand that Negro history be taught in the public schools so that our youngsters can learn that they are ancient citizens of this land. There must be open housing and fair employment practices, in law and in fact. And we will still demand preferential compensatory treatment (I shall discuss this more fully later). In brief, there should be no abatement in the efforts of the last years. At the same time we will enter the Negro community, working with those masses who couldn't care less about integrating and couldn't afford it if they did care. Our efforts in the ghettos to help the people build a community life and a community spirit will be spurred by the knowledge that desegregation is taking place simultaneously. In this way segregation will be transformed into separation. Perhaps "independence" is a better term than separation. We shall become independent men. We will accept, in other words, part of Malcolm's insight that segregation will become separation only with a separate effort of Negro heart and soul rejecting the notion of some of the older civil rights organizations (and of the original CORE) that desegregation and integration *in itself* will accomplish miracles. But we will correct the Muslims' belief that the Negro can do all things alone. There must be simultaneous desegregation and we must demand it. By this amendment we will affirm that we are Americans and that the civil rights movement is an American movement.

*   *   *   *

"Steady as She Goes," ROY WILKINS Keynote Address At NAACP 57th Annual Convention (July 5, 1966)

In the transition period of the civil rights movement, 1966 is developing into a critical year. The 57th annual convention of our NAACP is thus a gathering of more than ordinary significance.

All about us are alarums and confusions as well as great and challenging developments. Differences of opinion are sharper. For the first time since several organizations began to function where only two had functioned before, there emerges what seems to be a difference in goals.

Heretofore there were some differences in methods and in emphases, but none in ultimate goals. The end was always to be the inclusion of the Negro American, without racial discrimination, as a full-fledged equal in all phases of American citizenship. The targets were whatever barriers, crude or subtle, which blocked the attainment of that goal.

There has now emerged, first, a strident and threatening challenge to a strategy widely employed by civil rights groups, namely, non-violence. One organization, which has been meeting in Baltimore, has passed a resolution declaring for defense of themselves by Negro citizens if they are attacked.

This position is not new as far as the NAACP is concerned. Historically our Association has defended in court those persons who have defended themselves and their homes with firearms. Extradition cases are not as frequent or as fashionable as they once were, but in past years we have fought the extradition of men who had used firearms to defend themselves when attacked.

We freed seventy-nine Arkansas sharecroppers in a four-year court battle beginning in 1919. They had returned gunfire directed at a meeting they were holding in a church.

We employed the late Clarence Darrow in 1926 to defend a man and his family when a member of a mob threatening his newly-purchased Detroit home was shot and killed. The NAACP has subscribed to non-violence as a humane as well as a practical necessity in the realities of the American scene, but we have never required this as a deep personal commitment of our members. We never signed a pact either on paper or in our hearts to turn the other cheek forever and ever when we were assaulted.

But neither have we couched a policy of manly resistance in such a way that our members and supporters felt compelled to maintain themselves in an armed state, ready to retaliate instantly and in kind whenever attacked. We venture the observation that such a publicized posture could serve to stir counter-planning, counter-action and possible conflict. If carried out literally as instant retaliation, in cases adjudged by aggrieved persons to have been grossly unjust, this policy could produce —in extreme situations—lynchings, or, in better-sounding phraseology, private, vigilante vengeance.

Moreover, in attempting to substitute for derelict law enforcement machinery, the policy entails the risk of a broader, more indiscriminate crackdown by law officers under the ready-made excuse of restoring law and order.

It seems reasonable to assume that proclaimed protective violence is as likely to encourage counter-violence as it is to discourage violent persecution.

But the more serious division in the civil rights movement is the one posed by a word formulation that implies clearly a difference in goals.

No matter how endlessly they try to explain it, the term "black power" means anti-white power. In a racially pluralistic society, the concept, the formation and the exercise of an ethnically-tagged power, means opposition to other ethnic powers, just as the term "white supremacy" means subjection of all non-white people. In the black-white relationship, it has to mean that every other ethnic power is the rival and the antagonist of "black power." It has to mean "going-it-alone." It has to mean separatism.

Now, separatism, whether on the rarefield debate level of "black power" or on the wishful level of a secessionist Freedom City in Watts, offers a disadvantaged minority little except the chance to shrivel and die.

The only possible dividend of "black power" is embodied in its offer to millions of frustrated and deprived and persecuted black people of a solace, a tremendous psychological lift, quite apart from its political and economic implications.

Ideologically it dictates "up with black and down with white" in precisely the same fashion that South Africa reverses that slogan.

It is a reverse Mississippi, a reverse Hitler, a reverse Ku Klux Klan.

If these were evil in our judgment, what virtue can be claimed for black over white? If, as some proponents claim, this concept instills pride of race, cannot this pride be taught without preaching hatred or supremacy based upon race?

Though it be clarified and clarified again, "black power" in the quick, uncritical and highly emotional adoption it has received from some segments of a beleaguered people can mean in the end only black death. Even if, through some miracle, it should be enthroned briefly in an isolated area, the human spirit, which knows no color or geography or time, would die a little, leaving for wiser and stronger and more compassionate men the painful beating back to the upward trail.

We of the NAACP will have none of this. We have fought it too long. It is the ranging of race against race on the irrelevant basis of skin color. It is the father of hatred and the mother of violence.

It is the wicked fanaticism which has swelled our tears, broken our bodies, squeezed our hearts and taken the blood of our black and white loved ones. It shall not now poison our forward march.

We seek, therefore, as we have sought these many years, the inclusion of Negro Americans in the nation's life, not their exclusion. This is our land, as much so as it is any American's—every square foot of every city and town and village. The task of winning our share is not the easy one of disengagement and flight, but the hard one of work, of short as well as long jumps, of disappointments, and of sweet successes.

In our Fight for Freedom we choose:

1.   The power and the majesty of the ballot, the participation of free men in their government, both as voters and as honorable and competent elected and appointed public servants. Year in and year out, the NAACP voter registration work has proceeded. No one except the Federal Government has registered more Negro voters in Mississippi than the NAACP. In six weeks last summer more than twenty thousand new names were added by our workers alone, with additional thousands during an intensive renewal last winter. That work is continuing under the leadership of our Mississippi state president, Dr. Aaron Henry, and

of our state director, Charles Evers. Later this month a summer task force will be at work in Louisiana. Already our South Carolina NAACP is busy on registration, as is our Alabama organization.

We are aware that a Louisiana young man, born along the Mississippi border, has been named and confirmed as one of the seven governors of the Federal Reserve Bank. We know that his extraordinary ability finally tipped the scales, but we know also, that, without ballot power, he would not even have been on the scales ready to be tipped.

2. We choose employment for our people—jobs not hidden by racial labels or euphemisms, not limited by racial restrictions in access and promotion, whether by employers or organized labor. We commend a growing number of corporations for expanding their employment of Negro applicants in technical and professional posts, but we insist that only the surface has been scratched.

We commend the "good guys" among the trade unions for the improvement in opportunities and advancement for the Negro worker, but we condemn the policies of some unions which have either barred or heavily handicapped the Negro worker. Negro employment is in a crisis stage. The rate of unemployment ranges from twice that of whites to four and five times the white rate in some areas. The answer to the complaint of employers that workers are not trained is to institute in-plant training, just as they have in other shortages. The apprentice training stranglehold must be broken, the racially separate seniority lines, the still-persisting segregated local and the remaining crude segregation in plant facilities must be abolished. The demonstrations before the U. S. Steel Corporation offices and plants under the cooperative leadership of Dr. John Nixon, our Alabama president, and Henry Smith, our Pennsylvania president, had wide and beneficial impact.

The Negro migrant worker, the forgotten man in the employment picture, must have attention.

In the Watts district of Los Angeles last year the unemployment rate was more than 30 per cent, a rate higher than that during the great, nationwide Depression of the Nineteen Thirties. The Negro teenage rate is nearly 25 per cent as against 13 per cent for white teenagers.

Negro employment is a disaster area demanding the strict enforcement of Title VII of the 1964 Civil Rights Act. The NAACP has filed more than one thousand complaints with the Equal Employment Opportunity Commission and will file more until the law accomplishes what it was enacted to do. As evidence of his continuing concern, Congressman Augustus Hawkins of Los Angeles succeeded in having his bill relating to Federal employment passed by the House as an amendment to Title VII of the 1964 Civil Rights Act.

3. We choose to combat the color line in housing. In one breath

our opinion-makers decry the existence of the poverty and filth and crime and degradation of the slums, but in the next they decry low-cost housing and fair housing laws. Here in California the hysteria over whether Negro Americans should live in gullies or be pushed into the sea reached the Proposition 14 stage which the state's highest court has declared unconstitutional. But who cares about the Constitution when a Negro might be enabled to move into the neighborhood? One could think black Americans were men from Mars. Instead, we have been here, side by side with the white folks (some of whom just got here), for 345 years.

They tell us to work hard and save our money, to go to school and prepare ourselves, to be "responsible," to rear and educate our children in a wholesome and directed family atmosphere, to achieve, to "get up in the world."

After we do all this, they look us in the eye and bar us from renting or buying a home that matches our achievements and one in keeping with our aspirations for further advancement.

Some public officials, including mayors of cities, and many candidates for election to public office are not above public double talk and private single talk on this issue. Any candidate who orates about basic Americanism or "the American way," but who hems and haws over fair housing legislation is no friend of the Negro citizen.

The Administration's civil rights bill of 1966 with its vital section barring discrimination in the rental or sale of housing must be enacted with the amendment, already inserted by the committee, providing for administrative redress as well as court action.

Your Congressmen and Senators are at home until July 11 celebrating Independence Day—Freedom Day for the United States. See them or have your branch officers back home see them in person. Urge them to rub some freedom off on twenty million loyal Americans by voting for a strong civil rights bill. Of course the section on punishing in the Federal courts those who attack civil rights workers must pass. And we must have indemnification for victims.

4. Most of all, we choose to secure unsegregated, high quality public education for ourselves and our children. A new report, made public only last week, is a jolt for anyone who thought the 1954 Supreme Court decision or subsequent legislation solved the problem.

The report says officially and professionally what we have contended all along: that predominantly Negro schools are inferior to those attended largely by whites. Also that the achievement gap widens between the first grade and the twelfth. In other words, the longer our children attend racially segregated schools, the farther they fall behind white children.

And, lest the non-Southerners feel smug, the report found that segregation for both whites and Negroes is more complete in the South, but "is extensive in other regions where the Negro population is concentrated: the urban North, Midwest and West."

The Federal Government, whose Office of Education has made some strong statements, must follow up with a strong enforcement of Title VI of the 1964 law. The empty promises of school officials and the defiance of the whole State of Alabama must not be accepted meekly by Federal officials. The furor over the guidelines issued by HEW is another version of the Dixie bluff on race which has worked so well for so many decades. The guidelines are mild. They are legal and not illegal as Governor Wallace proclaimed to his state's educators. They ask the Southerners to do what is for them a strange thing: obey the school desegregation law. On this point the Federal Government must not yield. The Attorney General and the Department of Justice must back up resolutely the legality of Federal action. There can be no temporizing.

Outside the South the call is for unrelenting activity to wipe out de facto school segregation. Boston, Massachusetts, has proved to be the Mississippi of the North. In fact, in fairness to Mississippi and in consideration of the starting points and traditions of the two places, Boston is *below* Mississippi on this issue. The details, the traps, the methods and the progress will be covered in workshop discussions, but here it must be said that before we can get jobs to earn increased income to buy and rent better homes, before we can contribute to the enrichment of our nation, we must have free access to quality education.

The man who shoots and burns and drowns us is surely our enemy, but so is he who cripples our children for life with inferior public education.

5. We also choose to wrestle with the complex problems of urban life, all of which include an attitude toward and a treatment of millions of Negro citizens. The solution of urban problems will become the solution of living in the last third of our century since more than 70 per cent of Americans now live in urban communities.

If it has been asked once, it has been asked a hundred times: Are we going to have a long, hot summer? The answer has many facets, some extremely complex and difficult. But one quick answer is that the police everywhere can make or break urban racial tensions by their conduct toward minority group citizens.

Last summer you had here an upheaval that shook the world. To many of us who looked from afar, it appeared to be a wild, senseless rampage of hate and destruction. But that was far from the whole truth.

There was powder in Watts, piled up and packed down through the years: wide-scale unemployment, both adult and teenage, slum housing, crowded schools, non-existent health facilities, inadequate transportation and—the Parker police attitude. Everyone was suspect and everyone was subject to harassment in one form or another. The community smoldered under the peculiar brand that police place upon a whole section with their constant sirens, their contemptuous searches, their rough talk, their ready guns and their general "Godalmightiness."

The lesson they and city officials have learned from last year is to seek not correction and improvement, but still more repression. Mayor Yorty and whoever writes his scripts testified in Sacramento in support of a so-called riot-control bill.

The only thing one has to remember about this bill is that it would allow a policeman to judge whether an utterance or an act is an incitement to riot! On his own judgment he could arrest or club or otherwise deter—or shoot—a person whom he (not the law or the courts) deemed to be an inciter of riot. Down the drain goes freedom of speech and down too, possibly, goes a life.

The McCone Report on the 1965 riot called for "costly and extreme" remedies for Watts, undertaken with a "revolutionary attitude." The answer of the City of Los Angeles was to vote down a hospital bond issue. The answer of Mayor Yorty and of his man, Chief Parker, is a trampling-tough riot-control bill which, if enacted, would loose the police, almost without restraint, upon a populace sick to death—literally—of race control. To blot out any remaining fitful light, one of the gubernatorial candidates, full of disavowals, is the darling of those ultra-conservatives who believe in iron control of what they call "violence in the streets"—their code name for Negroes.

If this is the best that a great city can bring to a hard urban problem, one largely of its own making, then God pity both the whites and the Negroes!

We have no panacea for all these problems. We do not proclaim that what we declare here this week is going to change the course of the whole civil rights movement. We do not know all the answers to the George Wallace problem in Alabama, the James Eastland problem in Mississippi, or to the Boston, Massachusetts, school committee and its Louise Day Hicks problem. We certainly don't know the answers to foreign policy and to tax and interest rate puzzlers.

But in this unsettled time when shifts are the order of the day and when change is in the air, we can sail our NAACP ship "steady as she goes," with more drive to the turbines, more skill at the wheel, but no fancy capers for the sake of capers.

We can follow down into each community the really advanced blue-print of the White House Conference "To Fulfill These Rights," which covered four principal areas: economic security and welfare, education, housing, and the administration of justice.

We can expand and point up the community services of our NAACP branches, each of which is, in reality, a citizenship clinic. Just as medical clinics need specialists to cure physical ills, so our branch clinics should recruit volunteer specialists to diagnose and minister to social ills.

We must involve people in the communities in the solution of our problem—not limiting ourselves to our church or lodge or club group.

We must keep the pressure on our local and state education systems through the employment of every legitimate technique: protests, surveys, discussions, demonstrations, picketing and negotiation. Nothing should be overlooked in fighting for better education. Be persistent and ornery; this will be good for the lethargic educational establishment and will aid the whole cause of public education.

Our branches are at work in their territories. In Baltimore, the NAACP won a case against the police commissioner which the Fourth Circuit Court of Appeals declared revealed the most flagrant police practices ever to come before the court. The Blair County, Pennsylvania, NAACP is busy rooting out the remaining discrimination in public accommodations in Clearfield, Pennsylvania.

The Wilmington, Ohio, NAACP has a program for tutoring adults and drop-outs and has recruited college professors and students and textbooks to make the project effective. The Bay City, Michigan, NAACP also has a tutorial program under way as well as continuous work on industrial employment practices and housing. The Stillwater, Oklahoma, NAACP is active on a child care center project and on high school desegregation.

And the Mongomery County, West Virginia, NAACP, bless its heart, is 112 per cent above last year in membership and 500 per cent above last year in funds raised.

Thirty-one branches found time and funds to be present at the Meredith march rally in Jackson, Mississippi, even though the Association, at the last minute, was insulted by the barring of Charles Evers as an NAACP spokesman.

This is only part of the chronicle of "steady as she goes." In a world where the Mayor of Los Angeles is yelling "riot control," where Rhodesia says "never!" to black representation while in America SNCC raises the chant of black power, where the Federal Government at long last is committed, but both the far right and the far left offer vocal and vicious objection, someone has to drive the long haul toward the

group goal of Negro Americans and the larger ideal of our young nation.
Our objective is basically as it was laid down in 1909 by the inter-
racial founders of our NAACP. Back there William Lloyd Garrison
expressed the strong feeling that the first NAACP conference "will utter
no uncertain sound on any point affecting the vital subject. No part
of it is too delicate for plain speech. The republican experiment is at
stake, every tolerated wrong to the Negro reacting with double force
upon white citizens guilty of faithlessness to their brothers."

As it was then, so it is today. The republican experiment *is* at stake
in 1966. More than that, the dream of a brotherhood in equality and
justice is imperiled.

Our fraternity tonight, as it was then, is the fraternity of man, not
the white, or brown, or yellow, or black man, but man.

Power and Racism, STOKELY CARMICHAEL (1966)

One of the tragedies of the struggle against racism is that up to now
there has been no national organization which could speak to the growing militancy of young black people in the urban ghetto. There has
been only a civil rights movement, whose tone of voice was adapted to
an audience of liberal whites. It served as a sort of buffer zone between
them and angry young blacks. None of its so-called leaders could go
into a rioting community and be listened to. In a sense, I blame ourselves—together with the mass media—for what has happened in
Watts, Harlem, Chicago, Cleveland, Omaha. Each time the people in
those cities saw Martin Luther King get slapped, they became angry;
when they saw four little black girls bombed to death, they were angrier;
and when nothing happened, they were steaming. We had nothing to
offer that they could see, except to go out and be beaten again. We
helped to build their frustration.

For too many years, black Americans marched and had their heads
broken and got shot. They were saying to the country, "Look, you
guys are supposed to be nice guys and we are only going to do what
we are supposed to do—why do you beat us up, why don't you give
us what we ask, why don't you straighten yourselves out?" After years
of this, we are at almost the same point—because we demonstrated from
a position of weakness. We cannot be expected any longer to march
and have our heads broken in order to say to whites: come on, you're
nice guys. For you are not nice guys. We have found you out.

An organization which claims to speak for the needs of a community—as does the Student Nonviolent Coordinating Committee—must
speak in the tone of that community, not as somebody else's buffer

zone. This is the significance of black power as a slogan. For once, black people are going to use the words they want to use—not just the words whites want to hear. And they will do this no matter how often the press tries to stop the use of the slogan by equating it with racism or separatism.

An organization which claims to be working for the needs of a community—as SNCC does—must work to provide that community with a position of strength from which to make its voice heard. This is the significance of black power beyond the slogan.

Black power can be clearly defined for those who do not attach the fears of white America to their questions about it. We should begin with the basic fact that black Americans have two problems: they are poor and they are black. All other problems arise from this two-sided reality: lack of education, the so-called apathy of black men. Any program to end racism must address itself to that double reality.

Almost from its beginning, SNCC sought to address itself to both conditions with a program aimed at winning political power for impoverished Southern blacks. We had to begin with politics because black Americans are a propertyless people in a country where property is valued above all. We had to work for power, because this country does not function by morality, love, and non-violence, but by power. Thus we determined to win political power, with the idea of moving on from there into activity that would have economic effects. With power the masses could *make or participate in making* the decisions which govern their destinies, and thus create basic change in their day-to-day lives.

But if political power seemed to be the key to self-determination, it was also obvious that the key had been thrown down a deep well many years earlier. Disenfranchisement, maintained by racist terror, made it impossible to talk about organizing for political power in 1960. The right to vote had to be won, and SNCC workers devoted their energies to this from 1961 to 1965. They set up voter registration drives in the Deep South. They created pressure for the vote by holding mock elections in Mississippi in 1963 and by helping to establish the Mississippi Freedom Democratic Party (MFDP) in 1964. That struggle was eased, though not won, with the passage of the 1965 Voting Rights Act. SNCC workers could then address themselves to the questions "Who can we vote for, to have our needs met—how do we make our vote meaningful?"

SNCC had already gone to Atlantic City for recognition of the Mississippi Freedom Democratic Party by the Democratic convention and been rejected; it had gone with the MFDP to Washington for recognition by Congress and been rejected. In Arkansas, SNCC helped thirty

Negroes to run for School Board elections; all but one were defeated, and there was evidence of fraud and intimidation sufficient to cause their defeat. In Atlanta, Julian Bond ran for the state legislature and was elected—twice—and unseated—twice. In several states, black farmers ran in elections for agricultural committees which make crucial decisions concerning land use, loans, etc. Although they won places on a number of committees, they never gained the majorities needed to control them.

All of the efforts were attempts to win black power. Then, in Alabama, the opportunity came to see how blacks could be organized on an independent party basis. An unusual Alabama law provides that any group of citizens can nominate candidates for county office and, if they win 20 per cent of the vote, may be recognized as a county political party. The same then applies on a state level. SNCC went to organize in several counties such as Lowndes, where black people—who form 80 per cent of the population and have an average annual income of $943—felt they could accomplish nothing within the framework of the Alabama Democratic Party because of its racism and because the qualifying fee for this year's elections was raised from $50 to $500 in order to prevent most Negroes from becoming candidates. On May 3, five new county "freedom organizations" convened and nominated candidates for the offices of sheriff, tax assessor, members of the school boards. These men and women are up for election in November—if they live until then. Their ballot symbol is the black panther; a bold, beautiful animal, representing the strength and dignity of black demands today. A man needs a black panther on his side when he and his family must endure—as hundreds of Alabamians have endured—loss of job, eviction, starvation, and sometimes death, for political activity. He may also need a gun and SNCC reaffirms the right of black men everywhere to defend themselves when threatened or attacked. As for initiating the use of violence, we hope that such programs as ours will make that unnecesary; but it is not for us to tell black communities whether they can or cannot use any particular form of action to resolve their problems. Responsibility for the use of violence by black men, whether in self-defense or initiated by them, lies with the white community.

This is the specific historical experience from which SNCC's call for "black power" emerged on the Mississippi march last July. But the concept of "black power" is not a recent or isolated phenomenon: It has grown out of the ferment of agitation and activity by different people and organizations in many black communities over the years. Our last year of work in Alabama added a new concrete possibility. In Lowndes county, for example, black power will mean that if a Negro is elected sheriff, he can end police brutality. If a black man is elected tax assessor, he can collect and channel funds for the building of better roads and schools serving black people—thus advancing the move from political power into the economic arena. In such areas as Lowndes, where black men have a majority, they will attempt to use it to exercise control. This is what they seek: control. Where Negroes lack a majority, black power means proper representation and sharing of control. It means the creation of power bases from which black people can work to change statewide or nationwide patterns of oppression through pressure from strength—instead of weakness. Politically, black power means what it has always meant to SNCC: the coming-together of black people to elect representatives and *to force those representatives to speak to their needs.* It does not mean merely putting black faces into office. A man or woman who is black and from the slums cannot be automatically expected to speak to the needs of black people. Most of the black politicians we see around the country today are not what SNCC means by black power. The power must be that of a community, and emanate from there.

SNCC today is working in both North and South on programs of voter registration and independent political organizing. In some places, such as Alabama, Los Angeles, New York, Philadelphia, and New Jersey, independent organizing under the black panther symbol is in progress. The creation of a national "black panther party" must come about; it will take time to build, and it is much too early to predict its success. We have no infallible master plan and we make no claim to exclusive knowledge of how to end racism; different groups will work in their own different ways. SNCC cannot spell out the full logistics of self-determination but it can address itself to the problem by helping black communities define their needs, realize their strength, and go into action along a variety of lines which they must choose for themselves. Without knowing all the answers, it can address itself to the basic problem of poverty; to the fact that in Lowndes County, 86 white families own 90 per cent of the land. What are black people in that county going to do for jobs, where are they going to get money? There must be reallocation of land, of money.

Ultimately, the economic foundations of this country must be shaken if black people are to control their lives. The colonies of the United States—and this includes the black ghettoes within its borders, north and south—must be liberated. For a century, this nation has been like an octopus of exploitation, its tentacles stretching from Mississippi and Harlem to South America, the Middle East, southern Africa, and Vietnam; the form of exploitation varies from area to area but the essential result has been the same—a powerful few have been maintained and enriched at the expense of the poor and voiceless colored masses. This pattern must be broken. As its grip loosens here and there around the world, the hopes of black Americans become more realistic. For racism to die, a totally different America must be born.

This is what the white society does not wish to face; this is why that society prefers to talk about integration. But integration speaks not at all to the problem of poverty, only to the problem of blackness. Integration today means the man who "makes it," leaving his black brothers behind in the ghetto as fast as his new sports car will take him. It has no relevance to the Harlem wino or to the cottonpicker making three dollars a day. As a lady I know in Alabama once said, "the food that Ralph Bunche eats doesn't fill my stomach."

Integration, moreover, speaks to the problem of blackness in a despicable way. As a goal, it has been based on complete acceptance of the fact that *in order to have* a decent house or education, blacks must move into a white neighborhood or send their children to a white school. This reinforces, among both black and white, the idea that "white" is automatically better and "black" is by definition inferior. This is why integration is a subterfuge for the maintenance of white supremacy. It allows the nation to focus on a handful of Southern children who get into white schools, at great price, and to ignore the 94 per cent who are left behind in unimproved all-black schools. Such situations will not change until black people have power—to control their own school boards, in this case. Then Negroes become equal in a way that means something, and integration ceases to be a one-way street. Then integration doesn't mean draining skills and energies from the ghetto into white neighborhoods; then it can mean white people moving from Beverly Hills into Watts, white people joining the Lowndes County Freedom Organization. Then integration becomes relevant.

Last April, before the furor over black power, Christopher Jencks wrote in a *New Republic* article on white Mississippi's manipulation of the antipoverty program:

The war on poverty has been predicated on the notion that there is such a thing as *a community* which can be defined geographically and mobilized for a collective effort to help the poor. This theory has no relationship to reality in the Deep South. In every Mississippi county there are *two* communities. Despite all the pious platitudes of the moderates on both sides, these two communities habitually see their interests in terms of conflict rather than cooperation. Only when the Negro community can muster enough political, economic and professional strength to compete on somewhat equal terms, will Negroes believe in the possibility of true cooperation and whites accept its necessity. En route to integration, the Negro community needs to develop greater independence—a chance to run its own affairs and not cave in whenever "the man" barks . . . Or so it seems to me, and to most of the knowledgeable people with whom I talked in Mississippi. To OEO this judgment may sound like black nationalism . . .

Mr. Jencks, a white reporter, perceived the reason why America's antipoverty program has been a sick farce in both North and South. In the South, it is clearly racism which prevents the poor from running their own programs; in the North, it more often seems to be politicking and bureaucracy. But the results are not so different: In the North, non-whites make up 42 per cent of all families in metropolitan "poverty areas" and only 6 per cent of families in areas classified as not poor. SNCC has been working with local residents in Arkansas, Alabama, and Mississippi to achieve control by the poor of the program and its funds; it has also been working with groups in the North, and the struggle is no less difficult. Behind it all is a federal government which cares far more about winning the war on the Vietnamese than the war on poverty; which has put the poverty program in the hands of self-serving politicians and bureaucrats rather than the poor themselves; which is unwilling to curb the misuse of white power but quick to condemn black power.

To most whites, black power seems to mean that the Mau Mau are coming to the suburbs at night. The Mau Mau are coming, and whites must stop them. Articles appear about plots to "get Whitey," creating an atmosphere in which "law and order must be maintained." Once again, responsibility is shifted from the oppressor to the oppressed. Other whites chide, "Don't forget—you're only 10 per cent of the population; if you get too smart, we'll wipe you out." If they are liberals, they complain, "what about me?— don't you want my help any more?" These are people supposedly concerned about black Americans, but today they think first of themselves, of their feelings of rejection. Or they admonish, "you can't get anywhere without coalitions," without considering the problems of coalition with whom; on what terms (coalescing from weakness can mean absorption, betrayal); when? Or they accuse us of "polarizing the races" by our calls for black unity, when the true responsibility for polarization lies with whites who will not accept their responsibility as the majority power for making the democratic process work.

White America will not face the problem of color, the reality of it. The well-intended say: "We're all human, everybody is really decent, we must forget color." But color cannot be "forgotten" until its weight is recognized and dealt with. White America will not acknowledge that the ways in which this country sees itself are contradicted by being black—and always have been. Whereas most of the people who settled this country came here for freedom or for economic opportunity, blacks were brought here to be slaves. When the Lowndes County Freedom Organization chose the black panther as its symbol, it was christened by the press "the Black Panther Party"—but the Alabama Democratic Party, whose symbol is a rooster, has never been called the White Cock Party. No one ever talked about "white power" because power in this country *is* white. All this adds up to more than merely identifying a group phenomenon by some catchy name or adjective. The furor over that black panther reveals the problems that white America has with color and sex; the furor over "black power" reveals how deep racism runs and the great fear which is attached to it.

Whites will not see that I, for example, as a person oppressed because of my blackness, have common cause with other blacks who are oppressed because of blackness. This is not to say that there are no white people who see things as I do, but that it is black people I must speak to first. It must be the oppressed to whom SNCC addresses itself primarily, not to friends from the oppressing group.

From birth, black people are told a set of lies about themselves. We are told that we are lazy—yet I drive through the Delta area of Mississippi and watch black people picking cotton in the hot sun for fourteen hours. We are told, "If you work hard, you'll succeed"—but if that were true, black people would own this country. We are oppressed because we are black—not because we are ignorant, not because we are lazy, not because we're stupid (and got good rhythm), but because we're black.

I remember that when I was a boy, I used to go to see Tarzan movies on Saturday. White Tarzan used to beat up the black natives. I would sit there yelling, "Kill the beasts, kill the savages, kill 'em!" I was saying: Kill *me*. It was as if a Jewish boy watched Nazis taking Jews off to concentration camps and cheered them on. Today, I want the chief to beat hell out of Tarzan and send him back to Europe. But it takes time to become free of the lies and their shaming effect on black minds. It takes time to reject the most important lie: that black people inherently can't do the same things white people can do, unless white people help them.

The need for psychological equality is the reason why SNCC today believes that blacks must organize in the black community. Only black people can convey the revolutionary idea that black people are able to do things themselves. Only they can help create in the community an aroused and continuing black consciousness that will provide the basis for political strength. In the past, white allies have furthered white supremacy without the whites involved realizing it—or wanting it, I think. Black people must do things for themselves; they must get poverty money they will control and spend themselves, they must conduct tutorial programs themselves so that black children can identify with black people. This is one reason Africa has such importance: The reality of black men ruling their own nations gives blacks elsewhere a sense of possibility, of power, which they do not now have.

This does not mean we don't welcome help, or friends. But we want the right to decide whether anyone is, in fact, our friend. In the past, black Americans have been almost the only people whom everybody and his momma could jump up and call their friends. We have been tokens, symbols, objects—as I was in high school to many young whites, who liked having "a Negro friend." We want to decide who is our friend, and we will not accept someone who comes to us and says: "If you do X, Y, and Z, then I'll help you." We will not be told whom we should choose as allies. We will not be isolated from any group or nation except by our own choice. We cannot have the oppressors telling the oppressed how to rid themselves of the oppressor.

I have said that most liberal whites react to "black power" with the question, What about me?, rather than saying: Tell me what you want me to do and I'll see if I can do it. There are answers to the right question. One of the most disturbing things about almost all white supporters of the movement has been that they are afraid to go into their own communities—which is where the racism exists—and work to get rid of it. They want to run from Berkeley to tell us what to do in Mississippi; let them look instead at Berkeley. They admonish blacks to be nonviolent; let them preach nonviolence in the white community. They come to teach me Negro history; let them go to the suburbs and open up freedom schools for whites. Let them work to stop America's racist foreign policy; let them press this government to cease supporting the economy of South Africa.

There is a vital job to be done among poor whites. We hope to see, eventually, a coalition between poor blacks and poor whites. That is the only coalition which seems acceptable to us, and we see such a coalition as the major internal instrument of change in American society. SNCC has tried several times to organize poor whites; we are trying again now, with an initial training program in Tennessee. It is purely academic today to talk about bringing poor blacks and whites together, but the job of creating a poor-white power bloc must be attempted. The main responsibility for it falls upon whites. Black and white can work together in the white community where possible; it is not possible, however, to go into a poor Southern town and talk about integration. Poor whites everywhere are becoming more hostile—not less—partly because they see the nation's attention focussed on black poverty and nobody coming to them. Too many young middle-class Americans, like some sort of Pepsi generation, have wanted to come alive through the black community; they've wanted to be where the action is—and the action has been in the black community.

Black people do not want to "take over" this country. They don't want to "get Whitey"; they just want to get him off their backs, as the saying goes. It was for example the exploitation by Jewish landlords and merchants which first created black resentment toward Jews—not Judaism. The white man is irrelevant to blacks, except as an oppressive force. Blacks want to be in his place, yes, but not in order to terrorize and lynch and starve him. They want to be in his place because that is where a decent life can be had.

But our vision is not merely of a society in which all black men have enough to buy the good things of life. When we urge that black money go into black pockets, we mean the communal pocket. We want to see money go back into the community and used to benefit it. We want to see the cooperative concept applied in business and banking. We want to see black ghetto residents demand that an exploiting landlord or store keeper sell them, at minimal cost, a building or a shop that they will own and improve cooperatively; they can back their demand with a rent strike, or a boycott, and a community so unified behind them that no one else will move into the building or buy at the store. The society we seek to build among black people, then, is not a capitalist one. It is a society in which the spirit of community and humanistic love prevail. The word love is suspect; black expectations of what it might produce have been betrayed too often. But those were expectations of a response from the white community, which failed us. The love we seek to encourage is within the black community, the only American community where men call each other "brother" when they meet. We can build a community of love only where we have the ability and power to do so; among blacks.

As for white America, perhaps it can stop crying out against "black supremacy," "black nationalism," "racism in reverse," and begin facing reality. The reality is that this nation, from top to bottom, is racist; that racism is not primarily a problem of "human relations" but of an exploitation maintained—either actively or through silence—by the society as a whole. Camus and Sartre have asked, can a man condemn himself? Can whites, particularly liberal whites, condemn themselves?

Can they stop blaming us, and blame their own system? Are they capable of the shame which might become a revolutionary emotion?

We have found that they usually cannot condemn themselves, and so we have done it. But the rebuilding of this society, if at all possible, is basically the responsibility of whites—not blacks. We won't fight to save the present society, in Vietnam or anywhere else. We are just going to work, in the way *we* see fit, and on goals *we* define, not for civil rights but for all our human rights.

Testimony Before Congress, WHITNEY M. YOUNG, JR. (May 18, 1966)

Mr. Young. Thank you very much, Mr. Chairman and members of the committee.

My name is Whitney M. Young, Jr. I am executive director of the National Urban League.

The National Urban League is a nonprofit, charitable, and educational organization founded in 1910 to secure equal opportunities for Negro citizens. It is nonpartisan and interracial in its leadership and staff. . . .

I was about to continue my certification for this testimony. The National Urban League has affiliates in 76 cities, in 30 States and the District of Columbia. It maintains national headquarters in New York City, regional offices in Akron, Atlanta, Los Angeles, New York, and St. Louis, and a Washington bureau. I had already mentioned that the Urban League is some 56 years old.

We have a professional staff of some 800, trained in the techniques and disciplines of social work, which conducts the day-to-day activities of the Urban League throughout the country, aided and abetted by more than 8,000 volunteers who bring expert knowledge and experience to racial matters.

The National Urban League is deeply grateful for the invitation which this committee has given to appear before it today in order to add to your body of knowledge the information and evidence we have accumulated over the years as experts in the area and on the subject now before you.

I am aware that the proposed Civil Rights Act of 1966 (H.R. 14765) contains five titles of legislative substance and a sixth covering appropriations. On the basis of Urban League experience and in light of our attempts to give intelligent and balanced direction and guidance to the heightened aspirations and growing impatience of America's 20 million Negroes, I strongly recommend passage of the total package.

With respect to titles I, II, III, and V, I believe it is abundantly clear that they are but necessary supplements to the Civil Rights Act of 1964; that they constitute that amplification of the 1964 act which is necessary to give it significant meaning and establish a realistic basis for its implementation.

*   *   *   *

Title IV, however, mandating "the right of every person to be protected against discrimination on account of race, color, religion, or national origin in the purchase, rental, lease, financing, use, and occupancy of housing throughout the Nation," however, is a different matter, one around which there is a great deal of misunderstanding and misinterpretation.

*   *   *   *

The explosive increase of the Negro population in northern, central and western cities is one of the most dramatic social changes in urban history. Between 1940 and 1960, the Negro population living outside the 11 States of the Old Confederacy increased 2¼ times— from 4 million in 1940 to over 9 million in 1960. Most of this increase was concentrated in the central cities of the Nation's 12 largest metropolitan areas.

During the period 1940-60, the Negro population of New York increased nearly 2½ times. The Negro population of Chicago increased more than 2½ times. In Philadelphia, the Negro population doubled. In Detroit, it more than tripled. And the Negro population of Los Angeles County increased a phenomenal 600 per cent, from 75,000 to 464,000 in that 20-year period.

Today, here in Washington, D.C., and in Newark, N.J. Negroes constitute more than 50 per cent of the population. In Detroit, Baltimore, Cleveland and St. Louis Negroes represent one-third or more of the population. And in a number of others, including Chicago, Philadelphia, Cincinnati, Indianapolis and Oakland, they constitute well over one-fourth.

Even at the height of European immigration, no other ethnic group ever made up as large a proportion of the big cities' population and it is clear to the most casual observer that the vast bulk of the housing occupied by Negroes in these and other cities is segregated housing.

Thus the problem we are confronting is no longer confined to the plantations of the Mississippi Delta, nor to the sleepy towns of the Old South, nor even to the bustling cities of the New South. On the contrary, the most serious social problem confronting America today is to be found at the heart of its biggest cities, at the commercial nerve centers of the nation. And it is fanning out into a score of smaller cities like New Haven and Gary, San Diego, Buffalo and Rochester,

Toledo and Akron, Fort Wayne and Milwaukee, Kansas City and Wichita.

And yet the migration continues and the rigidity of residential segregation continues to increase. Here, in Washington, D.C., the number of census tracts where nonwhites made up 75 per cent or more of the population approximately doubled during the 1950's. An analysis by the Philadelphia Commission on Human Relations shows that in Philadelphia the number of census tracts with a nonwhite population of 80 per cent or more nearly tripled during the same decade. Newark, which was 34.4 per cent Negro at the time of the 1960 census, is now over 50 per cent Negro.

And what is the precise degree of residential segregation in such cities throughout the country? A recent study shows that in Washington, D.C., 80 per cent of the Negro population lives in segregated housing; in Newark, 71.6 per cent. These are the two cities where more than half of the population is now Negro.

In cities with a Negro population of one-third or more, the segregation index in Detroit is 84 per cent; in Baltimore, 89 per cent; and in Cleveland and St. Louis, it is 91 per cent.

In cities with a Negro population which exceeds one-fourth of the total population, we find the following picture: the segregation index in Oakland is 73 per cent; in Philadelphia, 87 per cent; in Cincinnati, 89 per cent; in Indianapolis, 91.6 per cent; and in Chicago, 92.6 per cent.

It may be reassuring to some to assume that these patterns of segregation, which have literally established a white ring—which some have chosen to call a "white noose"—around the central cities, developed quite by accident because of differences in socio-economic levels or because of taste.

The facts are completely at variance with this assumption. The facts show that the Negro has not been permitted to disperse. Members of other immigrant groups who initially settled in the central cities were able, upon acquiring education, money, and personal resources, to disperse freely, to buy and occupy housing wherever they could afford it. But the Negro has not had this opportunity. For the Negro, the port of entry in the central cities has become a prison.

And so, a man like Ralph Bunche, with his Ph.D., his Phi Beta Kappa key, a Nobel Prize, sufficient finances, and a triple A credit rating, could not until very recently move from the South Side of Chicago to Cicero, although criminal elements, as represented by Al Capone and others, could and did.

May I also refresh your memory on the terms under which the first subdivisions were built in this country. The first advertisements for suburban subdivisions in this country enumerated all the advantages of suburban living and then said quite bluntly, "No Negroes allowed."

Later these sentiments were more subtly expressed, but the message was loud and clear and the barriers were just as strong. The message was "exclusive," "restricted," or "homogeneous," and no Negro, however talented or gifted, no matter whether he wore the coveted Phi Beta Kappa key or the Distinguished Service Cross, could gain admittance.

Where there has been change, it has often been less than nominal. Recently in northern California, for example, fewer than 100 nonwhites were able to buy homes in unsegregated tracts in a period during which 350,000 new homes were built.

Ironically enough, the culprits in this undemocratic and immoral undertaking were not just the private lending agencies, nor just members of the real estate fraternity, nor even the builders. All of these were culpable, to be sure, but they were ably assisted and in effect given sanction for their actions by the Federal Government, which not only permitted residential segregation, but through its FHA programs required as a condition of loan insurance, an insistence upon the "homogeneous" neighborhood, the "compatible" neighborhood.

From 1935 to 1950, Federal public housing law mandated racial segregation as a condition of constructing public housing. So that in the last 30-odd years, residential segregation has been deliberately established in areas throughout the country where it had never existed before.

It should be clear that while today this society is, for a variety of reasons, more socially sensitive than at times in the past and that while broad segments within it find some of these conditions repulsive and morally reprehensible, the simple adoption of new attitudes will not significantly alter or eradicate the work of generations dedicated to calculated, planned, and deliberate racial segregation.

I believe we must face the fact that just as there were hotel and restaurant owners and public officials in the South and employers around the country who personally preferred to change segregationist and discriminatory patterns and practices, few had the courage to proceed or felt they could run the risk of change without the sanction of Federal law, and so it is in housing.

*   *   *   *

Any failure to enact title IV, a Federal fair housing law, has political as well as economic implications, though it is surely unnecessary to point out to men who are themselves politicians, the political significance of the picture emerging in our central cities; of the implications of finding our central cities occupied more and more fully by a dispossessed undereducated, underemployed, embittered, angry, impatient, low-income population.

For these reasons alone, I would think that responsible public officials and leaders in industry would find themselves in strong support of this legislation with its promise of permitting the ghetto population to disperse.

Do not misunderstand me. I feel strongly that there are many Negroes who are well qualified and capable of being mayors and Congressmen in all of our major cities, but I would get small comfort from their election if it were based mainly upon a superiority of numbers in the central cities rather than upon the personal qualifications of the individuals involved.

Finally, I would appeal to you on grounds which may on the surface seem emotional, but grounds which I honestly believe to be very realistic and practical in today's world. To a degree, the point I would make is already recognized by the more secure and enlightened citizens of our society. It is not only that Negro citizens would benefit from the enactment of this legislation—educationally and economically, culturally and socially—but that white citizens, especially our young people, would benefit equally.

Integration provides an opportunity for white citizens to help prepare their children in a natural, diversified setting for the world they're going to live in, a world in which it is 15 minutes by missile from Cape Kennedy to Africa. For a youngster to grow up today with no knowledge of social diversity in a world which is two-thirds nonwhite is a terrible handicap.

Unless such a youngster overcomes or outgrows these hindrances, he will not be able to work for any enlightened major corporation. He won't be able to work for the State Department or for the United Nations. He will not qualify for a $75-a-month job with the Peace Corps. He will certainly not be elected as a distinguished Congressman on this committee.

Increasingly it is the insecure, the frightened, the unsure who need to surround themselves with sameness. But there is richness in diversity and white citizens will benefit just as surely as Negroes from a solution of the racial problems to which title IV speaks.

In a way, I feel I may appear to have over-complicated the picture by talking of the economic, legal, and political implications of this legislation. I fear I may have obscured the basic human rights involved, such sacred things as freedom and dignity and equal rights for all men, the children of a Common Maker; that I may have obscured what should be the most persuasive argument of all, the elementary right of a human being to provide decent shelter for his family.

I may have obscured the fact that the only real qualifications that should matter in the selection of housing should be a man's desire, his determination, his thrift, his standards of decency, and in the case of the Negro, and additionally, his loyalty, his restraint, and his patience with a society to which he has given so much and from which he has received so little.

I would remind members of this committee that in the very soil on which this building rests lie the bones of Negro slaves and of Negro soldiers who died in the American Revolution, that the grass which we view out of these windows has been nourished by the blood and bodies of those for whom I now seek just to secure the right to buy a house.

Even today as we sit here, all of us must be conscious that though the Negro represents but 10 per cent of the population of this country, approximately 20 per cent of our troops in Vietnam are Negro and they are dying at a more rapid rate than other soldiers because they tend to choose the high-hazard assignments in a war 10,000 miles from home, a war our leaders have described as a war for freedom.

My hope is that this committee, through its deliberations, its determinations, and finally through its vote, will show that those who have died, and will die in behalf of this country, will not have done so in vain and that those who live through the battle will not return to find that the freedoms they fought for 10,000 miles away do not exist for them in their own home towns.

Some generation, it seems to me, must succumb to an excess of decency to make up for the generations where we have had an excess of callousness and brutality.

Gentlemen, I would submit to you that for the reasons I have given, both to the advantage of the white and the Negro community, economically, morally, politically, I think that this bill is not at all and should not be a controversial bill, but one that should flow normally and naturally from a sensitive Congress and Congressmen who themselves, I am sure, are aware of this situation.

IV
Education

SCHOOL SEGREGATION AND DESEGREGATION

The first selection dealing with education is an appendix to the brief filed in Brown *v.* Board of Education, *the Supreme Court decision ending school segregation. Prepared by a group of distinguished American psychologists and sociologists, it describes the effect of segregation and the consequences of desegregation on public school students both black and white. The analysis is as applicable today as it was 15 years ago.*

The Effects of Segregation and the Consequences of Desegregation: A Social Science Statement (September 22, 1952)

I

The problem of the segregation of racial and ethnic groups constitutes one of the major problems facing the American people today. It seems desirable, therefore, to summarize the contributions which contemporary social science can make toward its resolution. There are, of course, moral and legal issues involved with respect to which the signers of the present statement cannot speak with any special authority and which must be taken into account in the solution of the problem. There are, however, also factual issues involved with respect to which certain conclusions seem to be justified on the basis of the available scientific evidence. It is with these issues only that this paper is concerned. Some of the issues have to do with the consequences of segregation, some with the problems of changing from segregated to unsegregated practices. These two groups of issues will be dealt with in separate sections below. It is necessary, first, however, to define and delimit the problem to be discussed.

Definitions

For purposes of the present statement, *segregation* refers to that restriction of opportunities for different types of associations between the members of one racial, religious, national or geographic origin, or linguistic group and those of other groups, which results from or is supported by the action of any official body or agency representing some branch of government. We are not here concerned with such segregation as arises from the free movements of individuals which are neither enforced nor supported by official bodies, nor with the segregation of criminals or of individuals with communicable diseases which aims at protecting society from those who might harm it.

Where the action takes place in a social milieu in which the groups involved do not enjoy equal social status, the group that is of lesser social status will be referred to as the *segregated* group.

In dealing with the question of the effects of segregation, it must be recognized that these effects do not take place in a vacuum, but in a social context. The segregation of Negroes and of other groups in the United States takes place in a social milieu in which "race" prejudice and discrimination exist. It is questionable in the view of some students of the problem whether it is possible to have segregation without substantial discrimination. Myrdal states: "Segregation * * * is financially possible and, indeed, a device of economy only as it is combined with substantial discrimination." The imbeddedness of segregation in such a context makes it difficult to disentangle the effects of segregation *per se* from the effects of the context. Similarly, it is difficult to disentangle the effects of segregation from the effects of a pattern of social disorganization commonly associated with it and reflected in high disease and mortality rates, crime and delinquency, poor housing, disrupted family life and general substandard living conditions. We shall, however, return to this problem after consideration of the observable effects of the total complex in which segregation is a major component.

II

At the recent Mid-century White House Conference on Children and Youth, a fact-finding report on the effects of prejudice, discrimination and segregation on the personality development of children was prepared as a basis for some of the deliberations. This report brought together the available social science and psychological studies which were related to the problem of how racial and religious prejudices influenced the development of a healthy personality. It highlighted the fact that segregation, prejudices and discriminations, and their social concomitants potentially damage the personality of all children—the children of the majority group in a somewhat different way than the more obviously damaged children of the minority group.

The report indicates that as minority group children learn the inferior status to which they are assigned—as they observe the fact that they are almost always segregated and kept apart from others who are treated with more respect by the society as a whole—they often react with feelings of inferiority and a sense of personal humiliation. Many of them become confused about their own personal worth. On the one hand, like all other human beings they require a sense of personal dignity; on the other hand, almost nowhere in the large society do they find their own dignity as human beings respected by others. Under these conditions, the minority group child is thrown into a conflict with regard to his feelings about himself and his group. He wonders whether his group and he himself are worthy of no more respect than they receive. This conflict and confusion leads to self-hatred and rejection of his own group.

The report goes on to point out that these children must find ways with which to cope with this conflict. Not every child, of course, reacts with the same patterns of behavior. The particular pattern depends upon many interrelated factors, among which are: the stability and quality of his family relations; the social and economic class to which he belongs; the cultural and educational background of his parents; the particular minority group to which he belongs; his personal characteristics, intelligence, special talents, and personality pattern.

Some children, usually of the lower socio-economic classes, may react by overt aggressions and hostility directed toward their own group or members of the dominant group. Anti-social and delinquent behavior may often be interpreted as reactions to these racial frustrations. These reactions are self-destructive in that the larger society not only punishes those who commit them, but often interprets such aggressive and anti-social behavior as justification for continuing prejudice and segregation.

Middle class and upper class minority group children are likely to react to their frustrations and conflicts by withdrawal and submissive behavior. Or, they may react with compensatory and rigid conformity to the prevailing middle class values and standards and an aggressive determination to succed in these terms in spite of the handicap of their minority status.

The report indicates that minority group children of all social and economic classes often react with a generally defeatist attitude and a lowering of personal ambitions. This, for example, is reflected in a lowering of pupil morale and a depression of the educational aspiration level among minority group children in segregated schools. In producing such effects, segregated schools impair the ability of the child to profit from the educational opportunities provided him.

Many minority group children of all classes also tend to be hypersensitive and anxious about their relations with the larger society. They tend to see hostility and rejection even in those areas where these might not actually exist.

The report concludes that while the range of individual differences among members of a rejected minority group is as wide as among other peoples, the evidence suggests that all of these children are unnecessarily encumbered in some ways by segregation and its concomitants.

With reference to the impact of segregation and its concomitants on children of the majority group, the report indicates that the effects are somewhat more obscure. Those children who learn the prejudices of our society are also being taught to gain personal status in an unrealistic and non-adaptive way. When comparing themselves to members of the minority group, they are not required to evaluate themselves in terms of the more basic standards of actual personal ability and achievement. The culture permits and at times, encourages them to direct their feelings of hostility and aggression against whole groups of people the members of which are perceived as weaker than themselves. They often develop patterns of guilt feelings, rationalizations and other mechanisms which they must use in an attempt to protect themselves from recognizing the essential injustice of their unrealistic fears and hatreds of minority groups.

The report indicates further that confusion, conflict, moral cynicism, and disrespect for authority may arise in majority group children as a consequence of being taught the moral, religious and democratic principles of the brotherhood of man and the importance of justice and fair play by the same persons and institutions who, in their support of racial segregation and related practices, seem to be acting in a prejudiced and discriminatory manner. Some individuals may attempt to resolve this conflict by intensifying their hostility toward the minority group. Others may react by guilt feelings which are not necessarily reflected in more humane attitudes toward the minority group. Still others react by developing an unwholesome, rigid, and uncritical idealization of all authority figures—their parents, strong political and economic leaders. As described in *The Authoritarian Personality,* they despise the weak, while they obsequiously and unquestioningly conform to the demands of the strong whom they also, paradoxically, subconsciously hate.

With respect to the setting in which these difficulties develop, the report emphasized the role of the home, the school, and other social institutions. Studies have shown that from the earliest school years children are not only aware of the status differences among different groups in the society but begin to react with the patterns described above.

Conclusions similar to those reached by the Mid-century White House Conference Report have been stated by other social scientists who have concerned themselves with this problem. The following are some examples of these conclusions:

Segregation imposes upon individuals a distorted sense of social reality.

Segregation leads to a blockage in the communications and interaction between the two groups. Such blockages tend to increase mutual suspicion, distrust and hostility.

Segregation not only perpetuates rigid stereotypes and reinforces negative attitudes toward members of the other group, but also leads to the development of a social climate within which violent outbreaks of racial tensions are likely to occur.

We return now to the question, deferred earlier, of what it is about the total society complex of which segregation is one feature that produces the effects described above—or, more precisely, to the question of whether we can justifiably conclude that, as only one feature of a complex social setting, segregation is in fact a significantly contributing factor to these effects.

To answer this question, it is necessary to bring to bear the general fund of psychological and sociological knowledge concerning the role of various environmental influences in producing feelings of inferiority, confusions in personal roles, various types of basic personality structures and the various forms of personal and social disorganization.

On the basis of this general fund of knowledge, it seems likely that feelings of inferiority and doubts about personal worth are attributable to living in an underprivileged environment only insofar as the latter is itself perceived as an indicator of low social status and as a symbol of inferiority. In other words, one of the important determinants in producing such feelings is the awareness of social status difference. While there are many other factors that serve as reminders of the differences in social status, there can be little doubt that the fact of enforced segregation is a major factor.

This seems to be true for the following reasons among others: (1) because enforced segregation results from the decision of the majority group without the consent of the segregated and is commonly so perceived; and (2) because historically segregation patterns in the United States were developed on the assumption of the inferiority of the segregated.

In addition, enforced segregation gives official recognition and sanction to these other factors of the social complex, and thereby enhances the affects of the latter in creating the awareness of social status differences and feelings of inferiority. The child who, for example, is compelled to attend a segregated school may be able to cope with ordinary expressions of prejudice by regarding the prejudiced person as evil or misguided; but he cannot readily cope with symbols of authority, the full force of the authority of the State—the school or the school board, in this instance—in the same manner. Given both the ordinary expression of prejudice and the school's policy of segregation, the former takes on greater force and seemingly becomes an official expression of the latter.

Not all of the psychological traits which are commonly observed in the social complex under discussion can be related so directly to the awareness of status differences—which in turn is, as we have already noted, materially contributed to by the practices of segregation. Thus, the low level of aspiration and defeatism so commonly observed in segregated groups is undoubtedly related to the level of self-evaluation; but it is also, in some measure, related among other things to one's expectations with regard to opportunities for achievement and, having achieved, to the opportunities for making use of these achievements. Similarly, the hypersensitivity and anxiety displayed by many minority group children about their relations with the larger society probably reflects their awareness of status differences; but it may also be influenced by the relative absence of opportunities for equal status contact which would provide correctives for prevailing unrealistic stereotypes.

The preceding view is consistent with the opinion stated by a large majority (90%) of social scientists who replied to a questionnaire concerning the probable effects of enforced segregation under conditions of equal facilities. This opinion was that, regardless of the facilities which are provided, enforced segregation is psychologically detrimental to the members of the segregated group.

Similar considerations apply to the question of what features of the social complex of which segregation is a part contribute to the development of the traits which have been observed in majority group members. Some of these are probably quite closely related to the awareness of status differences, to which, as has already been pointed out, segregation makes a material contribution. Others have a more complicated relationship to the total social setting. Thus, the acquisition of an unrealistic basis for self-evaluation as a consequence of majority group membership probably reflects fairly closely the awareness of status differences. On the other hand, unrealistic fears and hatreds of minority groups, as in the case of the converse phenomenon among minority group members, are probably significantly influenced as well by the lack of opportunities for equal status contact.

With reference to the probable effects of segregation under conditions of equal facilities on majority group members, many of the social scientists who responded to the poll in the survey cited above felt that the evidence is less convincing than with regard to the probable effects of such segregation on minority group members, and the effects are possibly less widespread. Nonetheless, more than 80% stated it as their opinion that the effects of such segregation are psychologically detrimental to the majority group members.

It may be noted that many of these social scientists supported their opinions on the effects of segregation on both majority and minority groups by reference to one or another or to several of the following four lines of published and unpublished evidence. First, studies of children throw light on the relative priority of the awareness of status differentials and related factors as compared to the awareness of differences in facilities. On this basis, it is possible to infer some of the consequences of segregation as distinct from the influence of inequalities of facilities. Second, clinical studies and depth interviews throw light on the genetic sources and causal sequences of various patterns of psychological reaction; and, again, certain inferences are possible with respect to the effects of segregation *per se*. Third, there actually are some relevant but relatively rare instances of segregation with equal or even superior facilities, as in the cases of certain Indian reservations. Fourth, since there are inequalities of facilities in racially and ethnically homogeneous groups, it is possible to infer the kinds of effects attributable to such inequalities in the absence of effects of segregation and by a kind of subtraction to estimate the effects of segregation *per se* in situations where one finds both segregation and unequal facilities.

III

Segregation is at present a social reality. Questions may be raised, therefore, as to what are the likely consequences of desegregation.

One such question asks whether the inclusion of an intellectually inferior group may jeopardize the education of the more intelligent group by lowering educational standards or damage the less intelligent group by placing it in a situation where it is at a marked competitive disadvantage. Behind this question is the assumption, which is examined below, that the presently segregated groups actually are inferior intellectually.

The available scientific evidence indicates that much, perhaps all, of the observable differences among various racial and national groups may be adequately explained in terms of environmental differences. It has been found, for instance, that differences between the average intelligence test scores of Negro and white children decrease, and the overlap of the distributions increases, proportionately to the number of years that the Negro children have lived in the North. Related studies have shown that this change cannot be explained by the hypothesis of selective migration. It seems clear, therefore, that fears based on the assumption of innate racial differences in intelligence are not well founded.

It may also be noted in passing that the argument regarding the intellectual inferiority of one group as compared to another is, as applied to schools, essentially an argument for homogeneous groupings of children by intelligence rather than by race. Since even those who believe that there are innate differences between Negroes and whites in America in average intelligence grant that considerable overlap between the two groups exists, it would follow that it may be expedient to group together the superior whites and Negroes, the average whites and Negroes, and so on. Actually, many educators have come to doubt the wisdom of class groupings made homogeneous solely on the basis of intelligence. Those who are opposed to such homogeneous grouping believe that this type of segregation, too, appears to create generalized feelings of inferiority in the child who attends a below average class, leads to undesirable emotional consequences in the education of the gifted child, and reduces learning opportunities which result from the interaction of individuals with varied gifts.

A second problem that comes up in an evaluation of the possible consequences of desegregation involves the question of whether segregation prevents or stimulates inter-racial tension and conflict and the corollary question of whether desegregation has one or the other effect.

The most direct evidence available on this problem comes from observations and systematic study of instances in which desegregation has occurred. Comprehensive reviews of such instances clearly establish the fact that desegregation has been carried out successfully in a variety of situations although outbreaks of violence had been commonly predicted. Extensive desegregation has taken place without major incidents in the armed services in both Northern and Southern installations and involving officers and enlisted men from all parts of the country, including the South. Similar changes have been noted in housing and industry. During the last war, many factories both in the North and South hired Negroes on a non-segregated, non-discriminatory basis. While a few strikes occurred, refusal by management and unions to yield quelled all strikes within a few days.

Relevant to this general problem is a comprehensive study of urban race riots which found that race riots occurred in segregated neighborhoods, whereas there was no violence in sections of the city where the two races lived, worked and attended school together.

Under certain circumstances desegregation not only proceeds without major difficulties, but has been observed to lead to the emergence of more favorable attitudes and friendlier relations between races. Relevant studies may be cited with respect to housing, employment, the armed services and merchant marine, recreation agency, and general community life.

Much depends, however, on the circumstances under which members of previously segregated groups first come in contact with others in unsegregated situations. Available evidence suggests, first, that there is less likelihood of unfriendly relations when the change is simultaneously introduced into all units of a social institution to which it is applicable—*e.g.*, all of the schools in a school system or all of the shops in a given factory. When factories introduced Negroes in only some shops but not in others the prejudiced workers tended to classify the desegregated shops as inferior, "Negro work." Such objections were not raised when complete integration was introduced.

The available evidence also suggests the importance of consistent and firm enforcement of the new policy by those in authority. It indicates also the importance of such factors as: the absence of competition for a limited number of facilities or benefits; the possibility of contacts which permit individuals to learn about one another as individuals; and the possibility of equivalence of positions and functions among all of the participants within the unsegregated situation. These conditions can generally be satisfied in a number of situations, as in the armed services, public housing developments, and public schools.

IV

The problem with which we have here attempted to deal is admittedly on the frontiers of scientific knowledge. Inevitably, there must be some differences of opinion among us concerning the conclusiveness of certain items of evidence, and concerning the particular choice of words and placement of emphasis in the preceding statement. We are nonetheless in agreement that this statement is substantially correct and justified by the evidence, and the differences among us, if any, are of a relatively minor order and would not materially influence the preceding conclusions.

FLOYD H. ALLPORT, Syracuse, New York

GORDON W. ALLPORT, Cambridge, Mass.

CHARLOTTE BABCOCK, M.D., Chicago, Ill.

VIOLA W. BERNARD, M.D., N. Y., N. Y.

JEROME S. BRUNER, Cambridge, Mass.

HADLEY CANTRIL, Princeton, New Jersey
ISIDOR CHEIN, New York, New York
KENNETH B. CLARK, New York, N. Y.
MAMIE P. CLARK, New York, New York
STUART W. COOK, New York, New York
BINGHAM DAI, Durham, North Carolina
ALLISON DAVIS, Chicago, Illinois
ELSE FRENKEL-BRUNSWIK, Berkeley, Calif.
NOEL P. GIST, Columbia, Missouri
CHARLES S. JOHNSON, Nashville, Tennessee
DANIEL KATZ, Ann Arbor, Michigan
OTTO KLINEBERG, New York, New York
DAVID KRECH, Berkeley, California
ALFRED MCCLUNG LEE, Brooklyn, N. Y.
R. N. MACIVER, New York, New York
PAUL F. LAZARSFELD, New York, N. Y.
ROBERT K. MERTON, New York, N. Y.
GARDNER MURPHY, Topeka, Kans.
THEODORE M. NEWCOMB, Ann Arbor, Mich.
ROBERT REDFIELD, Chicago, Illinois
IRA DEA. REID, Haverford, Pennsylvania
ARNOLD M. ROSE, Minneapolis, Minn.
GERHART SAENGER, New York, New York
R. NEVITT SANFORD, Poughkeepsie, N. Y.
S. STANFIELD SARGENT, New York, N. Y.
M. BREWSTER SMITH, New York, N. Y.
SAMUEL A. STOUFFER, Cambridge, Mass.
WELLMAN WARNER, New York, N. Y.
GOODWIN WATSON, New York, New York
ROBIN M. WILLIAMS, Ithaca, New York

Dated: September 22, 1952.

DESEGREGATION AT LITTLE ROCK

Elizabeth Eckford, the courageous fifteen-year-old girl who attempted to enter Little Rock High School in 1957, describes her feelings about the event in a short section from Daisy Bates's Long Shadow of Little Rock. *Her description was used as the moving climax to Martin Duberman's play "In White America."*

Long Shadow of Little Rock, DAISY BATES (1962)

*   *   *   *

"You remember the day before we were to go in, we met Superintendent Blossom at the school board office. He told us what the mob might say and do but he never told us we wouldn't have any protection. He told our parents not to come because he wouldn't be able to protect the children if they did.

"That night I was so excited I couldn't sleep. The next morning I was about the first one up. While I was pressing my black and white dress—I had made it to wear on the first day of school—my little brother turned on the TV set. They started telling about a large crowd gathered at the school. The man on TV said he wondered if we were going to show up that morning. Mother called from the kitchen, where she was fixing breakfast, 'Turn that TV off!' She was so upset and worried. I wanted to comfort her, so I said, 'Mother, don't worry.'

"Dad was walking back and forth, from room to room, with a sad expression. He was chewing on his pipe and he had a cigar in his hand, but he didn't light either one. It would have been funny, only he was so nervous.

"Before I left home Mother called us into the living-room. She said we should have a word of prayer. Then I caught the bus and got off a block from the school. I saw a large crowd of people standing across the street from the soldiers guarding Central. As I walked on, the crowd suddenly got very quiet. Superintendent Blossom had told us to enter by the front door. I looked at all the people and thought, 'Maybe I will be safer if I walk down the block to the front entrance behind the guards.'

"At the corner I tried to pass through the long line of guards around the school so as to enter the grounds behind them. One of the guards pointed across the street. So I pointed in the same direction and asked whether he meant for me to cross the street and walk down. He nodded 'yes.' So, I walked across the street conscious of the crowd that stood there, but they moved away from me.

"For a moment all I could hear was the shuffling of their feet. Then someone shouted, 'Here she comes, get ready!' I moved away from the crowd on the sidewalk and into the street. If the mob came at me I could then cross back over so the guards could protect me.

"The crowd moved in closer and then began to follow me, calling me names. I still wasn't afraid. Just a little bit nervous. Then my knees started to shake all of a sudden and I wondered whether I could make it to the center entrance a block away. It was the longest block I ever walked in my whole life.

"Even so, I still wasn't too scared because all the time I kept thinking that the guards would protect me.

"When I got right in front of the school, I went up to a guard again. But this time he just looked straight ahead and didn't move to let me pass him. I didn't know what to do. Then I looked and saw that the path leading to the front entrance was a little further ahead. So I walked until I was right in front of the path to the front door.

"I stood looking at the school—it looked so big! Just then the guards let some white students go through.

"The crowd was quiet. I guess they were waiting to see what was going to happen. When I was able to steady my knees, I walked up to the guard who had let the white students in. He too didn't move. When I tried to squeeze past him, he raised his bayonet and then the other guards closed in and they raised their bayonets.

"They glared at me with a mean look and I was very frightened and didn't know what to do. I turned around and the crowd came toward me.

"They moved closer and closer. Somebody started yelling, 'Lynch her! Lynch her!'

"I tried to see a friendly face somewhere in the mob—someone who maybe would help. I looked into the face of an old woman and it seemed a kind face, but when I looked at her again, she spat on me.

"They came closer, shouting, 'No nigger bitch is going to get in our school. Get out of here!'

"I turned back to the guards but their faces told me I wouldn't get help from them. Then I looked down the block and saw a bench at the bus stop. I thought, 'If I can only get there I will be safe.' I don't know why the bench seemed a safe place to me, but I started walking toward it. I tried to close my mind to what they were shouting, and kept saying to myself, 'If I can only make it to the bench I will be safe.'

"When I finally got there, I don't think I could have gone another step. I sat down and the mob crowded up and began shouting all over again. Someone hollered, 'Drag her over to this tree! Let's take care of the nigger.' Just then a white man sat down beside me, put his arm around me and patted my shoulder. He raised my chin and said, 'Don't let them see you cry.'

"Then, a white lady—she was very nice—she came over to me on the bench. She spoke to me but I don't remember now what she said. She put me on the bus and sat next to me. She asked me my name and tried to talk to me but I don't think I answered. I can't remember much about the bus ride, but the next thing I remember I was standing in front of the School for the Blind, where Mother works.

"I thought, 'Maybe she isn't here. But she has to be here!' So I ran upstairs, and I think some teachers tried to talk to me, but I kept running until I reached Mother's classroom.

"Mother was standing at the window with her head bowed, but she must have sensed I was there because she turned around. She looked as if she had been crying, and I wanted to tell her I was all right. But I couldn't speak. She put her arms around me and I cried."

V
Voting

The harrassment and intimidation that southern Negroes suffered in their attempt to register and vote is epitomized in Hartman Turnbow's moving testimony before a Mississippi State Advisory Committee of the United States Commission on Civil Rights in January 1964. The long history of discrimination in Louisana was outlined in detail by Judge Wisdom of the Fifth Circuit Court of Appeals in his decision declaring unconstitutional Louisiana's interpretation test. The last of these pieces is a portion of a Civil Rights Commission report of 1965 entitled, "Voting in Mississippi," which showed the manner in which Mississippi had kept the Negro from obtaining the franchise.

Hartman Turnbow at Hearing of the Mississippi State Advisory Committee to the U.S. Commission on Civil Rights (January 8, 1964)

DR. BRITTON: Come right up, Mr. Turnbow. Now, this is in connection with an attempt to register. Have a seat there.

Q. Give us your name and address and tell us what happened.

A. My name is Hartman Turnbow. I lives at Tchula, Route 2, Box 25, Tchula, Mississippi. Well, I had been reading and hearing over the news about people trying to register in Tennessee, so finally I heard it had moved down to Greenwood, so finally somebody come and told me: "We are going to have a little registration meeting at your church—would you come over?"

I say: "A registration meeting?" They say: "Yeah." I say: "What's that for?" They said: "That's for to learn you how to register." I say: "Register?" They say: "Yeah." I say: "That mean we're going to start registering now in Holmes County." He said: "Yes." I say: "Well, I'll be down."

I comes home and I told my wife that one of my friends said they was going to have a registration meeting at the church, so I believe we'll go down. She say: "Yes, it's all right." So we got in the car and we drove on down to the church and it was a fellow from Greenwood, he made a talk about concerning registering, so I liked the story and I fell for it, so I started attending the meetings, so as I attended the meeting, they brought up these registration application forms to register.

So I read it. Well, it wasn't too complicated and I still liked it better, so after we had participated in the meeting for about three or four weeks, I said: "Well, why don't we go try it out now—who all know it—who all think they know it well enough to try it."

Well, it was about fourteen of us said: "We know it, we know it." I say: "Well, let's go then." So we had a citizenship teacher—was teaching us. His name is John Ball, so he made a pretty good job of teaching us to fill the forms, so fourteen of us felt we was qualified, so we got our cars and we went down to the Courthouse.

We left our cars parked. We didn't go right on the block. We left them outside the block on the curb—we got out. I say: "Well, now, they ain't going to want us to register in Holmes County no-way. Let's try to do everything we can, so they won't say we violated the law." They say: "Well, what you going to do, Turnbow?" I say: "Let's walk—let's not gang up—let's walk in twos." I say: "Let's don't walk too close together, so they can't say we demonstrating."

So we did that—fourteen of us. So when we went on around—Samuel Block, he was leading us. He was in front of us—it was two men—he was in the third—he was the third man in the little line we had formed of fourteen going to the Courthouse, so Mr. Andrew P. Smith is the Sheriff—well, at that time, his wife was Sheriff and he was the deputy. He had been the Sheriff before.

But we was met by Mr. Andrew P. Smith and he stopped—Samuel Block stopped. I mean the two men in head of Samuel Block—he was the third man, and the two in front stopped and Samuel Block said: "March forward," and Mr. Smith said: "None of that god damned forward stuff here," and throwed one hand on his pistol and the other one on his blackjack.

Samuel Block tightened his hat on his head. So right at that time, I was about four or five men down the line—about the fifth or the sixth man in the line—I stepped right out the line. Mr. Smith knowed me and I knowed him—had been knowing one another for quite a while.

I said: "Mr. Smith, we only come to register." Well, Mr. Smith called me by my name. He said: "Turnbow, go around to the north side of the Courthouse and stop under that tree" and said: "Don't go in no big droves." He said: "Go by twos." I say: "Yes, sir, we will."

So we did that, so after fourteen of us got around on the north side of the Courthouse and stopped under the tree in a little huddle, then Mr. Smith come around there, and he looked at us and he raised his voice. He say: "All right, now who will be first?" Then the little crowd of fourteen—when he raised his voice, he slapped one hand on his pistol and the other one on his blackjack and then raised his voice.

He say: "All right, now, who will be first." Well, the little bunch of fourteen of us commenced looking then one at another one right fast. So I seen what they was doing and I just stepped out. I say: "I'll be first—Hartman Turnbow will be fiirst." He said: "Well, all right"—he calmed his voice just at that moment. He said: "Well, all right, Turnbow, if you'll be first, just go right on down side the curb to the sidewalk and go into the Courthouse and the first door on the left, go in there and do what you're going to do."

I say: "Yes, sir," so I did that. So when I got in the Circuit Clerk's office, he wasn't in there. It was a lady in there. She say: "What you want?" I say: "I want to register to vote." She say: "Register to vote." I say: "Yes ma'am." She say: "Well, the Circuit Clerk ain't in here." I say: "Well, may I have a seat and wait on him." She say: "Yes, you may."

So I sat there until about five minutes to twelve. She say: "We're going to close now for lunch." I say: "I'll come back after lunch." She say: "Well, do so." So I went out head of her and she come on out and fastened the door. So I went back to the tree. So Samuel Block and John Ball—he's our teacher, so Ball decided we would go to Greenwood.

Well, I don't know anything about the purpose of that trip to Greenwood, but anyway, we rid to Greenwood, the most of the fourteen. Well, I didn't do anything but just sit in the car and stand around until they got ready to come back. So we come back to the Courthouse again afternoon—I guess it was about two-thirty or three o'clock.

We got right back under that tree and they said one had gone in. So when he come out, I went in and the Circuit Clerk was in. He said: "What you want?" I say: "I want to register to vote." He say: "For what—register to vote—what—what kind of voting? Folks votes on a lots of things." I say: "Well, I wants to register to vote for my governor or my sheriff or anybody that's running for a public office, where if I like what he doing, I wants to vote for him and if I don't I won't have to do it."

So he says: "All right"—he says: "Er ruh, go on around"—he give me a blank, a application form. It was similar to the one that we had been studying, so I went around in the room and filled it. So when I got it filled out, he brought another little writing. He say that was a section of the Constitution and say I had to copy it and interpret it, so I did so. I copied it and then I interpreted it and I gave it to him and I come out.

So it was about night, so about two of us got to register that day, but they say they kept going 'til finally the fourteen got registered. Well, I noticed the next day in the Lexington *Herald* it was a write-up that Hartman Turnbow was an integration leader, and I noticed in the next week—well, about between three and four o'clock—about three o'clock in the morning, my house was fired bombed—two fire bombs in the living room and one in the back bedroom.

And my wife jumped out the bed screaming: "The house is bombed." And my daughter—she was standing out—she is sixteen, she go to high school, she's eleven grade—and she was standing out in the little entry in the house there hollering: "Daddy, Daddy, the house is afire, come out."

So I didn't come out the house. When my wife run out, well, the smoke out the living room just filled our bedroom up, so I didn't go out then. I raised a window and took my foot and kicked out the screen and when I done that, I had to do that to keep the smoke from staggernating me, so when I got a little taste of air—I had a automatic twenty-two Remington sitting over in the corner in a scabbard.

It was brand new and it was loaded and I just reached over there and got my rifle and snatched that scabbard off and throwed it down and pushed the safety down and got it in shooting position, then I made my way through the smoke. And when I got outside of the back door I met my wife and my daughter coming back into the house.

My daughter went on the back porch and my wife stopped right at the back steps, but I kept going and when I got out in the open where I could see, the first thing I saw was two white men. One of them shot at me just the time I got out, and no sooner as he shot—well, I didn't take time to get my rifle up on him where I could kill him. I just got it up around his belt and commenced to pull on it.

So I put it right about his belt and I pulled it three or four times and he commenced to running, so about that time shooting started in the front of the house. They shot the front of it about five or six times with a forty-five, just shot holes all through the house, and by that time, well, they was gone. So my wife, she was fighting fire and then I reloaded my rifle and looked around and I didn't see no more people, so I started to fighting fire.

So for about a hour, myself, wife and daughter, we fought fire hard—took us about a hour to get it under control. So after we got it under control, well, we sat right on the back porch 'til day. I didn't want to move around 'cause I didn't know who was planted and I didn't want to get shot, so we just huddled on the back porch and we stayed 'til day.

And then when day come, we got in the car, myself, wife and daughter and we went to a friend's house, Ozelle Mitchell—we told him 'bout the story, and we had went to a singing that night, so one of the boys which was at the singing, he was there, and I waked him up and asked him could he get in touch with the F. B. I.

He said: "Yes, I can." I say: "Well, call them 'cause our house was set afire last night and shot in and shot at me and I shot at somebody." So he did that. So I went on to Jack Lewis—that's a friend. That's where our citizenship teacher was staying, John Ball, and I waked him up. He was in the bed asleep and I went in his room and waked him up, and I asked him, I say: "Say, can you get in touch with the Justice Department or the F. B. I.?" He say: "Yeah, I can. What happened?"

Well, I told him the story 'bout my house getting bombed and I got shot at and I shot at the man and I thought I hit him and so on. So he got up and say: "I'll go right now." I say: "Now, look, don't try to call them from Tchula 'cause they're going to be listening in and maybe you won't get the message through." I say: "You get in a car and go to Greenwood and then call." He say: "I will," and he took off for Greenwood.

So I come on back home and by that time—well, Mr. Moore and Mr. Bob Lester—Mr. Moore is the deputy Sheriff for Tchula, and Mr. Bob Lester, he is a country deputy there, too. So they came. They was the first white men to reach the scene. So they come—well, Mr. Moore, he didn't say very much, he didn't say anything much, but Mr. Bob Lester, he say: "Well, Turnbow, it's a reason for all of this"—say: "Don't you know it's a reason for all of this." I says: "I know it's a reason for it." I say: "Mr. Lester, you right, it's a reason for it." He say: "You keeping company with the wrong kind of associates—these outside agitators is getting paid to do it."

I say: "Well, I don't think I'm keeping company with the wrong kind of peoples." I say: "Anybody teaching me how to get my privilege and how to vote and helps elect somebody to dictate over me, I don't think that's the wrong kind of company." So he—er ruh—he just kept a-saying that, so finally the F. B. I. men came, so they was very nice mens.

They called me by my name and say: "Come in here, Turnbow," and we sat in the kitchen to the table and they commenced to asking me 'bout the story, so I told them the story just like it happened—told them where about seven-thirty—seven o'clock or seven-thirty, John Ball come by and say they was going to have a singing at the church and asked me to bring my daughter to the singing, and I told him I would.

So at about seven o'clock or seven-thirty, myself, wife and daughter went on to the church to the singing. Well, it was young peoples and I can't sing and I don't fool with singing much no-way, so I just stayed out in my car and laid down, so my wife and daughter, they went in the church to the singing, and my daughter and all of them, they sang.

So when we come out, it was about nine o'clock or nine-thirty when we got home. The first thing we noticed was—we had a little dog, a little tan dog, and he mousey around the house, then every time we come up, he run meet us, looking up and just switching his tail and shaking, so, er ruh, we didn't see the little dog. My wife said the dog must be asleep. I kinda smiled—I say: "Yeah, he could be. He could be asleep out in the highway somewhere for always."

DR. BRITTON: Q. Mr. Turnbow, this tape is about to run out and I want to ask you a question. I want to find out if there is any other type of brutality or anything that you suffered as a result of making this attempt to register. If you could just tell us briefly about that—did they shoot at you any more or burn your house any more?

A. Not since that first time.

Q. Well, did they do anything else that you think was the result of your making an attempt to register?

A. Yes, they did.

Q. Will you briefly tell us that?

A. Yes, yes, I can. Well, before then—well, I was born and raised at Lexington. I'm fifty-eight and I've spent all of my life in Holmes County except five years, three in Detroit, two in Chicago and all the rest of the fifty-eight years was spent right there in Holmes County, and I stood well with white and colored, never had no trouble with white or colored, and my credit was good. I could borrow anything I want. I borrowed as high as a hundred dollars from Mr. Ellis at the bank on an open note, no security whatever, and just anything I wanted around the block from white or colored, I could get it.

But the minute the news spread abroad that I had registered and I led a bunch of Negroes down on the Courthouse, all of my credit was cut off and where I was getting my gas to farm with, that man cut it off even. He told me: you have to pay cash for your gas from now on. That was Mr. Pate Johnson at Tchula, and so on and on and on. I could just tell you many things that really happened.

And it's a many other colored people right there at Tchula right now —well, they won't attempt to register. If you go to talking to them about participating in a registration or go down to the Courthouse to register, they'll say: "Yeah, if I go, I'll get fired, then what about it." They say: "If I go to register and my house gets bombed, then what about it." And all those kind of questions they'd ask, and those kind of questions has got all the colored people around Tchula vicinity blocked from registering.

They scared they'd get fired, they scared their house would get bombed and they scared they'd be framed in some kind of way. It's a plenty right there at Tchula.

REVEREND PAYNE: Q. Are you registered now? You are a registered voter now?

A. I'm not a registered voter, but I did attempt to register.

Q. That's all I wanted to get clear, that you attempted but you are not registered. He still didn't register you?

A. I filled out the form and give it to the Circuit Clerk and he said I didn't pass.

REVEREND PAYNE: That's what I wanted to get clear.

DR. BRITTON: Mr. Natalie would like to ask you a question.

MR. NATALIE: Q. Mr. Turnbow, was anyone ever arrested for arson in connection with the fire bombing of your house?

A. I was arrested myself. They said I did it.

Q. They said you set your own house afire?

A. That's what they said—put me in jail and put me under a five hundred dollar bond and say I fire bombed my own house.

Q. Did you find out who shot into your house?

A. No, never did find out who shot into it—never did. I don't know today who did it. They say I did it all.

Q. What is the status of your prosecution for arson? Where does it stand now?

A. Well, after the F.B.I.'s got in there and got it into the Federal Court, then they dropped the charges against me.

DR. BRITTON: Thank you very much, Mr. Turnbow.

Fifth Circuit Court of Appeals Decision in *United States v. Louisiana,* (November 27, 1963)

UNITED STATES OF AMERICA, Plaintiff, vs. STATE OF LOUISIANA, Jimmie H. Davis, C. C. Aycock, J. Thomas Jewel, as Members of the Board of Registration of the State of Louisiana, and Hugh E. Cutrer, Jr., Director and ex officio Secretary of the Board of Registration of the State of Louisiana, Defendants.

Before WISDOM, Circuit Judge, and CHRISTENBERRY and WEST, District Judges

WISDOM, Circuit Judge.

A wall stands in Louisiana between registered voters and unregistered, eligible Negro voters. The wall is the State constitutional requirement that an applicant for registration "understand and give a reasonable interpretation of any section" of the Constitutions of Louisiana or of the United States. It is not the only wall of its kind, but since the Supreme Court's demolishment of the white primary, the interpretation test has been the highest, best-guarded, most effective barrier to Negro voting in Louisiana.

When a Louisiana citizen seeks to register, the Parish Registrar of Voters may ask the applicant to interpret the provision, "The Supreme Court and the Court of Appeal, and each of the judges * * may also in aid of their respective jurisdictions, original, appellate, or supervisory, issue writs of mandamus, certiorari, prohibition, quo warranto, and all other needful writs." Or, the registrar may ask the applicant to interpret a less technical but more difficult provision, constitutionally, such as, "Every person has the natural right to worship God according to the dictates of his own conscience." In giving this test, the registrar selects the constitutional section and he must be satisfied with the explanation. In many parishes the registrar is not easily satisfied with constitutional interpretations from Negro applicants.

We hold: this wall, built to bar Negroes from access to the franchise, must come down. The understanding clause or interpretation test is *not* a literacy requirement. It has no rational relation to measuring the ability of an elector to read and write. It is a test of an elector's ability to interpret the Louisiana and United States Constitutions. Considering this law in its historical setting and considering too the actual operation and inescapable effect of the law, it is evident that the test is a sophisticated scheme to disfranchise Negroes. The test is unconstitutional as written and as administered.

*   *   *   *

To obtain some necessary pages of history, more valuable than volumes of logic, as Holmes has said, we sacrifice brevity.

The Louisiana interpretation test and its current variant, the citizenship test, are best understood as the latest, but perhaps not final, members of a long, logically connected series of socio-political events. These are rooted in the State's historic policy and the dominant white citizens' firm determination to maintain white supremacy in state and local government by denying to Negroes the right to vote.

A. There was, of course, no problem in colonial and territorial times; the *Codes Noir,* from the 1724 Code to Act 33 of the Territorial Legislature of 1806, disfranchised Negroes. Louisiana became a state in 1812. It limited the franchise to "free white male citizen[s]" who had paid state taxes or purchased land from the United States within six months prior to the election. For thirty-three years this constitutional limitation kept the ballot chiefly in the hands of landowners and merchants, disfranchised two-thirds of the electorate, and favored New Orleans and the southern parishes over the rest of the State. The Constitution of 1845, in many respects a progressive and broadly democratic document, did away with the tax-paying qualification for voters and established universal suffrage for free white males, regardless of wealth and literacy, but limited the vote to citizens of the United States who had resided in Louisiana for two years, and barred the vote to paupers and men in military service. The next Constitution, adopted in 1852, broadened the suffrage qualifications by lowering the state residential requirement to one year, and introduced registration of voters, a progressive step many years in advance of most states. This Constitution required registration for Orleans Parish and made it optional with the legislature for the other parishes.

Thus, from the *Code Noir* of 1724 until 1864, the organic law of the state ordained that only free white males could vote or hold office. This was in a state where there were thousands of free men of color. Many of these were well educated and owned slaves. Except for suffrage, they possessed the civil and legal rights of white citizens.

The Constitutional Convention of 1864 was the first convention in Louisiana to consider Negro suffrage. During the federal occupation of New Orleans, General N. P. Banks, Commander of the Gulf Department, at the direction of President Lincoln, ordered an election of delegates to a constitutional convention. Negroes could not vote for the delegates and were not represented in the Convention. It was attended by delegates from the federally occupied part of the State only: Orleans and eighteen southern parishes which recognized Michael Hahn as Governor. (Henry W. Allen was the Confederate Governor for the rest of the State.) The Constitution of 1864 abolished slavery and provided for free public schools for all children between six and eighteen years, regardless of race, but retained the previous limitation of suffrage to white males. In the early stages of the convention a strong sentiment existed against granting suffrage to the Negroes, and the delegates actually adopted a resolution declaring that the legislature should never pass a law authorizing Negroes to vote. Later in the session, the delegates established a voting qualification, without amending the suffrage ordinance restricting the vote to white males. This was based on an intelligence test, in the interest of permitting Negro suffrage. The resolution in question authorized the legislature "to pass laws extending suffrage to such other persons, citizens of the United States, as by military service, by taxation to support the

Government, or by intellectual fitness, may be deemed entitled thereto." The word "Negro" was not contained in the resolution as proposed in the Convention or in the ordinance as adopted and, at the time, which was before the adoption of the Civil War Amendments, it was generally thought that Negroes were not citizens. Nonetheless, in the debates over the resolution a number of delegates denounced it as a "nigger resolution," and at least one delegate stalked out of the Convention in protest against Negroes being allowed to vote.

The Constitution of 1864 required the registration of *all* voters in the State. In 1867 the State Board of Registration, making its first report, showed 45,189 white and 84,527 Negro registrants. The male population of voting age in Louisiana in 1860 was 94,711 whites and 92,502 Negroes.

Racial relations in Louisiana deteriorated rapidly. In the fall of 1865 the Democrats in Louisiana adopted resolutions "that this is a Government of white people, made and to be perpetuated for the exclusive benefit of the white race," and declared the Constitution of 1864 a creature of fraud. Radical Republicans, refusing to recognize the existing Democratic Government in Louisiana and adopting the Sumner theory that Louisiana was reduced to the status of a territory and as such was entitled to a territorial delegate to Congress, met in convention and called an election for November 6, 1865, to elect a delegate. Henry Clay Warmoth, later Governor, generally regarded in Louisiana histories as a carpetbagger, was elected as the delegate—without opposition. In that election, such as it was, for the first time in the history of the State, Negroes voted freely.

Ominous events progressively increased the friction between the races in the years between the Constitutions of 1864 and 1868. In 1864, relatively peacefully, the Free State Party attempted to establish a government "responsive to loyal white people; the demobilized Confederates, an administration which would restore Louisiana to its ante-bellum condition, except that peonage would replace slavery." By 1865 Confederate veterans had returned in number and in an orderly election that year defeated the Free Staters and gained control of the legislature, mainly by opposing Negro suffrage. The legislature and police juries promptly enacted new Black Codes which reduced the Negro to a "condition which lay between peonage and serfdom" and intensified the activities of Republicans and Northern radicals for Negro suffrage. July 30, 1866, a bloody riot took place in New Orleans at Mechanics Institute. This "massacre" was provoked, it has been said, by "the attempt of some irresponsible white radicals to transfer the franchise from Confederate veterans to freed men." In 1867 the Louisiana legislature rejected the

Fourteenth Amendment. "There followed, as night the day, military reconstruction."

In 1868 General Philip H. Sheridan, Commander of the Fifth Military District of Louisiana and Texas, called a constitutional convention to meet the conditions Congress imposed on the former States of the Confederacy: suffrage regardless of race and ratification of the Fourteenth Amendment. In the election of delegates to the convention, Confederate veterans and Democratic officeholders were barred from the polls. This was the first and last Louisiana constitutional convention to which Negro delegates were admitted; the president of the convention and forty-nine of the ninety-eight delegates were Negroes. In the 1868 Constitution Negroes finally received the right to vote and to hold office. This Constitution disfranchised all persons who had participated directly or indirectly in the War on the Confederate side and, pouring salt on open wounds, required, as a condition to voting, a certificate from Confederate soldiers and Democratic officeholders that "the late rebellion" was "morally and politically wrong." The Constitution of 1868 desegregated the schools, adopted the bill of rights, rejected a literacy test, and prohibited discrimination in public conveyances and places of public accommodation. This was all "that was needed to strengthen the determination of Southern whites to establish white supremacy, at whatever cost. The Constitution of 1868, therefore, instead of closing the breach between whites and blacks, served only to widen it."

As a result of the disfranchisement of many former Confederate soldiers and the enfranchisement of Negroes, the 1868 election resulted in the election of Warmoth as Governor, and of Oscar J. Dunn, a Negro ex-slave, as Lieutenant Governor. Between 1868 and 1896, a number of Negroes held high office in the State: two congressmen, six high state officials, thirty-two state senators, ninety-five state representatives, and one United States Senator, who was not seated; P. B. S. Pinchback served briefly as Governor.

The years from 1864 to 1876 in Louisiana were years of violence and disorder, notwithstanding the presence of federal troops during these years. In 1873 at Colfax, Grant Parish, fifty-nine Negroes and two white persons were killed. After the Colfax riot additional federal troops were sent to Louisiana and stationed at various points to aid officials in keeping order. Louisiana became an armed camp. In 1874 six white Republican officeholders of Red River Parish were killed, after they had surrendered and had agreed to leave the State. Elections were a farce, since "Governor [Kellogg] appointed the registrars, and through them returned his friends to the legislature"; "politicians bribed legislators for party and parish favors, and business men and corporations bribed the politicians for economic privileges." During most of the years between 1866 and 1877 there were two governors and two legislatures. The Republican governors and their elected associates were maintained in office only by the Returning Board and federal troops. Representative white citizens considered it a civic duty to belong first to The Knights of the White Camelia, a secret organization equivalent to the Ku Klux Klan in other states, and, later, to join the White League, a statewide organization which openly advocated white supremacy in a published platform. September 14, 1874, the Crescent City (New Orleans) White League, which was organized militarily, led by influential citizens, successfully fought a pitched battle in New Orleans against 3000 of Kellogg's Negro militia, 1000 Metropolitan Police under General Longstreet, and several hundred federal troops. The White League took over complete control of the City, then the Capitol of Louisiana, and established in the Statehouse Acting Governor Penn and, later, Governor McEnery. President Grant came to the rescue with sufficient troops to support Governor Kellogg's regime, and the White Leaguers returned to their homes without incident. Some years later, Liberty Place Monument was erected to the memory of the sixteen members of the White League who were killed. September 14 is still officially celebrated annually in New Orleans with public ceremonies as the day the tide turned in Louisiana against the Negroes, carpetbaggers, and scalawags who had been in control of state and local government.

The Battle at Liberty Place had an important effect on the election of 1876 when the "Redeemers," the White Democrats under Francis T. Nicholls, defeated the Negro Republican candidate, S. B. Packard. Throughout the State, and especially in New Orleans, armed members of the White League policed the election. Governor Nicholls, who ran as the White League's choice but who had also promised Negroes the continued enjoyment of their constitutional privileges, managed to attract enough Negro ballots to win by a substantial, if contested, vote. Governor Kellogg's Returning Board and, later, the Republican Legislature, declared S. B. Packard elected. Nicholls and Packard were each inaugurated. January 9, 1877, the White League numbering 6000, marched on the Cabildo in New Orleans, where Packard's troops were stationed. The troops surrendered. President Grant, unwilling to take sides because of the pending Hayes-Tilden controversy, ordered the status quo preserved. For four months armed White Leaguers patrolled the streets of New Orleans.

Louisiana was the last of the Southern States to be freed from carpet-bag government. In April 1877 President Hayes, as part of the Hayes-Tilden compromise, removed federal troops from Louisiana and recognized the Nicholls administration as the legal government of the state. These events foreshadowed the "lily white" primary, marked the emergence of the Democratic party in the south as "the institutionalized incarnation of the will to White Supremacy," and led inexorably to the "grandfather" clause, the understanding or interpretation test, and the tricky registration application form as techniques to avoid another Reconstruction.

In 1879, with the State firmly in the control of the White League, another Constitution was adopted. "Its chief objectives apparently, were to put 'white supremacy' back on a firm foundation and bring to an end the oppressive taxation, excessive public spending, and corrupt administration that had plagued the people for a decade." This was before the understanding clause was invented. The solution for the Negro problem devised by the Convention was to transfer powers to the Governor from the legislature and the police juries (county commissioners). The public acccommodations section and most of the provisions in the 1868 Constitution favorable to Negroes were eliminated, but the Constitution of 1879 did not restrict the Negro's right to vote. This may have been because of fear of another federal intervention or because the Negro-White unification movement under General Beauregard had collapsed. Article 188 of that Constitution provided, "No qualifications of any kind for suffrage or office, nor any restraint upon the same, on account of race, color or previous condition shall be made by law."

In the eighties and until 1898 Negroes in Louisiana continued to vote and to have their vote solicited by all parties. This is not surprising. In 1888 there were 127,923 Negro voters and 126,884 white voters on the registration rolls in Louisiana; the population of the state was about fifty per cent Negro.

In the election of 1892, the Louisiana Lottery issue split both parties. Murphy J. Foster, a Democrat, was the successful candidate for governor, but the Negro vote was a decisive factor in Governor Foster's favor in many parishes, a disquieting circumstance necessarily regarded as a mixed blessing. In a four-man race, the Democrats polled only 79,388 votes against a total of 98,647 cast for the Republicans and the newly organized people's Populist party. The next election, in 1896, was the turning point that led directly to the disfranchisement of the Negro in Louisiana. In that election, Governor Foster, running for re-election, defeated John N. Pharr, the choice of a Fusion Party of "National" (Lily white) Republicans, Regular (Radical) Republicans, Populists, and sugar-growers dissatisfied with low tariffs of 1894. It was a bitterly fought election. "The main issue * * * was the problem of Negro suffrage." Again the Negro vote was decisive in many parishes. Again, Foster, who ran on a "white supremacy" platform, had his heaviest majority in parishes where the Negro registration was the heaviest.

At this point, the handwriting on the wall could be read as easily in Louisiana as it was read earlier in Mississippi: something had to be done about Negro Suffrage. Local issues or national issues could split the Democratic party wide open, giving the Negroes the balance of power. And the political ecology of Louisiana made factionalism inevitable. In Louisiana, as in Mississippi and Alabama, there were, and still are, fundamental social and economic differences between the areas controlled by a plantation economy and the areas controlled by a small farm economy. Two potent additional facts of political life aggravate divisiveness in Louisiana: (1) North Louisiana is solidly Protestant, South Louisiana predominantly Catholic; (2) New Orleans and the rest of the State are like oil and water. See Fenton and Vines, Negro Registration in Louisiana, 51 Am.Pol.Sc.Rev. 704 (1957). By 1898, the moral as well as dollar-and-cents costs of buying victory at the polls were finally more than the purchasers were willing to pay.

Promptly after the important election of 1896, Governor Foster requested the Legislature to call a constitutional convention. Former Governor Nicholls, then Chief Justice of the Supreme Court of Louisiana, called the Convention to order February 8, 1898. Judge Thomas J. Semmes, Chairman of the Judiciary Committee of the Convention and a former president of the American Bar Association, described the purpose of the Convention: "We [meet] here to establish the supremacy of the white race, and the white race constitutes the Democratic party of this State." The Convention of 1898 "interpreted its mandate from the 'people' to be, to disfranchise as many Negroes and as few whites as possible."

The understanding clause, invented by Mississippi a few years before as an alternative to a literacy test, was strongly advocated by many of the delegates. After considerable debate, however, *"persuaded that the understanding clause was 'based on fraud'*, the Louisiana Convention rejected it and invented the 'grandfather clause'."

Under Article 197 of the 1898 Constitution, in order to register, an applicant had to meet educational and property qualifications—unless exempted by the "grandfather" clause. The educational test required the applicant to be able to read and write and demonstrate the ability to do so by filling out the application form without assistance. The property test required the applicant to own property assessed at $300 and to have paid the taxes due on the property. The grandfather clause exempted persons entitled to vote on or before January 1, 1867, or the son or grandson of such person. A similar provision exempted immigrants who came to this country after January 1, 1867. At the time, forty per cent of the registered voters in Louisiana were illiterate and most of the Negroes could not meet the property requirement. The result was disfranchisement of almost all of the Negro voters and of some twenty to thirty thousand white voters. Alcée Fortier, one of Louisiana's most respected historians, writing in 1904, succinctly stated the legislative purpose of the grandfather clause:

> "The purpose of this section, known as the 'Grandfather Clause' was to allow many honorable and intelligent but illiterate white men to retain the right of suffrage, and the purpose of the educational or property qualification was to disfranchise the ignorant negroes who had been a menace to the civilization of the state since the adoption of the Fifteenth Amendment to the Constitution of the United States." 4 Fortier, History of Louisiana 235.

On accepting the chair as President of the Convention, Ernest B. Kruttschnitt, a leading lawyer in New Orleans and a veteran of the White League, did not mince his words: "We have here no political antagonism and I am called upon to preside over what is little more than a family meeting of the Democratic Party of the State of Louisiana. * * * We are all aware that this Convention has been called * * * principally to deal with one question * * * to eliminate from the electorate the mass of corrupt and illiterate voters who have during the last quarter century degraded our politics." The Convention voted that no ordinance should be considered until the report of the Committee on Suffrage and Election was finally acted upon by the Convention. Near the end of the Convention, President Kruttschnitt announced:

> "We have not been free; we have not drafted the exact Constitution we should like to have drafted; otherwise we should have inscribed in it, if I know the popular sentiment of the State, Universal White Manhood Suffrage, and the exclusion from the suffrage of every man with a trace of African blood in his veins. * * * What care I whether it be more or less ridiculous or not? Doesn't it meet the case? Doesn't it let the white man vote, and doesn't it stop the negro from voting, and isn't that what we came here for?"

In his message to the legislature, Governor Foster was able to say:

> "The white supremacy for which we have so long struggled at the cost of so much precious blood and treasure, is now crystallized into the Constitution as a fundamental part and parcel of that organic instrument, and that, too, by no subterfuge or other evasions. With this great principle thus firmly imbedded in the Constitution, and honestly enforced, there need be no longer any fear as to the honesty and purity of our future elections."

Following the example of Mississippi, with respect to its 1890 Constitution, Louisana did not submit the 1898 Constitution to the vote of the people.

To make the disfranchisement effective, the legislature directed a complete new registration of all voters. Registration rolls before and after adoption of the Constitution show the prompt effect the grandfather clause had on Negro voters.

	January 1, 1897	March 17, 1900
Number of Negro Voters	130,344	5,320
Number of White Voters	164,088	125,437

The drop in Negro registration continued, so that by 1910 only 730 or less than 0.5 per cent of the adult male Negroes were registered. In the sixty parishes then in existence, there were no Negroes registered in twenty-seven parishes and only one Negro registered in each of another nine parishes. Only ten parishes had more than ten Negro registered voters each. By 1918, when there were sixty-four parishes, thirty-seven parishes had no Negroes registered. Eight other parishes had only a single Negro on the voter registration rolls. "With the adoption of the Constitution of 1898, Louisiana became in fact and practice a white man's state as far as its politics went."

The 1913 Constitution did not change the suffrage provisions of the 1898 Constitution.

In 1915, in *Guinn v. United States,* the Supreme Court declared the Oklahoma grandfather clause unconstitutional. Chief Justice Edward Douglass White, of Louisiana, who fought with "Louisiana's Own" at the Battle of Liberty Place and was the campaign manager for Governor Nicholls in 1888, wrote the opinion.

Against this background, a constitutional convention was called in 1921. Although there were several good reasons for Louisiana to revise its constitution, it was well understood, as reported in the New Orleans Times-Picayune: "Revision of the suffrage provision [was] necessary because the United States Supreme Court [had] declared the famous 'grandfather clause' invalid. * * * Already several substitutes have been proposed, among them the 'understanding clause' from Mississippi * * * and the plan of Ex-Governor R. G. Pleasant to confine the right of suffrage to those who inhabited the earth North of the twentieth degree of North latitude prior to October 12, 1492, when Columbus discovered America. The purpose of his plan is to shut out the Negro."

We are handicapped in studying the legislative history of the Constitution of 1921 because, at the request of Ruffin G. Pleasant, the former Governor, who was Chairman of the Committee on Suffrage and Elections, the Committee met in secrecy and no minutes were kept of any discussion or debate. The newspaper accounts of the proceedings, the next best evidence, quote Governor Pleasant as saying that this was because "there might be one subject coming up for discussion which we would not care to have preserved. * * *" Suffrage was "a delicate question" and the members preferred "not to debate it in the open." No one failed to hear and heed the thunder of the silence.

The Committee first considered and rejected Governor Pleasant's "Christopher Columbus" proposal. The plan finally agreed upon was the plan rejected in 1898 because of its "immorality"—Mississippi's understanding clause, the interpretation test. In reporting the proposal, newspapers of the period consistently referred to it as the Mississippi "understanding" clause, quoting Mr. C. E. Hardin of Vernon Parish and Judge Philip S. Pugh of Arcadia Parish, and described it as a "substitute" or "replacement" for the illegal grandfather clause. For example, a news report of the *Times-Picayune* characterized the plan as, "An ordinance designed to plug the hole shot through the suffrage provision when the United States Supreme Court declared the famous 'grandfather' clause invalid." The Negro community had no trouble recognizing the purpose of the test. A large delegation of Negro leaders from New Orleans, Baton Rouge, Shreveport, and the parishes appeared before the committee to plead in vain for the franchise, and for more educational facilities. "The Convention [also] placed the power to remove any registrar in the State in the hands of an *ex officio* board of registration composed of the governor, lieutenant governor, and speaker, a majority of whom were more likely to be white men. Should any registrar show a tendency to administer the new registration tests too liberally, or otherwise to conduct his office in a manner displeasing to the administration, the state board could remove him at will."

When the Committee on Suffrage and Elections finally agreed on the interpretation test, the Baton Rouge Times accurately reported:

"The grandfather clause is eliminated and there is substituted an understanding and good character clause. * * *"

As Professor Powell said in his study of Louisiana constitutions for the Louisiana Law Institute, "In justice to the Convention, it must be said that even its bitterest critics could not deny that the Negroes were almost completely disfranchised."

As an historical fact, and as appears from the evidence, the interpretation test was rarely, if ever, applied until the early fifties. It was not needed. The Democratic white primary made registration futile for Negroes. The Democratic State Central Committee, acting under authority granted to it by the State, restricted all candidates and voters in the Democratic Party primary elections for state officers to white persons.

"[D]ebarment from the nominating process is in effect disfranchisement. Denial of the privilege of participating in primaries also means, essentially, ineligibility to party membership in general and excludes the negro from all party proceedings such as mass meetings, conventions, or caucuses of voters in the precinct and from delegate conventions in larger areas, to say nothing of party offices and candidacies in the party primaries." Weeks, The White Primary, 8 Miss.L.J. 135, 136 (1935).

The white primary not only effectively kept Negroes from voting in the only election that had any significance in the Louisiana electoral process but it also correspondingly depressed Negro registration to insignificantly low numbers. During the period from 1921 to 1946 Negro registration was never in excess of one per cent of the total registered voters, although the Negro population of the state then constituted about one-third of the potential voters. In 1942 only 957 Negroes were registered to vote in Louisiana and no Negroes were registered in fifty-one of the sixty-four parishes of Louisiana.

In 1944, white primaries, even those conducted by a political party and not by the State, were declared unconstitutional. Smith v. Allwright, 1944, 321 U.S. 649, 64 S.Ct. 757, 88 L.Ed. 987. After the demise of the white primary, Negro registration in Louisiana rapidly increased, rising from 1,029 in 1944 to 7,561 in 1946, to 22,576 in 1948, and to 120,000 in 1952. In 1956 there were 161,410 Negro voters, 15 per cent of the total registered vote in Louisiana, the highest percentage of Negro voters in any state in the southeastern region of the country.

The decline and fall of the white primary, the return of Negro soldiers from World War II, the intensified tempo of activity in Negro organizations after the School Segregation Cases in 1954, and the civil rights explosion all worked toward increasing Negro interest in voting. These and correlative factors made it imperative for parish registrars in Louisiana to utilize the interpretation test, if the State intended to maintain its policy of segregation, historically indissolubly bound with disfranchisement of Negroes.

Immediately following the School Segregation Cases, two strong organizations dedicated to maintaining segregation in Louisiana were established, one by the legislature and one by private persons with official blessing. These two organizations have an important place in the history of the interpretation test. In our study, we see these organizations crossing and recrossing, publicizing and promoting the purpose and function of the test and how best to use it in order to prevent Negro participation in the electoral process. First, in 1954, the Louisiana legislature created a Joint Legislative Committee "to provide ways and means whereby our existing social order shall be preserved and our institutions and ways of life * * * maintained." This was to be accomplished by a program "to maintain segregation of the races in all phases of our life in accordance with the customs, traditions, and laws of our State." This Committee became known as the "Segregation Committee." Its chairman was William M. Rainach, State Senator from Claiborne Parish where there are more Negroes than white persons. Its counsel was William M. Shaw, also from Claiborne Parish. Second, at about the same time or before, Senator Rainach and Mr. Shaw and others organized and incorporated the Association of Citizens Councils of Louisiana to "protect and preserve by all legal means, our historical Southern Social Institutions in all of their aspects." Senator Rainach was the first president of the Citizens Councils. Mr. Shaw was its first secretary. Senator Rainach and Mr. Shaw organized local councils and spearheaded the operations of the Segregation Committee.

In 1956, the Association of Citizens' Councils published a pamphlet, prepared by Mr. Shaw and Senator Rainach, entitled, "Voter Qualification Laws in Louisiana—The Key to Victory in the Segregation Struggle." The pamphlet advocated a two-step program. First, the registration rolls should be purged of "the great numbers of unqualified voters who have been illegally registered," and who "invariably vote in blocks and constitute a menace to the community." Second, registrars should strictly enforce the interpretation test. The pamphlet concludes, "The whole purpose of our registration laws is to prevent the registration of ignorant, 'bloc' voters * * *" The foreword of the pamphlet makes clear who is referred to by the term "bloc" voter:

"The Communists and the NAACP plan to register and vote every colored person of age in the South * * *. They are not concerned with whether or not the colored bloc is registered in accordance with law."

No stress, no strain:

"If our laws are intelligently and fairly administered, they will accomplish our purpose automatically."

The "Key to Victory" is subtitled, "A Manual of Procedure for Registrars of Voters, Police Jurors and Citizens Councils." The booklet was the principal topic of discussion at State-sponsored meetings on voter registration attended by registrars and other public officials and was distributed to all persons attending such meetings. The State of Louisiana distributed it to parish registrars, with instructions to follow closely its purpose and intent. Senator Rainach and Mr. Shaw in their dual role as legislative and Citizens' Council leaders were clothed with State authority as they traveled about the State urging and even demanding that the registrars adopt their program.

Carrying out the first phase of the program, local Citizens Councils and their members conducted extensive purges, principally in 1956-58 in eight parishes throughout the state, under the provisions of the challenge statute, Louisiana R.S. 18:133 (1950) LSA. The evidence shows that primarily Negroes were removed from the rolls, although a few whites were also purged in a token effort to maintain an air of nondiscriminatory treatment. Most registrars cooperated fully with Citizens Council members in conducting the purges when requested to do so. Innumerable white persons whose registration cards showed deficiencies similar to those of the Negroes were not purged. One registrar said in her deposition that in her parish the Citizens Council members conducting the purges corrected the errors they made *on their own registration applications, while at the same time challenging Negroes for similar mistakes.* Many purges were for failure to take the interpretation test, *even though that test had not been administered at the time of the registrant's application.* When contested in federal court, these purges were found to be illegal deprivations of the Negroes' constitutional rights. . . .

In late 1958 and early 1959 the Segregation Committee and the State Board of Registration jointly sponsored meetings in each congressional district. Registrars were required to attend; sheriffs, police jurors, and other parochial officials, and officers of citizens councils also attended the meetings. At these meetings the Citizens Council's "Key to Victory" was officially distributed to the registrars. Senator Rainach, at that time still Chairman of the Segregation Committee and President of the Association of Citizens Councils, was the chairman at these meetings. Mr. Shaw, at that time was still counsel for the Segregation Committee and still counsel for the Association. They led these meetings, vigorously emphasizing the importance of maintaining segregation.

Senator Rainach would tell the registrars, "The fight for school integration in the South has shifted * * * to a fight for the voters of the Negro masses * * * *" He pointed out to the registrars that during the Reconstruction Period, when Negroes were permitted to vote, the public schools of Louisiana were integrated, and that, with the Negroes representing 32 per cent of the population of the state, the Negroes could easily do again what they did during the Reconstruction Era, if they should become registered to vote.

According to Senator Rainach, "In 1897, our forefathers in Louisiana started a program of voter qualification law enforcement, knowing that such a program would provide the solution to their problems." The present voter qualification laws "are adequate to solve our present problems * * *" Senator Rainach stressed that "registrars have become critically important officials * * * they have become the focal point of the solution to our problems."

Mr. Shaw would explain the registrar's part. The *"key to the solution of our whole problem lies in the interpretation of the Constitution," Mr. Shaw told the registrars.* He urged the registrars to require applicants to interpret the constitution and provided them with 25 test cards to be used for this purpose. Mr. Shaw instructed the registrars:

> "[T]he constitutional test and their ability to understand the duties and responsibilities under a republican form of government, which is another one of the tests, is basically a test of a person's understanding, which is native intelligence in that you can educate a fool, but you'd still have nothing but an educated fool when you get through, and he wouldn't be able to quality. And therefore, *if they were correctly and fairly administered*—that's the key to the whole thing—directed fairly—then it will amount to a test of ability, of a person's understanding, which is native ability.   It is not education. Education can merely refine native understanding.   If you have no native understanding to start out with, it can't be refined."   (Emphasis added.)

Mr. Shaw also told the registrars:

> "Constitutional tests are a test of native intelligence and not 'book learning.' Experience teaches that most of our own white people have this native intelligence while most Negroes do not."

Mrs. Mary C. Flournoy, former Registrar of Winn Parish, gives us some indication of the meaning of "correctly and fairly administer[ing]" the test.   She stated that Senator Rainach, while he was Chairman of the Segregation Committee, told her to discriminate on account of race in processing applications:

> "Rainach told me if * * * I can't fail them [Negro applicants] any other way, I could pull those Constitution reading cards on them.
> " * * * Rainach wanted me to pull those hard cards on colored people."

The Louisiana *Codes Noir* of Colonial times and the Black Codes of the eighteen sixties; the pre-Civil War denial of the vote to Negroes, even to wealthy and educated free men of color; the ebb and flow of Negro rights in the Constitutions of 1864 and 1868; the 1879 transfer of political power from police juries and the legislature to the Governor; the close election of 1892 and the 1896 victory for white supremacy; the grandfather clause and the complicated registration application form in the Constitution of 1898; the invalidity of the grandfather clause and the consequent resort to Mississippi's understanding and interpretation clause; the effectiveness of the white primary as a means of disfranchising Negroes; the invalidity of the white primary and the consequent need to revive enforcement of the interpretation test; the White League and the Citizens' Councils; the Black League and the NAACP; the Battle of Liberty Place in 1874 and the Ouachita voting purge of 1956—these are all related members of a series, all reactions to the same dynamics that produced the interpretation test and speak eloquently of its purpose.

In sum, the interpretation test is another grandfather clause. Its purpose is rooted in the same history. It has the same objective the delegates to the Constitutional Convention of 1898 envisaged for the grandfather clause. It is capable of producing the same effective disfranchisement of Negroes today that the grandfather clause produced sixty-five years ago.

Having determined the true reason for the interpretation test in its historical setting, we turn from *why* to *how* the test is used as a discriminatory device.

There are two reasons for a court to consider how a law is administered. The obvious reason is that any regulatory statute may be administered unfairly. If so, the court may enjoin the unfair acts without passing on the validity of the statute. But there is another reason. Just how a law is actually used by those charged with administering it is a proper guide to the purpose of the law and its necessary effect. Here, we find massive evidence that the registrars discriminated against Negroes not as isolated or accidental or unpredictable acts of unfairness by particular individuals, but as a matter of state policy in a pattern based on the regular, consistent, predictable unequal application of the test. This is the inescapable effect of a subjective requirement such as an understanding or interpretation test barren of standards and safeguards, the administration of which rests in the uncontrolled discretion of a registrar.

The United States introduced a great mass of evidence in the record, but with commendable diligence made it digestible by well-prepared indices and well-organized summaries. The evidence of discriminatory application of the interpretation test is especially well documented and supported by testimony with respect to the following parishes: Plaquemines, East Feliciana, Webster, Bienville, Red River, Jackson and Ouachita.

First of all, a Louisiana registrar has the power to use or not to use the interpretation test. The parties to this case stipulated that the test had never been used in the four largest parishes of the state, Caddo, Jefferson, East Baton Rouge, and Orleans. These parishes have almost forty per cent of the total number of registered voters in the State. The United States introduced evidence that the interpretation test was used in twenty-one parishes. No mention was made of the other thirty-nine parishes in the state. The evidence shows that the test was seldom, if ever, applied anywhere in Louisiana before 1954 because, as previously pointed out, until the white primary was invalidated there was no need for the test. This means that the *majority of Louisiana voters now registered under the permanent registration law have never taken the test.*

In the twenty-one parishes where it has been shown that the interpretation test has been used, as of December 31, 1962, only 8.6 per cent of the adult Negroes were registered as against 66.1 per cent of the adult white persons registered. Before the interpretation test was put into use, a total of 25,361 Negroes were registered in the twenty-one parishes using the test. By August 31, 1962, total Negro registration in these parishes was 10,351. During the same period, white registration was not discernibly affected.

The decision to enforce the interpretation test more than thirty years after its adoption was accompanied, in almost every parish where the test has been used, by a wholesale purge of Negro voters or by periodic registration so that Negro voters were required to re-register *after* the test came into use. Citizens Council members challenged the registration of large numbers of Negro voters on the ground that they had not satisfied all of the requirements of the Louisiana voter qualification laws at the time they registered. Actually, the challenged Negroes had satisfied all the requirements imposed by the registrar *at the time* they registered. White voters had registered under the same standards and procedures as the Negroes and their registrations suffered from the same alleged deficiencies as the Negroes who were purged. In at least two parishes, Ouachita and East Feliciana, one ground for challenging Negroes was that they had not interpreted or were not able to interpret a constitutional section, even though the test had not been used in either parish before the purge.

In most parishes where there was a purge, since the Negroes were unable to gain reinstatement in the manner prescribed by Louisiana law, they were required to re-register. And to do so they had to pass the interpretation test. The white voters, not having been challenged, in effect were exempted from the test. The discrimination brought about by the purge and the use of the interpretation test was frozen into the system in parishes such as Bienville, DeSoto, Jackson, Ouachita and Rapides, which have permanent registration. In parishes using periodic registration the purges had a deterrent effect on Negro registration which is still felt.

The registrar's whim alone determines which applicants will be tested. The Constitution merely states that applicants "shall *be able to* understand and give a reasonable interpretation" of a section of a constitution. Some registrars, for example, those in LaSalle, Lincoln, and Webster parishes, have interpreted this to mean that the applicant need not actually interpret the constitution, only that he have the ability to do so. The State Board of Registration maintained at one time that the correct interpretation was that the applicant must demonstrate his ability in all cases. It has, however, changed its understanding or interpretation of this very section of the Constitution. After the institution of this suit, the Board prescribed another test, instructing registrars to cease requiring an interpretation. The change in the interpretation given the interpretation-test provision of the Constitution by the State agency charged with enforcing it and the wide variety of interpretations adopted by the registrars reaffirm the impossibility of achieving objective standards for an interpretation of the Constitution acceptable to the State. Pity the applicant asked to interpret the interpretation test!

The Louisiana Constitution contains 443 sections, as against 56 sections in the United States Constitution, and is the longest and the most detailed of all state constitutions. The printed copy published by the State, unannotated, contains 600 pages, not counting an index of 140 pages. The evidence clearly demonstrates great abuses in the selection of sections of the constitutions to be interpreted. Some registrars have favorite sections which they apparently use regardless of an applicant's race. Some open a volume containing the United States and Louisiana Constitutions and, like soothsayers seeking divine help from the random flight of birds, require an applicant to interpret the section on the page where the book opens. The Segregation Committee distributed to registrars sets of twenty-four cards, each containing three sections of the Constitution with instructions that they be used in administering the interpretation test. The Registrar of Ouachita Parish used a set of test cards containing sections chosen by the Citizens' Council. The Registrar of Plaquemines used cards and answers prepared by Mr. Leander Perez, District Attorney for the Parish.

It is evident from the record that frequently the choice of difficult sections has made it impossible for many Negro applicants to pass. White applicants were more often given easy sections, many of which could be answered by short, stock phrases such as "freedom of speech," "freedom of religion," "States' rights," and so on. Negro applicants, on the other hand, were given parts of the Louisiana Constitution such as Article VII, § 41; Article X, § 1, § 16; Article XIV, § 23, § 24.2.

As in the selection process, gross abuses of discretion appear in the evaluation of the interpretations. One rejected Negro applicant stated that the registrar "said what I was saying was right, but it wasn't like she wanted me to say it."

Most of the interpretation tests have been administered orally, thus precluding the use of written records as a check on what the registrar accepted as reasonable interpretations. Nevertheless, the record shows that more interpretations far less responsive to the constitutional text selected have been accepted from whites than from Negroes. Compounding this with the fact that Negroes were often given more difficult sections to interpret, the bias in favor of the whites becomes readily apparent.

Some parishes administered written examinations and kept records of the questions asked and the responses accepted. In these examinations the registrar usually employed one or more of several sets of cards containing selected sections of the Constitution and a space for the applicant's interpretation of it. Even the most cursory glance at the records in these parishes underscores the heavy burden under which Negro applicants were laboring. In one set of cards, there is great disparity in the difficulty of the questions asked. This enables the registrar to select cards with simple sections for white applicants and difficult cards for Negroes. There is unmistakable evidence that many white applicants were shown cards with sample answers on them. Some applicants admitted this, and there is even an instance of a white applicant having, by mistake, signed the sample answer card. Negroes were not allowed to see the acceptable answers, let alone copy them. Similarly, the pattern of the answers indicates that the registrars often told white applicants the currently acceptable answers. The phraseology of almost every answer in one parish changed right along with the registrar's change in the wording of the acceptable answer.

Registrars were easily satisfied with answers from white voters. In one instance "FRDUM FOOF SPETGH" was an acceptable response to the request to interpret Article 1, § 3 of the Louisiana Constitution.

On the other hand, the record shows that Negroes whose application forms and answers indicate that they are highly qualified by literacy standards and have a high degree of intelligence have been turned down although they had given a reasonable interpretation of fairly technical clauses of the constitution. For example the Louisiana Constitution, Article X, § 16 provides: "Rolling stock operated in this State, the owners of which have no domicile therein, shall be assessed by the Louisiana Tax Commission, and shall be taxed for State purposes only, at a rate not to exceed forty mills on the dollar assessed value." The rejected interpretation was: "My understanding is that it means if the owner of which does not have residence within the State, his rolling stock shall be taxed not to exceed forty mills on the dollar."

In another instance the registrar rejected the following interpretation of the Search and Seizure provision of the Fourth Amendment: "[N]obody can just go into a person's house and take their belongings without a warrant from the law, and it had to specify in this warrant what they were to search and seize." Another rejected interpretation of the same Amendment by a Negro applicant was: "To search you would have to get an authorized authority to read a warrant." The Louisiana Constitution Article I, § 5 provides: "The people have the right peaceably to assemble." A registrar rejected the following interpretation: "That one may assemble or belong to any group, club, or organization he chooses as long as it is within the law."

Each of these incidents *could* conceivably be an isolated event, indicating personal dereliction by one registrar, regrettable, but basically trivial in the general adminstration of the interpretation test. However, the great number of these and other examples, illustrative of a conscious decision, show conclusively that the discriminatory acts were not isolated or accidental or peculiar to the individual registrar but were part of a pervasive pattern and practice of disfranchisement by discriminatory use of the interpretation test.

The State does not deny that unlimited discretion is vested in the registrars by the laws of Louisiana, but argues that officials must act reasonably and that their decisions are subject to review by district courts. Louisiana, however, provides no effective method whereby arbitrary and capricious action by registrars of voters may be prevented or redressed. Unreviewable discretion was built into the test.

The State Board of Registration recently recognized the arbitrary nature of the test, and, as indicated earlier in this opinion, abandoned its general use after the institution of this suit. However, the Constitution and statutes of Louisiana still require the use of the understanding and interpretation test. And registrars have not entirely abandoned it, despite the institution of the new test. For example, as late as April 1963 the Webster registrar was using the interpretation test because, as she explained, "it's still on the books"; sometimes she gave the citizenship test and sometimes the interpretation test. Voters registering now could be challenged and purged in the future for not taking the interpretation test—should history repeat itself. This is exactly what happened in the middle and late nineteen-fifties.

The statistics demonstrate strikingly the effect of resurrection of the interpretation test. A report of the Louisiana Sovereignty Committee, December 14, 1960, boasts:

"We would like to call your attention to the fact that, during this four year period of time, from 1956 until 1960, 81,214 colored people became of voting age, when the registration figures of colored people actually declined 2,377. Going further during this four year period, we had 114,529 white people who became of voting age and, during this four year period of time, the white registration increased 96,620."

The State of Louisiana accomplished its purpose in the parishes where the constitutional interpretation test was used. In those twenty-one parishes, registration of white persons between 1956 and December 31, 1960, increased from 161,069 to 162,427; registration of Negroes decreased from 25,361 to 10,256.

*   *   *   *

We summarize our holding. The Court holds that the interpretation test is unconstitutional because of its unlawful purpose, operation, and inescapably discriminatory effect. We enjoin its use in Louisiana. To make this decree effective and to exorcise past discrimination, the Court enjoins the use of the "citizenship test" in the Parishes of Bienville, Claiborne, DeSoto, East Carroll, East Feliciana, Franklin, Jackson, LaSalle, Lincoln, Morehouse, Ouachita, Plaquemines, Rapides, Red River, Richland, St. Helena, Union, Webster, West Carroll, West Feliciana, and Winn as to all persons of voting age who had the requisite residence in the parish before August 3, 1962. These are parishes where the registrars used the interpretation test. We enjoin the use of the citizenship test in the named parishes until there has been a general re-registration of all voters in a named parish, or until it has been shown, to the satisfaction of the court, that the interpretation test has lost its discriminatory effect in the parish.

Voting in Mississippi, U.S. Commission on Civil Rights (1965)

*   *   *   *

Chapter 4. Economic Dependence and Fear of Economic Reprisal

Since its organization in 1957 the Commission has received numerous reports from Mississippi of economic intimidation and reprisal in connection with registration and voting. At the hearing the Chairman of the Mississippi Advisory Committee to the Commission reported:

> Many other witnesses appearing before the advisory committee testified that those seeking to register to vote have been fired from their jobs, have had their loans called in, and their credit cut off, have been forced to leave their homes, and, in many cases, have been subjected to acts of physical violence.

Even before the hearing had closed, the Commission received a complaint that during the preceding two weeks three Negro residents of Carroll County had been discharged from employment following their attempt to register. While it is often difficult to determine whether a discharge or other economic sanction has been imposed in reprisal for registration, Commission investigation revealed that charges of such reprisal are widely circulated and that large numbers of Mississippi Negroes fear the economic consequences of an attempt to register and vote. This belief was reflected in the testimony given by Aaron Henry, a leader of the NAACP in Mississippi:

> Any step which will bring a Negro into the public view, in an effort to register to vote, will increase the likelihood that an employer, or a creditor, or a landlord will deprive him of the economic necessities of life.
> This problem is amplified manyfold by the extreme degree of poverty which exists among the Negro communities of Mississippi. To take an economic risk in Mississippi is to risk life itself.

Economic Dependence and Low Income

Fears of economic reprisal are rooted in the economic dependence of Negroes on whites in Mississippi. Most Negroes look to whites for employment, for loans, for credit to purchase food, seed and fertilizer, for use of farm equipment, or for a monthly welfare check.

The pattern of dependence appears particularly strong where Negroes are employed in agriculture. In the counties studied by the Commission between 60 and 85 percent of the Negroes were so employed. In 1959 about 35 percent of Mississippi's total Negro employment was in agriculture, while the comparable figure for white agricultural employment was about 13 percent. Approximately 60 percent of the Negro farmers worked as tenants, most of them on land owned by whites. Most of these tenants are classified as "croppers." Croppers differ from other farm tenants in that they are subject to close supervision by the landlord or his agent and are dependent upon them for work animals or tractor power.

Witnesses at the hearing from predominantly agricultural counties testified that the fear of economic reprisal prevented Negroes from attempting to register or vote. In Issaquena County Negro farmers were reportedly "afraid to go [register] and get cut off their welfare and get thrown off the farms and everything else * * *"

A witness from Humphreys County testified that Negroes were afraid to come forward and register. Asked why, he replied, "They're afraid they'll lose their jobs, afraid of not getting money * * *."

A Negro witness from Carroll County, who attempted unsuccessfully to persuade Negroes to register, testified that Negroes told him that they would be denied credit if they made the attempt.

A witness from Tallahatchie County reported that Negroes were afraid of "economic squeezes." Another believed that economic reprisal was the reason law enforcement officers photographed registration applicants:

> Well, I thought [the photographing] meant just about what it did mean, that they take your picture and if you had any credit with anybody they probably give them a picture to let them know you were up there and they probably cut out your credit * * *

The fears generated by dependence have been sharpened by extreme poverty. In 1959 the median income of Negro men in Mississippi was $984 a year, and of Negro women, $596 a year. White men in Mississippi earned more than three times as much as Negro men, and white women earned more than twice as much as Negro women. In 1959 more than 70 percent of occupied Negro rural housing was classed by the Bureau of Census as deteriorated or dilapidated—which means that the structures were becoming, or had become, unfit for human habitation. More than three-quarters of rural Negro homes were without plumbing.

In the counties studied by the Commission, median yearly income for Negro families ranged from $885 in Carroll County to slightly more than $1,600 in Washington County. The range for white families in the same counties was $2,500 in Carroll to $5,600 in Washington. In the Delta Negroes cut and chop cotton in the late spring and early summer at $3 per ten-hour day. In the fall they pick cotton for approximately $4 per ten-hour day. The near destitution of many Negroes makes any economic reprisal a major disaster.

The poverty of Mississippi Negroes also affects their ability to comply with Mississippi voting laws. A Negro desiring to qualify to vote for the first time must pay $4 in poll taxes. At the wage rates prevailing in the Delta, many Negroes would need a day or more of labor to earn this amount. Payment of the tax for each adult would constitute a significant expenditure for a family whose yearly income is less than $1,000.

Under Title I of the 1964 Civil Rights Act an applicant for registration is entitled upon written demand to receive a copy of any literacy test. Witnesses testified that the registrar of Issaquena County charged $2.50 for such copies and the registrar of Humphreys County testified that he charged $1.50. While the 1964 Act does not specify that no charge should be made, the imposition of fees in these counties has inhibited the exercise of a right conferred by Congress.

Teachers

Economic dependence and fear of economic reprisal are not confined to Negroes in the lowest economic status. Frequently Negroes with relatively good economic positions or with superior education are those who feel most vulnerable to the white community. School teachers and public employees with incomes well above the Negro median rely on white officials for their employment. In short, Negroes with the most to lose may be among the first to be deterred from registration or voting by the fear of economic consequences.

Among the best educated and best paid Negroes in Mississippi are the public school teachers. Prior to its recent investigation in Mississippi, the Commission had received reports that in some counties Negro teachers had failed to attempt to register because of fear of economic reprisal.

At the hearing the Commission heard testimony from the Executive Secretary of the all-Negro Mississippi Teachers Association. He stated that Negro teachers in Mississippi failed to register or vote because "they are afraid that they will lose their jobs. Their principal has been informed by their superintendent of education * * * if you try to register in this system, you won't have a job next year." He further stated that in his opinion teachers in many Mississippi counties were justified in this fear. He emphasized that all superintendents of education in Mississippi were white.

Two other witnesses, both of whom had taught school for many years in Mississippi, told the Commission that they knew of no Negro teachers registered to vote in their respective counties. One witness, a retired teacher, testified that he was the only teacher registered to vote in Carroll County. In the 1950's he had attempted unsuccessfully to convince other Negro school teachers to register. When asked why his efforts had failed, he replied:

> My opinion is they were afraid of their job. In the first place some of the teachers in the school went to the courthouse and paid their poll tax. The superintendent * * * heard of it and called them in and let them know if they are going to register for voting they wouldn't have a job, and consequently everybody had to back up.

Another retired teacher, who had taught school for 35 years in Tallahatchie County, testified she knew of no other Negro teacher in her county who was registered to vote. She became a registered voter only after she retired from teaching and began receiving social security payments. . . .

VI
Violence and Law Enforcement

OFFICIAL ABUSE

The chief focus of the President's Committee Report in 1947 was on the violence and injustice to which the Negroes were subjected. "Too many of our people still live under the harrowing fear of violence or death at the hands of the mob or of brutal treatment by police officers. Many fear entanglement with the law because of the knowledge that the justice rendered in some courts is not equal for all persons." There is perhaps no greater black mark against American society than that Negroes in many communities are still subject to the same fears of violence and brutality described in the 1947 report.

In 1964, a series of affidavits were obtained from Mississippi Negroes to show the extent of official interference with their rights in that state. The affidavits were collected in a book entitled, Mississippi Black Paper *and two of them are set out below.*

Mississippi Black Paper (1965)

HINDS COUNTY

I am a resident of Jackson, Negro, 22 years of age.

On July 5, 1961, I was in the Trailways bus station in Jackson, Mississippi, trying to get a ticket to New Orleans. Jackson police came up, asked me to move from the white section. I refused and the police hit me three times on the back of the neck with night sticks. This was during the Freedom Rides sponsored by CORE. I was then taken to city jail and charged with breach of the peace; and was eventually taken to the state penitentiary on conviction of $200 and four months. I served 45 days in the penitentiary. While I was still in city jail I had to see a doctor because my neck was bleeding from the beating in the Trailways station. The police allowed a doctor into the jail to give me treatment.

On March 9, 1962 (approximately), I went to the county courthouse in Jackson (Hinds County) to attend a trial of Diane Nash. I went into the courtroom and I took a seat on the so-called white side. I was approached by the bailiff of the court, asking me to move to the Negro side. I refused. The presiding judge, Russell Moore, then asked me to move from the bench. He stopped the trial for this purpose. I asked him why. He gave no reason and just said: "Are you going to move?" Then he said I was under arrest for contempt of court. I was then taken to county jail by the bailiff of the court. On the 22nd I had my trial. I had no lawyer. I asked Judge Russell Moore to continue my trial so that I could obtain a lawyer. He said: "Motion denied." I made another motion that he step down from the bench and have another judge in his place so he could take the witness stand and testify why he had placed me under arrest. He said: "Motion denied," again. He then put the bailiff on the witness stand, who testified that I had come into the court to start trouble and that I had been sitting "on the wrong side of the courtroom."

Then I asked the bailiff some questions. I asked him if he had authority to tell everyone in the courtroom where to sit and he said yes. Then I asked him why did he ask me to move. He said that the seats in my area had been reserved for some witnesses in the court. I then asked whether a white minister who had been sitting next to me and had come down from the North to observe the trial had been a witness. The bailiff said no. I asked why not. He said he had the right to ask whoever he wanted to move. Then he said: "We didn't want you to sit there." I then asked: "In other words the courtroom is segregated?" And he replied, "Yes." I then testified in my behalf. I said that my arrest had been unconstitutional, and that if released that day I would go right back into the courtroom and sit anywhere I pleased. I was then sentenced to $100 fine and 30 days on the county farm.

The bailiff who had testified was the one who took me back upstairs. And on our way back to the elevator, I asked him how long he had been working for the court. He said: "None of your damn business." I then said: "You guys are pretty smart. First you segregate us, and then you testify against us in court and tell lies." At this point he got mad and called over three deputy sheriffs. He said: "Ride on up in the elevator with me. This nigger's trying to get tough." The deputies told me to put my hands up against the wall of the elevator. Then they started to beat me. They beat me with their fists until I fell to the floor. Then they began to kick me in the face and side. All four officers took part in the beating. When they put me in the cell, I was bleeding from my nose, above my eyes, and on the back of my neck. I asked for a doctor. The jailer refused to call one.

I was in the county jail for about a week and was then shifted to the county farm. I was singled out as a "troublemaker." I was the only prisoner there dressed in completely striped uniform, most prisoners being dressed in overalls and a T-shirt. I was told that if I was seen talking to anybody, the person that I talked to would be beaten. I was told that I must address all the guards as "Captain" and that if I didn't obey the guards' orders I would be punished.

I was assigned to the road gang, under a Captain ————. He asked me what I was in for. I said contempt of court. He said: "You're one of those god-damn Freedom Riders." I said I didn't know what that meant. He said: "Well, I'm going to have to whip your ass." Then he called four other prisoners and said: "Take this nigger to the woods, and we're going to whip his ass." They threw me on the ground and started pulling off my clothes. He took up a long hose pipe and hit me about fifteen times on the back, neck, buttocks, etc. Then he said, "Get up and put on your clothes." I asked him what he did that for. He said: "We always break in new people like that." Then I said: "I'm going to have to report you to the superintendent, and file a complaint with federal officers." Then he looked at the other prisoners and said: "Well, we got a smart nigger here." I laid back down and pulled off my clothes again and asked if he was going to beat me again. He said: "No, get up." When we got back to the county farm I asked to see the superintendent. He came in and asked me what I wanted. I told him what had happened. He asked me what I was going to do about it. I told him I wanted to file a complaint against the guard, and if he didn't do anything about it I would file a complaint against him. He asked me not to do that, and that if I did I would "catch hell." Then he left. He seemed both worried and mad. He pleaded with me not to file a complaint, but he shook and acted like he'd like to shoot me.

About a week later, the same guard asked me to move a three-hundred-pound log. I told him I wouldn't. He started to hit me with a big stick he picked up off the ground. He hit me fifteen or twenty times. I grabbed the stick out of his hand and threw it away and said that if he ever hit me again, "me and him was going to have it." He pulled out his gun and started backing up and shaking and saying: "Nigger, I ought to kill you." Then he put me in a truck and took me back to the county farm, and took me to the superintendent and told the superintendent that I had hit him. Then they put me in a car and brought me back to the county jail and threw me in solitary.

I was in solitary for 36 hours. The cell was 9 by 12, a "sweatbox." I was naked. The cell was a big steel vault in the ground, with no windows. They turned on heated air into the vault, and left it on all the time I was in the cell. Then they came back and took me back to the county farm. They started asking me questions, such as whether I was ready to "act right." I said, "If somebody treat me right." They said that everything would be okay.

Then they put me back on the same road gang. After about one week, the guard (Captain ————), pulled out a long hose pipe and started to beat me one day without provocation. He struck me about 10 or fifteen times. I asked him why he had done that. He said: "You one of them smart-ass niggers. I don't like your ass." He took me back again to the county farm. I was put in a cell for about four days until I was released.

SIGNED: *Jesse Harris*

COAHOMA COUNTY

I am a Negro, 21 years old.

On February 6, 1962, when I was 19, I was walking with a young man down a Clarksdale street when Clarksdale police officers ———— and ———— stopped us and accused me of having been involved in a theft. I was taken to jail by the officers and they forced me to unclothe and lie on my back. One of the officers beat me between my legs with a belt. A few minutes later, the other officer began to beat me across my naked breasts.

SIGNED: *Bessie Turner*

*   *   *   *

EQUAL PROTECTION IN THE SOUTH

The Civil Rights Commission in its report "Law Enforcement—A Report on Equal Protection in the South" describes the failure of many southern officials to protect Negroes exercising their rights in a number of locales in the South.

Law Enforcement: A Report on Equal Protection in the South, United States Commission on Civil Rights (1965)

*   *   *   *

Chapter 3.   Failure to Protect or Prosecute

Many of the incidents of racial violence described in the preceding chapter were clandestine attacks. In some cases, however, violence occurred in circumstances where law enforcement officers were or could have been present to take preventive action or make arrests. Nevertheless, in only a few cases, were arrests made for crimes of racial violence. The Commission investigated the manner in which police performed their duty to prevent violence and make arrests. It also studied the conduct of prosecutors in seeking indictments and obtaining convictions.

Failure to Protect Persons Exercising Federal Rights

The failure of law enforcement officials to protect persons exercising Federal rights from violence interferes as decisively with the exercise of those rights as would a direct prohibition. The best known example of such interference is the 1961 Freedom Rides in Alabama.[1] In that instance, a Federal judge issued an injunction against the police requiring them to protect the Freedom Riders, stating that their prior failure was a direct interference with the right to travel in interstate commerce.[2] Since that time, as attempts by Negros to exercise Federal rights in the South have increased, violence by private citizens against persons exercising these rights has also increased. The Commission studied several cases in which law enforcement officers—although present and aware of the possibility of violence—failed to prevent such violence or to arrest the persons responsible.

GREENWOOD, MISSISSIPPI

In Greenwood, the county seat of Leflore County, two Negro brothers, Silas and Jake McGhee, tried repeatedly in July 1964 to attend the previously segregated Leflore Theater. The managed admitted them, as required by the Civil Rights Act of 1964, but angry crowds of whites gathered frequently at the theater, attempted to keep white patrons away by picketing with signs saying, "This is a nigger theater," and beat and harassed Negroes when they attended the theater. The building was also stoned by the crowds.

Silas McGhee first attempted to attend the theater on July 5. He was attacked by a group of men. Although he reported the incident immediately to the city police, no arrests were made. His brother Jake McGhee was attacked at the theater on July 8. Following this assault, the police attempted to persuade the manager of the theater to sign a warrant for his arrest. On July 16 Silas McGhee was abducted by a gang of men who referred to his having attended the theater and who then beat him

---

[1] See *1961 Report of the U.S. Commission on Civil Rights, Justice* 29-33. See also Marshall, *Federalism and Civil Rights* 66-68 (1964).

[2] *United States* v. *U.S. Klans*, 194 F. Supp. 897 (M.D. Ala. 1961).

with pipes and boards. Although McGhee swore out a warrant before the justice of the peace, no arrests were made by local officials.[3]

During this period the manager of the theater and the McGhees made repeated requests to city officials for protection but received none. The police made no attempt to stop the violence or to disperse the crowds which, for three weeks, gathered in front of the theater. The only action taken by city officials was to close the theater temporarily, pursuant to a special ordinance enacted for that purpose. According to the manager of the theater, on one occasion the city officials told him that they were occupied protecting the city's other theater, which continued to refuse to admit Negroes.

On July 26 the McGhees attended the theater and when they attempted to leave, they found a large, noisy, hostile crowd blocking their way. They called the police from inside the theater and requested protection. The police came but refused to escort the McGhees from the theater or to disperse the crowd. The McGhees were told: "You got yourselves in this damn mess, so get yourselves out." As they left the theater, Silas McGhee was struck in the face by a white man. Other whites in the crowd pummeled, kicked, and spat at them. When the McGhees drove away, a bottle was thrown through the car window, spraying glass in their faces. Followed by the hostile crowd, they were taken by a friend to a local hospital to be treated for injuries. The police chief refused to escort them home and, after several hours, the sheriff escorted them through the crowd. No arrests were made although numerous police officers were present at both the theater and the hospital.

A few weeks later Silas McGhee was shot and received a near fatal wound as he sat in a car in the Negro neighborhood. The police investigated but, again, no arrests were made.

Following these events, the Department of Justice brought suit against the police and city administration, contending that the failure to provide protection constituted a denial of the right to public accommodations in violation of the Civil Rights Act of 1964. An order was sought compelling the authorities to provide protection. Trial before a three-judge court was held in January 1965.

*   *   *   *

Failure to Prosecute Persons Responsible for Racial Violence

The Commission also investigated the conduct of prosecutors in the

---

[3] Interview with Silas McGhee, Oct. 4, 1964. The men were subsequently arrested by agents of the FBI, *United States* v. *Belk,* No. GCr-659 (N.D. Miss.). Trial has been delayed pending the decision in *United States* v. *Guest,* prob. juris noted, 381 U.S. 932 (1965), see Ch. 6, *infra,* pp. 109-12.

few cases in Mississippi in which persons were arrested for committing acts of racial violence. Most of these cases were never brought to trial and in the very few cases in which trials were held, defendants were either acquitted or received suspended sentences or minimal fines.

The officials responsible for instituting prosecutions to enforce State law are the county and district attorneys. Both are elected officials—the county attorney by the county and district attorney by a district composed of from two to seven counties. The district attorney is charged with the duty of attending "the deliberations of the grand jury" and with prosecuting all criminal cases for the State in the circuit court. The county attorney must "represent the State" before the grand jury and prosecute criminal cases in county and justice of the peace courts.

Neither district nor county attorneys investigate the cases they present to the grand jury. They are not authorized to have any legal or investigative staff, nor do they generally receive funds for investigation, for office expenses, or for secretarial assistance. As a result, both prosecuting attorneys tend to rely heavily on the sheriff's investigative services. As one prosecuting official described it:

> [The district and county attorneys] usually don't keep a lot of files in Mississippi; they depend on the sheriff. They don't get a lot of volu......ous reports and records; they have no facilities. The district attorneys have no investigators and must rely on the sheriff to furnish them any evidence they have.

*   *   *   *

FORREST COUNTY

On July 10, 1964, Rabbi Arthur J. Lelyveld, from Cleveland, Ohio, was walking along a street in Hattiesburg in Forrest County, Mississippi, accompanied by two white civil rights workers and two Negro girls. He was assaulted and seriously injured by three white men who struck him repeatedly with an iron bar. Two of his assailants subsequently surrendered to Hattiesburg police and were released on $2,500 bond on charges of assault with intent to maim. Rabbi Lelyveld received a subpoena in Cleveland and appeared before a Forrest County grand jury on August 7, 1964.

In an affidavit furnished to the Commission, Lelyveld stated that he was questioned by District Attorney James Finch before the grand jury and identified his assailants from photographs. His examination by Finch was confined almost entirely to these questions: why he had come to Hattiesburg; whether it was true that the white boys had been embracing the Negro girls before the attack took place; where he had slept during his visit to Hattiesburg; and whether Negroes were sleeping there as well.[4]

When the grand jury failed to indict those identified by Lelyveld, the district attorney filed an information charging them with simple assault— a misdemeanor. They pleaded no contest to these charges, were fined $500 and given 90 days hard labor, which was suspended.

*   *   *   *

Chapter 4. Official Interference With the Exercise of Federal Rights

Failures by State and local officials to prevent violence or punish those responsible has not been the only obstacle to the assertion of Federal rights by Negroes. State and local officials, by deliberately abusing legal processes, have thwarted or attempted to punish citizens exercising or attempting to exercise these rights.

In its study of these abuses, the Commission focused on the reactions of State and local officials to attempts by Negroes peacefully to assemble, publicly to protest denials of civil rights, and to obtain access to public facilities and public accommodations. The communities studied were Jackson, Greenwood, and Laurel, Mississippi; Gadsden, Alabama; Americus, Georgia; and St. Augustine, Florida.

Official response was manifested in various ways in these cities. Frequently it took the form of judicial and legislative efforts to prohibit constitutionally protected activity. Mass arrests of persons attempting to exercise rights were common. Discrimination and arbitrariness were prevalent in the setting of bail, in sentencing, and in the handling of juveniles. Prison conditions were alleged to be intolerable in several of the cities.

Federal Rights Involved

In recent years demonstrations and public protests have become a prime method of asserting and publicizing demands for equal rights for Negroes.[1] In cases resulting from efforts to suppress and interfere with

---

[4] According to his affidavit, Lelyveld told the grand jury that he had come to Hattiesburg for the National Council of Churches to participate in the Hattiesburg Ministers' Project. He denied that white boys had embraced Negro girls before the attack and stated that he had stayed at the headquarters of the Ministers' Project and slept beside a Negro colleague, the Reverend Dr. Donald Jacobs of Cleveland. In a letter to the Commission, dated Sept. 1, 1965, District Attorney James Finch stated, with respect to these allegations: "The State's Attorneys are not allowed, under the laws of Mississippi, to exert any influence upon the grand jury in their deliberations."
[1] In 1963 alone, more than 900 protest demonstrations occurred in 115 southern cities. Southern Regional Council, Inc., *Synopsis of Recent Developments*, No. 4, Dec. 31, 1963, p. 1.

demonstrations, the Supreme Court of the United States has held that peaceful protest demonstrations that do not unreasonably interfere with valid local functions—such as the regulation of traffic—are encompassed within the rights of free speech, assembly, and petition for redress of grievances guaranteed by the 1st and 14th amendments.

Because the communication of demands through public protest activity necessarily interferes with activities of other members of the community, courts have held that the right of public assembly is not entitled to as broad a protection as the right of free speech or the press. Thus, courts have attempted to delimit the scope of protected activity:

> A restriction . . . designed to promote the public convenience in the interest of all, and not susceptible to abuses of discriminatory application, cannot be disregarded by the attempted exercise of some civil right which, in other circumstances, would be entitled to protection. . . . [One could not] contrary to traffic regulations, insist upon a street meeting in the middle of Times Square at the rush hour as a form of freedom of speech or assembly. Governmental authorities have the duty and responsibility to keep their streets open and available for movement. A group of demonstrators could not insist upon the right to cordon off a street, or entrance to a public or private building, and allow no one to pass who did not agree to listen to their exhortations.

But the permissable extent of a demonstration may be related to the seriousness of the wrong protested:

> [I]t seems basic to our constitutional principles that the extent of the right to assemble, demonstrate and march peaceably along the highways and streets in an orderly manner should be commensurate with the enormity of the wrongs that are being protested and petitioned against.

Although it is valid for a municipality to regulate use of its streets by requiring a license to parade, licensing regulations may not be administered in a discriminatory manner. Neither may the regulation be so broadly drawn that the licensor may use his discretion to stifle free communication. In addition, the fact that a demonstration "induces a condition of unrest, creates dissatisfaction with conditions as they are or even stirs people to anger" will not remove it from constitutional protections, nor will it "permit a State to make criminal the peaceful expression of unpopular views."

The problems surrounding the legality of protest demonstrations are not raised by attempts to utilize previously segregated public facilities and public accommodations. The 14th amendment has long been held to prohibit a State, its agencies, its subdivisions, or its officials from enforcing or requiring or practicing segregation in public facilities or requiring segregation in public accommodations. Furthermore, the Civil

Rights Act of 1964 leaves no doubt as to the right to use public accommodations free from any interference from private citizens or public officials.

Legislative and Judicial Interference

Americus, Georgia.—In 1962, anticipating mass demonstrations, the Americus City Council amended the city's parade ordinance to require a permit if five or more persons desired to parade. Soon after demonstrations began, the Council enacted an ordinance restricting picketing to business hours, limiting the number of pickets to two per block, and requiring them to remain twenty feet apart. The Council later enacted ordinances that made it unlawful to refuse to comply with lawful orders or directions of police officers and required persons to leave any public or private building on request of the owner or person in charge. When large numbers of demonstrators were arrested for violating these ordinances, the Council passed another ordinance compelling city prisoners to pay jail fees in order to secure their release.

St. Augustine, Florida.—The St. Augustine City Commission, in June 1963, responded to picketing by enacting an ordinance that prohibited picketing which interfered with normal pedestrian traffic or sought to persuade persons not to do business with the establishments being picketed.

In May and June 1964 large groups of demonstrators staged a series of night mass marches. Police ordered the leaders to halt these marches, and a few days later the city council imposed a 9 p.m. curfew on all persons under the age of 18. As the demonstrations continued and met violent interference, Florida Governor Farris Bryant issued an executive order proclaiming a state of emergency and banning night marches during this emergency.

Mississippi.—In April 1963, three days after local Negroes and civil rights workers began marches to the county courthouse in Greenwood to protest denials of the right to vote, the city council reacted by issuing a proclamation prohibiting all large organized groups from going on the streets or sidewalks of the city. The council then broadened the city's parade ordinance to require a permit for virtually every use of the streets and sidewalks other than ordinary transit. City officials stated that no permits would be issued for demonstrations, explaining that this was necessary to prevent violence by whites. When demonstrations resumed in 1964, the council again issued a public order prohibiting organized groups from using public sidewalks or streets.

The most sweeping legislation adopted to restrict demonstration activity was passed by the Mississippi legislature early in 1964 in response to an announcement by civil rights workers that a "Summer Project" involving hundreds of persons was to be held in the State. Criminal measures were enacted which limited certain kinds of demonstrations, prohibited the printing or distribution of printed material advocating boycotts, provided municipal authorities with increased powers to deal with anticipated trouble, and prohibited advocating, teaching, or aiding in criminal acts designed to effect any political or social change.

In addition to legislation, officials in Jackson, Mississippi, and Gadsden, Alabama, sought and obtained State court injunctions prohibiting demonstrations. The injunctions were issued *ex parte*—without an opportunity for the demonstrators to present arguments against their issuance or terms. There were no arrests under the Jackson injunction but numerous arrests were made subsequently under the Gadsden injunction.

Arrests of Demonstrators

In the six communities studied, Commission investigation disclosed that persons who demonstrated or attempted to use public accommodations or facilities were immediately ordered to disperse and were arrested if they refused to do so. The action of local officials indicated they did not consider whether the activity of those arrested was statutorily or consitutionally protected or whether, in fact, the persons arrested were engaged in harmful activity.

Participants in mass marches rarely had an opportunity to proceed more than a few blocks before they were arrested—usually under an ordinance requiring a permit to parade. Officials often made arrests before the marchers could proceed past the Negro section of town. Since Negroes were unable to give public expression to their grievances through the use of public assembly, they submitted to arrest in order to publicize their protest.

*   *   *   *

Jail Conditions

A frequent charge by persons arrested in mass demonstrations was that they were subjected to primitive and, in some cases, inhuman jail conditions. The Commission did not investigate jail conditions at the time that demonstrators were incarcerated. However, judicial inquiries and other reliable reports indicate that in a number of cases the allegations were of substance.[2]

---

[2] Mistreatment of Negro prisoners arrested in Selma, Ala., for example, was reported by the federal court:

"This harrasment, intimidation and brutal treatment (by local law enforcement officials) has ranged from mass arrests without just cause to forced marches for several miles into the countryside, with the sheriff's deputies and members of his posse herding the Negro demonstrators at a rapid pace through the use of electrical shocking devices (designed for use on cattle) and night sticks to prod them along." *Williams* v. *Wallace*, 240 F. Supp. 100, 104 (M.D. Ala. 1965).

Americus, Georgia.—Following the arrests in Americus, most of the demonstrators were jailed temporarily in an abandoned office building and later transferred to jail facilities in neighboring counties. The complaints about all facilities were similar. Since the jails were mostly abandoned buildings, they had little or no functional plumbing. One building had to be fumigated by the prisoners, and in another there were not enough beds and no mattresses. Prisoners were not permitted outside; one group was confined in a barracks for 38 days during August and September. After a girl escaped from one jail, 26 girls were crowded into a dark punishment cell large enough for 12. At all of the jails the prisoners were served four hamburgers once a day and no other food. City officials admitted that jail conditions were below standard due to the absence of facilities to handle the large number of persons arrested. They did not dispute the existence of unsanitary conditions but alleged that they were the fault of the prisoners.

St. Augustine, Florida.—Federal Judge Simpson described Sheriff Davis' custodial procedures for demonstrators in St. Augustine:

[He forced the demonstrators] outside their cells to remain exposed to the elements in an open unshaded fenced compound through the midday hours, and sometimes all day. This place contained makeshift, exposed and inadequate toilet facilities, which were a source of humiliation, degradation and shame to the mixed group of males and females, juveniles and adults, whites and Negroes forced to share their use. This was used only for these plaintiffs, not for other jail inmates.

The use of this compound, in Florida's 90-degree-plus June temperature, and in one severe storm, was sought to be justified by the Defendant Davis as compliance with three successive Grand Jury reports that the jail must be equipped with an exercise yard so that inmates could get exercise outside their cells.

Further punishment devised by the Sheriff was the crowding of 9 or 10 male plaintiffs together overnight into concrete "sweatboxes," 7' x 8'. The females, 21 in number, on the other hand, were forced on one occasion for an hour and 18 minutes into a circular padded cell 10' in diameter. This group included one polio victim, Mrs. Georgia B. Reed, on crutches and unable to stand without them.

Both the sweatboxes and the padded cell were so small that the occupants had to sit or lie down in relays. These latter practices were imposed as punishment for singing religious songs or praying in the jail. As to the use of the compound, the good Sheriff said further that this was to make the Plaintiffs tired and ready for sleep at nightfall, to discourage singing in advance.

Judge Simpson concluded his findings of fact: "More than cruel and unusual punishment is shown. Here is exposed, in its raw ugliness, studied and cynical brutality, deliberately contrived to break men, physically and mentally."

Trial and Sentencing

When trials of civil rights demonstrators were finally held, in some cities only after extended delays, they generally resulted in convictions and the imposition of harsh sentences.

Americus, Georgia.—In Americus, trials of many of the demonstrators were postponed by the city recorder, the man responsible for hearing cases involving violations of city ordinances. During the height of the demonstrations, the recorder suspended court in order to attend summer military camp. Recorder's Court, which normally meets once a week, did not convene for four weeks. When the recorder returned, trials of demonstrators were held weekly and demonstrators were tried in order of arrest. As a consequence of this delay, and difficulty in obtaining bail, more than a hundred demonstrators were incarcerated for periods up to six weeks while awaiting trial for misdemeanors. Most of them were local teenagers.

All the Americus demonstrators were convicted and sentenced to the maximum penalty—$100 or 60 days labor on the streets. The recorder justified these sentences by stating that he had observed the violence that developed out of similar racial demonstrations in Albany, Georgia, and Birmingham, Alabama. When he sentenced demonstrators in Americus, he said, he "looked beyond what they had been doing" in order to discourage further demonstrations.

*   *   *   *

SOUTHERN JUSTICE

The Southern Regional Council in a report entitled "Southern Justice: An Indictment" outlined some of the reasons for the continued pattern of inequality in law enforcement.

Southern Justice: An Indictment, Southern Regional Council (1965)

If the public could ever plead ignorance to the double standard of justice in the South—one brand of justice for the white man, another for the Negro—that time is past. On television and on the front pages of newspapers, the stories have come.

An FBI informant testifies that he is in the same car with three Ku

Klux Klansmen as they shoot to death Mrs. Viola Liuzzo, a Detroit housewife, on an Alabama highway. The jury does not convict the first defendant charged in the crime—not even of manslaughter. While waiting for a new trial the Klansmen rush off to a Klan rally in North Carolina to sign autographs, openly confident that any new trial will end the same way.

A Hayneville, Alabama, community leader named Tom Coleman shoots down two civil rights workers at midday. Jonathan Daniels, a seminarian, dies at once and the Rev. Richard Morrisroe, a priest, is critically wounded. The trial, reportedly, turned into a circus, with Mr. Coleman not simply acquitted but almost proclaimed a hero.

The Liuzzo and Daniels cases were not isolated incidents, and Negroes can only reflect bitterly when white men—Southerners and Northerners alike—advise them, as they often do, to stop street demonstrations and take their grievances into the courts.

The Liuzzo case was not an isolated incident. From the sit-in demonstrations of 1960 through the spring of 1965, at least 26 Negroes and white civil rights workers died at the hands of racists in the South. Only one of the assailants was sentenced to prison, and he for 10 years. During the same period, "justice" was dispensed in double measure when white men were slain by Negroes. Two white segregationists died in the aftermath of racial demonstrations. Four Negroes went to prison, one of them for life.

The danger today is not that the public will fail to know about the double standard of justice, but that the public will think it limited only to civil rights cases, or will fail to act. If the problem were confined only to civil rights cases perhaps it could be solved with nothing more than a stern law making it a federal crime to kill a civil rights worker. The problem, however, goes far deeper.

From Birth to Death

In many areas of the South, dual justice is a standing abuse to all Negroes—the maid, the undertaker, the field hand, the school teacher, the minister. It exists from birth to death and the knowledge of it comes so early that a man may think he received it in his genes. It exists in the day to day brushes with "the law"; the policeman on his beat, at traffic court, in civil cases. It exists in the more awesome confrontations with judges and juries in rape and murder cases. To the extent that it exists, it provokes desperation among Negroes, shakes their faith in democracy, causes them to shun the policeman and the courts as enemies. More than any other factor it is responsible for what the white South views as increasing "radicalism" and "anarchy" in the civil rights movement.

Why is it Possible?

Why is it possible under the American judicial system for a white man to murder a Negro without fear of serious retribution? How widespread is dual justice and what is its impact?

The malignancy probably is far more prevalent than most white people, North and South, realize. Why that is so is one of the chief internal political problems of this country. There may be many reasons for the continued existence of dual justice, but these must surely be among them:

Dual justice survives because Presidents continue to treat federal judgeships as political rewards and pacifiers. It survives because the Justice Department fails to exercise the power that it has to correct abuses. It survives because the judicial network, federal, state, and municipal, is still one of the most segregated institutions in America. It survives through a built-in discrimination in the selection of juries, state and federal, and through the ill-concealed contempt of many courts and police officers for the rights of Negro citizens. It seems a fair estimate that it will continue to prosper, no matter how shrill the outrage in the distant pulpits and editorial towers, until the Negro gains adequate political power and until a sufficient number of white Southerners insist on equal rights for the minority.

Dual justice takes many forms, some merely disgusting and others so quietly terrifying that they balk the scrutiny of rational men.

Capital Cases

Consider the case of Thomas Wansley at Lynchburg, Virginia. In the winter of 1963, when he was 19 years old, he was accused of raping two women, one white and the other Japanese, and of stealing $1.36 from one of the victims.

The white woman was unable to identify Wansley—a Negro—as her assailant. Police, however, after a private talk with Wansley succeeded in getting a confession. The Japanese woman positively identified Wansley. The youth admitted to having sexual relations with the Japanese woman—not once but on several occasions. All-white juries deliberated, and handed down two death sentences for rape and a 20-year prison term for the $1.36 robbery. (The Virginia Supreme Court subsequently voided the sentences on grounds of trial error, and Wansley will be retried.)

Wansley, who had only one life to give, must have reflected bitterly on the knowledge that three months before in the same court room, a white man had received only a five-year sentence for raping an 11-year-old Negro girl.

Was this an isolated incident? Statistics amassed by the U. S. Bureau of Prisons answer, "no." Despite the fact that more than half of all convicted rapists are white, 87 per cent of all the persons executed for rape between 1930 and 1963 were Negroes convicted and sentenced by southern courts.

The wrath of southern judges and juries also falls on Negroes who are convicted of night-time burglaries and robberies. Between 1930 and 1961, 34 people were executed for this capital offense. Twenty-nine of them were Negroes and all but one were put to death in a southern or border state.

At first glance, Bureau of Prisons statistics would indicate that the Negro charged with murder receives better than equal treatment at the bar of justice. Negroes account for more than half of the murder arrests throughout the nation, but between 1930 and 1962 accounted for slightly less than half (49 per cent) of the executions. More detailed, if somewhat old, studies show, however, that the statistics conceal a double standard as menacing as any imposed for rape and burglary. Southern white juries are reluctant to hand down a stiff penalty to a Negro who kills a Negro, but are quick to exact the maximum penalty when a Negro kills a white person. Because most Negro murders are within the race, the execution statistics are relatively low.

The nature of the problem is shown in a study published by H. Garfinkel in a 1949 issue of *Social Forces.* Garfinkel examined murder convictions over an 11-year period in 10 North Carolina counties. He discovered that 26.6 per cent of all Negroes accused of killing white men received the death penalty. Most of the others received long sentences. Negroes accused of killing other Negroes fared far better. Only four per cent were executed; only five per cent received terms of 30 years or longer. Whites accused of killing Negroes had relatively little to fear at the hands of the court. None received life or death sentences.

*   *   *   *

The Jury Problem

Southern juries tend to be all-white and, all too often, inclined to support other whites in legal clashes with Negroes.

"Take for example, the killing of Clinton Melton, in Glendora, Mississippi, in the Delta, by a white man named Elmer Kimbell, a close friend of the man who had been acquitted of the murder of Emmett Till," Robert Penn Warren wrote in his book *Segregation*: "When the Lions Club met three days after the event, a resolution was drawn and signed by all members present: 'We consider the taking of the life of Clinton Melton an outrage against him, against all of the people of Glendora, against the people of Mississippi, as well as against the human family . . .'

And the town began to raise a fund to realize the ambition of the dead man, to send his children to college . . . " "But," Warren added, "in that division between man and man, the jury that tried Elmer Kimbell acquitted him."

The record of southern juries in racial cases is so depressingly anti-Negro that some observers have come to question the fairness of the jury system itself. Such sweeping criticism of one of man's sanest achievements—the right of trial by jury—is indicative of the danger of allowing the jury system to operate in crippled fashion. It is not merely a matter in the South of a rare, occasional miscarriage of justice growing out of the nature of the jury system at its best. "This is the price we have to pay for the jury system," Attorney General Katzenbach was quoted as saying after the Coleman acquittal in Hayneville, though not talking directly about that trial. The price is being paid for the crippled condition of the jury system. For there is no doubt that the jury system as it now operates in most parts of the South—and, it should be said, in many parts of the United States—is grossly unfair. It is unfair not only to Negroes but to poor whites, as well.

Much of the problem is in the selection of jurors. In almost no courts are jurors picked by thoroughly objective means to ensure a true cross-section of the community.

Charles Morgan, in a suit attacking the jury system of Jefferson County (Birmingham), Alabama, makes the point that most courts in the country use selection methods that work against obtaining a cross-section.

Mr. Morgan said in his brief, "Selection techniques now differ from state to state and within states from court to court. The federal system differs from the state system. Qualifications differ from state to state. Federal qualifications differ from state qualifications. Indeed, former Assistant Attorney General Burke Marshall recently noted: 'A justice department survey in 1961 showed that the 92 federal district courts had 92 different systems of selecting juries.'

"One jury commissioner's telephone book is another's city directory. A third may try voter registration lists. The Junior Chamber of Commerce; church membership lists (regardless of the First Amendment); lists of school teachers; American Legion posts or labor unions; lists of industrialists and lists of automobile owners; lists of householders or PTA members, or registered voters or real property tax payers—all are used."

Mr. Morgan pointed out that many of the federal courts rely on the "key man" system. Persons well known to the court—usually men of substance—are tapped and they in turn suggest their friends.

Mr. Morgan said, "One clear light shines through the forest of lists—

the United States in almost every one of its courts tries its citizens before *Literary Digest* juries."

That was an allusion to the old *Literary Digest* method of polling national issues and elections. The magazine went out of business after a spectacular polling failure in 1936 when it predicted that Landon would defeat Roosevelt. Subsequent evaluation of the *Digest* techniques indicated the reason for the failure: The magazine based its predictions on the opinions of middle and upper class Americans and paid no attention to the poor. Mr. Morgan concluded that present-day juries are selected by the same discredited method, ignoring the welfare and relief rolls and all other lists that would give the poor a voice on juries.

Governor Robert McNair of South Carolina was quoted recently as saying that the real threat of increased Negro votes is not so much at the polls as on juries. He said that adding large numbers of Negroes to the electorate would put more and more illiterates on juries, and he saw that as unfortunate.

If it is proper for a middle class public official charged with embezzlement to be tried by a jury of his peers—other members of the middle class—why is it improper for a penniless Negro to have his fate decided by a jury that includes his peers?

*   *   *   *

Democracy Damaged

Of all the forces that urge the Negro away from the American democracy, none is more vicious or more effective than the dual system of justice. His ingrained knowledge of the dual system causes a Negro instinctively to dodge a policeman. The same wretched awareness leads him to think of the courts as a white man's game, and, since to the Negro in poverty the court is one of the most visible arms of the government, it tempts him to consider the entire governing system as a device for maintaining the white man in charge and the Negro in "his place." From the Deep South, he carries his fear, resentment, and distrust to the ghetto slums of the rest of the nation, like the Watts area of Los Angeles where rioting was touched off when policemen made an arrest. Too often, he finds, out of the South, the familiar taints of dual justice.

The duality is so successfully pernicious that multitudes of Negroes have gone to their graves without doubting the rightness of the scheme.

*   *   *   *

LAW ENFORCEMENT IN THE NORTH

The law enforcement problems facing the Negro in the North center primarily around his relations with the police. A long history of conflict, claims of abuse and brutality and mistrust has recently blossomed into a matter of national concern. The 1964, 1965 and 1966 summer riots in various northern cities were in almost every instance set off by an incident involving the police. In its analysis of the Watts riot, the McCone report recognized that relations between the Negro community and the police must be improved by better lines of communication. However, its conclusion that a civilian review board is not necessary has been disputed by most civil rights organizations. An example of the kind of police activities which Negro groups claim require such a board is found in a recent decision of the Federal Court of Appeals for the Fourth Circuit in Lankford v. Gelston, set out below.

McCone Report on Negro-Police Relations (1965)

Law Enforcement—The Thin Thread

"As the patriots of seventy-six did to the support of the Declaration of Independence, so to the support of the Constitution and laws let every American pledge his life, his property, and his sacred honor — let every man remember that to violate the law is to trample on the blood of his father and to tear the charter of his own children's liberty. Let reverence for the laws . . . become the political religion of the nation; and let the old and the young, the rich and the poor, the grave and the gay of all sexes and tongues and colors and conditions, sacrifice unceasingly upon its altars."

Abraham Lincoln, January 27, 1837

Maintenance of law and order is a prerequisite to the enjoyment of freedom in our society. Law enforcement is a critical responsibility of government, and effective enforcement requires mutual respect and understanding between a law enforcement agency and the residents of the community which it serves.

The Problem — Deep and Serious

The conduct of law enforcement agencies, most particularly the Los Angeles Police Department, has been subject to severe criticism by many Negroes who have appeared before the Commission as witnesses. The bitter criticism we have heard evidences a deep and longstanding schism between a substantial portion of the Negro community and the Police Department. "Police brutality" has been the recurring charge. One witness after another has recounted instances in which, in their opinion, the police have used excessive force or have been disrespectful and abusive in their language or manner.*

On the other hand, the police have explained to us the extent to which the conduct of some Negroes when apprehended has required the use of force in making arrests. Example after example has been recited of arrestees, both men and women, becoming violent, struggling to resist arrest, and thus requiring removal by physical force. Other actions, each provocative to the police and each requiring more than normal action by the police in order to make an arrest or to perform other duties, have been described to us.

Chief of Police Parker appears to be the focal point of the criticism within the Negro community. He is a man distrusted by most Negroes and they carefully analyze for possible anti-Negro meaning almost every action he takes and every statement he makes. Many Negroes feel that he carries a deep hatred of the Negro community. However, Chief Parker's statements to us and collateral evidence such as his record of fairness to Negro officers are inconsistent with his having such an attitude. Despite the depth of the feeling against Chief Parker expressed to us by so many witnesses, he is recognized, even by many of his most vocal critics, as a capable Chief who directs an efficient police force that serves well this entire community.

With respect to the Los Angeles County Sheriff's Department, the situation is somewhat different. Generally speaking, the Negro community does not harbor the same angry feeling toward the Sheriff or his staff as it does toward the Los Angeles police. Nevertheless, witnesses recited to us instances of alleged brutality and excessive use of force by deputy sheriffs on duty.

The reasons for the feeling that law enforcement officers are the enemy of the Negro are manifold and it is well to reflect on them before they are accepted. An examination of seven riots in northern cities of the United States in 1964 reveals that each one was started over a police incident, just as the Los Angeles riot started with the arrest of Marquette Frye. In each of the 1964 riots, "police brutality" was an issue, as it was here, and, indeed, as it has been in riots and insurrections elsewhere in the world. The fact that this charge is repeatedly made must not go unnoticed, for there is a real danger that persistent criticism will reduce and perhaps destroy the effectiveness of law enforcement.

---

* The more than seventy cases of alleged police brutality which were submitted to the Commission contributed to our understanding of the depths of the feelings of a segment of the Negro community toward the Police Department. Because our responsibility has been to review the general policy and procedure for handling citizen complaints rather than to review individual cases, we have referred all of the cases to the appropriate and responsible agencies.

Our society is held together by respect for law. A group of officers who represent a tiny fraction of one percent of the population is the thin thread that enforces observance of law by those few who would do otherwise. If police authority is destroyed, if their effectiveness is impaired, and if their determination to use the authority vested in them to preserve a law abiding community is frustrated, all of society will suffer because groups would feel free to disobey the law and inevitably their number would increase. Chaos might easily result. So, while we must examine carefully the claim of police brutality and must see that justice is done to all groups within our society, we must, at the same time, be sure that law enforcement agencies, upon which so much depends, are not rendered impotent.

Solution is Possible — But Action by Both Police and the Negro Community Is Essential

Much can be done to correct the existing impressions and to promote an understanding between the police and the Negro community, and this, we believe, is essential in the interest of crime prevention. The steps that have been taken appear to us to be insufficient. Further action is indicated.

Basically, on the one hand, we call for a better understanding by the law enforcement agencies of Negro community attitudes and, on the other hand, a more widespread understanding within the Negro community of the value of the police and the extent to which the law enforcement agencies provide it with security. Although the criminal element among the Negroes is only a small fraction of the Negro population, over half of all crimes of violence committed in the City of Los Angles are committed by Negroes, and the great majority of the victims of these crimes are Negroes. Thus, the police, in their effort to suppress crime, are doing so to protect the entire community, including the Negro community.

The Board of Police Commissioners — Strengthening is Needed

The Board of Police Commissioners, as the civilian head of the Police Department, has a great responsibility. It is charged with establishing policies for the Department, supervising and managing the Department, and seeing to it that its policies are followed. In discharging its duties, the Board should have a major role in the improvement and maintenance of police-community relationships. In addition, the Board has extensive responsibilities for the issuance and revocation of permits for carrying on a large number of businesses.

The Commission believes that this Board, meeting one afternoon a week, with compensation of the members of the Board at $10.00 per meeting, cannot and does not exercise the control and direction of the Police Department which is prescribed by the City Charter. It is significant to us that the Board and its actions have not been drawn into the recent criticisms of police conduct in the predominantly Negro areas of the city. Almost without exception, the complaints that we have heard have been directed against Chief Parker and the police officers. No one, not a single witness, has criticized the Board for the conduct of the police, although the Board is the final authority in such matters. We interpret this as evidence that the Board of Police Commissioners is not visibly exercising the authority over the Department vested in it by the City Charter. Our own investigation and evaluation, and the testimony of witnesses, confirm this.

Therefore, we urge that steps be taken immediately to arm the Board of Police Commissioners with all the necessary tools to discharge its City Charter responsibilities. This will mean increased compensation for the Commissioners, more frequent meetings of the Board, a larger staff, and a revision of procedures that have been followed in the past. A Board, shouldering the responsibilities envisaged here, must be composed of capable and dedicated men, chosen by the Mayor and confirmed by the City Council, willing to devote the necessary time and thoughtful effort to the task.

Complaint Procedures — A New Approach to an Old Problem

A strained relationship such as we have observed as existing between the police and the Negro community can be relieved only if the citizen knows that he will be fairly and properly treated, that his complaints of police misconduct will be heard and investigated, and that, if justified, disciplinary action will be taken against the offending officer.

Under the present Police Department procedure, citizen complaints are received by the Police Department or by the Board of Police Commissioners. All investigations of citizen complaints, wherever received, are conducted under the overall supervision of the Internal Affairs Division of the Police Department. In the vast majority of cases, primary responsibility for investigating allegations of officer misconduct has in the past been placed with the division commander of the individual officer involved. After the investigation has been completed, the determination whether a complaint should be sustained is made either by the Chief of Police or by the Board of Police Commissioners, depending upon where the complaint was originally filed. Where a complaint is sustained, responsibility for discipline is vested in the Chief of Police and the Board of Rights, which provides a departmental hearing to an accused officer before serious sanctions can be imposed.

The Commission has concluded that there are several deficiencies in this existing procedure. We believe that division commanders and those in the command structure should not conduct investigations of complaints with respect to their own subordinate officers. Moreover, existing procedures are not sufficiently visible to or understood by the public. Finally, we do not think there should be a difference, as there now is, in the handling of a complaint depending solely upon whether it was filed with the Board or the Police Department.

Under the existing procedure, the impression is widespread that complaints by civilians go unnoticed, that police officers are free to conduct themselves as they will, and that the manner in which they handle the public is of little concern to the higher authorities. This impression is not consistent with fact. Department policies set high standards of conduct for police officers in their contacts with citizens, and these standards are conscientiously enforced. In 1964, 412 complaints of police misconduct were received from citizens. Forty-two complaints alleging police misconduct in contacts with citizens were sustained.* Despite these facts, the impression that citizen complaints are ignored continues because of deficiencies in the existing procedure. Thus, the clamor is raised from many sources for an independent civilian review board.

The Commission feels that a civilian review board, authorized to investigate, and perhaps to decide, complaints, but with no other law enforcement responsibilities, would endanger the effectiveness of law enforcement, would be intolerable at a time when crime is on the increase throughout the country. Experience in two cities which have such Boards —and in which alleged misconduct of police officers was a major issue in connection with riots which occurred in those cities in 1964—has not demonstrated the advantages of such a review board. From our observations and from testimony of knowledgeable law enforcement administrators, we are persuaded that the value of an independent board would not outweigh the likely deleterious effects on law enforcement. We, therefore, propose improvements in the existing procedure which will go far toward establishing the widest possible confidence in the handling of all complaints but which will not destroy the authority vested by the City Charter in the Board of Police Commissioners and the Chief of Police.

To insure independent investigation of complaints, we recommend that an "Inspector General" should be established in the Police Department, under the authority of the Chief of Police but outside the chain of com-

---

* Of the 42 complaints which were sustained, 10 were for alleged excessive force, 23 were alleged discourtesy or profanity, and nine alleged unlawful arrest or unreasonable search. In 1964, 470 officers, approximately 10% of the police force, were assessed disciplinary penalties of some type.

mand. Properly staffed with sworn officers and civilian personnel, the Inspector General would perform the functions of the present Internal Affairs Division and would be responsible for making investigations and recommendations on all citizen complaints, whether filed with the Board or the Department. An adequate hearing process for the complaint should be made available at some point in the procedure, and he should be informed of the action taken on his complaint. The "Inspector General" concept has proved, through years of experience, to be effective in the four military services, each of which has such an independent and objective agency under the Chief of Staff of the service. The Inspector General's investigations can be visible to the public. He would report to the Chief of Police, and his findings and recommendations on all complaints would be the basis for the Chief's report to the Board on all such complaints. The Board would act on all complaints as it now acts on some complaints initially presented to it; that is, it would pass on whether the complaint is or is not sustained. Under the procedure suggested here, responsibility for discipline would remain with the Chief of Police and the Board of Rights as provided by the City Charter.

These improvements, we believe, would provide a satisfactory procedure for processing citizen complaints both from the viewpoint of the Los Angeles Police Department and the community. We have focused our discussion on the existing procedure in the Police Department. We encourage the Los Angeles Sheriff's Department to adopt those aspects of our conclusions which may be applicable to its procedures for handling citizen complaints.

*   *   *   *

Community-Police Relations — A Responsibility for Crime Prevention

In 1963, the Los Angeles Police Department issued an excellent statement of the need for and purpose of a community relations program. The order stated:

"The mutual advantages of a friendly relationship between the people of a community and their police force should be widely understood and more fully appreciated. The success of a police force in the performance of its duties is largely measured by the degree of support and cooperation it receives from the people it serves. It is of paramount importance, therefore, to secure for this department the confidence, respect, and approbation of the public. The cultivation of such desirable attitudes on the part of the public is dependent upon reciprocal attitudes on the part of this department."

Witness after witness, in discussing the question of police-community relations, emphasized the importance of "non-punitive contacts" as basic to the problem. But, from the statements of many witnesses it appears that the steps taken by the Los Angeles Police Department, although commendable, have been faltering. The worthwhile Deputy Auxiliary Police program, which was designed to bring youth into closer contact with police organizations, has been permitted to lapse and pass out of existence. The staff assigned to community relations activities is not large enough, and the range of community relations activities has been limited.

Moreover, little has been done in recent years to encourage the Negro youth's support of the police, or to implant in the youth's mind the true value of the Police Department with respect to the welfare of the youth. Productive programs can and must be developed in Los Angeles, as they have been developed elsewhere.

We commend the Board of Police Commissioners and the Chief of Police for the community relations activities which the Department has undertaken in 1965. These have included the appointment of a Coordinator of Community Relations Activity and a Community-Police Relations Advisory Committee, and an increase in the staff of the community relations unit. Visitation programs to elementary schools and command level seminars on community relations have also been useful steps. But, we believe, a greater effort is indicated.

We propose more intensive in-service human relations training programs for officer personnel; youth programs such as the Deputy Auxiliary Police program; periodic open forums and workshops in which the police and residents of the minority communities will engage in discussions of law enforcement; and frequent contact between the police and the students in junior and senior high schools.

Such programs are a basic responsibility of the Police Department. They serve to prevent crime, and, in the opinion of this Commission, crime prevention is a responsibility of the Police Department, equal in importance to law enforcement.

Programs of this nature, and the underlying philosophies that support them, can only be initiated through determined leadership at the top. If these actions are pursued energetically, we can expect a gratifying improvement in the relationship between the police and the community. Succssful implementation of these programs will require additional personnel and funds and we believe that the City Council should authorize both without delay.

Again, while we have focused our discussion on the Police Department, we encourage the Los Angeles Sheriff's Department to introduce community relations activities of the character we have recommended for the Police Department.

*More Negroes and Mexican-Americans Must Enter Careers
in Law Enforcement*

Finally, the Commission expresses its concern over the reltaively few sworn officer personnel in the Police Department and the Sheriff's Department who are Negroes or Mexican-Americans. Only four percent of the sworn personnel of the Police Department and six percent of the Sheriff's Department are Negroes and an even smaller percentage are Mexican-American. Both of these departments recruit their personnel through the civil service agencies and selections are made on a basis of qualifications without regard for race, religion, or national origin. Despite efforts by the civil service agencies, the law enforcement departments, and some elected officials to encourage Negroes and Mexican-Americans to enter the law enforcement field, the results have been unsatisfactory.

We believe it essential that the number of sworn officers of each minority group should be increased substantially. To bring this about, more active recruitment by the Police and Sheriff's Departments and the civil service must be undertaken. Furthermore, educational and private institutions and organizations, and political leaders as well, should encourage members of the minority groups to enter careers in law enforcement. Finally, budget support for extensive efforts in recruitment, which should include pre-employment preparatory training, should be provided by both the City Council and the Board of Supervisors.

To implement our conclusions, we offer the following recommendations:

1) The Board of Police Commissioners should be strengthened.

2) Investigation of all citizen complaints should be conducted by an independent Inspector General under the authority of the Chief of Police in the implementation of procedures established by the Board of Police Commissioners.

3) The Police Department should institute expanded community relations programs.

4) The Sheriff's Department should effectuate these recommendations to the extent that they are applicable to it.

Fourth Circuit Court of Appeals Decision in *Lankford* v. *Gelston* (June 23, 1966)

Samuel James LANKFORD and Corinthia Julia Lankford, his wife, Claude Tompkins and Rev. Elizabeth Tompkins, his wife, Walter Summers and Regina Summers, his wife, and Arthur Rayner, Appellants,

v.
George GELSTON, as Commissioner of Police of Baltimore City,
Appellee.*

No. 10384.
United States Court of Appeals
Fourth Circuit
Argued June 2, 1966.
Decided June 23, 1966.

Before HAYNSWORTH, Chief Judge, and SOBELOFF, BOREMAN,
BRYAN and J. SPENCER BELL, Circuit Judges, sitting en banc.

SOBELOFF, Circuit Judge:

Negro families of Baltimore City, four in number but acting in behalf
of others similarly situated, as well as in their own behalf, instituted an
action in the United States District Court for the District of Maryland,
seeking injunctive relief against the Police Commissioner of Baltimore
City to prevent further invasions of their right to privacy guaranteed by
the Fourth and Fourteenth Amendments to the Constitution. Jurisdiction
is grounded on 28 U.S.C.A. §1343, as authorized by 42 U.S.C.A. §1983,

The District Court heard the testimony of forty-two witnesses and received a summary of the police records from a team of special masters
chosen from the membership of the Junior Bar Association of Baltimore
City. This case, which has attained considerable notoriety, stems from the
efforts of the Baltimore Police Department to capture Samuel and Earl
Veney, two brothers who shot and killed one policeman and seriously
wounded another. During a nineteen-day period in December, 1964, and
January, 1965, the police conducted searches of more than 300 houses,
most of them private dwellings. The searches were based in almost every
instance on unverified anonymous tips. In none did the police have a
search warrant. Although the court found that the police, in conducting
these searches at all hours of the day and night, upon telephone tips from
unknown persons, had deprived plaintiffs and others of their constitutional rights, it refused to issue an injunction and denied plaintiffs relief.
The court, however, retained jurisdiction of the case in order to process
expeditiously any future claim of invasion of the plaintiffs' rights. 240
F.Supp. 550 (D.Md. 1965).

There is no dispute over the facts. On the evening of December 24,
1964, several persons committed an armed robbery of a liquor store in
Baltimore City, in the course of which Police Lieutenant James Maskell

---

* (Bernard J. Schmidt, Police Commissioner when this case was heard below, has retired from office and was succeeded by General George M. Gelston as Interim Police
Commissioner. The latter has been substituted as appellee at the instance of counsel
for appellants.)

was shot and seriously wounded. A suspect was soon apprehended near the scene of the crime and after questioning him, several police officers visited homes in the area in search of other suspects. At about 4:50 a.m., on December 25, Police Sergeant Jack Cooper, a uniformed officer in a cruising car and a member of the search party, was found fatally shot near his cruiser.

Early in the morning of December 25, warrants were issued for the arrest of Samuel Veney and his brother Earl, charging them with the robbery of the liquor store and with assaulting and shooting Lieutenant Maskell. The Veney brothers were justifiably believed by the police to be armed and extremely dangerous. Later that day, the then Police Commissioner, Bernard Schmidt, authorized a special squad to be formed under the command of Captain Joseph Mahrer to search for the Veneys. About 50 or 60 police officers were members of the squad at one time or another.

Between December 25 and January 12, the Baltimore police made more than 300 "turn-ups" in an unsuccessful effort to locate and arrest the Veneys. In police parlance a turn-up is an investigation of a location and usually includes a search of the premises. Most of the searches here were of private residences. The Veneys are Negroes, and most of the dwellings searched were occupied by Negroes.

The court found that:

> The police records with respect to many of the searches are sketchy and incomplete. Frequently all that is shown is that a particular address was turned-up on a particular day.
> The police did not apply for or obtain search warrants for the search of any of the more than 300 premises they entered.

A police emergency vehicle carrying shotguns, submachine guns, tear gas apparatus, and bulletproof vests accompanied the men on every search. Before each turn-up a surveillance team of plainclothesmen would drive past the building to locate exits, alleyways, etc., but there were no inquiries in the neighborhoods about the houses to be searched nor was there any other investigation of the tips, except to observe the character of the neighborhood.

Four officers carrying shotguns or submachine guns and wearing bulletproof vests would go to the front door and knock. They would be accompanied or followed by supervising officers, a sergeant or lieutenant. Other men would surround the house, training their weapons on windows and doors. "As soon as an occupant opened the door, the first man would enter the house to look for any immediate danger, and the supervising officer would then talk to the person who had answered the door.

Few stated any objection to the entry; some were quite willing to have the premises searched for the Veneys, while others acquiesced because of the show of force."

The officers involved worked exceptionally long hours. Some were polite and considerate of the occupants. Others were abrupt, and without adequate explanation of their purpose, flashed lights on beds where children were sleeping and otherwise upset the occupants of the home being searched.

Few specific instances need be detailed to illustrate the consequences of police reliance on anonymous tips and the terrifying experiences to which occupants of the searched homes were subjected.

Samuel Lankford and his wife, who have six children, have resided at 2707 Parkwood Avenue since 1949. Mr. Lankford has worked at the U.S. Post Office in Baltimore for over ten years. At about 1:15 a.m. on January 2, 1965, Lieutenant Robert Hewes was told by a communications center officer that he had received a call that the Veney brothers were at this address with a family named Garrett. A few minutes before 2:00 a.m. Lieutenant Hewes and his search party converged upon Parkwood Avenue. Upon their arrival in the neighborhood they met on the street a Negro man, described by the lieutenant as "respectable looking," who identified himself as the person that had called the communications center. He told Lieutenant Hewes that he had been told by a newspaper boy that two men resembling the Veneys had entered a house on Parkwood Avenue. At 2:00 a.m. a search party led by the lieutenant knocked on the door, and Mrs. Lankford, awakened by the knock, opened the door. The officers entered the house and began their search while the lieutenant talked with the woman. She told him that her name was not Garrett. At the trial she denied that the officers asked for or were given permission to search, and Lieutenant Hewes acknowledged that his men had already gone to the second floor while he was talking with her. The husband was awakened in his second floor bedroom by two flashlights shining in his face and four men with shotguns in his room. They questioned him, while other officers searched the remaining rooms including the children's bedrooms, and left.

Mr. and Mrs. Wallace have made their home at 2408 Huron Street for 21 years. They live with a three-year old son, three daughters, Lucinda (a Baltimore public school teacher), Harrietta (a college student), and Sharon (a high school student), and two other relatives. At 8:30 p.m. on December 30, 1964, Lieutenant Coll of the Southwest District was told by a clerk at another police station that she had received an anonymous call from a man who said that the Veneys were being sheltered at this address. Lieutenant Coll testified that since this was the first time that the

Veneys had been placed in this neighborhood, he felt that an investigation was in order. A little after 9:00 p.m. Lieutenant Coll led about 14 officers to the house. When the police arrived, Lucinda Wallace was showing slides to a group of her family and guests. Mr. and Mrs. Wallace were both out, Mrs. Wallace at a beauty shop she operated four doors away. Six officers armed with shotguns and rifles entered and searched the home; others who were stationed outside would not allow Mrs. Wallace to enter and refused to explain what was happening. Reduced to tears, she was finally admitted to her home, where she was joined by her children, all crying hysterically. As the policemen were departing, they told Lucinda and her mother that they had received an anonymous call that the Veneys were in the house.

At the trial several police officers, each with long experience on the Baltimore police force, testified that in serious cases it was routine practice to make searches of homes on the basis of anonymous calls. They recognized the difference in authenticating such tips, and testified that they attempted to do so by evaluating the tone of voice used by the caller. The officers further stated that not infrequently they would also conduct searches based on tips received from the outside and transmitted to them by police telephone clerks.

On January 8, 1966, plantiffs' attorneys brought the complaint to the chambers of the District Judge and asked for a temporary restraining order. At a hearing held that afternoon, the Deputy Attorney General represented to the court that the Police Commissioner would promptly issue a general order dealing with the problems raised in the complaint. Based on that representation, the District Court denied the request for a temporary restraining order, and set the case for trial on January 14.

On January 11 the Police Commissioner did issue General Order No. 10388. In essence the Order forbids police officers from searching "any premises for the purpose of arresting a person for whom an arrest warrant has been issued" unless "the officer has probable cause to believe the accused person to be on the premises to be searched." The determination of what constitutes probable cause is still left to the policeman, and there is nothing in the Order which specifically prohibits officers from conducting searches grounded only on anonymous tips, which is precisely the evil to which the Complaint was addressed. We therefore find nothing in General Order No. 10388 which would make the issuance of an injunction unnecessary.

In refusing injunctive relief, the District Court, emphasized the reluctance of the federal judiciary to employ its equity power to control police practices and noted that

"this Court has now stated the basic principles which must be observed by the police in determining whether there are reasonable grounds for a contemplated entry. The Court is satisfied that the Police Commissioner and other police officers will make a bona fide effort to observe those rules. They did observe them during the remainer of the search for the Veneys after the Commissioner issued General Order No. 10388 on January 11." 240 F. Supp. at 561.

We conclude, however, that in striking the balance between the role of the federal court in the preservation of the constitutional rights of the appellants and the independence of state officials, the District Court erred when it refused to issue an injunction prohibiting the police from conducting searches based only on uncorroborated anonymous tips and hence without probable cause.

This case reveals a series of the most flagrant invasions of privacy ever to come under the scrutiny of a federal court. The undisputed testimony indicates that the police in conducting the wholesale Veney raids were engaging in a practice which on a smaller scale has routinely attended efforts to apprehend persons accused of serious crime. If denying relief in these circumstances should be held a proper exercise of judicial restraint, it would be difficult to envision any case justifying judicial intervention. The parties seeking redress have committed no acts warranting violation of the privacy of their homes; there has never been any suspicion concerning them or their associations. It was not contended by the Attorney General, nor could it have been contended, that information from an anonymous and unverifiable source is probable cause for the search of a home.

Instances have often come to the attention of courts in which persons accused of crime have sought to prevent the use against them of illegally seized incriminating evidence. But it is only in the rare instance that a person not accused or even suspected of any crime petitions the court for redress of police invasion of his home. The reason is not that such invasions do not occur but, as Mr. Justice Jackson eloquently put it:

Only occasional and more flagrant abuses come to the attention of the courts, and then only those where the search and seizure yields incriminating evidence and the defendant is at least sufficiently compromised to be indicted. If the officers raid a home, an office, or stop and search an automobile but find nothing incriminating, this invasion of the personal liberty of the innocent too often finds no practical redress. There may be, and I am convinced that there are, many unlawful searches of homes and automobiles of innocent people which turn up nothing incriminating, in which no arrest is made, about which courts do nothing, and about which we never hear.
* * * There is no opportunity for injunction or appeal to disinterested intervention. The citizen's choice is quietly to submit to whatever the officers undertake or to resist at risk of arrest or immediate violence.—Brinegar v.

United States, 338 U.S. 160, 181-182, 69 S.Ct. 1302, 1314, 93 L.Ed. 1879 (1949). (Mr. Justice Jackson dissenting).

*   *   *   *

The appellants' position has been lucidly articulated by their attorneys:

> Unless equity courts find means to protect the innocent homeowners, who are the principal beneficiaries of the Fourth Amendment, their rights will not be protected. It would be a grotesque irony if our courts protect only against the unlawful search which actually uncovers contraband (by the exclusionary rule), while offering no relief against an admittedly unlawful pattern and practice affecting hundreds of innocent homeowners.—Brief of Appellants, p. 38.

We are persuaded that the injunction should issue even though the Veney raids have ceased and notwithstanding the Police Commissioner's General Order No. 10388. These raids were not isolated instances undertaken by individual police officers. They were rather the effectuation of a plan conceived by high ranking officials. All members of the Police Department, from the Commissioner down to the raw recruit, are expected to be familiar with the principle that if the police intend to conduct a search of a man's home for a suspect, they must at least have probable cause to believe that he is on the premises. The doctrine is not subtle; it touches the very heart of law enforcement practices, and has found expression in numerous judicial opinions. Its force could not have escaped the Commissioner and other members of the police hierarchy, yet the raids were carried on relentlessly for 19 days. The grave character of the department's conduct places a strong obligation on the court to make sure that similar conduct will not recur. Police protestations of repentance and reform timed to anticipate or to blunt the force of a lawsuit offer insufficient assurance that similar raids will not ensue when another aggravated crime occurs. . . . In fact, it is perhaps more reasonable to view the cessation of the raids and the promulgation of General Order No. 10388 not as belated acts of repentance but as the recognition of the futility of continuing the searches when it had become manifest that the Veneys had made their escape. They were later apprehended in New York State.

The General Order, in reciting no more than that probable cause is required to conduct a search, is in no sense a recognition that the conduct complained of fell short of established legal standards; it adds nothing to the general rule with which the rank-and-file policeman should already have been familiar. It is too vague to provide even a faint warning that searches based only on anonymous tips do not constitute proper police tactics. It would not have been too much to expect in these circumstances a forthright statement that officers conducting such illegal searches in the future will subject themselves to disciplinary action.

The plaintiffs, in their argument in the District Court maintained that the police behavior was racially discriminatory since most of the homes searched were occupied by Negroes. This contention the District Court rejected, reasoning that the police concentrated on Negro residences because the Veneys are Negroes and most of the information received related to their supposed presence in Negro neighborhoods. While this ruling of the District Court is not contested on appeal, we think that it has a substantial bearing on the question of whether injunctive relief is appropriate. The District Judge himself noted that "[t]he evidence does show what has become common knowledge in Baltimore—that the relations between the Negro community and the police have deteriorated seriously." 240 F.Supp. at 556 n. 4.

Baltimore City has escaped thus far the agony and brutality of the riots experienced in New York City, Los Angeles, Chicago, and other urban centers. Courts cannot shut their eyes to events that have been widely publicized throughout the nation and the world. Lack of respect for the police is conceded to be one of the factors generating violent outbursts in Negro communities. The invasions so graphically depicted in this case "could" happen in prosperous suburban neighborhoods, but the innocent victims know only that wholesale raids do not happen elsewhere and did happen to them. Understandably they feel that such illegal treatment is reserved for those elements who the police believe cannot or will not challenge them. It is of the highest importance to community morale that the courts shall give firm and effective reassurance, especially to those who feel that they have been harassed by reason of their color or their poverty.

After so vast a demonstration of disregard of private rights, the complainants are entitled to a clear response. While the immediate pressure of wholesale raids has been withdrawn, the practice of indiscriminate searches of homes has been renounced only obliquely, if at all, and the danger of repetition has not been removed. The sense of impending crisis in police-community relations persists, and nothing would so directly ameliorate it as a judicial decree forbidding the practices complained of.

In ordering the issuance of an injunction we have not blotted from our consideration the serious problems faced by the law enforcement officer in his daily work. His training stresses the techniques of the prevention of crime and the apprehension of criminals, and what seems to him to be the logical and practical means to solve a crime or to arrest a suspect may turn out to be a deprivation of another's constitutional rights. And where one policeman is killed and another wounded, the police, and the public, too, are understandably outraged and impatient with any obstacle in the search for the murderer. While fully appreciating the exceedingly difficult task of the policeman, a court must not be deterred from protecting rights secured to all by the Constitution.

The police department is society's instrumentality to maintain law and order, and to be fully effective it must have public confidence and cooperation. Confidence can exist only if it is generally recognized that the department uses its enforcement procedures with integrity and zeal, according to law and without resort to oppressive measures. Law observance by the police cannot be divorced from law enforcement. When official conduct feeds a sense of injustice, raises barriers between the department and segments of the community, and breeds disrespect for the law, the difficulties of law enforcement are multiplied.

Baltimore now has a new Interim Police Commissioner whose enlightened efforts to foster better relations between the Negro community and the Police Department have been widely applauded by all elements of the community. The clear assurance which the injunction is designed to give is nevertheless still necessary in the interest of public tranquility. The issuance of the injunction will not prove harmful, but helpful, to the Interim Commissioner temporarily in office and to his successors in the lawful and effective exercise of their authority and in the administration of the department.

*   *   *   *

VII
The Government Responds

FIRST CONGRESSIONAL ACTION

The Government's response to the civil rights movement has been a checkered one. Following the report of the President's Committee in 1947, President Truman urged the enactment of a Fair Employment Practices Committee Law, the outlawing of poll taxes and lynching and the elimination of segregation in interstate transportation. None of his proposals was passed by Congress. On July 26, 1948, however, he issued an Executive Order banning segregation in the Armed Forces.

During the Eisenhower Administration, the government pressed school desegregation cases and the President did order troops into Little Rock in 1957. However, his preference for state over federal action and his laissez-faire attitude toward government precluded any strong action in the field. He said at one point, "I don't believe you can change the hearts of men with laws or decisions."

The only important civil rights legislation passed by the Eisenhower Administration was the Civil Rights Act of 1957 and that of 1960. The 1957 statute authorized the Justice Department to bring suits in the Federal Courts against voting discrimination. However, only a handful of suits was brought in the next three years. Because of a number of adverse court decisions under the 1957 Act, Congress passed a new Act in 1960 permitting the Department of Justice to bring voting suits against a state and requiring local officials to produce voting records for the federal government. The text of these Acts is set out below.

Civil Rights Act of 1957

PART I

ESTABLISHMENT OF THE COMMISSION ON CIVIL RIGHTS

Sec. 101. (a) There is created in the executive branch of the Government a Commission on Civil Rights (hereinafter called the "Commission").

(b) The Commission shall be composed of six members who shall be appointed by the President by and with the advice and consent of the Senate. Not more than three of the members shall at any one time be of the same political party.

(c) The President shall designate one of the members of the Commission as Chairman and one as Vice Chairman. The Vice Chairman shall act as Chairman in the absence or disability of the Chairman, or in the event of a vacancy in that office.

(d) Any vacancy in the Commission shall not affect its powers and shall be filled in the same manner, and subject to the same limitation with respect to party affiliations as the original appointment was made.

(e) Four members of the Commission shall constitute a quorum.

Rules of Procedure of the Commission

Sec. 102. (a) The Chairman or one designated by him to act as Chairman at a hearing of the Commission shall announce in an opening statement the subject of the hearing.

(b) A copy of the Commission's rules shall be made available to the witness before the Commission.

(c) Witnesses at the hearings may be accompanied by their own counsel for the purpose of advising them concerning their constitutional rights.

(d) The Chairman or Acting Chairman may punish breaches of order and decorum and unprofessional ethics on the part of counsel, by censure and exclusion from the hearings.

(e) If the Commission determines that evidence or testimony at any hearing may tend to defame, degrade, or incriminate any person, it shall (1) receive such evidence or testimony in executive session; (2) afford such person an opportunity voluntarily to appear as a witness; and (3) receive and dispose of requests from such person to subpena additional witnesses.

(f) Except as provided in sections 102 and 105(f) of this Act, the Chairman shall receive and the Commission shall dispose of requests to subpena additional witnesses.

(g) No evidence or testimony taken in executive session may be released or used in public sessions without the consent of the Commission. Whoever releases or uses in public without the consent of the Commission evidence or testimony taken in executive session shall be fined not more than $1,000, or imprisoned for not more than one year.

(h) In the discretion of the Commission, witnesses may submit brief and pertinent sworn statements in writing for inclusion in the record. The Commission is the sole judge of the pertinency of testimony and evidence adduced at its hearings.

(i) Upon payment of the cost thereof, a witness may obtain a transcript copy of his testimony given at a public session or, if given at an executive session, when authorized by the Commission.

(j) A witness attending any session of the Commission shall receive $4 for each day's attendance and for the time necessarily occupied in going to and returning from the same, and 8 cents per mile for going from and returning to his place of residence. Witnesses who attend at points so far removed from their respective residences as to prohibit return thereto from day to day shall be entitled to an additional allowance of $12 per day for expenses of subsistence, including the time necessarily occupied in going to and returning from the place of attendance. Mileage payments shall be tendered to the witness upon service of a subpena issued on behalf of the Commission or any subcommittee thereof.

(k) The Commission shall not issue any subpena for the attendance and testimony of witnesses or for the production of written or other matter which would require the presence of the party subpenaed at a hearing to be held outside of the State, wherein the witness is found or resides or transacts business.

Compensation of Members of the Commission

Sec. 103. (a) Each member of the Commission who is not otherwise in the service of the Government of the United States shall receive the sum of $50 per day for each day spent in the work of the Commission, shall be reimbursed for actual and necessary travel expenses, and shall receive a per diem allowance of $12 in lieu of actual expenses for subsistence when away from his usual place of residence, inclusive of fees or tips to porters and stewards.

(b) Each member of the Commission who is otherwise in the service of the Government of the United States shall serve without compensation in addition to that received for such other service, but while engaged in the work of the Commission shall be reimbursed for actual and necessary travel expenses, and shall receive a per diem allowance of $12 in lieu of actual expenses for subsistence when away from his usual place of residence, inclusive of fees or tips to porters and stewards.

Duties of the Commission

Sec. 104. (a) The Commission shall—

(1) investigate allegations in writing under oath or affirmation that certain citizens of the United States are being deprived of their right to vote and have that vote counted by reason of their color, race, religion, or national origin; which writing, under oath or affirmation, shall set forth the facts upon which such belief or beliefs are based;

(2) study and collect information concerning legal developments constituting a denial of equal protection of the laws under the Constitution; and

(3) appraise the laws and policies of the Federal Government with respect to equal protection of the laws under the Constitution.

(b) The Commission shall submit interim reports to the President and to the Congress at such times as either the Commission or the President shall deem desirable, and shall submit to the President and to the Congress a final and comprehensive report of its activities, findings, and recommendations not later than two years from the date of the enactment of this Act.

(c) Sixty days after the submission of its final report and recommendations the Commission shall cease to exist.

Powers of the Commission

Sec. 105. (a) There shall be a full-time staff director for the Commission who shall be appointed by the President by and with the advice and consent of the Senate and who shall receive compensation at a rate, to be fixed by the President, not in excess of $22,500 a year. The President shall consult with the Commission before submitting the nomination of any person for appointment to the position of staff director. Within the limitations of its appropriations, the Commission may appoint such other personnel as it deems advisable, in accordance with the civil service and classification laws, and may procure services as authorized by section 15 of the Act of August 2, 1946 (60 Stat. 810; 5 U.S.C. 55a), but at rates for individuals not in excess of $50 per diem.

(b) The Commission shall not accept or utilize services of voluntary or uncompensated personnel, and the term "whoever" as used in paragraph (g) of section 102 hereof shall be construed to mean a person whose services are compensated by the United States.

(c) The Commission may constitute such advisory committees within States composed of citizens of that State and may consult with governors, attorneys general, and other representatives of State and local governments, and private organizations, as it deems advisable.

(d) Members of the Commission, and members of advisory committees constituted pursuant to subsection (c) of this section, shall be exempt from the operation of sections 281, 283, 284, 434, and 1914 of title 18 of the United States Code, and section 190 of the Revised Statutes (5 U.S.C. 99).

(e) All Federal agencies shall cooperate fully with the Commission to the end that it may effectively carry out its functions and duties.

(f) The Commission, or on the authorization of the Commission any subcommittee of two or more members, at least one of whom shall be of each major political party, may, for the purpose of carrying out the provisions of this Act, hold such hearings and act at such times and places as the Commission or such authorized subcommittee may deem advisable. Subpenas for the attendance and testimony of witnesses or the production of written or other matter may be issued in accordance with the rules of the Commission as contained in section 102(j) and (k) of this Act, over the signature of the Chairman of the Commission or of such subcommittee, and may be served by any person designated by such Chairman.

(g) In case of contumacy or refusal to obey a subpena, any district court of the United States or the United States court of any Territory or possession, or the District Court of the United States for the District of Columbia, within the jurisdiction of which the inquiry is carried on or within the jurisdiction of which said person guilty of contumacy or refusal to obey is found or resides or transacts business, upon application by the Attorney General of the United States shall have jurisdiction to issue to such person an order requiring such person to appear before the Commission or a subcommittee thereof, there to produce evidence if so ordered, or there to give testimony touching the matter under investigation; and any failure to obey such order of the court may be punished by said court as a contempt thereof.

Appropriations

Sec. 106. There is hereby authorized to be appropriated, out of any money in the Treasury not otherwise appropriated, so much as may be necessary to carry out the provisions of this Act.

PART II
TO PROVIDE FOR AN ADDITIONAL ASSISTANT ATTORNEY GENERAL

Sec. 111. There shall be in the Department of Justice one additional Assistant Attorney General, who shall be appointed by the President, by and with the advice and consent of the Senate, who shall assist the Attorney General in the performance of his duties, and who shall receive compensation at the rate prescribed by law for other Assistant Attorneys General.

PART III
TO STRENGTHEN THE CIVIL RIGHTS STATUTES, AND FOR OTHER PURPOSES

Sec. 121. Section 1343 of title 28, United States Code, is amended as follows:

(a) Amend the catch line of said section to read,

"§ 1343. Civil rights and elective franchise"

(b) Delete the period at the end of paragraph (3) and insert in lieu thereof a semicolon.

(c) Add a paragraph as follows:

"(4) To recover damages or to secure equitable or other relief under any Act of Congress providing for the protection of civil rights, including the right to vote."

Sec. 122. Section 1989 of the Revised Statutes (42 U.S.C. 1993) is hereby repealed.

PART IV
TO PROVIDE MEANS OF FURTHER SECURING AND PROTECTING THE RIGHT TO VOTE

Sec. 131. Section 2004 of the Revised Statutes (42 U.S.C. 1971), is amended as follows:

(a) Amend the catch line of said section to read, "Voting rights".

(b) Designate its present text with the subsection symbol "(a)".

(c) Add, immediately following the present text, four new subsections to read as follows:

"(b) No person, whether acting under color of law or otherwise, shall intimidate, threaten, coerce, or attempt to intimidate, threaten, or coerce any other person for the purpose of interfering with the right of such other person to vote or to vote as he may choose, or of causing such other person to vote for, or not to vote for, any candidate for the office of President, Vice President, presidential elector, Member of the Senate, or Member of the House of Representatives, Delegates or Commissioners from the Territories or possessions, at any general, special, or primary election held solely or in part for the purpose of selecting or electing any such candidate.

"(c) Whenever any person has engaged or there are reasonable grounds to believe that any person is about to engage in any act or practice which would deprive any other person of any right or privilege secured by subsection (a) or (b), the Attorney General may institute for the United States, or in the name of the United States, a civil action or other proper proceeding for preventive relief, including an application for a permanent or temporary injunction, restraining order, or other order. In any proceeding hereunder the United States shall be liable for costs the same as a private person.

"(d) The district courts of the United States shall have jurisdiction of proceedings instituted pursuant to this section and shall exercise the same without regard to whether the party aggrieved shall have exhausted any administrative or other remedies that may be provided by law.

"(e) Any person cited for an alleged contempt under this Act shall be allowed to make his full defense by counsel learned in the law; and the court before which he is cited or tried, or some judge thereof, shall immediately, upon his request, assign to him such counsel, not exceeding two, as he may desire, who shall have free access to him at all reasonable hours. He shall be allowed, in his defense to make any proof that he can produce by lawful witnesses, and shall have the like process of the court to compel his witnesses to appear at his trial or hearing, as is usually granted to compel witnesses to appear on behalf of the prosecution. If such person shall be found by the court to be financially unable to provide for such counsel, it shall be the duty of the court to provide such counsel."

PART V

TO PROVIDE TRIAL BY JURY FOR PROCEEDINGS TO PUNISH CRIMINAL CONTEMPTS OF COURT GROWING OUT OF CIVIL RIGHTS CASES AND TO AMEND THE JUDICIAL CODE RELATING TO FEDERAL JURY QUALIFICATIONS

Sec. 151. In all cases of criminal contempt arising under the provisions of this Act, the accused, upon conviction, shall be punished by fine or imprisonment or both: *Provided however,* That in case the accused is a natural person the fine to be paid shall not exceed the sum of $1,000, nor shall imprisonment exceed the term of six months: *Provided further,* That in any such proceeding for criminal contempt, at the discretion of the judge, the accused may be tried with or without a jury: *Provided further, however,* That in the event such proceeding for criminal contempt be tried before a judge without a jury and the sentence of the court upon conviction is a fine in excess of the sum of $300 or imprisonment in excess of forty-five days, the accused in said proceeding, upon demand therefor, shall be entitled to a trial de novo before a jury, which shall conform as near as may be to the practice in other criminal cases.

This section shall not apply to contempts committed in the presence of the court or so near thereto as to interfere directly with the administration of justice nor to the misbehavior, misconduct, or disobedience, of any officer of the court in respect to the writs, orders, or process of the court.

Nor shall anything herein or in any other provision of law be construed to deprive courts of their power, by civil contempt proceedings, without a jury, to secure compliance with or to prevent obstruction of, as distinguished from punishment for violations of, any lawful writ, process, order, rule, decree, or command of the court in accordance with the prevailing usages of law and equity, including the power of detention.

Sec. 152. Section 1861, title 28, of the United States Code is hereby amended to read as follows:

"§ 1861. Qualifications of Federal jurors

"Any citizen of the United States who has attained the age of twenty-one years and who has resided for a period of one year within the judicial district, is competent to serve as a grand or petit juror unless—

"(1) He has been convicted in a State or Federal court of record of a crime punishable by imprisonment for more than one year and his civil rights have not been restored by pardon or amnesty.

"(2) He is unable to read, write, speak, and understand the English language.

"(3) He is incapable, by reason of mental or physical infirmities to render efficient jury service."

Sec. 161. This Act may be cited as the "Civil Rights Act of 1957".

Approved September 9, 1957.

Civil Rights Act of 1960

TITLE I

OBSTRUCTION OF COURT ORDERS

Sec. 101. Chapter 73 of title 18, United States Code, is amended by adding at the end thereof a new section as follows:

"§ 1509. Obstruction of court orders

"Whoever, by threats or force, willfully prevents, obstructs, impedes, or interferes with, or willfully attempts to prevent, obstruct, impede, or interfere with, the due exercise of rights or the performance of duties under any order, judgment, or decree of a court of the United States, shall be fined not more than $1,000 or imprisoned not more than one year, or both.

"No injunctive or other civil relief against the conduct made criminal by this section shall be denied on the ground that such conduct is a crime."

Sec. 102. The analysis of chapter 73 of such title is amended by adding at the end thereof the following:

"1509. Obstruction of court orders."

TITLE II

FLIGHT TO AVOID PROSECUTION FOR DAMAGING OR DESTROYING ANY BUILDING OR OTHER REAL OF PERSONAL PROPERTY; AND, ILLEGAL TRANSPORTATION, USE OR POSSESSION OF EXPLOSIVES; AND, THREATS OR FALSE INFORMATION CONCERNING ATTEMPTS TO DAMAGE OR DESTROY REAL OR PERSONAL PROPERTY BY FIRE OR EXPLOSIVES

Sec. 201. Chapter 49 of title 18, United States Code, is amended by adding at the end thereof a new section as follows:

"§ 1074. Flight to avoid prosecution for damaging or destroying any building or other real or personal property

"(a) Whoever moves or travels in interstate or foreign commerce with intent either (1) to avoid prosecution, or custody, or confinement after conviction, under the laws of the place from which he flees, for willfully attempting to or damaging or destroying by fire or explosive any building, structure, facility, vehicle, dwelling house, synagogue, church, religious center or educational institution, public or private, or (2) to avoid giving testimony in any criminal proceeding relating to any such offense shall be fined not more than $5,000 or imprisoned not more than five years, or both.

"(b) Violations of this section may be prosecuted in the Federal judicial district in which the original crime was alleged to have been committed or in which the person was held in custody or confinement: *Provided, however,* That this section shall not be construed as indicating an intent on the part of Congress to prevent any State, Territory, Commonwealth, or possession of the United States of any jurisdiction over any offense over which they would have jurisdiction in the absence of such section."

Sec. 202. The analysis of chapter 49 of such title is amended by adding thereto the following:

"1074. Flight to avoid prosecution for damaging or destroying any building or other real or personal property."

Sec. 203. Chapter 39 of title 18 of the United States Code is amended by adding at the end thereof the following new section:

"§ 837. Explosives; illegal use or possession; and, threats or false information concerning attempts to damage or destroy real or personal property by fire or explosives

"(a) As used in this section—

" 'commerce' means commerce between any State, Territory, Commonwealth, District, or possession of the United States, and any place outside thereof; or between points within the same State, Territory, or possession, or the District of Columbia, but through any place outside thereof; or within any Territory, or possession of the United States, or the District of Columbia;

" 'explosive' means gunpowders, powders used for blasting, all forms of high explosives, blasting materials, fuzes (other than electric circuit breakers), detonators, and other detonating agents, smokeless powders, and any chemical compounds or mechanical mixture that contains any oxidizing and combustible units, or other ingredients, in such proportions, quantities, or packing that ignition by fire, by friction, by concussion, by percussion, or by detonation of the compound or mixture or any part thereof may cause an explosion.

"(b) Whoever transports or aids and abets another in transporting in interstate or foreign commerce any explosive, with the knowledge or intent that it will be used to damage or destroy any building or other real or personal property for the purpose of interfering with its use for educational, religious, charitable, residential, business, or civic objectives or of intimidating any person pursuing such objectives, shall be subject to imprisonment for not more than one year, or a fine of not more than $1,000, or both; and if personal injury results shall be subject to imprisonment for not more than ten years or a fine of not more than $10,000, or both; and if death results shall be subject to imprisonment for any term of years or for life, but the court may impose the death penalty if the jury so recommends.

"(c) The possession of an explosive in such a manner as to evince an intent to use, or the use of, such explosive, to damage or destroy any building or other real or personal property used for educational, religious, charitable, residential, business, or civic objectives or to intimidate any person pursuing such objectives, creates rebuttable presumptions that the explosive was transported in interstate or foreign commerce or caused to be transported in interstate or foreign commerce by the person so possessing or using it, or by a person aiding or abetting the person so possessing or using it; *Provided, however,* That no person may be convicted under this section unless there is evidence independent of the presumptions that this section has been violated.

"(d) Whoever, through the use of the mail, telephone, telegraph, or other instrument of commerce, willfully imparts or conveys, or causes to be imparted or conveyed, any threat, or false information knowing the same to be false, concerning an attempt or alleged attempt being made, or to be made, to damage or destroy any building or other real or personal property for the purpose of interfering with its use for educational, religious, charitable, residential, business, or civic objectives, or of intimidating any person pursuing such objectives, shall be subject to imprisonment for not more than one year or a fine of not more than $1,000, or both.

"(e) This section shall not be construed as indicating an intent on the part of Congress to occupy the field in which this section operates to the exclusion of a law of any State, Territory, Commonwealth, or possession of the United States, and no law of any State, Territory, Commonwealth, or possession of the United States which would be valid in the absence of the section shall be declared invalid, and no local authorities shall be deprived of any jurisdiction over any offense over which they would have jurisdiction in the absence of this section."

Sec. 204. The analysis of chapter 39 of title 18 is amended by adding thereto the following:

"837. Explosives; illegal use or possession; and threats or false information concerning attempts to damage or destroy real or personal property by fire or explosives."

TITLE III

FEDERAL ELECTION RECORDS

Sec. 301. Every officer of election shall retain and preserve, for a period of twenty-two months from the date of any general, special, or primary election of which candidates for the office of President, Vice President, presidential elector, Member of the Senate, Member of the House of Representatives, or Resident Commissioner from the Commonwealth of Puerto Rico are voted for, all records and papers which come into his possession relating to any application, registration, payment of poll tax, or other act requisite to voting in such election, except that, when required by law, such records and papers may be delivered to another officer of election and except that, if a State or the Commonwealth of Puerto Rico designates a custodian to retain and preserve these records and papers at a specified place, then such records and papers may be deposited with such custodian, and the duty to retain and preserve any record or paper so deposited shall devolve upon such custodian. Any officer of election or custodian who willfully fails to comply with this section shall be fined not more than $1,000 or imprisoned not more than one year, or both.

Sec. 302. Any person, whether or not an officer of election or custodian, who willfully steals, destroys, conceals, mutilates, or alters any record or paper required by section 301 to be retained and preserved shall be fined not more than $1,000 or imprisoned not more than one year, or both.

Sec. 303. Any record or paper required by section 301 to be retained and preserved shall, upon demand in writing by the Attorney General or his representative directed to the person having custody, possession, or control of such record or paper, be made available for inspection, reproduction, and copying at the principal office of such custodian by the Attorney General or his representative. This demand shall contain a statement of the basis and the purpose therefor.

Sec. 304. Unless otherwise ordered by a court of the United States, neither the Attorney General nor any employee of the Department of Justice, nor any other representative of the Attorney General, shall disclose any record or paper produced pursuant to this title, or any reproduction or copy, except to Congress and any committee thereof, governmental agencies, and in the presentation of any case or proceeding before any court or grand jury.

Sec. 305. The United States district court for the district in which a demand is made pursuant to section 303, or in which a record or paper so demanded is located, shall have jurisdiction by appropriate process to compel the production of such record or paper.

Sec. 306. As used in this title, the term "officer of election" means any person who, under color of any Federal, State, Commonwealth, or local law, statute, ordinance, regulation, authority, custom, or usage, performs or is authorized to perform any function, duty, or task in connection with any application, registration, payment of poll tax, or other act requisite to voting in any general, special, or primary election at which votes are cast for candidates for the office of President, Vice President, presidential elector, Member of the

Senate, Member of the House of Representatives, or Resident Commissioner from the Commonwealth of Puerto Rico.

TITLE IV
EXTENSION OF POWERS OF THE CIVIL RIGHTS COMMISSION

Sec. 401. Section 105 of the Civil Rights Act of 1957 (41 U.S.C. Supp. V 1975d) (71 Stat. 635) is amended by adding the following new subsection at the end thereof:

"(h) Without limiting the generality of the foregoing, each member of the Commission shall have the power and authority to administer oaths or take statements of witnesses under affirmation."

TITLE V
EDUCATION OF CHILDREN OF MEMBERS OF ARMED FORCES

Sec. 501. (a) Subsection (a) of section 6 of the Act of September 30, 1950 (Public Law 874, Eighty-first Congress), as amended, relating to arrangements for the provision of free public education for children residing on Federal property where local educational agencies are unable to provide such education, is amended by inserting after the first sentence the following new sentence: "Such arrangements to provide free public education may also be made for children of members of the Armed Forces on active duty, if the schools in which free public education is usually provided for such children are made unavailable to them as a result of official action by State or local governmental authority and it is the judgment of the Commissioner, after he has consulted with the appropriate State educational agency, that no local educational agency is able to provide suitable free public education for such children."

(b) (1) The first sentence of subsection (d) of such section 6 is amended by adding before the period at the end thereof: "or, in the case of children to whom the second sentence of subsection (a) applies, with the head of any Federal department or agency having jurisdiction over the parents of some or all of such children".

(2) The second sentence of such subsection (d) is amended by striking out "Arrangements" and inserting in lieu thereof "Except where the Commissioner makes arrangements pursuant to the second sentence of subsection (a), arrangements".

Sec. 502. Section 10 of the Act of September 23, 1950 (Public Law 815, Eighty-first Congress), as amended, relating to arrangements for facilities for the provision of free public education for children residing on Federal property where local educational agencies are unable to provide such education, is amended by inserting after the first sentence the following new sentence: "Such arrangements may also be made to provide, on a temporary basis, minimum school facilities for children of members of the Armed Forces on active duty, if the schools in which free public education is usually provided for such children are made unavailable to them as a result of official action by State or local governmental authority and it is the judgment of the Commissioner, after he has consulted with the appropriate State educational agency, that no local educational agency is able to provide suitable free public education for such children."

TITLE VI

Sec. 601. That section 2004 of the Revised Statutes (42 U.S.C. 1971), as amended by section 131 of the Civil Rights Act of 1957 (71 Stat. 637), is amended as follows:

(a) Add the following as subsection (e) and designate the present subsection (e) as subsection "(f)":

"In any proceeding instituted pursuant to subsection (c) in the event the court finds that any person has been deprived on account of race or color of any right or privilege secured by subsection (a), the court shall upon request of the Attorney General and after each party has been given notice and the opportunity to be heard make a finding whether such deprivation was or is pursuant to a pattern or practice. If the court finds such pattern or practice, any person of such race or color resident within the affected area shall, for one year and thereafter until the court subsequently finds that such pattern or practice has ceased, be entitled, upon his application therefor, to an order declaring him qualified to vote, upon proof that at any election or elections (1) he is qualified under State law to vote, and (2) he has since such finding by the court been (a) deprived of or denied under color of law the opportunity to register to vote or otherwise to qualify to vote, or (b) found not qualified to vote by any person acting under color of law. Such order shall be effective as to any election held within the longest period for which such applicant could have been registered or otherwise qualified under State law at which the applicant's qualifications would under State law entitle him to vote.

"Notwithstanding any inconsistent provision of State law or the action of any State officer or court, an applicant so declared qualified to vote shall be permitted to vote in any such election. The Attorney General shall cause to be transmitted certified copies of such order to the appropriate election officers. The refusal by any such officer with notice of such order to permit any person so declared qualified to vote at an appropriate election shall constitute contempt of court.

"An application for an order pursuant to this subsection shall be heard within ten days, and the execution of any order disposing of such application shall not be stayed if the effect of such stay would be to delay the effectiveness of the order beyond the date of any election at which the applicant would otherwise be enabled to vote.

"The court may appoint one or more persons who are qualified voters in the judicial district, to be known as voting referees, who shall subscribe to the oath of office required by Revised Statutes, section 1757; (5 U.S.C. 16) to serve for such period as the court shall determine, to receive such applications and to take evidence and report to the court findings as to whether or not at any election or elections (1) any such applicant is qualified under State law to vote, and (2) he has since the finding by the court heretofore specified been (a) deprived of or denied under color of law the opportunity to register to vote or otherwise to qualify to vote, or (b) found not qualified to vote by any person acting under color of law. In a proceeding before a voting referee, the applicant shall be heard ex parte at such times and places as the court shall direct. His statement under oath shall be prima facie evidence as to his age, residence, and his prior efforts to register or otherwise qualify to vote. Where proof of literacy or an understanding of other subjects is required by valid provisions of State law, the answer of the applicant, if written, shall be included in such report to the court; if oral, it shall be taken down stenographically and a transcription included in such report to the court.

"Upon receipt of such report, the court shall cause the Attorney General to transmit a copy thereof to the State attorney general and to each party to such proceeding together with an order to show cause within ten days, or such shorter time as the court may fix, why an order of the court should not be entered in accordance with such report. Upon the expiration of such period, such order shall be entered unless prior to that time there has been filed with the court and served upon all parties a statement of exceptions to such report. Exceptions as to matters of fact shall be considered only if supported by a duly verified copy of a public record or by affidavit of persons having personal knowledge of such facts or by statements or matters contained in such report; those relating to matters of law shall be supported by an appropriate memorandum of law. The issues of fact and law raised by such exceptions shall be determined by the court or, if the due and speedy administration of justice requires, they may be referred to the voting referee to determine in accordance with procedures prescribed by the court. A hearing as to an issue of fact shall be held only in the event that the proof in support of the exception disclose the existence of a genuine issue of material fact. The applicant's literacy and understanding of other subjects shall be determined solely on the basis of answers included in the report of the voting referee.

"The court, or at its direction the voting referee, shall issue to each applicant so declared qualified a certificate identifying the holder thereof as a person so qualified.

"Any voting referee appointed by the court pursuant to this subsection shall to the extent not inconsistent herewith have all the powers conferred upon a master by rule 53(c) of the Federal Rules of Civil Procedure. The compensation to be allowed to any persons appointed by the court pursuant to this subsection shall be fixed by the court and shall be payable by the United States.

"Applications pursuant to this subsection shall be determined expeditiously. In the case of any application filed twenty or more days prior to an election which is undetermined by the time of such election, the court shall issue an order authorizing the applicant to vote provisionally: *Provided, however,* That such applicant shall be qualified to vote under State law. In the case of an application filed within twenty days prior to an election, the court, in its discretion, may make such an order. In either case the order shall make appropriate provision for the impounding of the applicant's ballot pending determination of the application. The court may take any other action, and may authorize such referee or such other person as it may designate to take any other action, appropriate or necessary to carry out the provisions of this subsection and to enforce its decrees. This subsection shall in no way be construed as a limitation upon the existing powers of the court.

"When used in the subsection, the word 'vote' includes all action necessary to make a vote effective including, but not limited to, registration or other action required by State law prerequisite to voting, casting a ballot, and having such ballot counted and included in the appropriate totals of votes cast with respect to candidates for public office and propositions for which votes are received in an election; the words 'affected area' shall mean any subdivision of the State in which the laws of the State relating to voting are or have been to any extent administered by a person found in the proceeding to have violated subsection (a); and the words 'qualified under State law' shall mean qualified according to the laws, customs, or usages of the State, and shall not, in any event, imply qualifications more stringent than those used by the persons found in the proceeding to have violated subsection (a) in qualifying persons other than those of the race or color against which the pattern or practice of discrimination was found to exist."

(b) Add the following sentence at the end of subsection (c):

"Whenever, in a proceeding instituted under this subsection any official of a State or subdivision thereof is alleged to have committed any act or practice constituting a deprivation of any right or privilege secured by subsection (a), the act or practice shall also be deemed that of the State and the State may be joined as a party defendant and, if, prior to the institution of such proceeding, such official has resigned or has been relieved of his office and no successor has assumed such office, the proceeding may be insituted against the State."

TITLE VII
SEPARABILITY

Sec. 701. If any provision of this Act is held invalid, the remainder of this Act shall not be affected thereby.

Approved May 6, 1960.

Civil Rights Act of 1964

The Kennedy Administration was committed to strong civil rights action. During his campaign President Kennedy upbraided Eisenhower for not moving by way of Executive Order wherever possible. He claimed that by a "stroke of the pen," segregation in numerous federal programs could be eliminated. However, once he became President, Kennedy did not use his pen (to ban discrimination in federally financed housing) until almost two years after he was elected, largely because of his concern about his legislative program in Congress. It was only after the Birmingham crisis in 1963 that strong civil rights legislation was introduced by the Kennedy Administration.

President Kennedy's June 1963 message to Congress (included below), outlining a new Civil Rights Bill, showed the need for this legislation. However, it took a year before Congress passed the law. Only the strong support of Senator Dirksen and other Republicans insured its passage.

President Kennedy's Report to Congress Outlining a Civil Rights Bill (June 19, 1963)

To the Congress of the United States:

Last week I addressed to the American people an appeal to conscience —a request for their cooperation in meeting the growing moral crisis in American race relations. I warned of "a rising tide of discontent that threatens the public safety" in many parts of the country. I emphasized that "the events in Birmingham and elsewhere have so increased the cries for equality that no city or State or legislative body can prudently choose to ignore them." "It is a time to act," I said, "in the Congress, in State and local legislative bodies, and, above all, in all of our daily lives."

In the days that have followed, the predictions of increased violence have been tragically borne out. The "fires of frustration and discord" have burned hotter than ever.

At the same time, the response of the American people to this appeal to their principles and obligations has been reassuring. Private progress— by merchants and unions and local organizations—has been marked, if not uniform, in many areas. Many doors long closed to Negroes, North and South, have been opened. Local biracial committees, under private and public sponsorship, have mushroomed. The mayors of our major cities, whom I earlier addressed, have pledged renewed action. But persisting inequalities and tensions make it clear that Federal action must lead the way, providing both the Nation's standard and a nationwide solution. In short, the time has come for the Congress of the United States to join with the executive and judicial branches in making it clear to all that race has no place in American life or law.

On February 28, I sent to the Congress a message urging the enactment this year of three important pieces of civil rights legislation:

1. Voting: Legislation to assure the availability to all of a basic and powerful right—the right to vote in a free American election—by providing for the appointment of temporary Federal voting referees while voting suits are proceeding in areas of demonstrated need; by giving such suits preferential and expedited treatment in the Federal courts; by prohibiting in Federal elections the application of different tests and standards to

different voter applicants; and by providing that, in voting suits pertaining to such elections, the completion of the sixth grade by any applicant creates a presumption that he is literate. Armed with the full and equal right to vote, our Negro citizens can help win other rights through political channels not now open to them in many areas.

2. Civil Rights Commission: Legislation to renew and expand the authority of the Commission on Civil Rights, enabling it to serve as a national civil rights clearinghouse offering information, advice, and technical assistance to any public or private agency that so requests.

3. School desegregation: Legislation to provide Federal technical and financial assistance to aid school districts in the process of desegregation in compliance with the Constitution.

Other measures introduced in the Congress have also received the support of this administration, including those aimed at assuring equal employment opportunity.

Although these recommendations were transmitted to the Congress some time ago, neither House has yet had an opportunity to vote on any of these essential measures. The Negro's drive for justice, however, has not stood still—nor will it, it is now clear, until full equality is achieved. The growing and understandable dissatisfaction of Negro citizens with the present pace of desegregation, and their increased determination to secure for themselves the equality of opportunity and treatment to which they are rightfully entitled, have underscored what should already have been clear: the necessity of the Congress enacting this year—not only the measures already proposed—but also additional legislation providing legal remedies for the denial of certain individual rights.

The venerable code of equity law commands "for every wrong, a remedy." But in too many communities, in too many parts of the country, wrongs are inflicted on Negro citizens for which no effective remedy at law is clearly and readily available. State and local laws may even affirmatively seek to deny the rights to which these citizens are fairly entitled—and this can result only in a decreased respect for the law and increased violations of the law.

In the continued absence of congressional action, too many State and local officials as well as businessmen will remain unwilling to accord these rights to all citizens. Some local courts and local merchants may well claim to be uncertain of the law, while those merchants who do recognize the justice of the Negro's request—and I believe these constitute the great majority of merchants, North and South—will be fearful of being the first to move, in the face of official, customer, employee, or competitive pressures. Negroes, consequently, can be expected to continue increasingly to seek the vindication of these rights through organized direct action, with all its potentially explosive consequences, such as we have seen in Birmingham, in Philadelphia, in Jackson, in Boston, in Cambridge, Md., and in many other parts of the country.

In short, the result of continued Federal legislative inaction will be continued, if not increased, racial strife—causing the leadership on both sides to pass from the hands of reasonable and responsible men to the purveyors of hate and violence, endangering domestic tranquility, retarding our Nation's economic and social progress, and weakening the respect with which the rest of the world regards us. No American, I feel sure, would prefer this course of tension, disorder, and division—and the great majority of our citizens simply cannot accept it.

For these reasons, I am proposing that the Congress stay in session this year until it has enacted—preferably as a single omnibus bill—the most responsible, reasonable and urgently needed solutions to this problem, solutions which should be acceptable to all fair-minded men. This bill would be known as the Civil Rights Act of 1963, and would include—in addition to the aforementioned provisions on voting rights and the Civil Rights Commission—additional titles on public accommodations, employment, federally assisted programs, a community relations service, and education, with the latter including my previous recommendation on this subject. In addition, I am requesting certain legislative and budget amendments designed to improve the training, skills and economic opportunities of the economically distressed and discontented, white and Negro alike. Certain executive actions are also reviewed here; but legislative action is imperative.

I. Equal Accommodations in Public Facilities

Events of recent weeks have again underlined how deeply our Negro citizens resent the injustice of being arbitrarily denied equal access to those facilities and accommodations which are otherwise open to the general public. That is a daily insult which has no place in a country proud of its heritage—the heritage of the melting-pot, of equal rights, of one nation and one people. No one has been barred on account of his race from fighting or dying for America—there are no "white" or "colored" signs on the foxholes or graveyards of battle. Surely, in 1963, 100 years after emancipation, it should not be necessary for any American citizen to demonstrate in the streets for the opportunity to stop at a hotel, or to eat at a lunch counter in the very department store in which he is shopping, or to enter a motion picture house, on the same terms as any other customer. As I stated in my message to the Congress of February 28, "no action is more contrary to the spirit of our democracy and Constitution—or more rightfully resented by a Negro citizen who seeks only equal treatment—than the barring of that citizen from restaurants, hotels, theaters, recreational areas and other public accommodations and facilities."

The U.S. Government has taken action through the courts and by other means to protect those who are peacefully demonstrating to obtain access to these public facilities; and it has taken action to bring an end to discrimination in rail, bus, and airline terminals, to open up restaurants and other public facilities in all buildings leased as well as owned by the Federal Government, and to assure full equality of access to all federally owned parks, forests, and other recreational areas. When uncontrolled mob action directly threatened the nondiscriminatory use of transportation facilities in May 1961, Federal marshals were employed to restore order and prevent potentially widespread personal and property damage. Growing nationwide concern with this problem, however, makes it clear that further Federal action is needed now to secure the right of all citizens to the full enjoyment of all facilities which are open to the general public.

Such legislation is clearly consistent with the Constitution and with our concepts of both human rights and property rights. The argument that such measures constitute an unconstitutional interference with property rights has consistently been rejected by the courts in upholding laws on zoning, collective bargaining, minimum wages, smoke control, and countless other measures designed to make certain that the use of private property is consistent with the public interest. While the legal situations are not parallel, it is interesting to note that Abraham Lincoln, in issuing the Emancipation Proclamation 100 years ago, was also accused of violating the property rights of slaveowners. Indeed, there is an age-old saying that "property has its duties as well as its rights"; and no property owner who holds those premises for the purpose of serving at a profit the American public at large can claim any inherent right to exclude a part of that public on grounds of race or color. Just as the law requires common carriers to serve equally all who wish their services, so it can require public accommodations to accommodate equally all segments of the general public. Both human rights and property rights are foundations of our society—and both will flourish as the result of this measure.

In a society which is increasingly mobile and in an economy which is increasingly interdependent, business establishments which serve the public—such as hotels, restaurants, theaters, stores, and others—serve not only the members of their immediate communities but travelers from other States and visitors from abroad. Their goods come from all over the Nation. This participation in the flow of interstate commerce has given these business establishments both increased prosperity and an increased responsibility to provide equal access and service to all citizens. Some 30 States, the District of Columbia and numerous cities—covering some two-thirds of this country and well over two-thirds of its people —have already enacted laws of varying effectiveness against discrimination in places of public accommodation, many of them in response to the recommendation of President Truman's Committee on Civil Rights in 1947. But while their efforts indicate that legislation in this area is not extraordinary, the failure of more States to take effective action makes it clear that Federal legislation is necessary. The State and local approach has been tried. The voluntary approach has been tried. But these approaches are insufficient to prevent the free flow of commerce from being arbitrarily and inefficiently restrained and distorted by discrimination in such establishments.

Clearly the Federal Government has both the power and the obligation to eliminate these discriminatory practices: First, because they adversely affect the national economy and the flow of interstate commerce; and secondly, because Congress has been specifically empowered under the 14th amendment to enact legislation making certain that no State law permits or sanctions the unequal protection or treatment of any of its citizens.

There have been increasing public demonstrations of resentment directed against this kind of discrimination—demonstrations which too often breed tension and violence. Only the Federal Government, it is clear, can make these demonstrations unnecessary by providing peaceful remedies for the grievances which set them off.

For these reasons, I am today proposing, as part of the Civil Rights Act of 1963, a provision to guarantee all citizens equal access to the services and facilities of hotels, restaurants, places of amusement, and retail establishments.

This seems to me to be an elementary right. Its denial is an arbitrary indignity that no American in 1963 should have to endure. The proposal would give the person aggrieved the right to obtain a court order against the offending establishment or persons. Upon receiving a complaint in a case sufficiently important to warrant his conclusion that a suit would materially further the purposes of the act, the Attorney General—if he finds that the aggrieved party is unable to undertake or otherwise arrange for a suit on his own (for lack of financial means or effective representation, or for fear of economic or other injury)—will first refer the case for voluntary settlement to the Community Relations Service described below, give the establishment involved time to correct its practices, permit State and local equal access laws (if any) to operate first, and then, and only then, initiate a suit for compliance. In short, to the extent that these unconscionable practices can be corrected by the individual owners, localities and States (and recent experience demonstrates how effectively and uneventfully this can be done), the Federal Government has no desire to intervene.

But an explosive national problem cannot await city-by-city solutions; and those who loudly abhor Federal action only invite it if they neglect or evade their own obligations.

This provision will open doors in every part of the country which never should have been closed. Its enactment will hasten the end to practices which have no place in a free and united nation, and thus help move this potentially dangerous problem from the streets to the courts.

II. Desegregation of Schools

In my message of February 28, while commending the progress already made in achieving desegregation of education at all levels as required by the Constitution, I was compelled to point out the slowness of progress toward primary and secondary school desegregation. The Supreme Court has recently voiced the same opinion. Many Negro children entering segregated grade schools at the time of the Supreme Court decision in 1954 will enter segregated high schools this year, having suffered a loss which can never be regained. Indeed, discrimination in education is one basic cause of the other inequities and hardships inflicted upon our Negro citizens. The lack of equal educational opportunity deprives the individual of equal economic opportunity, restricts his contribution as a citizen and community leader, encourages him to drop out of school and imposes a heavy burden on the effort to eliminate discriminatory practices and prejudices from our national life.

The Federal courts, pursuant to the 1954 decision of the U.S. Supreme Court and earlier decisions on institutions of higher learning, have shown both competence and courage in directing the desegregation of schools on the local level. It is appropriate to keep this responsibility largely within the judicial arena. But it is unfair and unrealistic to expect that the burden of initiating such cases can be wholly borne by private litigants. Too often those entitled to bring suit on behalf of their children lack the economic means for instituting and maintaining such cases or the ability to withstand the personal, physical and economic harassment which sometimes descends upon those who do institute them. The same is true of students wishing to attend the college of their choice but unable to assume the burden of litigation.

These difficulties are among the principal reasons for the delay in carrying out the 1954 decision; and this delay cannot be justified to those who have been hurt as a result. Rights such as these, as the Supreme

Court recently said, are "present rights. They are not merely hopes to some future enjoyment of some formalistic constitutional promise. The basic guarantees of our Constitution are warrants for the here and now."

In order to achieve a more orderly and consistent compliance with the Supreme Court's school and college desegregation decisions, therefore, I recommend that the Congress assert its specific constitutional authority to implement the 14th amendment by including in the Civil Rights Act of 1963 a new title providing the following:

(A) Authority would be given the Attorney General to initiate in the Federal district courts appropriate legal proceedings against local public school boards or public institutions of higher learning—or to intervene in existing cases—whenever

(1) he has received a written complaint from students or from the parents of students who are being denied equal protection of the laws by a segregated public school or college; and

(2) he certifies that such persons are unable to undertake or otherwise arrange for the initiation and maintenance of such legal proceedings for lack of financial means or effective legal representation or for fear of economic or other injury; and

(3) he determines that his initiation of or intervention in such suit will materially further the orderly progress of desegregation in public education. For this purpose, the Attorney General would establish criteria to determine the priority and relative need for Federal action in those districts from which complaints have been filed.

(B) As previously recommended, technical and financial assistance would be given to those school districts in all parts of the country which, voluntarily or as the result of litigation, are engaged in the process of meeting the educational problems flowing from desegregation or racial imbalance but which are in need of guidance, experienced help or financial assistance in order to train their personnel for this changeover, cope with new difficulties and complete the job satisfactorily (including in such assistance loans to a district where State or local funds have been withdrawn or withheld because of desegregation).

Public institutions already operating without racial discrimination, of course, will not be affected by this statute. Local action can always make Federal action unnecessary. Many school boards have peacefully and voluntarily desegregated in recent years. And while this act does not include private colleges and schools, I strongly urge them to live up to their responsibilities and to recognize no arbitrary bar of race or color—

for such bars have no place in any institution, least of all one devoted to the truth and to the improvement of all mankind.

III. Fair and Full Employment

Unemployment falls with special cruelty on minority groups. The unemployment rate of Negro workers is more than twice as high as that of the working force as a whole. In many of our larger cities, both North and South, the number of jobless Negro youth—often 20 percent or more—creates an atmosphere of frustration, resentment and unrest which does not bode well for the future. Delinquency, vandalism, gang warfare, disease, slums and the high cost of public welfare and crime are all directly related to unemployment among whites and Negroes alike—and recent labor difficulties in Philadelphia may well be only the beginning if more jobs are not found in the larger Northern cities in particular.

Employment opportunities, moreover, play a major role in determining whether the rights described above are meaningful. There is little value in a Negro's obtaining the right to be admitted to hotels and restaurants if he has no cash in his pocket and no job.

Relief of Negro unemployment requires progress in three major areas:

(1) More jobs must be created through greater economic growth: The Negro—too often unskilled, too often the first to be fired and the last to be hired—is a primary victim of recessions, depressed areas and unused industrial capacity. Negro unemployment will not be noticeably diminished in this country until the total demand for labor is effectively increased and the whole economy is headed toward a level of full employment. When our economy operates below capacity, Negroes are more severely affected than other groups. Conversely, return to full employment yields particular benefits to the Negro. Recent studies have shown that for every 1 percentage point decline in the general unemployment rate there tends to be a 2-percentage point reduction in Negro unemployment.

Prompt and substantial tax reduction is a key to achieving the full employment we need. The promise of the area redevelopment program—which harnesses local initiative toward the solution of deep-seated economic distress—must not be stifled for want of sufficient authorization or adequate financing. The accelerated public works program is now gaining momentum; States, cities, and local communities should press ahead with the projects financed by this measure. In addition, I have instructed the Departments of Labor, Commerce, and Health, Education, and Welfare to examine how their programs for the relief of unemployment and economic hardship can be still more intensively focused on those areas of hard-core, long-term unemployment, among both white and nonwhite workers. Our concern with civil rights must not cause any diversion or dilution of our efforts for economic progress—for without such progress the Negro's hopes will remain unfulfilled.

(2) More education and training to raise the level of skills: A distressing number of unemployed Negroes are illiterate and unskilled, refugees from farm automation, unable to do simple computations or even to read a help-wanted advertisement. Too many are equipped to work only in those occupations where technology and other changes have reduced the need for manpower—as farm labor or manual labor, in mining or construction. Too many have attended segregated schools that were so lacking in adequate funds and faculty as to be unable to produce qualified job applicants. And too many who have attended nonsegregated schools dropped out for lack of incentive, guidance, or progress. The unemployment rate for those adults with less than 5 years of schooling is around 10 percent; it has consistently been double the prevailing rate for high school graduates; and studies of public welfare recipients show a shockingly high proportion of parents with less than a primary school education.

Although the proportion of Negroes without adequate education and training is far higher than the proportion of whites, none of these problems is restricted to Negroes alone. This Nation is in critical need of a massive upgrading in its education and training effort for all citizens. In an age of rapidly changing technology, that effort today is failing millions of our youth. It is especially failing Negro youth in segregated schools and crowded slums. If we are ever to lift them from the morass of social and economic degradation, it will be through the strengthening of our education and training services—by improving the quality of instruction; by enabling our schools to cope with rapidly expanding enrollments; and by increasing opportunities and incentives for all individuals to complete their education and to continue their self-development during adulthood.

I have therefore requested of the Congress and request again today the enactment of legislation to assist education at every level from grade school through graduate school.

I have also requested the enactment of several measures which provide, by various means and for various age and educational groups, expanded job training and job experience. Today, in the new and more urgent context of this message, I wish to renew my request for these measures, to expand their prospective operation and to supplement them with additional provisions. The additional $400 million which will be required beyond that contained in the January budget is more than offset by the various budget reductions which I have already sent to the Congress in the last 4 months. Studies show, moreover, that the loss of 1 year's income due to unemployment is more than the total cost of 12 years of education through high school; and, when welfare and other social costs are added, it is clear that failure to take these steps will cost us far more than their enactment. There is no more profitable investment than education, and no greater waste than ill-trained youth.

Specifically, I now propose:

(A) That additional funds be provided to broaden the manpower development and training program, and that the act be amended, not only to increase the authorization ceiling and to postpone the effective date of State matching requirements, but also (in keeping with the recommendations of the President's Committee on Youth Employment) to lower the age for training allowances from 19 to 16, to allocate funds for literacy training, and to permit the payment of a higher proportion of the program's training allowances to out-of-school youths, with provisions to assure that no one drops out of school to take advantage of this program;

(B) That additional funds be provided to finance the pending youth employment bill which is designed to channel the energies of out-of-school, out-of-work youth into the constructive outlet offered by hometown improvement projects and conservation work;

(C) That the pending vocational education amendments, which would greatly update and expand this program of teaching job skills to those in school, be strengthened by the appropriation of additional funds, with some of the added money earmarked for those areas with a high incidence of school dropouts and youth unemployment, and by the addition of a new program of demonstration youth training projects to be conducted in these areas;

(D) That the vocational education program be further amended to provide a work-study program for youth of high school age, with Federal funds helping their school or other local public agency employ them part time in order to enable and encourage them to complete their training;

(E) That the ceiling be raised on the adult basic education provisions in the pending education program, in order to help the States teach the fundamental tools of literacy and learning to culturally deprived adults. More than 22 million Americans in all parts of the country have less than 8 years of schooling; and

(F) That the public welfare work-relief and training program, which the Congress added last year, be amended to provide Federal financing of the supervision and equipment costs, and more Federal demonstration and training projects, thus encouraging State and local welfare agencies to put employable but unemployed welfare recipients to work on local projects which do not displace other workers.

To make the above recommendations effective, I call upon more States to adopt enabling legislation covering unemployed fathers under the aid-to-dependent children program, thereby gaining their services for work-relief jobs, and to move ahead more vigorously in implementing the man-power development and training program. I am asking the Secretaries of Labor and Health, Education, and Welfare to make use of their auth-ority to deal directly with communities and vocational schools whenever State cooperation or progress is insufficient, particularly in those areas where youth unemployment is too high. Above all, I urge the Congress to enact all of these measures with alacrity and foresight.

For even the complete elimination of racial discrimination in em-ployment—a goal toward which this Nation must strive (as discussed below)—will not put a single unemployed Negro to work unless he has the skills required and unless more jobs have been created—and thus the passage of the legislation described above (under both sections (1) and (2)) is essential if the objectives of this message are to be met.

(3) Finally racial discrimination in employment must be eliminated: Denial of the right to work is unfair, regardless of its victim. It is doubly unfair to throw its burden on an individual because of his race or color. Men who served side by side with each other on the field of battle should have no difficulty working side by side on an assembly line or construc-tion project.

Therefore, to combat this evil in all parts of the country,

(A) The Committee on Equal Employment Opportunity, under the chairmanship of the Vice President, should be given a permanent statu-tory basis, assuring it of adequate financing and enforcement procedures. That Committee is now stepping up its efforts to remove racial barriers in the hiring practices of Federal departments, agencies, and Federal contractors, covering a total of some 20 million employees and the Nation's major employers. I have requested a company-by-company, plant-by-plant, union-by-union report to assure the implementation of this policy.

(B) I will shortly issue an Executive order extending the authority of the Committee on Equal Employment Opportunity to include the con-struction of buildings and other facilities undertaken wholly or in part as a result of Federal grant-in-aid programs.

(C) I have directed that all Federal construction programs be re-viewed to prevent any racial discrimination in hiring practices, either directly in the rejection of presently available qualified Negro workers or indirectly by the exclusion of Negro applicants for apprenticeship training.

(D) I have directed the Secretary of Labor, in the conduct of his duties under the Federal Apprenticeship Act and Executive Order No.

10925, to require that the admission of young workers to apprenticeship programs be on a completely nondiscriminatory basis.

(E) I have directed the Secretary of Labor to make certain that the job counseling and placement responsibilities of the Federal-State Employment Service are carried out on a nondiscriminatory basis, and to help assure that full and equal employment opportunity is provided all qualified Negro applicants. The selection and referral of applicants for employment and for training opportunities, and the administration of the employment offices' other services and facilities, must be carried on without regard to race or color. This will be of special importance to Negroes graduating from high school or college this month.

(F) The Department of Justice has intervened in a case now pending before the NLRB involving charges of racial discrimination on the part of certain union locals.

(G) As a part of its new policy on Federal employee organizations, this Government will recognize only those that do not discriminate on grounds of race or color.

(H) I have called upon the leaders of organized labor to end discrimination in their membership policies; and some 118 unions, representing 85 percent of the AFL-CIO membership, have signed nondiscrimination agreements with the Committee on Equal Employment Opportunity. More are expected.

(I) Finally, I renew my support of pending Federal fair employment practices legislation, applicable to both employers and unions. Approximately two-thirds of the Nation's labor force is already covered by Federal, State, and local equal employment opportunity measures—including those employed in the 22 States and numerous cities which have enacted such laws as well as those paid directly or indirectly by Federal funds. But, as the Secretary of Labor testified in January 1962, Federal legislation is desirable, for it would help set a standard for all the Nation and close existing gaps.

This problem of unequal job opportunity must not be allowed to grow, as the result of either recession or discrimination. I enlist every employer, every labor union, and every agency of government—whether affected directly by these measures or not—in the task of seeing to it that no false lines are drawn in assuring equality of the right and opportunity to make a decent living.

IV. Community Relations Service

I have repeatedly stressed the fact that progress in race relations, while it cannot be delayed, can be more solidly and more peacefully accomplished to the extent that legislation can be buttressed by voluntary action.

I have urged each member of the U.S. Conference of Mayors to establish biracial human relations committees in every city; and I hope all communities will establish such a group, preferably through official action. Such a board or committee can provide invaluable services by identifying community tensions before they reach the crisis stage, by improving cooperation and communication between the races, and by advising local officials, merchants, and organizations on the steps which can be taken to insure prompt progress.

A similar agency is needed on the Federal level—to work with these local committees, providing them with advice and assistance—to work in those communities which lack a local committee—and generally to help ease tensions and suspicions, to help resolve interracial disputes and to work quietly to improve relations in any community threatened or torn with strife. Such an effort is in no way a substitute for effective legislative guarantees of human rights. But conciliation and cooperation can facilitate the achievement of those rights, enabling legislation to operate more smoothly and more effectively.

The Department of Justice and its Civil Rights Division have already performed yeoman service of this nature, in Birmingham, in Jackson, and throughout the country. But the problem has grown beyond the time and energies which a few otherwise burdened officials can make available—and, in some areas, the confidence of all will be greater in an intermediary whose duties are completely separated from departmental functions of investigation or litigation.

It is my intention, therefore, to establish by Executive order (until such time as it can be created by statute) an independent Community Relations Service—to fulfill the functions described above, working through regional, State, and local committees to the extent possible, and offering its services in tension-torn communities either upon its own motion or upon the request of a local official or other party. Authority for such a Service is included in the proposed omnibus bill. It will work without publicity and hold all information imparted to its officers in strict confidence. Its own resources can be preserved by its encouraging and assisting the creation of State and local committees, either on a continuing basis or in emergency situations.

Without powers of enforcement or subpena, such a Service is no substitute for other measures; and it cannot guarantee success. But dialog and discussion are always better than violence—and this agency, by enabling all concerned to sit down and reason together, can play a major role in achieving peaceful progress in civil rights.

V. Federal Programs

Simple justice requires that public funds, to which all taxpayers of all races contribute, not be spent in any fashion which encourages, entrenches, subsidizes, or results in racial discrimination. District discrimination by Federal, State, or local governments is prohibited by the Constitution. But indirect discrimination, through the use of Federal funds, is just as invidious; and it should not be necessary to resort to the courts to prevent each individual violation. Congress and the Executive have their responsibilities to uphold the Constitution also; and, in the 1960's, the executive branch has sought to fulfill its responsibilities by banning discrimination in federally financed housing, in NDEA and NSF institutes, in federally affected employment, in the Army and Air Force Reserve, in the training of civilian defense workers, and in all federally owned and leased facilities.

Many statutes providing Federal financial assistance, however, define with such precision both the Administrator's role and the conditions upon which specified amounts shall be given to designated recipients that the amount of administrative discretion remaining—which might be used to withhold funds if discrimination were not ended—is at best questionable. No administrator has the unlimited authority to invoke the Constitution in opposition to the mandate of the Congress. Nor would it always be helpful to require unconditionally—as is often proposed—the withdrawal of all Federal funds from programs urgently needed by Negroes as well as whites; for this may only penalize those who least deserve it without ending discrimination.

Instead of permitting this issue to become a political device often exploited by those opposed to social or economic progress, it would be better at this time to pass a single comprehensive provision making it clear that the Federal Government is not required, under any statute, to furnish any kind of financial assistance—by way of grant, loan, contract, guarantee, insurance, or otherwise—to any program or activity in which racial discrimination occurs. This would not permit the Federal Government to cut off all Federal aid of all kinds as a means of punishing an area for the discrimination occurring therein—but it would clarify the authority of any administrator with respect to Federal funds or financial assistance and discriminatory practices.

Conclusion

Many problems remain that cannot be ignored. The enactment of the legislation I have recommended will not solve all our problems of race relations. This bill must be supplemented by action in every branch of government at the Federal, State, and local level. It must be supplemented as well by enlightened private citizens, private businesses and private labor and civic organizations, by responsible educators and editors, and certainly by religious leaders who recognize the conflict between racial bigotry and the Holy Word.

This is not a sectional problem—it is nationwide. It is not a partisan problem. The proposals set forth above are based on a careful consideration of the views of leaders of both parties in both Houses of Congress. In 1957 and 1960, members of both parties rallied behind the civil rights measures of my predecessor; and I am certain that this tradition can be continued, as it has in the case of world crises. A national domestic crisis also calls for bipartisan unity and solutions.

We will not solve these problems by blaming any group or section for the legacy which has been handed down by past generations. But neither will these problems be solved by clinging to the patterns of the past. Nor, finally, can they be solved in the streets, by lawless acts on either side, or by the physical actions or presence of any private group or public official, however appealing such melodramatic devices may seem to some.

During the weeks past, street demonstrations, mass picketing and parades have brought these matters to the Nation's attention in dramatic fashion in many cities throughout the United States. This has happened because these racial injustices are real and no other remedy was in sight. But, as feelings have risen in recent days, these demonstrations have increasingly endangered lives and property, enflamed emotions and unnecessarily divided communities. They are not the way in which this country should rid itself of racial discrimination. Violence is never justified; and, while peaceful communication, deliberation, and petitions of protest continue, I want to caution against demonstrations which can lead to violence.

This problem is now before the Congress. Unruly tactics or pressures will not help and may hinder the effective consideration of these measures. If they are enacted, there will be legal remedies available; and, therefore, while the Congress is completing its work, I urge all community leaders, Negro and white, to do their utmost to lessen tensions and to exercise self-restraint. The Congress should have an opportunity to freely work its will. Meanwhile, I strongly support action by local public officials and merchants to remedy these grievances on their own.

The legal remedies I have proposed are the embodiment of this Nation's basic posture of commonsense and common justice. They involve every American's right to vote, to go to school, to get a job, and to be served in a public place without arbitrary discrimination—rights which most Americans take for granted.

In short, enactment of the Civil Rights Act of 1963 at this session of the Congress—however long it may take and however troublesome it may be—is imperative. It will go far toward providing reasonable men with the reasonable means of meeting these problems; and it will thus help end the kind of racial strife which this Nation can hardly afford. Rancor, violence, disunity, and national shame can only hamper our national standing and security. To paraphrase the words of Lincoln: "In giving freedom to the Negro, we assure freedom to the free—honorable alike in what we give and what we preserve."

I therefore ask every Member of Congress to set aside sectional and political ties, and to look at this issue from the viewpoint of the Nation. I ask you to look into your hearts—not in search of charity, for the Negro neither wants nor needs condescension—but for the one plain, proud and priceless quality that unites us all as Americans; a sense of justice. In this year of the emancipation centennial, justice requires us to insure the blessings of liberty for all Americans and their posterity— not merely for reasons of economic efficiency, world diplomacy, and domestic tranquility—but, above all, because it is right.

JOHN F. KENNEDY.

THE WHITE HOUSE, *June 19, 1963.*

VOTING RIGHTS ACT OF 1965

After "Bloody Sunday" in Selma and the murder of the Reverend James Reeb, President Johnson, in perhaps the most moving speech of his career, threw the full force of the Federal Government behind an effective voting law. The Congressional Report on the Voting Rights Act showed the strong need for this legislation.

President Johnson's Selma Speech (March 15, 1965)

The PRESIDENT. Mr. Speaker, Mr. President, Members of the Congress, I speak tonight for the dignity of man and the destiny of democracy.

I urge every member of both parties—Americans of all religions and of all colors—from every section of this country—to join me in that cause.

At times history and fate meet at a single time in a single place to shape a turning point in man's unending search for freedom. So it was at Lexington and Concord. So it was a century ago at Appomattox. So it was last week in Selma, Ala.

There, long-suffering men and women peacefully protested the denial of their rights as Americans. Many were brutally assaulted. One good man—a man of God—was killed.

There was no cause for pride in what has happened in Selma.

There is no cause for self-satisfaction in the long denial of equal rights of millions of Americans.

But there is cause for hope and for faith in our democracy in what is happening here tonight.

For the cries of pain, and the hymns and protests of oppressed people, have summoned into convocation all the majesty of this great Government, the Government of the greatest Nation on earth.

Our mission is at once the oldest and most basic of this country: to right wrong, to do justice, to serve man.

In our time we have come to live with the moments of great crisis. Our lives have been marked with debate about great issues—issues of war and peace, issues of prosperity and depression. But rarely, in any time, does an issue lay bare the secret heart of America itself. Rarely are we met with the challenge, not to our growth or abundance, or our welfare or our security—but rather to the values and the purposes and the meaning of our beloved Nation.

The issue of equal rights for American Negroes is such an issue. And should we defeat every enemy, and should we double our wealth and conquer the stars and still be unequal to this issue, then we will have failed as a people and as a nation.

For with a country as with a person, "What is a man profited, if he shall gain the whole world, and lose his own soul?"

There is no Negro problem. There is no southern problem. There is no northern problem. There is only an American problem.

And we are met here tonight as Americans—not as Democrats or Republicans—we are met here as Americans to solve that problem.

This was the first nation in the history of the world to be founded with a purpose. The great phrases of that purpose still sound in every American heart, north and south: "All men are created equal"—"Government by consent of the governed"—"Give me liberty or give me death." And those are not just clever words and those are not just empty theories. In their name Americans have fought and died for two centuries and tonight around the world they stand there as guardians of our liberty risking their lives.

Those words are a promise to every citizen that he shall share in the dignity of man. This dignity cannot be found in a man's possessions. It cannot be found in his power or in his position. It really rests on his right to be treated as a man equal in opportunity to all others. It says that he shall share in freedom, he shall choose his leaders, educate his children, provide for his family according to his ability and his merits as a human being.

To apply any other test—to deny a man his hopes because of his color or race or his religion or the place of his birth—is not only to do injustice, it is to deny America and to dishonor the dead who gave their lives for American freedom.

Our fathers believed that if this noble view of the rights of man was to flourish, it must be rooted in democracy. The most basic right of all was the right to choose your own leaders. The history of this country in large measure, is the history of the expansion of that right to all of our people.

Many of the issues of civil rights are very complex and most difficult. But about this there can and should be no argument. Every American citizen must have an equal right to vote. There is no reason which can excuse the denial of that right. There is no duty which weighs more heavily on us than the duty we have to insure that right.

Yet the harsh fact is that in many places in this country men and women are kept from voting simply because they are Negroes.

Every device of which human ingenuity is capable has been used to deny this right. The Negro citizen may go to register only to be told that the day is wrong, or the hour is late, or the official in charge is absent.

And if he persists, and if he manages to present himself to the registrar, he may be disqualified because he did not spell out his middle name or because he abbreviated a word on the application.

And if he manages to fill out an application he is given a test. The registrar is the sole judge of whether he passes this test. He may be asked to recite the entire Constitution, or explain the most complex provisions of State law and even a college degree cannot be used to prove that he can read and write.

For the fact is that the only way to pass these barriers is to show a white skin.

Experience has clearly shown that the existing process of law cannot overcome systematic and ingenious discrimination. No law that we now have on the books—and I have helped to put three of them there—can insure the right to vote when local officials are determined to deny it.

In such a case our duty must be clear to all of us. The Constitution says that no person shall be kept from voting because of his race or his color. We have all sworn an oath before God to support and to defend that Constitution.

We must now act in obedience to that oath.

Wednesday I will send to Congress a law designed to eliminate illegal barriers to the right to vote.

The broad principles of that bill will be in the hands of the Democratic and Republican leaders tomorrow. After they have reviewed it, it will come here formally as a bill.

I am grateful for this opportunity to come here tonight at the invitation of the leadership to reason with my friends, to give them my views, and to visit with my former colleagues.

I have had prepared a more comprehensive analysis of the legislation which I had intended to transmit to the Clerk tomorrow, but which I will submit to the Clerk tonight. But I want to really discuss with you now, briefly, the main proposals of this legislation.

This bill will strike down restrictions to voting in all elections—Federal, State, and local—which have been used to deny Negroes the right to vote.

This bill will establish a simple, uniform standard which cannot be used however ingenious the effort to flout our Constitution.

It will provide for citizens to be registered by officials of the U.S. Government if the State officials refuse to register them.

It will eliminate tedious, unnecessary lawsuits which delay the right to vote.

Finally, this legislation will insure that properly registered individuals are not prohibited from voting.

I will welcome the suggestions from all the Members of Congress—I have no doubt that I will get some—on ways and means to strengthen this law and to make it effective. But experience has plainly shown that this is the only path to carry out the command of the Constitution.

To those who seek to avoid action by their National Government in their home communities—who want to and who seek to maintain purely local control over elections—the answer is simple.

Open your polling places to all your people.

Allow men and women to register and vote whatever the color of their skin.

Extend the rights of citizenship to every citizen of this land.

There is no constitutional issue here. The command of the Constitution is plain.

There is no moral issue. It is wrong—deadly wrong—to deny any of your fellow Americans the right to vote in this country.

There is no issue of States rights or National rights. There is only the struggle for human rights.

I have not the slightest doubt what will be your answer.

But the last time a President sent a civil rights bill to the Congress it contained a provision to protect voting rights in Federal elections. That civil rights bill was passed after 8 long months of debate. And when that bill came to my desk from the Congress for my signature, the heart of the voting provision had been eliminated.

This time, on this issue, there must be no delay, or no hesitation, or no compromise with our purpose.

We cannot, we must not refuse to protect the right of every American to vote in every election that he may desire to participate in.

And we ought not and we cannot and we must not wait another 8 months before we get a bill. We have already waited a hundred years and more. And the time for waiting is gone.

So I ask you to join me in working long hours, nights, and weekends if necessary to pass this bill. And I do not make this request lightly, for from the window where I sit with the problems of our country I recognize that from outside this Chamber is the outraged conscience of a nation—the grave concern of many nations—and the harsh judgment of history on our acts.

But even if we pass this bill, the battle will not be over. What happened in Selma is part of a far larger movement which reaches into every section and State of America. It is the effort of American Negroes to secure for themselves the full blessings of American life.

Their cause must be our cause too, because it is not just Negroes but really it is all of us, who must overcome the crippling legacy of bigotry and injustice. And we shall overcome.

As a man whose roots go deeply into southern soil I know how agonizing racial feelings are. I know how difficult it is to reshape the attitudes and the structure of our society.

But a century has passed—more than 100 years—since the Negro was freed. And he is not fully free tonight. It was more than 100 years ago that Abraham Lincoln, a great President of another party, signed the Emancipation Proclamation. But emancipation is a proclamation and not a fact.

A century has passed—more than 100 years—since equality was promised. And yet the Negro is not equal.

A century has passed since the day of promise. And the promise is unkept.

The time of justice has now come. And I tell you that I believe sincerely that no force can hold it back. It is right—in the eyes of man and God—that it should come. And when it does, I think that day will brighten the lives of every American.

For Negroes are not the only victims. How many white children have gone uneducated and how many white families have lived in stark poverty—how many white lives have been scarred by fear because we have wasted our energy and our substance to maintain the barriers of hatred and terror.

And so I say to all of you here and to all in the Nation tonight that those who appeal to you to hold on to the past do so at the cost of denying you your future.

This great, rich, restless country can offer opportunity and education and hope to all—all black and white, all North and South, sharecropper and city dweller. These are the enemies—poverty, ignorance, disease— they are our enemies, not our fellow man, not our neighbor. And these enemies too—poverty, disease, and ignorance—we shall overcome.

Now let none of us, in any section, look with prideful righteousness on the troubles in another section or the problems of our neighbors. There is really no part of America where the promise of equality has been fully kept. In Buffalo as well as in Birmingham, in Philadelphia as well as Selma, Americans are struggling for the fruits of freedom.

This is one nation. What happens in Selma or in Cincinnati is a matter of legitimate concern to every American. But let us look within our own hearts and our own communities, and let each of us put our shoulder to the wheel to root out injustice wherever it exists.

As we meet here in this peaceful, historic Chamber tonight, men from the South, some of whom were at Iwo Jima, men from the North, who have carried Old Glory to far corners of the world and brought it back without a stain on it, men from the East and from the West, are all fighting together without regard to religion or color or region in Vietnam. Men from every region fought for us across the world 20 years ago.

And now, in these common dangers and these common sacrifices, the South made its contribution of honor and gallantry no less than any other region of the Great Republic, and in some instances—a great many of them—more.

And I have not the slightest doubt that good men from everywhere in this country—from the Great Lakes to the Gulf of Mexico, from the Golden Gate to the harbors along the Atlantic—will rally now together in this cause to vindicate the freedom of all Americans. For all of us owe this duty, and I believe that all of us will respond to it.

Your President makes that request of every American.

The real hero of this struggle is the American Negro. His actions and protests—his courage to risk safety, and even to risk his life—have awakened the conscience of this Nation. His demonstrations have been designed to call attention to injustice, designed to provoke change, designed to stir freedom. He has called upon us to make good the promise of America. And who among us can say that we would have made the same progress were it not for his persistent bravery and his faith in American democracy?

For at the real heart of battle for equality is a deep-seated belief in the democratic process. Equality depends not on the force of arms or tear gas, but depends upon the force of moral right—not on recourse to violence but on respect for law and order.

There have been many pressures upon your President—and there will be others as the days come and go—but I pledge you tonight that we intend to fight this battle where it should be fought, in the courts and in the Congress and in the hearts of men.

We must preserve the right of free speech and the right of free assembly. But the right of free speech does not carry with it, as has been said, the right to holler "fire" in a crowded theater. We must preserve the right to free assembly, but free assembly does not carry with it the right to block public thoroughfares to traffic.

We do have a right to protest and a right to march under conditions that do not infringe the constitutional rights of our neighbors. And I intend to protect all those rights as long as I am permitted to serve in this office.

We will guard against violence, knowing it strikes from our hands the very weapons with which we seek progress—obedience to law, and belief in American values.

In Selma, as elsewhere, we seek and pray for peace. We seek order. We seek unity.

But we will not accept the peace of stifled rights, or the order imposed by fear, or the unity that stifles protest. For peace cannot be purchased at the cost of liberty.

In Selma tonight—and we had a good day there—as in every city, we are working for a just and peaceful settlement. And we must all remember—after this speech I am making tonight, after the police and the FBI and the marshals have all gone, and after you have promptly passed this bill—the people of Selma and the other cities of the Nation must still live and work together. And when the attention of the Nation has gone elsewhere they must try to heal the wounds and to build a new community. This cannot be easily done on a battleground of violence, as the history of the South itself shows. It is in recognition of this that men of both races have shown such an outstandingly impressive responsibility in recent days—last Tuesday, and again today.

The bill that I am presenting to you will be known as a civil rights bill. But, in a larger sense, most of the program I am recommending is a civil rights program. Its object is to open the city of hope to all people of all races.

Because all Americans just must have the right to vote. And we are going to give them that right.

All Americans must have the privileges of citizenship regardless of race. And they are going to have those privileges of citizenship regardless of race.

But I would like to caution you and remind you that to exercise these privileges takes much more than legal right. It requires a trained mind and a healthy body. It requires a decent home, and the chance to find a job, and the opportunity to escape from the clutches of poverty.

Of course people cannot contribute to the Nation if they are never taught to read or write, if their bodies are stunted from hunger, if their sickness goes untended, if their life is spent in hopeless poverty just drawing a welfare check.

So we want to open the gates to opportunity. But we are also going to give all our people—black and white—the help that they need to walk through those gates.

My first job after college was as a teacher in Cotulla, Tex., in a small Mexican-American school. Few of them could speak English and I could not speak much Spanish. My students were poor and they often came to class without breakfast—hungry. And they knew, even in their youth the pain of prejudice. They never seemed to know why people disliked them, but they knew it was so because I saw it in their eyes.

I often walked home late in the afternoon after the classes were finished wishing there was more that I could do. But all I knew was to teach them the little that I knew—hoping that it might help them against the hardships that lay ahead.

Somehow you never forget what poverty and hatred can do when you see its scars on the hopeful face of a young child.

I never thought then in 1928 that I would be standing here in 1965. It never even occurred to me in my fondest dreams that I might have the chance to help the sons and daughters of those students—and to help people like them all over this country.

But now I do have that chance and I will let you in on a secret—I mean to use it.

And I hope that you will use it with me.

This is the richest and most powerful country which ever occupied this globe. The might of past empires is little compared to ours.

But I do not want to be the President who built empires, or sought grandeur, or extended dominion.

I want to be the President who educated young children to the wonders of their world.

I want to be the President who helped to feed the hungry and to prepare them to be taxpayers instead of tax-eaters.

I want to be the President who helped the poor to find their own way and who protected the right of every citizen to vote in every election.

I want to be the President who helped to end hatred among his fellow men and who promoted love among the people of all races and all regions and all parties.

I want to be the President who helped to end war among the brothers of this earth.

And so at the request of your beloved Speaker and the Senator from Montana, the majority leader, Mr. MANSFIELD, and the Senator from Illinois, the minority leader, Mr. DIRKSEN, and Mr. McCULLOCH and others, members of both parties, I come here tonight not as President Roosevelt came down one time in person to veto a bonus bill; not as President Truman came down one time to urge the passage of a railroad bill. But I come here to ask you to share this task with me and to share it with the people we both work for.

I want this to be the Congress—Republicans and Democrats alike—which did all these things for all these people.

Beyond this great Chamber—out yonder in the 50 States are the people we serve. Who can tell what deep and unspoken hopes are in their hearts tonight as they sit there and listen? We all can guess, from our own lives, how difficult they often find their own pursuit of happiness; how many problems each little family has. They look most of all to themselves for their future.

But I think that they also look to each of us.

Above the pyramid on the great seal of the United States it says in Latin, "God has favored our undertaking."

God will not favor everything that we do. It is rather our duty to divine His will. I cannot help but believe that He truly understands and that He really favors the undertaking that we begin here tonight.

Congressional Report on the Voting Rights Act of 1965

Purpose of the Legislation

The bill, as amended, is designed primarily to enforce the 15th amendment to the Constitution of the United States and is also designed to enforce the 14th amendment and article I, section 4. To accomplish this objective the bill (1) suspends the use of literacy and other tests and devices in areas where there is reason to believe that such tests and devices have been and are being used to deny the right to vote on account of race or color; (2) authorizes the appointment of Federal examiners in such areas to register persons who are qualified under State law, except insofar as such law is suspended by this act, to vote in State, local, and Federal elections; (3) empowers the Federal courts, in any action instituted by the Attorney General, to enforce the guarantees of the 15th amendment, to authorize the appointment of Federal examiners, pending final determination of the suit or after a final judgment in which the court finds that violations of the 15th amendment have occurred; (4) provides criminal penalties for intimidating, threatening, or coercing any person for voting or attempting to vote, or for urging or aiding any person to vote or to attempt to vote. In addition, civil and criminal remedies are provided for the enforcement of the act.

Upon the basis of findings that poll taxes as a prerequisite to voting violate the 14th and 15th amendments to the Constitution, the bill abolishes the poll tax in any State or subdivision where it still exists.

*   *   *   *

Enforcement Experience in Recent Years

What has been the effect of the 1957, 1960, and 1964 voting rights statutes? Although these laws were intended to supply strong and effective remedies, their enforcement has encountered serious obstacles in various regions of the country. Progress has been painfully slow, in part because of the intransigence of State and local officials and repeated delays in the judicial process. Judicial relief has had to be gaged not in terms of months—but in terms of years. With reference to the 71 voting rights cases filed to date by the Department of Justice under the 1957, 1960, and 1964 Civil Rights Acts, the Attorney General testified before a judiciary subcommittee that an incredible amount of time has had to be devoted to analyzing voting records—often as much as 6,000 man-hours —in addition to time spent on trial preparation and the almost inevitable appeal. The judicial process affords those who are determined to resist plentiful opportunity to resist. Indeed, even after apparent defeat resisters seek new ways and means of discriminating. Barring one contrivance too often has caused no change in result, only in methods. See dissenting opinion of Judge John Brown in United States v. Mississippi, 229 F.Supp. 925, reversed and remanded, 380 U.S. 128 (1965); see also United States v. Penton, 212 F.Supp. 193 (M.D.Ala.). And even where some registration has been achieved, Negro voters have sometimes been discriminatorily purged from the rolls. E. g., United States v. McElveen, 180 F.Supp. 10, 12-13 (E.D.La.1960), affirmed sub. nom. United States v. Thomas, 80 S.Ct. 612, 362 U.S. 58 (1960); United States v. Assn. of Citizens Councils, 196 F.Supp. 908, 910 (W.D.La.1961). Such experience amply demonstrates that the case-by-case approach has been unsatisfactory.

Another measure of the effectiveness of existing civil rights statutes and their case-by-case enforcement is to be found in voter registration statistics in those areas where Federal litigation has been previously concentrated. For example, in Alabama, the number of Negroes registered to vote has increased by only 5.2 percent between 1958 and 1964 to 19.4 percent; in Mississippi, approximately 6.4 percent of voting age Negroes were registered in 1964 compared to 4.4 percent in 1954; and in Louisiana, the increase in Negro registration has been imperceptible— from approximately 31.7 percent in 1956 to approximately 31.8 percent of the eligible Negroes registered as of January 1, 1965. Meanwhile, the percentage of registered white voters in Louisiana is 80.2 percent.

* * * * *

Provisions Suspending Tests and Devices and Authorizing Appointment of Examiners

Section 3 of the bill makes additional remedies available to deal with denials or abridgements of the right to vote in so-called "pockets of discrimination"—areas outside the States and subdivisions to which the prohibitions of section 4 are in effect. Section 3 follows the traditional case-by-case approach, authorizes the suspension of tests and devices and the appointment of Federal examiners after a judicial determination that violations of the 15th amendment have occurred (and also the appointment of examiners by interlocutory order of the court). In such cases, section 3 further authorizes the court to determine the validity of any voting standard or practice which is different from that which was in effect when the suit was instituted.

Suspension of "tests and devices"

Sections 4, 5, and 6 of the bill, as amended, provide for "automatic" suspension of literacy tests and other devices in certain areas and for appointment of Federal examiners to register applicants to vote in Federal, State, and local elections. Under the bill, the use of specified voting qualifications, defined as "tests and devices", would be suspended in States and subdivisions upon the coincidence of two factors, namely, where (1) such tests or devices were maintained on November 1, 1964, and (2) less than 50 percent of the voting-age population was registered or voted in the presidential election of 1964.

The record before the committee indicates that where these two factors are present there is a strong probability that low registration and voting are a result of racial discrimination in the use of such tests. To illustrate, in the presidential election of 1964, although ballots were cast by 62 percent of the national electorate, there nine States in which fewer than 50 percent voted. Of these nine States, seven maintained literacy tests. In addition, a preliminary survey, suggests that there are certain counties in States which maintained literacy tests in November 1964, in which counties fewer than 50 percent voted, although the statewide percentage exceeded 50 percent. From the foregoing, it would appear that the voting qualifications of the following States and political subdivisions would be affected by the bill: The States of Alabama, Alaska, Georgia, Louisiana, Mississippi, South Carolina, and Virginia; and Apache County (Arizona), Elmore County (Idaho), Aroostook County (Maine), and 34 counties in the State of North Carolina.

*   *   *   *

CIVIL RIGHTS BILL OF 1966

The final selection is part of President Johnson's message to Congress on the 1966 Civil Rights Bill, which was not passed largely because of opposition to its open-housing provisions.

President Johnson's Message on the 1966 Civil Rights Bill (May 2, 1966)

*   *   *   *

VI

We undertake to expand and reform the civil rights laws this year with the clear understanding that legal reforms can be counted only a small part of a national program for the Negro American.

We know that the more important challenges of racial inequality today are emphatically national.

Negro ghettos indict our cities North and South, from coast to coast. Hope of cutting back the severe unemployment rate among Negroes is tied directly to the expansion of our national economy. And the ultimate need in human terms—of a more generous idea of brotherhood and a more responsible conception of equality—are part of the unfinished business in every State.

The time has passed when we could realistically deal effectively with racial problems by the passage of what could be strictly defined as civil rights laws.

In fact, the most disturbing current measures of the impact of discrimination are economic facts that cover the entire Nation:

Nonwhite Americans constitute only 11 percent of the national labor force, but they make up 20 percent of the unemployed. They take home less than 7 percent of the total personal income of all Americans.
One-fifth of the entire population lives in poverty. One-half of nonwhite Americans live in poverty.
In junior high schools across the country, 12 percent of white children are in school grades below their age level—compared to 30 percent of Negro children.

Poor housing, unemployment, and poverty, while they affect racial minorities particularly, will not be defeated by new civil rights laws. Thus, the programs that Congress has adopted go far beyond the vindication of civil rights.

The Elementary and Secondary Education Act of 1965 will enrich the quality of our public schools.

The Housing Act of 1965 will provide part of the decent low-and middle-income housing our cities desperately need. Beyond this, adoption of the Demonstration Cities Act this year will launch a major attack on the blight of urban ghettos.

Amendments to the Manpower Development and Training Act adopted in 1965 will help unskilled Negroes, as well as whites, prepare for a role in the economies of today and tomorrow.

The Economic Opportunity Act of 1965—the Anti-Poverty Act—is reaching out with new hope for the disadvantaged—for those pre-school children, teenagers, and older men and women who have never before had cause to hope.

We do not call any of these "civil rights programs." Nevertheless, they are crucial, and perhaps decisive elements in the Negro American's long struggle for a fair chance in life.

It is self-evident that the problems we are struggling with form a complicated chain of discrimination and lost opportunities. Employment is often dependent on education, education on neighborhood schools and housing, housing on income, and income on employment. We have learned by now the folly of looking for any single crucial link in the chain that binds the ghetto.

All the links—poverty, lack of education, underemployment, and now discrimination in housing—must be attacked together. If we are to include the Negro in our society, we must do more than give him the education he needs to obtain a job and a fair chance for useful work.

We must give the Negro the right to live in freedom among his fellow Americans.

I ask the Congress to enact the first effective Federal law against discrimination in the sale and rental of housing.

The time has come for the Congress to declare resoundingly that discrimination in housing and all the evils it breeds are a denial of justice and a threat to the development of our growing urban areas.

The time has come to combat unreasoning restrictions on any family's freedom to live in the home and the neighborhood of its choice.

This year marks the hundredth anniversary of the first statute enacted by the Congress in an attempt to deal with discrimination in housing. It reads:

> All citizens of the United States shall have the same right, in every State and territory, as is enjoyed by white citizens thereof to inherit, purchase, lease, sell, hold, and convey real and personal property.

For 100 years this law has reflected an ideal favoring equality of housing opportunity. Acting under this statute and the 14th amendment, the Supreme Court has invalidated State and local laws prohibiting the sale of houses to Negroes. It has prohibited the enforcement of racially restrictive covenants. It has struck down State legislation imposing undue burdens upon minority groups with respect to real estate transactions.

There is nothing novel about the congressional concern with housing that I now ask you to expand. Programs enacted by Congress have, for more than three decades, stimulated the development of private housing, and directly financed hundreds of thousands of public housing units.

The historic Housing Act of 1949 proclaimed a national goal for the first time: "a decent home and suitable living environment for every American family."

The great boom in housing construction since the Second World War is, in large part, attributable to congressional action to carry out this objective.

Yet not enough has been done to guarantee that *all* Americans shall benefit from the expanding housing market Congress has made possible.

Executive Order No. 11063, signed by President Kennedy on November 20, 1962, prohibited housing discrimination where Federal Housing Administration and Veterans' Administration insurance programs are involved. That Executive order clearly expressed the commitment of the executive branch to the battle against housing discrimination.

But that order, and all the amendments that could validly be added to it, are inevitably restricted to those elements of the housing problem which are under direct Executive authority.

Our responsibility is to deal with discrimination directly at the point of sale or refusal, as well as indirectly through financing. Our need is to reach discrimination practiced by financial institutions operating outside the FHA and VA insurance programs, and not otherwise regulated by the Government.

Our task is to end discrimination in all housing, old and new—not simply in the new housing covered by the Executive order.

I propose legislation that is constitutional in design, comprehensive in scope, and firm in enforcement. It will cover the sale, rental, and financing of all dwelling units. It will prohibit discrimination, on either racial or religious grounds, by owners, brokers, and lending corporations' in their housing commitments.

Under this legislation, private individuals could sue in either State or Federal courts to block discrimination.

The Attorney General would be empowered to sue directly for appropriate relief, wherever he has reasonable cause to believe that a pattern of discrimination exists.

The legislation would direct the Secretary of Housing and Urban Development to make factual studies, and to give technical assistance to the Community Relations Service and all other public and private organizations working to eliminate discriminatory housing patterns.

The bill I am submitting to the Congress this year would leave in effect the many State laws that have preceded the Federal Government in the field of fair housing. We would hope to enact a law that will not only open the fight against discrimination where there are no State laws against it, but also strengthen the enforcement efforts of States which have fair housing programs now.

The ghettos of our major cities—North and South, from coast to coast—represent fully as severe a denial of freedom and the fruits of American citizenship as more obvious injustices. As long as the color of a man's skin determines his choice of housing, no investment in the physical rebuilding of our cities will free the men and women living there.

The fair housing law I propose this year is an essential part of our attempt to rejuvenate and liberate America's growing urban areas—and more importantly, to expand the liberty of all the people living in them.

A nation that aspires to greatness cannot be a divided nation—with whites and Negroes entrenched behind barriers of mutual suspicion and fear.

It cannot tolerate:

Overcrowded ghetto schools, producing new thousands of ill-trained citizens for whom the whole community must be responsible.

Rising health hazards and crime rates in the ghettos' ugly streets and homes.

The failure of expensive social programs, such as urban renewal, where there is no way out and up for Negro residents.

The truly insufferable cost of imprisoning the Negro in the slums is borne by our national conscience.

When we restrict the Negro's freedom, inescapably we restrict a part of our own.

Negro Americans comprise 22 percent of the enlisted men in our Army combat units in Vietnam—and 22 percent of those who have lost their lives in battle there. We fall victim to a profound hypocrisy when we say that they cannot buy or rent dwellings among citizens they fight to save.

VII

No civil rights act, however historic, will be final. We would look in vain for one definitive solution to an injustice as old as the Nation itself—an injustice that leaves no section of the country and no level of American life unstained. This administration has pledged that as long as racial discrimination denies opportunity and equal rights in America, we will honor our constitutional and moral responsibility to restore the balance of justice.

Yet no amount of legislation, no degree of commitment on the part of the National Government, can by itself bring equal opportunity and achievement to Negro Americans. It must be joined by a massive effort on the part of the States and local governments, of industry, and of all citizens, white and Negro.

Hundreds of thousands of Negro Americans in every part of the country are making that effort now. They know that the responsibilities of citizenship follow inevitably from the achievement of civil rights and economic opportunity.

They know that an obligation lies before them, to take full advantage of the improved education and training that is now becoming available to them—in the public schools, in vocational training, in the universities.

They know that it is their task to lead others in the quest for achievement and social justice—to inspire them with confidence, with perseverance, with the mutual forbearance on which our democracy depends.

VIII

We are engaged in a great adventure—as great as that of the last century, when our fathers marched to the western frontier. Our frontier today is of human beings, not of land.

If we are able to open that frontier, to free each child to become the best that is in him to become, our reward—both spiritual and material—will exceed any that we gained a century ago through territorial expansion.

Whether we shall succeed is an issue that rests in the heart of every American. It rests in the determination of Negro Americans to use the opportunities for orderly progress that are now becoming—at last—a reality in their lives. It rests in our common willingness to expand those opportunities in the years ahead.

That issue can and will be decided in only one way. For we have not come this far to fail within sight of our goal.

LYNDON B. JOHNSON.

THE WHITE HOUSE *April 28, 1966.*

VIII
The Future

The future progress of the civil rights movement is now in doubt. The recent split in leadership on the question of "Black Power," Congressional refusal to enact any civil rights legislation in 1966, and the lack of easily definable goals in the future have created a pause. To hope that the Negro will pass easily into the main stream of American life as the European immigrants did fifty years ago ignores the core of the problem. As Charles E. Silberman writes in "The Crisis in Black and White": "The Negro is unlike any other immigrant group in one crucial regard: he is colored. And that makes all the difference . . . The European ethnic groups, in short, could move into the main stream of American life without forcing beforehand any drastic rearrangements of attitudes or institutions. For the Negro to do so, however, will require the most radical changes in the whole structure of American society."

All observers agree that the problems facing the Negro community are extraordinarily numerous, complex and interrelated. Progress in one area—such as legal rights—is often offset by retreat in other areas—such as employment. Economic advance depends upon adequate education and training, which require higher quality schools, which are directly related to better, integrated housing—all of which can come about only after a change in the underlying psychological attitude of white America toward the Negro.

Thomas Pettigrew has examined the "special and debilitating stigma placed upon Negro status" in the United States. Pettigrew points out that the Negro has been stereotyped with an "id" stigma, as superstitious, lazy, ignorant, dirty, irresponsible and sexually uninhibited. This stereotype serves an important psychological purpose for white Americans: they can project onto the Negro their own unacceptable inner impulses and attack the Negro for possessing them. As Pettigrew adds: "Yet the

Negro American inherits the id stigma with special force. Not only is he typically confronted by class barriers at the bottom of the social structure, but he is also confronted by caste barriers as the degrading legacy of three centuries of slavery and segregation."

Only increased contact and interchange between the races can break the stereotype and destroy the stigma. Employment contact, which is increasing, will help in this direction. However de facto *segregation in school and housing can only slow down the process. In addition* de facto *segregation has always meant inferior training and living accommodations for the Negro, which make his economic advance difficult and his frustration and anger significantly stronger.*

Daniel Moynihan, while a member of the Department of Labor's Policy Planning and Research Office examined another facet of the Negro problem. His analysis of "The Negro Family" (the complete text of which appears below), shows how economic and social deprivation causes the basic family unit to deteriorate, making the possibility of advance much more difficult.

Developments in the war on poverty will be very important in the civil rights movement. An increased political awareness by Negro groups and maximum use of their political power is also crucial. The two articles by James Tobin and Bayard Rustin appearing below offer new possibilities in the economic and political sphere.

The Moynihan Report—*The Negro Family: The Case for National Action* (1965)

The United States is approaching a new crisis in race relations.

In the decade that began with the school desegregation decision of the Supreme Court, and ended with the passage of the Civil Rights Act of 1964, the demand of Negro Americans for full recognition of their civil rights was finally met.

The effort, no matter how savage and brutal, of some State and local governments to thwart the exercise of those rights is doomed. The nation will not put up with it—least of all the Negroes. The present moment will pass. In the meantime, a new period is beginning.

In this new period the expectations of the Negro Americans will go beyond civil rights. Being Americans, they will now expect that in the near future equal opportunities for them as a group will produce roughly equal results, as compared with other groups. This is not going to happen. Nor will it happen for generations to come unless a new and special effort is made.

There are two reasons. First, the racist virus in the American blood stream still afflicts us: Negroes will encounter serious personal prejudice for at least another generation. Second, three centuries of sometimes unimaginable mistreatment have taken their toll on the Negro people. The harsh fact is that as a group, at the present time, in terms of ability to win out in the competitions of American life, they are not equal to most of those groups with which they will be competing. Individually, Negro Americans reach the highest peaks of achievement. But collectively, in the spectrum of American ethnic and religious and regional groups, where some get plenty and some get none, where some send eighty percent of their children to college and others pull them out of school at the 8th grade, Negroes are among the weakest.

The most difficult fact for white Americans to understand is that in these terms the circumstances of the Negro American community in recent years has probably been getting *worse, not better.*

Indices of dollars of income, standards of living, and years of education deceive. The gap between the Negro and most other groups in American society is widening.

The fundamental problem, in which this is most clearly the case, is that of family structure. The evidence—not final, but powerfully persuasive—is that the Negro family in the urban ghettos is crumbling. A middle-class group has managed to save itself, but for vast numbers of the unskilled, poorly educated city working class the fabric of conventional social relationships has all but disintegrated. There are indications that the situation may have been arrested in the past few years, but the general postwar trend is unmistakable. So long as this situation persists, the cycle of poverty and disadvantage will continue to repeat itself.

The thesis of this paper is that these events, in combination, confront the nation with a new kind of problem. Measures that have worked in the past, or would work for most groups in the present, will not work here. A national effort is required that will give a unity of purpose to the many activities of the Federal government in this area, directed to a new kind of national goal: the establishment of a stable Negro family structure.

This would be a new departure for Federal policy. And a difficult one. But it almost certainly offers the only possibility of resolving in our time what is, after all, the nation's oldest, and most intransigent, and now its most dangerous social problem. What Gunnar Myrdal said in *An American Dilemma* remains true today: *"America is free to choose whether the Negro shall remain her liability or become her opportunity."*

Chapter 1. The Negro American Revolution

The Negro American revolution is rightly regarded as the most important domestic event of the postwar period in the United States.

Nothing like it has occurred since the upheavals of the 1930's which led to the organization of the great industrial trade unions, and which in turn profoundly altered both the economy and the political scene. There have been few other events in our history—the American Revolution itself, the surge of Jacksonian Democracy in the 1830's, the Abolitionist movement, and the Populist movement of the late 19th century—comparable to the current Negro movement.

There has been none more important. The Negro American revolution holds forth the prospect that the American Republic, which at birth was flawed by the institution of Negro slavery, and which throughout its history has been marred by the unequal treatment of Negro citizens, will at last redeem the full promise of the Declaration of Independence.

Although the Negro leadership has conducted itself with the strictest propriety, acting always and only as American citizens asserting their rights within the framework of the American political system, it is no less clear that the movement has profound international implications.

It was in no way a matter of chance that the nonviolent tactics and philosophy of the movement, as it began in the South, were consciously adapted from the techniques by which the Congress Party undertook to free the Indian nation from British colonial rule. It was not a matter of chance that the Negro movement caught fire in America at just that moment when the nations of Africa were gaining their freedom. Nor is it merely incidental that the world should have fastened its attention on events in the United States at a time when the possibility that the nations of the world will divide along color lines seems suddenly not only possible, but even imminent.

(Such racist views have made progress within the Negro American community itself—which can hardly be expected to be immune to a virus that is endemic in the white community. The Black Muslim doctrines, based on total alienation from the white world, exert a powerful influence. On the far left, the attraction of Chinese Communism can no longer be ignored.)

It is clear that what happens in America is being taken as a sign of what can, or must, happen in the world at large. The course of world events will be profoundly affected by the success or failure of the Negro American revolution in seeking the peaceful assimilation of the races in the United States. The award of the Nobel Peace Prize to Dr. Martin Luther

King was as much an expression of the hope for the future, as it was recognition for past achievement.

It is no less clear that carrying this revolution forward to a successful conclusion is a first priority confronting the Great Society.

The End of the Beginning

The major events of the onset of the Negro revolution are now behind us.

The *political events* were three: First, the Negroes themselves organized as a mass movement. Their organizations have been in some ways better disciplined and better led than any in our history. They have established an unprecedented alliance with religious groups throughout the nation and have maintained close ties with both political parties and with most segments of the trade union movement. Second, the Kennedy-Johnson Administration committed the Federal government to the cause of Negro equality. This had never happened before. Third, the 1964 Presidential election was practically a referendum on this commitment: if these were terms made by the opposition, they were in effect accepted by the President.

The overwhelming victory of President Johnson must be taken as emphatic popular endorsement of the unmistakable, and openly avowed course which the Federal government has pursued under his leadership.

The *administrative events* were threefold as well: First, beginning with the establishment of the President's Committee on Equal Employment Opportunity and on to the enactment of the Manpower Development and Training Act of 1962, the Federal government has launched a major national effort to redress the profound imbalance between the economic position of the Negro citizens and the rest of the nation that derives primarily from their unequal position in the labor market. Second, the Economic Opportunity Act of 1964 began a major national effort to abolish poverty, a condition in which almost half of Negro families are living. Third, the Civil Rights Act of 1964 marked the end of the era of legal and formal discrimination against Negroes and created important new machinery for combating covert discrimination and unequal treatment. (The Act does not guarantee an end to harassment in matters such as voter registration, but does make it more or less incumbent upon government to take further steps to thwart such efforts when they do occur.)

The *legal events* were no less specific. Beginning with *Brown* v. *Board of Education* in 1954, through the decade that culminated in the recent decisions upholding Title II of the Civil Rights Act, the Federal judiciary, led by the Supreme Court, has used every opportunity to combat unequal treatment of Negro citizens. It may be put as a general proposition that the laws of the United States now look upon any such treatment as obnoxious, and that the courts will strike it down wherever it appears.

The Demand for Equality

With these events behind us, the nation now faces a different set of challenges, which may prove more difficult to meet, if only because they cannot be cast as concrete propositions of right and wrong.

The fundamental problem here is that the Negro revolution, like the industrial upheaval of the 1930's, is a movement for equality as well as for liberty.

Liberty and Equality are the twin ideals of American democracy. But they are not the same thing. Nor, most importantly, are they equally attractive to all groups at any given time; nor yet are they always compatible, one with the other.

Many persons who would gladly die for liberty are appalled by equality. Many who are devoted to equality are puzzled and even troubled by liberty. Much of the political history of the American nation can be seen as a competition between these two ideals, as for example, the unending troubles between capital and labor.

By and large, liberty has been the ideal with the higher social prestige in America. It has been the middle-class aspiration, par excellence. (Note the assertions of the conservative right that ours is a republic, not a democracy.) Equality, on the other hand, has enjoyed tolerance more than acceptance. Yet it has roots deep in Western civilization and "is at least coeval with, if not prior to, liberty in the history of Western political thought."

American democracy has not always been successful in maintaining a balance between these two ideals, and notably so where the Negro American is concerned. "Lincoln freed the slaves," but they were given liberty, not equality. It was therefore possible in the century that followed to deprive their descendants of much of their liberty as well.

The ideal of equality does not ordain that all persons end up, as well as start out equal. In traditional terms, as put by Faulkner, "there is no such thing as equality *per se*, but only equality *to*: equal right and opportunity to make the best one can of one's life within one's capability, without fear of injustice or oppression or threat of violence." But the evolution of American politics, with the distinct persistence of ethnic and religious groups, has added a profound significant new dimension to that egalitarian ideal. It is increasingly demanded that the distribution of success and failure within one group be roughly comparable to that within other groups. It is not enough that all individuals start out on even terms, if the members of one group almost invariably end up well to the fore, and those of another far to the rear. This is what ethnic politics are all about in America, and in the main the Negro American demands are being put forth in this now traditional and established framework.

Here a point of semantics must be grasped. The demand for Equality of Opportunity has been generally perceived by white Americans as a demand for liberty, a demand not to be excluded from the competitions of life—at the polling place, in the scholarship examinations, at the personnel office, on the housing market. Liberty does, of course, demand that everyone be free to try his luck, or test his skill in such matters. But these opportunities do not necessarily produce equality: on the contrary, to the extent that winners imply losers, equality of opportunity almost insures inequality of results.

The point of semantics is that equality of opportunity now has a different meaning for Negroes than it has for whites. It is not (or at least no longer) a demand for liberty alone, but also for equality—in terms of group results. In Bayard Rustin's terms, "It is now concerned not merely with removing the barriers to full *opportunity* but with achieving the fact of *equality*." By equality Rustin means a distribution of achievements among Negroes roughly comparable to that among whites.

As Nathan Glazer has put it, "The demand for economic equality is now not the demand for equal opportunities for the equally qualified: it is now the demand for equality of economic results . . . The demand for equality in education . . . has also become a demand for equality of results, of outcomes."

Some aspects of the new laws do guarantee results, in the sense that upon enactment and enforcement they bring about an objective that is an end in itself, e.g., the public accommodations title of the Civil Rights Act.

Other provisions are at once terminal and intermediary. The portions of the Civil Rights Act dealing with voting rights will achieve an objective that is an end in itself, but the exercise of those rights will no doubt lead to further enlargements of the freedom of the Negro American.

But by and large, the programs that have been enacted in the first phase of the Negro revolution—Manpower Retraining, the Job Corps, Community Action, et al.—only make opportunities available. They cannot insure the outcome.

The principal challenge of the next phase of the Negro revolution is to make certain that equality of results will now follow. If we do not, there will be no social peace in the United States for generations.

The Prospect for Equality

The time, therefore, is at hand for an unflinching look at the present potential of Negro Americans to move from where they now are to where they want, and ought to be.

There is no very satisfactory way, at present, to measure social health or social pathology within an ethnic, or religious, or geographical community. Data are few and uncertain, and conclusions drawn from them, including the conclusions that follow, are subject to the grossest error. Nonetheless, the opportunities, no less than the dangers, of the present moment, demand that an assessment be made.

That being the case, it has to be said that there is a considerable body of evidence to support the conclusion that Negro social structure, in particular the Negro family, battered and harassed by discrimination, injustice, and uprooting, is in the deepest trouble. While many young Negroes are moving ahead to unprecedented levels of achievement, many more are falling further and further behind.

After an intensive study of the life of central Harlem, the board of directors of Harlem Youth Opportunities Unlimited, Inc. summed up their findings in one statement: "Massive deterioration of the fabric of society and its institutions . . ."

It is the conclusion of this survey of the available national data, that what is true of central Harlem, can be said to be true of the Negro American world in general.

If this is so, it is the single most important social fact of the United States today.

Chapter 2. The Negro American Family

At the heart of the deterioration of the fabric of Negro society is the deterioration of the Negro family.

It is the fundamental source of the weakness of the Negro community at the present time.

There is probably no single fact of Negro American life so little understood by whites. The Negro situation is commonly perceived by whites in terms of the visible manifestations of discrimination and poverty, in part because Negro protest is directed against such obstacles, and in part, no doubt, because these are facts which involve the actions and attitudes of the white community as well. It is more difficult, however, for whites to perceive the effect that three centuries of exploitation have had on the fabric of Negro society itself. Here the consequences of the historic injustices done to Negro Americans are silent and hidden from view. But here is where the true injury has occurred: unless this damage is repaired, all the effort to end discrimination and poverty and injustice will come to little.

The role of the family in shaping character and ability is so pervasive as to be easily overlooked. The family is the basic social unit of American life; it is the basic socializing unit. By and large, adult conduct in society is learned as a child.

A fundamental insight of psychoanalytic theory, for example, is that the child learns a way of looking at life in his early years through which all later experience is viewed and which profoundly shapes his adult conduct.

It may be hazarded that the reason family structure does not loom larger in public discussion of social issues is that people tend to assume that the nature of family life is about the same throughout American society. The mass media and the development of suburbia have created an image of the American family as a highly standardized phenomenon. It is therefore easy to assume that whatever it is that makes for differences among individuals or groups of individuals, it is not a different family structure.

There is much truth to this; as with any other nation, Americans are producing a recognizable family system. But that process is not completed by any means. There are still, for example, important differences in family patterns surviving from the age of the great European migration to the United States, and these variations account for notable differences in the progress and assimilation of various ethnic and religious groups. A number of immigrant groups were characterized by unusually strong family bonds; these groups have characteristically progressed more rapidly than others.

But there is one truly great discontinuity in family structure in the United States at the present time: that between the white world in general and that of the Negro American.

The white family has achieved a high degree of stability and is maintaining that stability.

By contrast, the family structure of lower class Negroes is highly unstable, and in many urban centers is approaching complete breakdown.

N.B. There is considerable evidence that the Negro community is in fact dividing between a stable middle-class group that is steadily growing stronger and more successful, and an increasingly disorganized and disadvantaged lower-class group. There are indications, for example, that the middle-class Negro family puts a higher premium on family stability and the conserving of family resources than does the white middle-class family. The discussion of this paper is not, obviously, directed to the first group excepting as it is affected by the experiences of the second—an important exception. (See Chapter 4, The Tangle of Pathology.)

There are two points to be noted in this context.

First, the emergence and increasing visibility of a Negro middle-class may beguile the nation into supposing that the circumstances of the remainder of the Negro community are equally prosperous, whereas just the opposite is true at present, and is likely to continue so.

Second, the lumping of all Negroes together in one statistical measurement very probably conceals the extent of the disorganization among the lower-class group. If conditions are improving for one and deteriorating for the other, the resultant statistical averages might show no change. Further, the statistics on the Negro family and most other subjects treated in this paper refer only to a specific point in time. They are a vertical measure of the situation at a given moment. They do not measure the experience of individuals over time. Thus the average monthly unemployment rate for Negro males for 1964 is recorded as 9 percent. But *during* 1964, some 29 percent of Negro males were unemployed at one time or another. Similarly, for example, if 36 percent of Negro children are living in broken homes *at any specific moment*, it is likely that a far higher proportion of Negro children find themselves in that situation *at one time or another* in their lives.

Nearly A Quarter of Urban Negro Marriages are Dissolved

Nearly a quarter of Negro women living in cities who have ever married are divorced, separated, or are living apart from their husbands.

The rates are highest in the urban Northeast where 26 percent of Negro women ever married are either divorced, separated, or have their husbands absent.

On the urban frontier, the proportion of husbands absent is even higher. In New York City in 1960, it was 30.2 percent, *not* including divorces.

Among ever-married nonwhite women in the nation, the proportion with husbands present *declined* in *every* age group over the decade 1950-60, as follows:

Age	Percent with Husbands Present	
	1950	1960
15-19 years	77.8	72.5
20-24 years	76.7	74.2
25-29 years	76.1	73.4
30-34 years	74.9	72.0
35-39 years	73.1	70.7
40-44 years	68.9	68.2

Although similar declines occurred among white females, the proportion of white husbands present never dropped below 90 percent except for the first and last age group.

Nearly One-Quarter of Negro Births are Now Illegitimate.

Both white and Negro illegitimacy rates have been increasing, although from dramatically different bases. The white rate was 2 percent in 1940; it was 3.07 percent in 1963. In that period, the Negro rate went from 16.8 percent to 23.6 percent.

The number of illegitimate children per 1,000 live births increased by 11 among whites in the period 1940-63, but by 68 among nonwhites. There are, of course, limits to the dependability of these statistics. There are almost certainly a considerable number of Negro children who, although technically illegitimate, are in fact the offspring of stable unions. On the other hand, it may be assumed that many births that are in fact illegitimate are recorded otherwise. Probably the two opposite effects cancel each other out.

On the urban frontier, the nonwhite illegitimacy rates are usually higher than the national average, and the increase of late has been drastic.

In the District of Columbia, the illegitimacy rate for nonwhites grew from 21.8 percent in 1950, to 29.5 percent in 1964.

A similar picture of disintegrating Negro marriages emerges from the divorce statistics. Divorces have increased of late for both whites and nonwhites, but at a much greater rate for the latter. In 1940 both groups had a divorce rate of 2.2 percent. By 1964 the white rate had risen to 3.6 percent, but the nonwhite rate had reached 5.1 percent—40 percent greater than the formerly equal white rate.

Almost One-Fourth of Negro Families are Headed by Females

As a direct result of this high rate of divorce, separation, and desertion, a very large percent of Negro families are headed by females. While the percentage of such families among whites has been dropping since 1940, it has been rising among Negroes.

The percent of nonwhite families headed by a female is more than double the percent for whites. Fatherless nonwhite families increased by a sixth between 1950 and 1960, but held constant for white families.

It has been estimated that only a minority of Negro children reach the age of 18 having lived all their lives with both their parents.

Once again, this measure of family disorganization is found to be diminishing among white families and increasing among Negro families.

The Breakdown of the Negro Family Has Led to a Startling Increase in Welfare Dependency

The majority of Negro children receive public assistance under the ADC program at one point or another in their childhood.

At present, 14 percent of Negro children are receiving ADC assist-ance, as against 2 percent of white children. Eight percent of white chil-dren receive such assistance at some time, as against 56 percent of non-whites, according to an extrapolation based on HEW data. (Let it be noted, however, that out of a total of 1.8 million nonwhite illegitimate children in the nation in 1961, 1.3 million were *not* receiving aid under the ADC program, although a substantial number have, or will, receive aid at some time in their lives.)

Again, the situation may be said to be worsening. The ADC pro-gram, deriving from the long established Mothers' Aid programs, was established in 1935 principally to care for widows and orphans, although the legislation covered all children in homes deprived of parental support because one or both of their parents are absent or incapacitated.

In the beginning, the number of ADC families in which the father was absent because of desertion was less than a third of the total. Today it is two-thirds. HEW estimates "that between two-thirds and three-fourths of the 50 percent increase from 1948 to 1955 in the number of absent-father families receiving ADC may be explained by an increase in broken homes in the population."

A 1960 study of Aid to Dependent Children in Cook County, Ill. stated:

> The 'typical' ADC mother in Cook County was married and had children by her husband, who deserted; his whereabouts are unknown, and he does not contribute to the support of his children. She is not free to remarry and has had an illegitimate child since her husband left. (Almost 90 percent of the ADC families are Negro.)

The steady expansion of this welfare program, as of public assistance programs in general, can be taken as a measure of the steady disintegra-tion of the Negro family structure over the past generation in the United States.

Chapter 3. The Roots of the Problem

Slavery

The most perplexing question about American slavery, which has never been altogether explained, and which indeed most Americans hardly know exists, has been stated by Nathan Glazer as follows: "Why was Ameri-can slavery the most awful the world has ever known?" The only thing that can be said with certainty is that this is true: it was.

American slavery was profoundly different from, and in its lasting effects on individuals and their children, indescribably worse than, any recorded servitude, ancient or modern. The peculiar nature of American slavery was noted by Alexis de Tocqueville and others, but it was not until 1948 that Frank Tannenbaum, a South American specialist, pointed to the striking differences between Brazilian and American slavery. The feudal, Catholic society of Brazil had a legal and religious tradition which accorded the slave a place as a human being in the hierarchy of society—a luckless, miserable place, to be sure, but a place withal. In contrast, there was nothing in the tradition of English law or Protestant theology which could accommodate to the fact of human bondage—the slaves were therefore reduced to the status of chattels—often, no doubt, well cared for, even privileged chattels, but chattels nevertheless.

Glazer, also focusing on the Brazil-United States comparison, continues:

In Brazil, the slave had many more rights than in the United States: he could legally marry, he could, indeed had to, be baptized and become a member of the Catholic Church, his family could not be broken up for sale, and he had many days on which he could either rest or earn money to buy his freedom. The Government encouraged manumission, and the freedom of infants could often be purchased for a small sum at the baptismal font. In short: the Brazilian slave knew he was a man, and that he differed in degree, not in kind, from his master.

[In the United States,] the slave was totally removed from the protection of organized society (compare the elaborate provisions for the protection of slaves in the Bible), his existence as a human being was given no recognition by any religious or secular agency, he was totally ignorant of and completely cut off from his past, and he was offered absolutely no hope for the future. His children could be sold, his marriage was not recognized, his wife could be violated or sold (there was something comic about calling the woman with whom the master permitted him to live a "wife"), and he could also be subject, without redress, to frightful barbarities—there were presumably as many sadists among slaveowners, men and women, as there are in other groups. The slave could not, by law, be taught to read or write; he could not practice any religion without the permission of his master, and could never meet with his fellows, for religious or any other purposes, except in the presence of a white; and finally, if a master wished to free him, every legal obstacle was used to thwart such action. This was not what slavery meant in the ancient world, in medieval and early modern Europe, or in Brazil and the West Indies.

More important, American slavery was also awful in its effects. If we compared the present situation of the American Negro with that of, let us say, Brazilian Negroes (who were slaves 20 years longer), we begin to suspect that the differences are the result of very different patterns of slavery. Today the Brazilian Negroes are Brazilians; though most are poor and do the hard and dirty work of the country, as Negroes do in the United States, they are not cut off from society. They reach into its highest strata, merging there — in smaller and smaller numbers, it is true, but with complete acceptance —

with other Brazilians of all kinds. The relations between Negroes and whites in Brazil show nothing of the mass irrationality that prevails in this country.

Stanley M. Elkins, drawing on the aberrant behavior of the prisoners in Nazi concentration camps, drew an elaborate parallel between the two institutions. This thesis has been summarized as follows by Thomas F. Pettigrew:

> Both were closed systems, with little chance of manumission, emphasis on survival, and a single, omnipresent authority. The profound personality change created by Nazi internment, as independently reported by a number of psychologists and psychiatrists who survived, was toward childishness and total acceptance of the SS guards as father-figures—a syndrome strikingly similar to the "Sambo" caricature of the Southern slave. Nineteenth-century racists readily believed that the "Sambo" personality was simply an inborn racial type. Yet no African anthropological data have ever shown any personality type resembling Sambo; and the concentration camps molded the equivalent personality pattern in a wide variety of Caucasian prisoners. Nor was Sambo merely a product of "slavery" in the abstract, for the less devastating Latin American system never developed such a type.
>
> Extending this line of reasoning, psychologists point out that slavery in all its forms sharply lowered the need for achievement in slaves . . . Negroes in bondage, stripped of their African heritage, were placed in a completely dependent role. All of their rewards came, not from individual initiative and enterprise, but from absolute obedience — a situation that severely depresses the need for achievement among all peoples. Most important of all, slavery vitiated family life . . . Since many slaveowners neither fostered Christian marriage among their slave couples nor hesitated to separate them on the auction block, the slave household often developed a fatherless matrifocal (mother-centered) pattern.

The Reconstruction

With the emancipation of the slaves, the Negro American family began to form in the United States on a widespread scale. But it did so in an atmosphere markedly different from that which has produced the white American family.

The Negro was given liberty, but not equality. Life remained hazardous and marginal. Of the greatest importance, the Negro male, particularly in the South, became an object of intense hostility, an attitude unquestionably based in some measure on fear.

When Jim Crow made its appearance towards the end of the 19th century, it may be speculated that it was the Negro male who was most humiliated thereby; the male was more likely to use public facilities, which rapidly became segregated once the process began, and just as important, segregation, and the submissiveness it exacts, is surely more destructive to the male than to the female personality. Keeping the Negro "in his place" can be translated as keeping the Negro male in his place: the female was not a threat to anyone.

Unquestionably, these events worked against the emergence of a strong father figure. The very essence of the male animal, from the bantam rooster to the four-star general, is to strut. Indeed, in 19th century America, a particular type of exaggerated male boastfulness became almost a national style. Not for the Negro male. The "sassy nigger" was lynched.

In this situation, the Negro family made but little progress toward the middle-class pattern of the present time. Margaret Mead has pointed out that "In every known human society, everywhere in the world, the young male learns that when he grows up one of the things which he must do in order to be a full member of society is to provide food for some female and her young." This pattern is not immutable, however: it can be broken, even though it has always eventually reasserted itself.

> Within the family, each new generation of young males learn the appropriate nurturing behavior and superimpose upon their biologically given maleness this learned parental role. When the family breaks down — as it does under slavery, under certain forms of indentured labor and serfdom, in periods of extreme social unrest during wars, revolutions, famines, and epidemics, or in periods of abrupt transition from one type of economy to another — this delicate line of transmission is broken. Men may flounder badly in these periods, during which the primary unit may again become mother and child, the biologically given, and the special conditions under which man has held his social traditions in trust are violated and distorted.

E. Franklin Frazier makes clear that at the time of emancipation Negro women were already "accustomed to playing the dominant role in family and marriage relations" and that this role persisted in the decades of rural life that followed.

Urbanization

Country life and city life are profoundly different. The gradual shift of American society from a rural to an urban basis over the past century and a half has caused abundant strains, many of which are still much in evidence. When this shift occurs suddenly, drastically, in one or two generations, the effect is immensely disruptive of traditional social patterns.

It was this abrupt transition that produced the wild Irish slums of the 19th Century Northeast. Drunkenness, crime, corruption, discrimination, family disorganization, juvenile delinquency were the routine of that era. In our own time, the same sudden transition has produced the Negro slum—different from, but hardly better than its predecessors, and fundamentally the result of the same process.

Negroes are now more urbanized than whites.

Urban Population as Percent of Total, by Color, by Region, 1960

REGION	WHITE	NEGRO
United States	69.5	73.2
Northeast	79.1	95.7
North Central	66.8	95.7
South	58.6	58.4
West	77.6	92.6

Source: *U.S. Census of Population*, PC (1)-1D, 1960, *U.S. Summary*, table 155 and 233; PC (2)-1C, *Nonwhite Population by Race*, table 1.

Negro families in the cities are more frequently headed by a woman than those in the country. The difference between the white and Negro proportions of families headed by a woman is greater in the city than in the country.

Percent of Negro Families with Female Head, by Region and Area, 1960

REGION	URBAN	RURAL NONFARM	RURAL FARM
United States	23.1	19.5	11.1
Northeast	24.2	14.1	4.3
North Central	20.8	14.7	8.4
South	24.2	20.0	11.2
West	20.7	9.4	5.5

Source: *U.S. Census of Population 1960, Nonwhite Population by Race*, PC (2) IC,, table 9, pp. 9-10.

The promise of the city has so far been denied the majority of the Negro migrants, and most particularly the Negro family.

In 1939, E. Franklin Frazier described its plight movingly in that part of *The Negro Family* entitled "In the City of Destruction":

The impact of hundreds of thousands of rural southern Negroes upon northern metropolitan communities presents a bewildering spectacle. Striking contrasts in levels of civilization and economic well-being among these new-comers to modern civilization seem to baffle any attempt to discover order and direction in their mode of life.

In many cases, of course, the dissolution of the simple family organization has begun before the family reaches the northern city. But, if these families have managed to preserve their integrity until they reach the northern city, poverty, ignorance, and color force them to seek homes in deteriorated slum areas from which practically all institutional life has disappeared. Hence, at the same time that these simple rural families are losing their internal cohesion, they are being freed from the controlling force of public opinion and communal institutions. Family desertion among Negroes in cities appears, then, to be one of the inevitable consequences of the impact of urban life on the simple family organization and folk culture which the Negro has evolved in the rural South. The distribution of desertions in relation to the general economic and cultural organization of Negro communities that have grown up in our American cities shows in a striking manner the influence of selective factors in the process of adjustment to the urban environment.

Frazier concluded his classic study, *The Negro Family,* with the prophesy that the "travail of civilization is not yet ended."

First, it appears that the family which evolved within the isolated world of the Negro folk will become increasingly disorganized. Modern means of communication will break down the isolation of the world of the black folk, and, as long as the bankrupt system of southern agriculture exists, Negro families will continue to seek a living in the towns and cities of the country. They will crowd the slum areas of southern cities or make their way to northern cties where their family life will become disrupted and their poverty will force them to depend upon charity.

In every index of family pathology—divorce, separation, and desertion, female family head, children in broken homes, and illegitimacy—the contrast between the urban and rural environment for Negro families is unmistakable.

Harlem, into which Negroes began to move early in this century, is the center and symbol of the urban life of the Negro American. Conditions in Harlem are not worse, they are probably better than in most Negro ghettos. The social disorganization of central Harlem, comprising ten health areas, was thoroughly documented by the HARYOU report, save for the illegitimacy rates. These have now been made available to the Labor Department by the New York City Department of Health. There could hardly be a more dramatic demonstration of the crumbling—the breaking—of the family structure on the urban frontier.

Unemployment and Poverty

The impact of unemployment on the Negro family, and particularly on the Negro male, is the least understood of all the developments that have contributed to the present crisis. There is little analysis because there has been almost no inquiry. Unemployment, for whites and non-whites alike, has on the whole been treated as an economic phenomenon, with almost no attention paid for at least a quarter-century to social and personal consequences.

In 1940, Edward Wight Bakke described the effects of unemployment on family structure in terms of six stages of adjustment. Although the families studied were white, the pattern would clearly seem to be a general one, and apply to Negro families as well.

The first two stages end with the exhaustion of credit and the entry of the wife into the labor force. The father is no longer the provider and the elder children become resentful.

The third stage is the critical one of commencing a new day-to-day existence. At this point two women are in charge:

> Consider the fact that relief investigators or case workers are normally women and deal with the housewife. Already suffering a loss in prestige and authority in the family because of his failure to be the chief bread winner, the male head of the family feels deeply this obvious transfer of planning for the family's well-being to two women, one of them an outsider. His role is reduced to that of errand boy to and from the relief office.

If the family makes it through this stage Bakke finds that it is likely to survive, and the rest of the process is one of adjustment. *The critical element of adjustment was not welfare payments, but work.*

> Having observed our families under conditions of unemployment with no public help, or with that help coming from direct [sic] and from work relief, we are convinced that after the exhaustion of self-produced resources, work relief is the only type of assistance which can restore the strained bonds of family relationship in a way which promises the continued functioning of that family in meeting the responsibilities imposed upon it by our own culture.

Work is precisely the one thing the Negro family head in such circumstances has not received over the past generation.

The fundamental, overwhelming fact is that *Negro unemployment,* with the exception of a few years during World War II and the Korean War, *has continued at disaster levels for 35 years.*

Once again, this is particularly the case in the northern urban areas to which the Negro population has been moving.

The 1930 Census (taken in the spring, before the depression was in full swing) showed Negro unemployment at 6.1 percent, as against 6.6 percent for whites. But taking out the South reversed the relationship: white 7.4 percent, nonwhite 11.5 percent.

By 1940, the 1 to 2 white-Negro unemployment relationship that persists to this day had clearly emerged. Taking out the South again, whites were 14.8 percent, nonwhites 29.7 percent.

Since 1929, the Negro worker has been tremendously affected by the movements of the business cycle and of employment. He has been hit worse by declines than whites, and proportionately helped more by recoveries.

From 1951 to 1963, the level of Negro male unemployment was on a long-run rising trend, while at the same time following the short-run ups and downs of the business cycle. During the same period, the number of broken families in the Negro world was also on a long-run rise, with intermediate ups and downs.

The series move in the same directions—up and down together, with a long-run rising trend—but the peaks and troughs are 1 year out of phase. Thus unemployment peaks 1 year before broken families, and so on. By plotting these series in terms of deviation from trend, and moving the unemployment curve *1 year ahead,* we see the clear relation of the two otherwise seemingly unrelated series of events; the cyclical swings in unemployment have their counterpart in increases and decreases in separations.

The effect of recession unemployment on divorces further illustrates the economic roots of the problem. The nonwhite divorce rates dipped slightly in high unemployment years like 1954-55, 1958, and 1961-62.

Divorce is expensive: those without money resort to separation or desertion. While divorce is not a desirable goal for a society, it recognizes the importance of marriage and family, and for children some family continuity and support is more likely when the institution of the family has been so recognized.

The conclusion from these and similar data is difficult to avoid: During times when jobs were reasonably plentiful (although at no time during this period, save perhaps the first 2 years, did the unemployment rate for Negro males drop to anything like a reasonable level) the Negro family became stronger and more stable. As jobs became more and more difficult to find, the stability of the family became more and more difficult to maintain.

This relation is clearly seen in terms of the illegitimacy rates of census tracts in the District of Columbia compared with male unemployment rates in the same neighborhoods.

In 1963, a prosperous year, 29.2 percent of all Negro men in the labor force were unemployed at some time during the year. Almost half of these men were out of work 15 weeks or more.

The impact of poverty on Negro family structure is no less obvious, although again it may not be widely acknowledged. There would seem to be an American tradition, agrarian in its origins but reinforced by attitudes of urban immigrant groups, to the effect that family morality and stability decline as income and social position rise. Over the years this may have provided some consolation to the poor, but there is little evidence that it is true. On the contrary, higher family incomes are unmistakably associated with greater family stability—which comes first may be a matter for conjecture, but the conjunction of the two characteristics is unmistakable.

The Negro family is no exception. In the District of Columbia, for example, census tracts with median incomes over $8,000 had an illegitimacy rate one-third that of tracts in the category under $4,000.

The Wage System

The American wage system is conspicuous in the degree to which it provides high incomes for individuals, but is rarely adjusted to insure that family, as well as individual needs are met. Almost without exception, the social welfare and social insurance systems of other industrial democracies provide for some adjustment or supplement of a worker's income to provide for the extra expenses of those with families. American arrangements do not, save for income tax deductions.

The Federal minimum wage of $1.25 per hour provides a basic income for an individual, but an income well below the poverty line for a couple, much less a family with children.

The 1965 Economic Report of the President revised the data on the number of persons living in poverty in the United States to take account of the varying needs of families of different sizes, rather than using a flat cut off at the $3,000 income level. The resulting revision illustrates the significance of family size. Using these criteria, the number of poor families is smaller, but the number of large families who are poor increases, and the number of children in poverty rises by more than one-third—from 11 million to 15 million. This means that one-fourth of the Nation's children live in families that are poor.

A third of these children belong to families in which the father was not only present, but was employed the year round. In overall terms, median family income is lower for large families than for small families. Families of six or more children have median incomes 24 percent below families with three. (It may be added that 47 percent of young men who fail the Selective Service education test come from families of six or more.)

During the 1950-60 decade of heavy Negro migration to the cities of the North and West, the ratio of nonwhite to white family income in cities increased from 57 to 63 percent. Corresponding declines in the ratio in the rural nonfarm and farm areas kept the national ratio virtually unchanged. But between 1960 and 1963, median nonwhite family income slipped from 55 percent to 53 percent of white income. The drop occurred in three regions, with only the South, where a larger proportion of Negro families have more than one earner, showing a slight improvement.

Because in general terms Negro families have the largest number of children and the lowest incomes, many Negro fathers literally cannot support their families. Because the father is either not present, is unemployed, or makes such a low wage, the Negro woman goes to work. Fifty-six percent of Negro women, age 25 to 64, are in the work force, against 42 percent of white women. This dependence on the mother's income undermines the position of the father and deprives the children of the kind of attention, particularly in school matters, which is now a standard feature of middle-class upbringing.

The Dimensions Grow

The dimensions of the problems of Negro Americans are compounded by the present extraordinary growth in Negro population. At the founding of the nation, and into the first decade of the 19th century, 1 American in 5 was a Negro. The proportion declined steadily until it was only 1 in 10 by 1920, where it held until the 1950's, when it began to rise. Since 1950, the Negro population has grown at a rate of 2.4 percent per year compared with 1.7 percent for the total population. If this rate continues, in seven years 1 American in 8 will be nonwhite.

These changes are the result of a declining Negro death rate, now approaching that of the nation generally, and a fertility rate that grew steadily during the postwar period. By 1959, the ratio of white to nonwhite fertility rates reached 1:1.42. Both the white and nonwhite fertility rates have declined since 1959, but the differential has not narrowed.

Family size increased among nonwhite families between 1950 and 1960—as much for those without fathers as for those with fathers. Average family size changed little among white families, with a slight increase in the size of husband-wife families balanced by a decline in the size of families without fathers.

Negro women not only have more children, but have them earlier. Thus in 1960, there were 1,247 children ever born per thousand ever-married nonwhite women 15 to 19 years of age, as against only 725 among white women, a ratio of 1.7:1. The Negro fertility rate over-all is now 1.4 times the white, but what might be called the generation rate is 1.7 times the white.

This population growth must inevitably lead to an unconcealable crisis in Negro unemployment. The most conspicuous failure of the American social system in the past 10 years has been its inadequacy in providing jobs for Negro youth. Thus, in January 1965 the unemployment rate for Negro teenagers stood at 29 percent. This problem will now become steadily more serious.

Population and Labor Force Projections, by Color

	PERCENT INCREASE	
	Actual 1954-64	Projected* 1964-70
Civilian population age 14 and over		
White	15.6	9.7
Nonwhite	23.9	19.9
Civilian labor force		
White	14.6	10.8
*Nonwhite	19.3	20.0

* Population and labor force projections by color were made by the Bureau of Labor Statistics. They have not been revised since the total population and labor force were re-estimated, but are considered accurate measures of the relative magnitudes of increase.
Source: Bureau of Labor Statistics.

During the rest of the 1960's the nonwhite civilian population 14 years of age and over will increase by 20 percent—more than double the white rate. The nonwhite labor force will correspondingly increase 20 percent in the next 6 years, double the rate of increase in the nonwhite labor force of the past decade.

Family income in 1959	Number of Children per Nonwhite Mother Age 35-39, 1960
Under $2,000	5.3
$2,000 to $3,999	4.3
$4,000 to $4,999	4.0
$5,000 to $5,999	3.8
$6,000 to $6,999	3.5
$7,000 to $9,999	3.2
$10,000 to $14,999	2.9
$15,000 and over	2.9

Source: 1960 Census, *Women by Number of Children Ever Born,* PC (2) 3A, table 38, p. 188.

As with the population as a whole, there is much evidence that children are being born most rapidly in those Negro families with the least financial resources. This is an ancient pattern, but because the needs of children are greater today it is very possible that the education and opportunity gap between the offspring of these families and those of stable middle-class unions is not closing, but is growing wider.

A cycle is at work; too many children too early make it most difficult for the parents to finish school. (In February, 1963, 38 percent of the white girls who dropped out of school did so because of marriage or pregnancy, as against 49 percent of nonwhite girls.) An Urban League study in New York reported that 44 percent of girl dropouts left school because of pregnancy.

Low education levels in turn produce low income levels, which deprive children of many opportunities, and so the cycle repeats itself.

Chapter 4. The Tangle of Pathology

That the Negro American has survived at all is extraordinary—a lesser people might simply have died out, as indeed others have. That the Negro community has not only survived, but in this political generation has entered national affairs as a moderate, humane, and constructive national force is the highest testament to the healing powers of the democratic ideal and the creative vitality of the Negro people.

But it may not be supposed that the Negro American community has not paid a fearful price for their incredible mistreatment to which it has been subjected over the past three centuries.

In essence, the Negro community has been forced into a matriarchal structure which, because it is so out of line with the rest of the American society, seriously retards the progress of the group as a whole, and imposes a crushing burden on the Negro male and, in consequence, on a great many Negro women as well.

There is, presumably, no special reason why a society in which males are dominant in family relationships is to be preferred to a matriarchal arrangement. However, it is clearly a disadvantage for a minority group to be operating on one principle, while the great majority of the population, and the one with the most advantages to begin with, is operating on another. This is the present situation of the Negro. Ours is a society which presumes male leadership in private and public affairs. The arrangements of society facilitate such leadership and reward it. A subculture, such as that of the Negro American, in which this is not the pattern, is placed at a distinct disadvantage.

Here an earlier word of caution should be repeated. There is much evidence that a considerable number of Negro families have managed to break out of the tangle of pathology and to establish themselves as stable, effective units, living according to patterns of American society in general. E. Franklin Frazier has suggested that the middle-class Negro American family is, if anything, more patriarchal and protective of its children than the general run of such families. Given equal opportunities, the children of these families will perform as well or better than their white peers. They need no help from anyone, and ask none.

While this phenomenon is not easily measured, one index is that middle-class Negroes have even fewer children than middle-class whites, indicating a desire to conserve the advances they have made and to insure that their children do as well or better. Negro women who marry early to uneducated laborers have more children than white women in the same situation; Negro women who marry at the common age for the middle class to educated men doing technical or professional work have only four-fifths as many children as their white counterparts.

It might be estimated that as much as half of the Negro community falls into the middle class. However, the remaining half is in desperate and deteriorating circumstances. Moreover, because of housing segregation it is immensely difficult for the stable half to escape from the cultural influences of the unstable one. The children of middle-class Negroes often as not must grow up in, or next to the slums, an experience almost unknown to white middle-class children. They are therefore constantly exposed to the pathology of the disturbed group and constantly in danger of being drawn into it. It is for this reason that the propositions put forth in this study may be thought of as having a more or less general application.

In a word, most Negro youth are in *danger* of being caught up in the tangle of pathology that affects their world, and probably a majority are so entrapped. Many of those who escape do so for one generation only: as things now are, their children may have to run the gauntlet all over again. That is not the least vicious aspect of the world that white America has made for the Negro.

Obviously, not every instance of social pathology afflicting the Negro community can be traced to the weakness of family structure. If, for example, organized crime in the Negro community were not largely controlled by whites, there would be more capital accumulation among Negroes, and therefore probably more Negro business enterprises. If it were not for the hostility and fear many whites exhibit toward Negroes, they in turn would be less afflicted by hostility and fear and so on. There is no one Negro community. There is no one Negro problem. There is no one solution. Nonetheless, at the center of the tangle of pathology is the weakness of the family structure. Once or twice removed, it will be found to be the principal source of most of the aberrant, inadequate, or antisocial behavior that did not establish, but now serves to perpetuate the cycle of poverty and deprivation.

It was by destroying the Negro family under slavery that white America broke the will of the Negro people. Although that will has reasserted itself in our time, it is a resurgence doomed to frustration unless the viability of the Negro family is restored.

Matriarchy

A fundamental fact of Negro American family life is the often reversed roles of husband and wife.

Robert O. Blood, Jr. and Donald M. Wolfe, in a study of Detroit families, note that "Negro husbands have unusually low power," and while this is characteristic of all low income families, the pattern pervades the Negro social structure: "the cumulative result of discrimination in jobs . . ., the segregated housing, and the poor schooling of Negro men." In 44 percent of the Negro families studied, the wife was dominant, as against 20 percent of white wives. "Whereas the majority of white families are equalitarian, the largest percentage of Negro families are dominated by the wife."

The matriarchal pattern of so many Negro families reinforces itself over the generations. This process begins with education. Although the gap appears to be closing at the moment, for a long while, Negro females were better educated than Negro males, and this remains true today for the Negro population as a whole.

Educational Attainment of the Civilian Noninstitutional Population
18 Years of Age and Over, March 1964

Color and sex	Median school years completed
White:	
Male	12.1
Female	12.1
Nonwhite:	
Male	9.2
Female	10.0

Source: Bureau of Labor Statistics, unpublished data.

The difference in educational attainment between nonwhite men and women in the labor force is even greater; men lag 1.1 years behind women.

The disparity in educational attainment of male and female youth age 16 to 21 who were out of school in February 1963, is striking. Among the nonwhite males, 66.3 percent were not high school graduates, compared with 55.0 percent of the females. A similar difference existed at the college level, with 4.5 percent of the males having completed 1 to 3 years of college compared with 7.3 percent of the females.

The poorer performance of the male in school exists from the very beginning, and the magnitude of the difference was documented by the 1960 Census in statistics on the number of children who have fallen one or more grades below the typical grade for children of the same age. The boys have more frequently fallen behind at every age level. (White boys also lag behind white girls, but at a differential of 1 to 6 percentage points.)

Percent of Nonwhite Youth Enrolled in School Who are
1 or More Grades Below Mode for Age, by Sex, 1960

Age	Male	Female
7 to 9 years old	7.8	5.8
10 to 13 years old	25.0	17.1
14 and 15 years old	35.5	24.8
16 and 17 years old	39.4	27.2
18 and 19 years old	57.3	46.0

Source: 1960 Census, *School Enrollment*, PC (2) 5A, table 3, p. 24.

In 1960, 39 percent of all white persons 25 years of age and over who had completed 4 or more years of college were women. Fifty-three percent of the nonwhites who had attained this level were women.

However, the gap is closing. By October 1963, there were slightly more Negro men in college than women. Among whites there were almost twice as many men as women enrolled.

There is much evidence that Negro females are better students than their male counterparts.

Daniel Thompson of Dillard University, in a private communication on January 9, 1965, writes:

> As low as is the aspirational level among lower class Negro girls, it is considerably higher than among the boys. For example, I have examined the honor rolls in Negro high schools for about 10 years. As a rule, from 75 to 90 percent of all Negro honor students are girls.

Dr. Thompson reports that 70 percent of all applications for the National Achievement Scholarship Program financed by the Ford Foundation for outstanding Negro high school graduates are girls, despite special efforts by high school principals to submit the names of boys.

The finalists for this new program for outstanding Negro students were recently announced. Based on an inspection of the names, only about 43 percent of all the 639 finalists were male. (However, in the regular National Merit Scholarship program, males received 67 percent of the 1964 scholarship awards.)

Inevitably, these disparities have carried over to the area of employment and income.

In 1 out of 4 Negro families where the husband is present, is an earner, and someone else in the family works, the husband is not the principal earner. The comparable figure for whites is 18 percent.

More important, it is clear that Negro females have established a strong position for themselves in white collar and professional employment, precisely the areas of the economy which are growing most rapidly, and to which the highest prestige is accorded.

The President's Committee on Equal Employment Opportunity, making a preliminary report on employment in 1964 of over 16,000 companies with nearly 5 million employees, revealed this pattern with dramatic emphasis.

> In this work force, Negro males outnumber Negro females by a ratio of 4 to 1. Yet Negro males represent only 1.2 percent of all males in white collar occupations, while Negro females represent 3.1 percent of the total female white collar work force. Negro males represent 1.1 percent of all male professionals. Again, in technician occupations, Negro males represent 2.1 per-

cent of all male technicians while Negro females represent roughly 10 percent of all female technicians. It would appear therefore that there are
proportionately 4 times as many Negro females in significant white collar
jobs than Negro males.

Although it is evident that office and clerical jobs account for approximately
50 percent of all Negro female white collar workers, it is significant that 6
out of every 100 Negro females are in professional jobs. This is substantially
similar to the rate of all females in such jobs. Approximately 7 out of every
100 Negro females are in technician jobs. This exceeds the proportion of all
females in technician jobs—approximately 5 out of every 100.

Negro females in skilled jobs are almost the same as that of all females in
such jobs. Nine out of every 100 Negro males are in skilled occupations
while 21 out of 100 of all males are in such jobs.

This pattern is to be seen in the Federal government, where special
efforts have been made recently to insure equal employment opportunity
for Negroes. These efforts have been notably successful in Departments such
as Labor, where some 19 percent of employees are now Negro. (A not
disproportionate percentage, given the composition of the work force in
the areas where the main Department offices are located.) However, it
may well be that these efforts have redoubled mostly to the benefit of Negro
women, and may even have accentuated the comparative disadvantage of
Negro men. Seventy percent of the Negro employees of the Department
of Labor are women, as contrasted with only 42 percent of the white
employees.

Among nonprofessional Labor Department employees—where the most
employment opportunities exist for all groups—Negro women outnumber
Negro men 4 to 1, and average almost one grade higher in classification.

The testimony to the effects of these patterns in Negro family structure
is widespread, and hardly to be doubted.

WHITNEY YOUNG: Historically, in the matriarchal Negro society, mothers
made sure that if one of their children had a chance for higher education the
daughter was the one to pursue it.

The effect on family functioning and role performance of this historical
experience [economic deprivation] is what you might predict. Both as a
husband and as a father the Negro male is made to feel inadequate, not
because he is unlovable or unaffectionate, lacks intelligence or even a gray
flannel suit. But in a society that measures a man by the size of his pay
check, he doesn't stand very tall in a comparison with his white counterpart.
To this situation he may react with withdrawal, bitterness toward society,
aggression both within the family and racial group, self-hatred, or crime. Or
he may escape through a number of avenues that help him to lose himself in
fantasy or to compensate for his low status through a variety of exploits.

THOMAS PETTIGREW: The Negro wife in this situation can easily become disgusted with her financially dependent husband, and her rejection of him further alienates the male from family life. Embittered by their experiences with men, many Negro mothers often act to perpetuate the mother-centered pattern by taking a greater interest in their daughters than their sons.

DETON BROOKS: In a matriarchal structure, the women are transmitting the culture.

DOROTHY HEIGHT: If the Negro woman has a major underlying concern, it is the status of the Negro man and his position in the community and his need for feeling himself an important person, free and able to make his contribution in the whole society in order that he may strengthen his home.

DUNCAN M. MACINTYRE: The Negro illegitimacy rate always has been high —about eight times the white rate in 1940 and somewhat higher today even though the white illegitimacy rate also is climbing. The Negro statistics are symptomatic of some old socioeconomic problems, not the least of which are underemployment among Negro men and compensating higher labor force propensity among Negro women. Both operate to enlarge the mother's role, undercutting the status of the male and making many Negro families essentially matriarchal. The Negro man's uncertain employment prospects, matriarchy, and the high cost of divorces combine to encourage desertion (the poor man's divorce), increases the number of couples not married, and thereby also increases the Negro illegitimacy rate. In the meantime, higher Negro birth rates are increasing the nonwhite population, while migration into cities like Detroit, New York, Philadelphia, and Washington, D.C. is making the public assistance rolls in such cities heavily, even predominantly, Negro.

ROBIN M. WILLIAMS, JR. *in a study of Elmira, New York:* Only 57 percent of Negro adults reported themselves as married—spouse present, as compared with 78 percent of native white American gentiles, 91 percent of Italian-American, and 96 percent of Jewish informants. Of the 93 unmarried Negro youths interviewed, 22 percent did not have their mother living in the home with them, and 42 percent reported that their father was not living in their home. One-third of the youths did not know their father's present occupation, and two-thirds of a sample of 150 Negro adults did not know what the occupation of their father's father had been. Forty percent of the youths said that they had brothers and sisters living in other communities: another 40 percent reported relatives living in their home who were not parents, siblings, or grandparent.

The Failure of Youth

Williams' account of Negro youth growing up with little knowledge of their fathers, less of their fathers' occupations, still less of family occupational traditions, is in sharp contrast to the experience of the white child. The white family, despite many variants, remains a powerful agency not only for transmitting property from one generation to the next, but also for transmitting no less valuable contracts with the world of education and work. In an earlier age, the Carpenters, Wainwrights, Weavers, Mercers, Farmers, Smiths acquired their names as well as their trades from their fathers and grandfathers. Children today still learn the patterns of work from their fathers even though they may no longer go into the same jobs.

White children without fathers at least perceive all about them the pattern of men working.

Negro children without fathers flounder—and fail.

Not always, to be sure. The Negro community produces its share, very possibly more than its share, of young people who have the something extra that carries them over the worst obstacles. But such persons are always a minority. The common run of young people in a group facing serious obstacles to success do not succeed.

A prime index of the disadvantage of Negro youth in the United States is their consistently poor performance on the mental tests that are a standard means of measuring ability and performance in the present generation.

There is absolutely no question of any genetic differential: Intelligence potential is distributed among Negro infants in the same proportion and pattern as among Icelanders or Chinese or any other group. American society, however, impairs the Negro potential. The statement of the HARYOU report that "there is no basic disagreement over the fact that central Harlem students are performing poorly in school" may be taken as true of Negro slum children throughout the United States.

Eighth grade children in central Harlem have a median IQ of 87.7, which means that perhaps a third of the children are scoring at levels perilously near to those of retardation. IQ *declines* in the first decade of life, rising only slightly thereafter.

The effect of broken families on the performance of Negro youth has not been extensively measured, but studies that have been made show an unmistakable influence.

Martin Deutch and Bert Brown, investigating intelligence test differences between Negro and white 1st and 5th graders of different social classes, found that there is a direct relationship between social class and IQ. As the one rises so does the other: but more for whites than Negroes. This is surely a result of housing segregation, referred to earlier, which makes it difficult for middle-class Negro families to escape the slums.

The authors explain that "it is much more difficult for the Negro to attain identical middle- or upper-middle-class status with whites, and the social class graduations are less marked for Negroes because Negro life in a caste society is considerably more homogeneous than is life for the majority group."

Therefore, the authors look for background variables other than social class which might explain the difference: "One of the most striking differences between the Negro and white groups is the consistently higher frequency of broken homes and resulting family disorganization in the Negro group."

Father Absent From the Home

Lowest social class level		Middle social class level		Highest social class level	
Percent of White	Negro	Percent of White	Negro	Percent of White	Negro
15.4	43.9	10.3	27.9	0.0	13.7

(Adapted from authors' table)

Further, they found that children from homes where fathers are present have significantly higher scores than children in homes without fathers.

	Mean Intelligence Scores
Father Present	97.83
Father Absent	90.79

The influence of the father's presence was then tested *within* the social classes and school grades for Negroes alone. They found that a "consistent trend within both grades at the lower SES [social class] level appears, and in no case is there a reversal of this trend: for males, females, and the combined group, the IQ's of children with fathers in the home are always higher than those who have no father in the home."

The authors say that broken homes "may also account for some of the differences between Negro and white intelligence scores."

The sources of fifth graders with fathers absent were lower than the scores of first graders with fathers absent, and while the authors point out that it is cross sectional data and does not reveal the duration of the fathers' absence, "What we might be tapping is the cumulative effect of fatherless years."

This difference in ability to perform has its counterpart in statistics on actual school performance. Nonwhite boys from families with both parents present are more likely to be going to school than boys with only one parent present, and enrollment rates are even lower when neither parent is present.

When the boys from broken homes are in school, they do not do as well as the boys from whole families. Grade retardation is higher when only one parent is present, and highest when neither parent is present.

The loneliness of the Negro youth in making fundamental decisions about education is shown in a 1959 study of Negro and white dropouts in Connecticut high schools.

Only 29 percent of the Negro male dropouts discussed their decision to drop out of school with their fathers, compared with 65 percent of the white males (38 percent of the Negro males were from broken homes). In fact, 26 percent of the Negro males did not discuss this major decision in their lives with anyone at all, compared with only 8 percent of white males.

A study of Negro apprenticeship by the New York State Commission Against Discrimination in 1960 concluded:

> Negro youth are seldom exposed to influences which can lead to apprenticeship. Negroes are not apt to have relatives, friends, or neighbors in skilled occupations. Nor are they likely to be in secondary schools where they receive encouragement and direction from alternate role models. Within the minority community, skilled Negro 'models' after whom the Negro youth might pattern himself are rare, while substitute sources which could provide the direction, encouragement, resources, and information needed to achieve skilled craft standing are nonexistent.

Delinquency and Crime

The combined impact of poverty, failure, and isolation among Negro youth has had the predictable outcome in a disastrous delinquency and crime rate.

In a typical pattern of discrimination, Negro children in all public and private orphanages are a smaller proportion of all children than their proportion of the population although their needs are clearly greater.

On the other hand Negroes represent a third of all youth in training schools for juvenile delinquents.

Children in Homes for Dependent and
Neglected Children, 1960

	Number	Percent
White	64,807	88.4
Negro	6,140	8.4
Other races	2,359	3.2
All races	73,306	100.0

Source: 1960 Census, *Inmates of Institutions,* PC (2) 3A, table 31, p. 44.

It is probable that at present, a majority of the crimes against the person, such as rape, murder, and aggravated assault are committed by Negroes. There is, of course, no absolute evidence; inference can only be made from arrest and prison population statistics. The data that follow unquestionably are biased against Negroes, who are arraigned much more casually than are whites, but it may be doubted that the bias is great enough to affect the general proportions.

Number of Arrests in 1963

	White	Negro
Offenses charged total	31,988	38,549
Murder and nonnegligent manslaughter	2,288	2,948
Forcible rape	4,402	3,935
Aggravated assault	25,298	31,666

Source: *Crime in the United States* (Federal Bureau of Investigation, 1963) table 25, p. 111.

Again on the urban frontier the ratio is worse: 3 out of every 5 arrests for these crimes were of Negroes.

In Chicago in 1963, three-quarters of the persons arrested for such crimes were Negro; in Detroit, the same proportions held.

In 1960, 37 percent of all persons in Federal and State prisons were Negro. In that year, 56 percent of the homicide and 57 percent of the assault offenders committed to State institutions were Negro.

The overwhelming number of offenses committed by Negroes are directed toward other Negroes: the cost of crime to the Negro community is a combination of that to the criminal and to the victim.

Some of the research on the effects of broken homes on delinquent behavior recently surveyed by Thomas F. Pettigrew in *A Profile of the Negro American* is summarized below, along with several other studies of the question.

Mary Diggs found that three-fourths—twice the expected ratio—of Philadelphia's Negro delinquents who came before the law during 1948 did not live with both their natural parents.

In predicting juvenile crime, Eleanor and Sheldon Glueck also found that a higher proportion of delinquent than nondelinquent boys came from broken homes. They identified five critical factors in the home environment that made a difference in whether boys would become delinquents: discipline of boy by father, supervision of boy by mother, affection of father for boy, affection of mother for boy, and cohesiveness of family.

In 1952, when the New York City Youth Board set out to test the validity of these five factors as predictors of delinquency, a problem quickly emerged. The Glueck sample consisted of white boys of mainly Irish, Italian, Lithuanian, and English descent. However, the Youth Board group was 44 percent Negro and 14 percent Puerto Rican, and the frequency of broken homes within these groups was out of proportion to the total number of delinquents in the population.

In the majority of these cases, the father was usually never in the home at all, absent for the major proportion of the boy's life, or was present only on occasion.

(The final prediction table was reduced to three factors: supervision of boy by mother, discipline of boy by mother, and family cohesiveness within what family, in fact, existed, but was, nonetheless, 85 percent accurate in predicting delinquents and 96 percent accurate in predicting nondelinquents.)

Researchers who have focussed upon the "good" boy in high delinquency neighborhoods noted that they typically come from exceptionally stable, intact families.

Recent psychological research demonstrates the personality effects of being reared in a disorganized home without a father. One study showed that children from fatherless homes seek immediate gratification of their desires far more than children with fathers present. Others revealed that children who hunger for immediate gratification are more prone to delinquency, along with other less social behavior. Two psychologists, Pettigrew says, maintain that inability to delay gratification is a critical factor in immature, criminal, and neurotic behavior.

Finally, Pettigrew discussed the evidence that a stable home is a crucial factor in counteracting the effects of racism upon Negro personality.

A warm, supportive home can effectively compensate for many of the restrictions the Negro child faces outside of the ghetto; consequently, the type of home life a Negro enjoys as a child may be far more crucial for governing the influence of segregation upon his personality than the form the segregation takes — legal or informal, Southern or Northern.

A Yale University study of youth in the lowest socioeconomic class in New Haven in 1950 whose behavior was followed through their 18th year revealed that among the delinquents in the group, 38 percent came from broken homes, compared with 24 percent of nondelinquents.

The President's Task Force on Manpower Conservation in 1963 found that of young men rejected for the draft for failure to pass the mental tests, 42 percent of those with a court record came from broken homes, compared with 30 percent of those without a court record. Half of all the nonwhite rejectees in the study with a court record came from broken homes.

An examination of the family background of 44,448 delinquency cases in Philadelphia between 1949 and 1954 documents the frequency of broken homes among delinquents. Sixty-two percent of the Negro delinquents and 36 percent of white delinquents were not living with both parents. In 1950, 33 percent of nonwhite children and 7 percent of white children in Philadelphia were living in homes without both parents. Repeaters were even more likely to be from broken homes than first offenders.

The Armed Forces

The ultimate mark of inadequate preparation for life is the failure rate on the Armed Forces mental test. The Armed Forces Qualification Test is not quite a mental test, nor yet an education test. It is a test of ability to perform at an acceptable level of competence. It roughly measures ability that ought to be found in an average 7th or 8th grade student. A grown young man who cannot pass this test is in trouble.

Fifty-six percent of Negroes fail it.

This is a rate almost four times that of the whites.

The Army, Navy, Air Force, and Marines conduct by far the largest and most important education and training activities of the Federal Government, as well as provide the largest single source of employment in the nation.

Military service is disruptive in some respects. For those comparatively few who are killed or wounded in combat, or otherwise, the personal sacrifice is inestimable. But on balance service in the Armed Forces over the past quarter-century has worked greatly to the advantage of those involved. The training and experience of military duty itself is unique; the advantages that have generally followed in the form of the G.I. Bill, mortgage guarantees, Federal life insurance, Civil Service preference, veterans' hospitals, and veterans' pensions are singular, to say the least.

Although service in the Armed Forces is at least nominally a duty of all male citizens coming of age, it is clear that the present system does not enable Negroes to serve in anything like their proportionate numbers. This is not a question of discrimination. Induction into the Armed Forces is based on a variety of objective tests and standards, but these tests nonetheless have the effect of keeping the number of Negroes disproportionately small.

In 1963 the United States Commission on Civil Rights reported that "A decade ago, Negroes constituted 8 percent of the Armed Forces. Today . . . they continue to constitute 8 percent of the Armed Forces."

In 1964 Negroes constituted 11.8 percent of the population, but probably remain at 8 percent of the Armed Forces.

Enlisted Men:	Percent Negro
Army	12.2
Navy	5.2
Air Force	9.1
Marine Corps	7.6

Officers:

Army	3.2
Navy	.2
Air Force	1.2
Marine Corps	.2

The significance of Negro under-representation in the Armed Forces is greater than might at first be supposed. If Negroes were represented in the same proportions in the military as they are in the population, they would number 300,000 plus. This would be over 100,000 more than at present (using 1964 strength figures). If the more than 100,000 unemployed Negro men were to have gone into the military the Negro male unemployment rate would have been 7.0 percent in 1964 instead of 9.1 percent.

In 1963 the Civil Rights Commission commented on the occupational aspect of military service for Negroes. "Negro enlisted men enjoy relatively better opportunities in the Armed Forces than in the civilian economy in every clerical, technical, and skilled field for which the data permit comparison."

There is, however, an even more important issue involved in military service for Negroes. Service in the United States Armed Forces is the *only* experience open to the Negro American in which he is truly treated as an equal: not as a Negro equal to a white, but as one man equal to any other man in a world where the category "Negro" and "white" do not exist. If this is a statement of the ideal rather than reality, it is an ideal that is close to realization. In food, dress, housing, pay, work—the Negro in the Armed Forces *is* equal and is treated that way.

There is another special quality about military service for Negro men: it is an utterly masculine world. Given the strains of the disorganized and matrifocal family life in which so many Negro youth come of age, the Armed Forces are a dramatic and desperately needed change: a world away from women, a world run by strong men of unquestioned authority, where discipline, if harsh, is nonetheless orderly and predictable, and where rewards, if limited, are granted on the basis of performance.

The theme of a current Army recruiting message states it as clearly as can be: "In the U.S. Army you get to know what it means to feel like a man."

At the recent Civil Rights Commission hearings in Mississippi a witness testified that his Army service was in fact "the only time I ever felt like a man."

Yet a majority of Negro youth (and probably three-quarters of Mississippi Negroes) fail the Selective Service education test and are rejected. Negro participation in the Armed Forces would be less than it is, were it not for a proportionally larger share of voluntary enlistments and reen-listments. (Thus 16.3 percent of Army sergeants are Negro.)

Alienation

The term alienation may by now have been used in too many ways to retain a clear meaning, but it will serve to sum up the equally numerous ways in which large numbers of Negro youth appear to be withdrawing from American society.

One startling way in which this occurs is that the men are just not there when the Census enumerator comes around.

According to Bureau of Census population estimates for 1963, there are only 87 nonwhite males for every 100 females in the 30-to-34-year age group. The ratio does not exceed 90 to 100 throughout the 25-to-44-year age bracket. In the urban Northeast, there are only 76 males per 100 females 20-to-24-years of age, and males as a percent of females are below 90 percent throughout all ages after 14.

There are not really fewer men than women in the 20-to-40 age bracket. What obviously is involved is an error in counting: the surveyors simply do not find the Negro man. Donald J. Bogue and his associates, who have studied the Federal count of the Negro man, place the error as high as 19.8 percent at age 28; a typical error of around 15 percent is estimated from age 19 through 43. Preliminary research in the Bureau of the Census on the 1960 enumeration has resulted in similar conclusions, although not necessarily the same estimates of the extent of the error. The Negro male *can* be found at age 17 and 18. On the basis of birth records and mortality records, the conclusion must be that he is there at age 19 as well.

When the enumerators do find him, his answers to the standard questions asked in the monthly unemployment survey often result in counting him as "not in the labor force." In other words, Negro male unemployment may in truth be somewhat greater than reported.

The labor force participation rates of nonwhite men have been falling since the beginning of the century and for the past decade have been lower than the rates for white men. In 1964, the participation rates were 78.0 percent for white men and 75.8 percent for nonwhite men. Almost one percentage point of this difference was due to a higher proportion of nonwhite men unable to work because of long-term physical or mental illness; it seems reasonable to assume that the rest of the difference is due to discouragement about finding a job.

If nonwhite male labor force participation rates were as high as the white rates, there would have been 140,000 more nonwhite males in the labor force in 1964. If we further assume that the 140,000 would have been unemployed, the unemployment rate for nonwhite men would have been 11.5 percent instead of the recorded rate of 9 percent, and the ratio between the nonwhite rate and the white rate would have jumped from 2:1 to 2.4:1.

Understated or not, the official unemployment rates for Negroes are almost unbelievable.

The unemployment statistics for Negro teenagers—29 percent in January 1965—reflect lack of training and opportunity in the greatest measure, but it may not be doubted that they also reflect a certain failure of nerve.

"Are you looking for a job?" Secretary of Labor Wirtz asked a young man on a Harlem street corner. "Why?" was the reply.

Richard A. Cloward and Robert Ontell have commented on this withdrawal in a discussion of the Mobilization for Youth project on the lower East Side of New York.

> What contemporary slum and minority youth probably lack that similar children in earlier periods possessed is not motivation but some minimal sense of competence.
> We are plagued, in work with these youth, by what appears to be a low tolerance for frustration. They are not able to absorb setbacks. Minor irritants and rebuffs are magnified out of all proportion to reality. Perhaps they react as they do because they are not equal to the world that confronts them, and they know it. And it is the knowing that is devastating. Had the occupational structure remained intact, or had the education provided to them kept pace with occupational changes, the situation would be a different one. But it is not, and that is what we and they have to contend with.

Narcotic addiction is a characteristic form of withdrawal. In 1963, Negroes made up 54 percent of the addict population of the United States. Although the Federal Bureau of Narcotics reports a decline in the Negro proportion of new addicts, HARYOU reports the addiction rate in central Harlem rose from 22.1 per 10,000 in 1955 to 40.4 in 1961.

There is a larger fact about the alienation of Negro youth than the tangle of pathology described by these statistics. It is a fact particularly difficult to grasp by white persons who have in recent years shown increasing awareness of Negro problems.

The present generation of Negro youth growing up in the urban ghettos has probably less personal contact with the white world than any generation in the history of the Negro American.

Until World War II it could be said that in general the Negro and white worlds lived, if not together, at least side by side. Certainly they did, and do, in the South.

Since World War II, however, the two worlds have drawn physically apart. The symbol of this development was the construction in the 1940's and 1950's of the vast white, middle- and lower-middle-class suburbs around all of the Nation's cities. Increasingly the inner cities have been left to Negroes—who now share almost no community life with whites.

In turn, because of this new housing pattern—most of which has been financially assisted by the Federal government—it is probable that the American school system has become *more,* rather than less segregated in the past two decades.

School integration has not occurred in the South, where a decade after *Brown v. Board of Education* only 1 Negro in 9 is attending school with white children.

And in the North, despite strenuous official efforts, neighborhoods and therefore schools are becoming more and more of one class and one color.

In New York City, in the school year 1957-58 there were 64 schools that were 90 percent or more Negro or Puerto Rican. Six years later there were 134 such schools.

Along with the diminution of white middle-class contacts for a large percentage of Negroes, observers report that the Negro churches have all but lost contact with men in the Northern cities as well. This may be a normal condition of urban life, but it is probably a changed condition for the Negro American and cannot be a socially desirable development.

The only religious movement that appears to have enlisted a considerable number of lower-class Negro males in Northern cities of late is that of the Black Muslims: a movement based on total rejection of white society, even though it emulates white mores.

In a word: the tangle of pathology is tightening.

Chapter 5. The Case for National Action

The object of this study has been to define a problem, rather than propose solutions to it. We have kept within these confines for three reasons.

First, there are many persons, within and without the Government, who do not feel the problem exists, at least in any serious degree. These persons feel that, with the legal obstacles to assimilation out of the way, matters will take care of themselves in the normal course of events. This is a fundamental issue, and requires a decision within the Government.

Second, it is our view that the problem is so inter-related, one thing with another, that any list of program proposals would necessarily be incomplete, and would distract attention from the main point of inter-relatedness. We have shown a clear relation between male employment, for example, and the number of welfare dependent children. Employment in turn reflects educational achievement, which depends in large part on family stability, which reflects employment. Where we should break into this cycle, and how, are the most difficult domestic questions facing the United States. We must first reach agreement on what the problem is, then we will know what questions must be answered.

Third, it is necessary to acknowledge the view, held by a number of responsible persons, that this problem may in fact be out of control. This is a view with which we emphatically and totally disagree, but the view must be acknowledged. The persistent rise in Negro educational achievement is probably the main trend that belies this thesis. On the other hand our study has produced some clear indications that the situation may indeed have begun to feed on itself. It may be noted, for example, that for most of the postwar period male Negro unemployment and the number of new ADC cases rose and fell together as if connected by a chain from 1948 to 1962. The correlation between the two series of data was an astonishing .91. (This would mean that 83 percent of the rise and fall in ADC cases can be statistically ascribed to the rise and fall in the unemployment rate.) In 1960, however, for the first time, unemployment declined, but the number of new ADC cases rose. In 1963 this happened a second time. In 1964 a third. The possible implications of these and other data are serious enough that they, too, should be understood before program proposals are made.

However, the argument of this paper does lead to one central conclusion: Whatever the specific elements of a national effort designed to resolve this problem, those elements must be coordinated in terms of one general strategy.

What then is that problem? We feel the answer is clear enough. Three centuries of injustice have brought about deep-seated structural distortions in the life of the Negro American. At this point, the present tangle of pathology is capable of perpetuating itself without assistance from the white world. The cycle can be broken only if these distortions are set right.

In a word, a national effort towards the problems of Negro Americans must be directed towards the question of family structure. The object should be to strengthen the Negro family so as to enable it to raise and support its members as do other families. After that, how this group of Americans chooses to run its affairs, take advantage of its opportunities, or fail to do so, is none of the nation's business.

The fundamental importance and urgency of restoring the Negro American Family structure has been evident for some time. E. Franklin Frazier put it most succinctly in 1950:

As the result of family disorganization a large proportion of Negro children and youth have not undergone the socialization which only the family can provide. The disorganized families have failed to provide the discipline and habits which are necessary for personality development. Because the disorganized family has failed in its function as a socializing agency, it has handicapped the children in their relations to the institutions in the community. Moreover, family disorganization has been partially responsible for a large amount of juvenile delinquency and adult crime among Negroes. Since the widespread family disorganization among Negroes has resulted from the failure of the father to play the role in family life required by American society, the mitigation of this problem must await those changes in the Negro and American society which will enable the Negro father to play the role required of him.

Nothing was done in response to Frazier's argument. Matters were left to take care of themselves, and as matters will, grew worse not better. The problem is now more serious, the obstacles greater. There is, however, a profound change for the better in one respect. The President has committed the nation to an all out effort to eliminate poverty wherever it exists, among whites or Negroes, and a militant, organized, and responsible Negro movement exists to join in that effort.

Such a national effort could be stated thus:

The policy of the United States is to bring the Negro American to full and equal sharing in the responsibilities and rewards of citizenship. To this end, the programs of the Federal government bearing on this objective shall be designed to have the effect, directly or indirectly, of enhancing the stability and resources of the Negro American family.

On Improving the Economic Status of the Negro, JAMES TOBIN (1965)

I start from the presumption that the integration of Negroes into the American society and economy can be accomplished within existing political and economic institutions. I understand the impatience of those who think otherwise, but I see nothing incompatible between our peculiar mixture of private enterprise and government, on the one hand, and the liberation and integration of the Negro, on the other. Indeed the present position of the Negro is an aberration from the principles of our society, rather than a requirement of its functioning. Therefore, my suggestions are directed to the aim of mobilizing existing powers of government to bring Negroes into full participation in the main stream of American economic life.

The economic plight of individuals, Negroes and whites alike, can always be attributed to specific handicaps and circumstances: discrimination, immobility, lack of education and experience, ill health, weak motivation, poor neighborhood, large family size, burdensome family responsibilities. Such diagnoses suggest a host of specific remedies, some in the domain of civil rights, others in the war on poverty. Important as these remedies are, there is a danger that the diagnoses are myopic. They explain why certain individuals rather than others suffer from the economic maladies of the time. They do not explain why the over-all incidence of the maladies varies dramatically from time to time—for example, why personal attributes which seemed to doom a man to unemployment in 1932 or even in 1954 or 1961 did not so handicap him in 1944 or 1951 or 1956.

Public health measures to improve the environment are often more productive in conquering disease than a succession of individual treatments. Malaria was conquered by oiling and draining swamps, not by quinine. The analogy holds for economic maladies. Unless the global incidence of these misfortunes can be diminished, every individual problem successfully solved will be replaced by a similar problem somewhere else. That is why an economist is led to emphasize the importance of the over-all economic climate.

Over the decades, general economic progress has been the major factor in the gradual conquest of poverty. Recently some observers, J. K. Galbraith and Michael Harrington most eloquently, have contended that this process no longer operates. The economy may prosper and labor may become steadily more productive as in the past, but "the other America" will be stranded. Prosperity and progress have already eliminated almost all the easy cases of poverty, leaving a hard core beyond the reach of national economic trends. There may be something to the "backwash" thesis as far as whites are concerned. But it definitely does not apply to Negroes. Too many of them are poor. It cannot be true that half of a race of twenty million human beings are victims of specific disabilities which insulate them from the national economic climate. It cannot be true, and it is not. Locke Anderson has shown that the pace of Negro economic progress is peculiarly sensitive to general economic growth. He estimates that if nationwide per capita personal income is stationary, nonwhite median family income falls by .5 per cent per year, while if national per capita income grows 5 per cent, nonwhite income grows nearly 7.5 per cent.

National prosperity and economic growth are still powerful engines for improving the economic status of Negroes. They are not doing enough and they are not doing it fast enough. There is ample room for a focused attack on the specific sources of Negro poverty. But a favorable over-all economic climate is a necessary condition for the global success—as distinguished from success in individual cases—of specific efforts to remedy the handicaps associated with Negro poverty.

The Importance of a Tight Labor Market

But isn't the present over-all economic climate favorable? Isn't the economy enjoying an upswing of unprecedented length, setting new records almost every month in production, employment, profits, and income? Yes, but expansion and new records should be routine in an economy with growing population, capital equipment, and productivity. The fact is that the economy has not operated with reasonably full utilization of its manpower and plant capacity since 1957. Even now, after four and one-half years of uninterrupted expansion, the economy has not regained the ground lost in the recessions of 1958 and 1960. The current expansion has whittled away at unemployment, reducing it from 6.5 to 7 per cent to 4.5 to 5 per cent. It has diminished idle plant capacity correspondingly. The rest of the gains since 1960 in employment, production, and income have just offset the normal growth of population, capacity, and productivity.

The magnitude of America's poverty problem already reflects the failure of the economy in the second postwar decade to match its performance in the first. Had the 1947-56 rate of growth of median family income been maintained since 1957, and had unemployment been steadily limited to 4 per cent, it is estimated that the fraction of the population with poverty incomes in 1963 would have been 16.6 per cent instead of 18.5 per cent. The educational qualifications of the labor force have continued to improve. The principal of racial equality, in employment as in other activities, has gained ground both in law and in the national conscience. If, despite all this, dropouts, inequalities in educational attainment, and discrimination in employment seem more serious today rather than less, the reason is that the over-all economic climate has not been favorable after all.

The most important dimension of the over-all economic climate is the tightness of the labor market. In a tight labor market unemployment is low and short in duration, and job vacancies are plentiful. People who stand at the end of the hiring line and the top of the layoff list have the most to gain from a tight labor market. It is not surprising that the position of Negroes relative to that of whites improves in a tight labor market and declines in a slack market. Unemployment itself is only one way in which a slack labor market hurts Negroes and other disadvantaged groups, and the gains from reduction in unemployment are by no means confined to the employment of persons counted as unemployed. A tight labor market means not just jobs, but better jobs, longer hours, higher wages. Because of the heavy demands for labor during the second world war and its economic aftermath, Negroes made dramatic relative gains between 1940 and 1950. Unfortunately this momentum has not been maintained, and the blame falls largely on the weakness of labor markets since 1957.

The shortage of jobs has hit Negro men particularly hard and thus has contributed mightily to the ordeal of the Negro family, which is in turn the cumulative source of so many other social disorders. The unemployment rate of Negro men is more sensitive than that of Negro women to the national rate. Since 1949 Negro women have gained in median income relative to white women, but Negro men have lost ground to white males. In a society which stresses breadwinning as the expected role of the mature male and occupational achievement as his proper goal, failure to find and to keep work is devastating to the mans' self-respect and family status. Matriarchy is in any case a strong tradition in Negro society, and the man's role is further downgraded when the family must and can depend on the woman for its livelihood. It is very important to increase the proportion of Negro children who grow up in stable families with two parents. Without a strong labor market it will be extremely difficult to do so.

Unemployment. It is well known that Negro unemployment rates are multiples of the general unemployment rate. This fact reflects both the lesser skills, seniority, and experience of Negroes and employers' discrimination against Negroes. These conditions are a deplorable reflection on American society, but as long as they exist Negroes suffer much more than others from a general increase in unemployment and gain much more from a general reduction. A rule of thumb is that changes in the nonwhite unemployment rate are twice those in the white rate. The rule works both ways. Nonwhite unemployment went from 4.1 per cent in 1953, a tight labor market year, to 12.5 per cent in 1961, while the white rate rose from 2.3 per cent to 6 per cent. Since then, the Negro rate has declined by 2.4 per cent, the white rate by 1.2.

Even the Negro teenage unemployment rate shows some sensitivity to general economic conditions. Recession increased it from 15 per cent in 1955-56 to 25 per cent in 1958. It decreased to 22 per cent in 1960 but rose to 28 per cent in 1963; since then it has declined somewhat. Teenage unemployment is abnormally high now, relative to that of other age groups, because the wave of postwar babies is coming into the labor market. Most of them, especially the Negroes, are crowding the end of the hiring line. But their prospects for getting jobs are no less dependent on general labor market conditions.

Part-time work. Persons who are involuntarily forced to work part-time instead of full time are not counted as unemployed, but their number goes

up and down with the unemployment rate. Just as Negroes bear a disproportionate share of unemployment, they bear more than their share of
involuntary part-time unemployment. A tight labor market will not only
employ more Negroes; it will also give more of those who are employed
full-time jobs. In both respects, it will reduce disparities between whites
and Negroes.

Labor-force participation. In a tight market, of which a low unemployment rate is a barometer, the labor force itself is larger. Job opportunities
draw into the labor force individuals who, simply because the prospects
were dim, did not previously regard themselves as seeking work and were
therefore not enumerated as unemployed. For the economy as a whole,
it appears that an expansion of job opportunities enough to reduce unemployment by one worker will bring another worker into the labor force.

This phenomenon is important for many Negro families. Statistically,
their poverty now appears to be due more often to the lack of a breadwinner in the labor force than to unemployment. But in a tight labor
market many members of these families, including families now on public
assistance, would be drawn into employment. Labor-force participation
rates are roughly 2 per cent lower for nonwhite men than for white men,
and the disparity increases in years of slack labor markets. The story is
different for women. Negro women have always been in the labor force
to a much greater extent than white women. A real improvement in the
economic status of Negro men and in the stability of Negro families would
probably lead to a reduction in labor-force participation by Negro women.
But for teenagers, participation rates for Negroes are not so high as for
whites; and for women twenty to twenty-four they are about the same.
These relatively low rates are undoubtedly due less to voluntary choice
than to the same lack of job opportunities that produces phenomenally
high unemployment rates for young Negro women.

Duration of unemployment. In a tight labor market, such unemployment as does exist is likely to be of short duration. Short-term unemployment is less damaging to the economic welfare of the unemployed. More
will have earned and fewer will have exhausted private and public unemployment benefits. In 1953 when the over-all unemployment rate was 2.9
per cent, only 4 per cent of the unemployed were out of work for longer
than twenty-six weeks and only 11 per cent for longer than fifteen weeks.
In contrast, the unemployment rate in 1961 was 6.7 per cent; and of the
unemployed in that year, 17 per cent were out of work for longer than
twenty-six weeks and 32 per cent for longer than fifteen weeks. Between
the first quarter of 1964 and the first quarter of 1965, over-all unemployment fell 11 per cent, while unemployment extending beyond half a year
was lowered by 22 per cent.

As Rashi Fein points out, one more dimension of society's inequity to the Negro is that an unemployed Negro is more likely to stay unemployed than an unemployed white. But his figures also show that Negroes share in the reduction of long-term unemployment accompanying economic expansion.

Migration from agriculture. A tight labor market draws the surplus rural population to higher paying non-agricultural jobs. Southern Negroes are a large part of this surplus rural population. Migration is the only hope for improving their lot, or their children's. In spite of the vast migration of past decades, there are still about 775,000 Negroes, 11 per cent of the Negro labor force of the country, who depend on the land for their living and that of their families. Almost a half million live in the South, and almost all of them are poor.

Migration from agriculture and from the South is the Negroes' historic path toward economic improvement and equality. It is a smooth path for Negroes and for the urban communities to which they move only if there is a strong demand for labor in towns and cities North and South. In the 1940's the number of Negro farmers and farm laborers in the nation fell by 450,000 and one and a half million Negroes (net) left the South. This was the great decade of Negro economic advance. In the 1950's the same occupational and geographical migration continued undiminished. The movement to higher-income occupations and locations should have raised the relative economic status of Negroes. But in the 1950's Negroes were moving into increasingly weak job markets. Too often disguised unemployment in the countryside was simply transformed into enumerated unemployment, and rural poverty into urban poverty.

Quality of jobs. In a slack labor market, employers can pick and choose, both in recruiting and in promoting. They exaggerate the skill, education, and experience requirements of their jobs. They use diplomas, or color, or personal histories as convenient screening devices. In a tight market, they are forced to be realistic, to tailor job specifications to the available supply, and to give on-the-job training. They recruit and train applicants whom they would otherwise screen out, and they upgrade employees whom they would in slack times consign to low-wage, low-skill, and part-time jobs.

Wartime and other experience shows that job requirements are adjustable and that men and women are trainable. It is only in slack times that people worry about a mismatch between supposedly rigid occupational requirements and supposedly unchangeable qualifications of the labor force. As already noted, the relative status of Negroes improves in a tight labor market not only in respect to unemployment, but also in respect to wages and occupations.

Cyclical fluctuation. Sustaining a high demand for labor is important. The in-and-out status of the Negro in the business cycle damages his long-term position because periodic unemployment robs him of experience and seniority.

Restrictive practices. A slack labor market probably accentuates the discriminatory and protectionist proclivities of certain crafts and unions. When jobs are scarce, opening the door to Negroes is a real threat. Of course prosperity will not automatically dissolve the barriers, but it will make it more difficult to oppose efforts to do so.

I conclude that the single most important step the nation could take to improve the economic position of the Negro is to operate the economy steadily at a low rate of unemployment. We cannot expect to restore the labor market conditions of the second world war, and we do not need to. In the years 1951-1953, unemployment was roughly 3 per cent, teenage unemployment around 7 per cent, Negro unemployment about 4.5 per cent, long-term unemployment negligible. In the years 1955-57, general unemployment was roughly 4 per cent, and the other measures correspondingly higher. Four per cent is the official target of the Kennedy-Johnson administration. It has not been achieved since 1957. Reaching and maintaining 4 per cent would be a tremendous improvement over the performance of the last eight years. But we should not stop there; the society and the Negro can benefit immensely from tightening the labor market still further, to 3.5 or 3 per cent unemployment. The administration itself has never defined 4 per cent as anything other than an "interim" target.

Why Don't We Have a Tight Labor Market?

We know how to operate the economy so that there is a tight labor market. By fiscal and monetary measures the federal government can control aggregate spending in the economy. The government could choose to control it so that unemployment *averaged* 3.5 or 3 per cent instead of remaining over 4.5 per cent except at occasional business cycle peaks. Moreover, recent experience here and abroad shows that we can probably narrow the amplitude of fluctuations around whatever average we select as a target.

Some observers have cynically concluded that a society like ours can achieve full employment only in wartime. But aside from conscription into the armed services, government action creates jobs in wartime by exactly the same mechanism as in peacetime—the government spends more money and stimulates private firms and citizens to spend more too. It is the *amount* of spending, not its purpose, that does the trick. Public or private spending to go to the moon, build schools, or conquer poverty can be just as effective in reducing unemployment as spending to build air-planes and submarines—if there is enough of it. There may be more political constraints and ideological inhibitions in peacetime, but the same techniques of economic policy are available if we want badly enough to use them. The two main reasons we do not take this relatively simple way out are two obsessive fears, inflation and balance of payments deficits.

Running the economy with a tight labor market would mean a some-what faster upward creep in the price level. The disadvantages of this are, in my view, exaggerated and are scarcely commensurable with the real economic and social gains of higher output and employment. Moreover, there are ways of protecting "widows and orphans" against erosion in the purchasing power of their savings. But fear of inflation is strong both in the U.S. financial establishment and in the public at large. The vast com-fortable white middle class who are never touched by unemployment pre-fer to safeguard the purchasing power of their life insurance and pension rights than to expand opportunities for the disadvantaged and unemployed.

The fear of inflation would operate anyway, but it is accentuated by U.S. difficulties with its international balance of payments. These difficul-ties have seriously constrained and hampered U.S. fiscal and monetary policy in recent years. Any rise in prices might enlarge the deficit. An aggressively expansionary monetary policy, lowering interest rates, might push money out of the country.

In the final analysis what we fear is that we might not be able to defend the parity of the dollar with gold, that is, to sell gold at thirty-five dollars an ounce to any government that wants to buy. So great is the gold mystique that this objective has come to occupy a niche in the hierarchy of U.S. goals second only to the military defense of the country, and not always to that. It is not fanciful to link the plight of Negro teenagers in Harlem to the monetary whims of General de Gaulle. But it is only our own attachment to "the dollar" as an abstraction which makes us cringe before the European appetite for gold.

This topic is too charged with technical complexities, real and imagined, and with confused emotions to be discussed adequately here. I will confine myself to three points. First, the United States is the last country in the world which needs to hold back its own economy to balance its interna-tional accounts. To let the tail wag the dog is not in the interests of the rest of the world, so much of which depends on us for trade and capital, any more than in our own.

Second, forces are at work to restore balance to American international accounts—the increased competitiveness for our exports and the income from the large investments our firms and citizens have made overseas since the war. Meanwhile we can finance deficits by gold reserves and lines of credit at the International Monetary Fund and at foreign central banks, Ultimately we have one foolproof line of defense—letting the dollar depreciate relative to foreign currencies. The world would not end. The sun would rise the next day. American products would be more competitive in world markets. Neither God nor the Constitution fixed the gold value of the dollar. The U.S. would not be the first country to let its currency depreciate. Nor would it be the first time for the U.S.—not until we stopped "saving" the dollar and the gold standard in 1933 did our recovery from the Great Depression begin.

Third, those who oppose taking such risks argue that the dollar today occupies a unique position as international money, that the world as a whole has an interest, which we cannot ignore, in the stability of the gold value of the dollar. If so, we can reasonably ask the rest of the world, especially our European friends, to share the burdens which guaranteeing this stability imposes upon us.

This has been an excursion into general economic policy. But the connection between gold and the plight of the Negro is no less real for being subtle. We are paying much too high a social price for avoiding creeping inflation and for protecting our gold stock and "the dollar." But it will not be easy to alter these national priorities. The interests of the unemployed, the poor, and the Negroes are under-represented in the comfortable consensus which supports and confines current policy.

Another approach, which can be pursued simultaneously, is to diminish the conflicts among these competing objectives, in particular to reduce the degree of inflation associated with low levels of unemployment. This can be done in two ways. One way is to improve the mobility of labor and other resources to occupations, locations, and industries where bottlenecks would otherwise lead to wage and price increases. This is where many specific programs, such as the training and retraining of manpower and policies to improve the technical functioning of labor markets, come into their own.

A second task is to break down the barriers to competition which now restrict the entry of labor and enterprise into certain occupations and industries. These lead to wage- and price-increasing bottlenecks even when resources are not really short. Many barriers are created by public policy itself, in response to the vested interests concerned. Many reflect concentration of economic power in unions and in industry. These barriers represent another way in which the advantaged and the unemployed purchase their standards of living and their security at the expense of unprivileged minorities.

In the best of circumstances, structural reforms of these kinds will be slow and gradual. They will encounter determined economic and political resistance from special interests which are powerful in Congress and state legislatures. Moreover, Congressmen and legislators represent places rather than people and are likely to oppose, not facilitate, the increased geographical mobility which is required. It is no accident that our manpower programs do not include relocation allowances.

Increasing the Earning Capacity of Negroes

Given the proper over-all economic climate, in particular a steadily tight labor market, the Negro's economic condition can be expected to improve, indeed to improve dramatically. But not fast enough. Not as fast as his aspirations or as the aspirations he has taught the rest of us to have for him. What else can be done? This question is being answered in detail by experts elsewhere. I shall confine myself to a few comments and suggestions that occur to a general economist.

Even in a tight labor market, the Negro's relative status will suffer both from current discrimination and from his lower earning capacity, the result of inferior acquired skill. In a real sense both factors reflect discrimination, since the Negro's handicaps in earning capacity are the residue of decades of discrimination in education and employment. Nevertheless for both analysis and policy it is useful to distinguish the two.

Discrimination means that the Negro is denied access to certain markets where he might sell his labor, and to certain markets where he might purchase goods and services. Elementary application of "supply and demand" makes it clear that these restrictions are bound to result in his selling his labor for less and buying his livelihood for more than if these barriers did not exist. If Negro women can be clerks only in certain stores, those storekeepers will not need to pay them so much as they pay whites. If Negroes can live only in certain houses, the prices and rents they have to pay will be high for the quality of accommodation provided.

Successful elimination of discrimination is not only important in itself but will also have substantial economic benefits. Since residential segregation is the key to so much else and so difficult to eliminate by legal fiat alone, the power of the purse should be unstintingly used. I see no reason that the expenditure of funds for this purpose should be confined to new construction. Why not establish private or semi-public revolving funds to purchase, for resale or rental on a desegregated basis, strategically located existing structures as they become available?

The effects of past discrimination will take much longer to eradicate. The sins against the fathers are visited on the children. They are deprived of the intellectual and social capital which in our society is supposed to be transmitted in the family and the home. We have only begun to realize how difficult it is to make up for this deprivation by formal schooling, even when we try. And we have only begun to try, after accepting all too long the notion that schools should acquiesce in, even re-enforce, inequalities in home backgrounds rather than overcome them.

Upgrading the earning capacity of Negroes will be difficult, but the economic effects are easy to analyze. Economists have long held that the way to reduce disparities in earned incomes is to eliminate disparities in earning capacities. If college-trained people earn more money than those who left school after eight years, the remedy is to send a larger proportion of young people to college. If machine operators earn more than ditchdiggers, the remedy is to give more people the capacity and opportunity to be machine operators. These changes in relative supplies reduce the disparity both by competing down the pay in the favored line of work and by raising the pay in the less remunerative line. When there are only a few people left in the population whose capacities are confined to garbage-collecting, it will be a high-paid calling. The same is true of domestic service and all kinds of menial work.

This classical economic strategy will be hampered if discrimination, union barriers, and the like stand in the way. It will not help to increase the supply of Negro plumbers if the local unions and contractors will not let them join. But exerience also shows that barriers give way more easily when the pressures of unsatisfied demand and supply pile up.

It should therefore be the task of educational and manpower policy to engineer over the next two decades a massive change in the relative supplies of people of different educational and professional attainments and degrees of skill and training. It must be a more rapid change than has occurred in the past two decades, because that has not been fast enough to alter income differentials. We should try particularly to increase supplies in those fields where salaries and wages are already high and rising. In this process we should be very skeptical of self-serving arguments and calculations—that an increase in supply in this or that profession would be bound to reduce quality, or that there are some mechanical relations of "need" to population or to Gross National Product that cannot be exceeded.

Such a policy would be appropriate to the "war on poverty" even if there were no racial problem. Indeed, our objective is to raise the earning capacities of low-income whites as well as of Negroes. But Negroes have the most to gain, and even those who because of age or irreversible environmental handicaps must inevitably be left behind will benefit by reduction in the number of whites and other Negroes who are competing with them.

Assuring Living Standards in the Absence of Earning Capacity

The reduction of inequality in earning capacity is the fundamental solution, and in a sense anything else is stopgap. Some stopgaps are useless and even counter-productive. People who lack the capacity to earn a decent living need to be helped, but they will not be helped by minimum wage laws, trade union wage pressures, or other devices which seek to compel employers to pay them more than their work is worth. The more likely outcome of such regulations is that the intended beneficiaries are not employed at all.

A far better approach is to supplement earnings from the public fisc. But assistance can and should be given in a way that does not force the recipients out of the labor force or give them incentive to withdraw. Our present system of welfare payments does just that, causing needless waste and demoralization. This application of the means test is bad economics as well as bad sociology. It is almost as if our present programs of public assistance had been consciously contrived to perpetuate the conditions they are supposed to alleviate.

These programs apply a strict means test. The amount of assistance is an estimate of minimal needs, less the resources of the family from earnings. The purpose of the means test seems innocuous enough. It is to avoid wasting taxpayer's money on people who do not really need help. But another way to describe the means test is to note that it taxes earnings at a rate of 100 per cent. A person on public assistance cannot add to his family's standard of living by working. Of course, the means test provides a certain incentive to work in order to get off public assistance altogether. But in many cases, especially where there is only one adult to provide for and take care of several children, the adult simply does not have enough time and earning opportunities to get by without financial help. He, or more likely she, is essentially forced to be both idle and on a dole. The means test also involves limitation on property holdings which deprive anyone who is or expects to be on public assistance of incentive to save.

In a society which prizes incentives for work and thrift, these are surprising regulations. They deny the country useful productive services, but that economic loss is minor in the present context. They deprive individuals and families both of work experience which could teach them skills, habits, and self-discipline of future value and of the self-respect and satisfaction which comes from improving their own lot by their own efforts.

Public assistance encourages the disintegration of the family, the key to so many of the economic and social problems of the American Negro. The main assistance program, Aid for Dependent Children, is not available if there is an able-bodied employed male in the house. In most states it is not available if there is an able-bodied man in the house, even if he is not working. All too often it is necessary for the father to leave his children so that they can eat. It is bad enough to provide incentives for idleness but even worse to legislate incentives for desertion.

The bureaucratic surveillance and guidance to which recipients of public assistance are subject undermine both their self-respect and their capacity to manage their own affairs. In the administration of assistance there is much concern to detect "cheating" against the means tests and to ensure approved prudent use of the public's money. Case loads are frequently too great and administrative regulation too confining to permit the talents of social maladies of their clients. The time of the clients is considered a free good, and much of it must be spent in seeking or awaiting the attention of the officials on whom their livelihood depends.

The defects of present categorical assistance programs could be in my opinion, greatly reduced by adopting a system of basic income allowances, integrated with and administered in conjunction with the federal income tax. In a sense the proposal is to make the income tax symmetrical. At present the federal government takes a share of family income in excess of a certain amount (for example, a married couple with three children pays no tax unless their income exceeds $3700). The proposal is that the Treasury pay any family who falls below a certain income a fraction of the shortfall. The idea has sometimes been called a negative income tax.

The payment would be a matter of right, like an income tax refund. Individuals expecting to be entitled to payments from the government during the year could receive them in periodic installments by making a declaration of expected income and expected tax withholdings. But there would be a final settlement between the individual and the government based on a "tax" return after the year was over, just as there is now for taxpayers on April 15.

A family with no other income at all would receive a basic allowance scaled to the number of persons in the family. For a concrete example, take the basic allowance to be $400 per year per person. It might be desirable and equitable, however to reduce the additional basic allowance for children after, say, the fourth. Once sufficient effort is being made to disseminate birth control knowledge and technique, the scale of allowances by family size certainly should provide some disincentive to the creation of large families.

A family's allowance would be reduced by a certain fraction of every dollar of other income it received. For a concrete example, take this fraction to be one-third. This means that the family has considerable incentive to earn income, because its total income including allowances will be increased by two-thirds of whatever it earns. In contrast, the means test connected with present public assistance is a 100 per cent "tax" on earnings. With a one-third "tax" a family will be on the receiving end of the allowance and income tax system until its regular income equals three times its basic allowance.

Families above this "break-even" point would be taxpayers. But the less well-off among them would pay less taxes than they do now. The first dollars of income in excess of this break-even point would be taxed at the same rate as below, one-third in the example. At some income level, the tax liability so computed would be the same as the tax under the present income tax law. From that point up, the present law would take over; taxpayers with incomes above this point would not be affected by the plan.

*   *   *   *

Beneficiaries under Federal Old Age Survivors and Disability Insurance would not be eligible for the new allowances. Congress should make sure that minimum benefits under OASDI are at least as high as the allowances. Some government payments, especially those for categorical public assistance, would eventually be replaced by basic allowances. Others, like unemployment insurance and veterans' pensions, are intended to be rights earned by past services regardless of current need. It would therefore be wrong to withhold allowances from the beneficiaries of these payments, but it would be reasonable to count them as income in determining the size of allowances, even though they are not subject to tax.

Although the numbers used above are illustrative, they are indicative of what is needed for an effective program. It would be expensive for the federal budget, involving an expenditure of perhaps fifteen billion dollars a year. Partially offsetting this budgetary cost are the savings in public assistance, on which governments now spend five and six-tenths billion dollars a year, of which three and two-tenths billion are federal funds. In addition, savings are possible in a host of other income maintenance programs, notably in agriculture.

The program is expensive, but it need not be introduced all at once. The size of allowances can be gradually increased as room in the budget becomes available. This is likely to happen fairly rapidly. First of all, there is room right now. The budget, and the budget deficit, can and should be larger in order to create a tight labor market. Second, the normal growth of the economy increases federal revenues from existing tax rates by some six to seven billion dollars a year. This is a drag on the economy, threatening stagnation and rising unemployment unless it is matched by a similar rise in federal spending or avoided by cutting taxes. With defense spending stable or declining, there is room both for increases in civilian spending, as in the war on poverty, and for further tax cuts. Indeed, periodic tax reduction is official administration policy, and President Johnson agrees that the next turn belongs to low-income families. Gradually building an allowance system into the federal income tax would be the best way to lower the net yield of the tax— fairer and more far-reaching than further cuts in tax rates.

I referred to programs which make up for lack of earning capacity as stopgaps, but that is not entirely fair. Poverty itself saps earning capacity. The welfare way of life, on the edge of subsistence, does not provide motivation or useful work experience either to parents or to children. A better system, one which enables people to retain their self-respect and initiative, would in itself help to break the vicious circle.

The proposed allowance system is of course not the only thing which needs to be done. Without attempting to be exhaustive, I shall mention three other measures for the assistance of families without adequate earning capacity.

It hardly needs emphasizing that the large size of Negro families or non-families is one of the principal causes of Negro poverty. There are too many mouths to feed per breadwinner, and frequently the care of children keeps the mother, the only possible breadwinner, at home. A program of day care and pre-school education for children five and under could meet several objectives at once—enriching the experience of the children and freeing the mother for training or for work.

The quality of the medical care of Negroes is a disgrace in itself and contributes to their other economic handicaps. Even so the financing of the care of "the medically indigent" is inadequate and chaotic. Sooner or later we will extend the principle of Medicare to citizens under sixty-five. Why not sooner?

As mentioned above, much Negro poverty in the South reflects the inability of Negroes to make a livelihood in agriculture. As far as the traditional cash crop, cotton, is concerned, mechanization and the competition of larger-scale units in the Southwest are undermining the plantation and share-cropping system of the Southeast. The Negro subsistence farmer has too little land, equipment, and know-how to make a decent income. Current government agricultural programs, expensive as they are to the taxpayer, do very little to help the sharecropper or subsistence farmer. Our whole agricultural policy needs to be recast, to give income support to people rather than price support to crops and to take people off the land rather than to take land out of cultivation. The effects on the social system of the South may be revolutionary, but they can only be salutary. Obviously there will be a tremendous burden on educational and training facilities to fit people for urban and industrial life. And I must emphasize again that substantial migration from agriculture is only possible, without disaster in the cities, in a booming economy with a tight labor market.

Conclusion

By far the most powerful factor determining the economic status of Negroes is the over-all state of the U.S. economy. A vigorously expanding economy with a steadily tight labor market will rapidly raise the position of the Negro, both absolutely and relatively. Favored by such a climate, the host of specific measures to eliminate discrimination, improve education and training, provide housing, and strengthen the family can yield substantial additional results. In a less beneficent economic climate, where jobs are short rather than men, the wars against racial inequality and poverty will be uphill battles, and some highly touted weapons may turn out to be dangerously futile.

The forces of the market place, the incentives of private self-interest, the pressures of supply and demand—these can be powerful allies or stubborn opponents. Properly harnessed, they quietly and impersonally accomplish objectives which may elude detailed legislation and administration. To harness them to the cause of the American Negro is entirely possible. It requires simply that the federal government dedicate its fiscal and monetary policies more wholeheartedly and singlemindedly to achieving and maintaining genuinely full employment. The obstacles are not technical or economic. One obstacle is a general lack of understanding that unemployment and related evils are remediable by national fiscal and monetary measures. The other is the high priority now given to competing financial objectives.

In this area, as in others, the administration has disarmed its conservative opposition by meeting it halfway, and no influential political voices challenge the tacit compromise from the "Left." Negro rights movements have so far taken no interest in national fiscal and monetary policy. No doubt gold, the federal budget, and the actions of the Federal Reserve System seem remote from the day-to-day firing line of the movements. Direct local actions to redress specific grievances and to battle visible enemies are absorbing and dramatic. They have concrete observable results. But the use of national political influence on behalf of the goals of the Employment Act of 1946 is equally important. It would fill a political vacuum, and its potential long-run pay-off is very high.

The goal of racial equality suggests that the federal government should provide more stimulus to the economy. Fortunately, it also suggests constructive ways to give the stimulus. We can kill two birds with one stone. The economy needs additional spending in general; the wars on poverty and racial inequality need additional spending of particular kinds. The needed spending falls into two categories: government programs to diminish economic inequalities by building up the earning capacities of the poor and their children, and humane public assistance to citizens who temporarily or permanently lack the capacity to earn a decent living for themselves and their families. In both categories the nation, its conscience aroused by the plight of the Negro, has the chance to make reforms which will benefit the whole society.

From Protest to Politics: The Future of the Civil Rights Movement, BAYARD RUSTIN (1965)

The decade spanned by the 1954 Supreme Court decision on school desegregation and the Civil Rights Act of 1964 will undoubtedly be recorded as the period in which the legal foundations of racism in America were destroyed. To be sure, pockets of resistance remain; but it would be hard to quarrel with the assertion that the elaborate legal structure of segregation and discrimination, particularly in relation to public accommodations, has virtually collapsed. On the other hand, without making light of the human sacrifices involved in the direct-action tactics (sit-ins, freedom rides, and the rest) that were so instrumental to this achievement, we must recognize that in desegregating public accommodations, we affected institutions which are relatively peripheral both to the American socio-economic order and to the fundamental conditions of life of the Negro people. In a highly industrialized, 20th-century civilization, we hit Jim Crow precisely where it was most anachronistic, dispensable, and vulnerable—in hotels, lunch counters, terminals, libraries, swimming pools, and the like. For in these forms, Jim Crow does impede the flow of commerce in the broadest sense: it is a nuisance in a society on the move (and on the make). Not surprisingly, therefore, it was the most mobility-conscious and relatively liberated groups in the Negro community—lower-middle-class college students—who launched the attack that brought down this imposing but hollow structure.

The term "classical" appears especially apt for this phase of the civil rights movement. But in the few years that have passed since the first flush of sit-ins, several developments have taken place that have complicated matters enormously. One is the shifting focus of the movement in the South, symbolized by Birmingham; another is the spread of the revolution to the North; and the third, common to the other two, is the expansion of the movement's base in the Negro community. To attempt to disentangle these three strands is to do violence to reality. David Danzig's perceptive article, "The Meaning of Negro Strategy" (*Commentary*, February 1964), correctly saw in the Birmingham events the victory of the concept of collective struggle over individual achievement as the road to Negro freedom. And Birmingham remains the unmatched symbol of grass-roots protest involving all strata of the black community. It was also in this most industrialized of Southern cities that the single-issue demands of the movement's classical stage gave way to the "package deal." No longer were Negroes satisfied with integrating lunch counters. They now sought advances in employment, housing, school integration, police protection, and so forth.

Thus, the movement in the South began to attack areas of discrimination which were not so remote from the Northern experience as were Jim Crow lunch counters. At the same time, the interrelationship of these apparently distinct areas became increasingly evident. What is the value of winning access to public accommodations for those who lack money to use them? The minute the movement faced this question, it was compelled to expand its vision beyond race relations to economic relations, including the role of education in modern society. And what also became clear is that all these interrelated problems, by their very nature, are not soluble by private, voluntary efforts but require government action—or politics. Already Southern demonstrators had recognized that the most effective way to strike at the police brutality they suffered from was by getting rid of the local sheriff—and that meant political action, which in turn meant, and still means, political action within the Democratic party where the only meaningful primary contests in the South are fought.

And so, in Mississippi, thanks largely to the leadership of Bob Moses, a turn toward political action has been taken. More than voter registration is involved here. A conscious bid for *political power* is being made, and in the course of that effort a tactical shift is being effected: direct-action techniques are being subordinated to a strategy calling for the building of community institutions or power bases. Clearly, the implications of this shift reach far beyond Mississippi. What began as a protest movement is being challenged to translate itself into a political movement. Is this the right course? And if it is, can the transformation be accomplished?

II

The very decade which has witnessed the decline of legal Jim Crow has also seen the rise of *de facto* segregation in our most fundamental socio-economic institutions. More Negroes are unemployed today than in 1954, and the unemployment gap between the races is wider. The median income of Negroes has dropped from 57 per cent to 54 per cent of that of whites. A higher percentage of Negro workers is now concentrated in jobs vulnerable to automation than was the case ten years ago. More Negroes attend *de facto* segregated schools today than when the Supreme Court handed down its famous decision; while school integration proceeds at a snail's pace in the South, the number of Northern schools with an excessive proportion of minority youth proliferates. And behind this is the continuing growth of racial slums, spreading over our central cities and trapping Negro youth in a milieu which, whatever its legal definition, sows an unimaginable demoralization. Again, legal niceties aside, a resident of a racial ghetto lives in segregated housing, and more Negroes fall into this category than ever before.

These are the facts of life which generate frustration in the Negro community and challenge the civil rights movement. At issue, after all, is not *civil rights,* strictly speaking, but social and economic conditions. Last summer's riots were not race riots; they were outbursts of class aggression in a society where class and color definitions are converging disastrously. How can the (perhaps misnamed) civil rights movement deal with this problem?

Before trying to answer, let me first insist that the task of the movement is vastly complicated by the failure of many whites of good will to understand the nature of our problem. There is a widespread assumption that the removal of artificial racial barriers should result in the automatic integration of the Negro into all aspects of American life. This myth is fostered by facile analogies with the experience of various ethnic immigrant groups, particularly the Jews. But the analogies with the Jews do not hold for three simple but profound reasons. First, Jews have a long history as a literate people, a resource which has afforded them opportunities to advance in the academic and professional worlds, to achieve intellectual status even in the midst of economic hardship, and to evolve sustaining value systems in the context of ghetto life. Negroes, for the greater part of their presence in this country, were forbidden by law to read or write. Second, Jews have a long history of family stability, the importance of which in terms of aspiration and self-image is obvious. The Negro family structure was totally destroyed by slavery and with it the possibility of cultural transmission (the right of Negroes to marry and rear children is barely a century old). Third, Jews are white and have the *option* of relinquishing their cultural-religious identity, intermarrying, passing, etc. Negroes, or at least the overwhelming majority of them, do not have this option. There is also a fourth, vulgar reason. If the Jewish and Negro communities are not comparable in terms of education, family structure, and color, it is also true that their respective economic roles bear little resemblance.

This matter of economic role brings us to the greater problem—the fact that we are moving into an era in which the natural functioning of the market does not by itself ensure every man with will and ambition a place in the productive process. The immigrant who came to this country during the late 19th and early 20th centuries entered a society which was expanding territorially and/or economically. It was then possible to start at the bottom, as an unskilled or semi-skilled worker, and move up the ladder, acquiring new skills along the way. Especially was this true when industrial unionism was burgeoning, giving new dignity and higher wages to organized workers. Today the situation has changed. We are not expanding territorially, the western frontier is settled, labor organizing has leveled off, our rate of economic growth has been stagnant for a decade. And we are in the midst of a technological revolution which is altering the fundamental structure of the labor force, destroying unskilled and semi-skilled jobs—jobs in which Negroes are disproportionately concentrated.

Whatever the pace of this technological revolution may be, the *direction* is clear: the lower rungs of the economic ladder are being lopped off. This means that an individual will no longer be able to start at the bottom and work his way up; he will have to start in the middle or on top, and hold on tight. It will not even be enough to have certain specific skills, for many skilled jobs are also vulnerable to automation. A broad educational background, permitting vocational adaptability and flexibility, seems more imperative than ever. We live in a society where, as Secretary of Labor Willard Wirtz puts it, machines have the equivalent of a high school diploma. Yet the average educational attainment of American Negroes is 8.2 years.

Negroes, of course, are not the only people being affected by these developments. It is reported that there are now 50 per cent fewer unskilled and semi-skilled jobs than there are high school dropouts. Almost one-third of the 26 million young people entering the labor market in the 1960's will be dropouts. But the percentage of Negro dropouts nationally is 57 per cent, and in New York City, among Negroes 25 years of age or over, it is 68 per cent. They are without a future.

To what extent can the kind of self-help compaign recently prescribed by Eric Hoffer in the *New York Times Magazine* cope with such a situation? I would advise those who think that self-help is the answer to familiarize themselves with the long history of such efforts in the Negro community, and to consider why so many foundered on the shoals of ghetto life. It goes without saying that any effort to combat demoralization and apathy is desirable, but we must understand that demoralization in the Negro community is largely a common-sense response to an objective reality. Negro youths have no need of statistics to perceive, fairly accurately, what their odds are in American society. Indeed, from the point of view of motivation, some of the healthiest Negro youngsters I know are juvenile delinquents: vigorously pursuing the American Dream of material acquisition and status, yet finding the conventional means of attaining it blocked off, they do not yield to defeatism but resort to illegal (and often ingenious) methods. They are not alien to American culture. They are, in Gunnar Myrdal's phrase, "exaggerated Americans." To want a Cadillac is not un-American; to push a cart in the garment center is. If Negroes are to be persuaded that the conventional path (school, work, etc.) is superior, we had better provide evidence which is now sorely lacking. It is a double cruelty to harangue Negro youth about education and training when we do not know what jobs will be available for them. When a Negro youth can reasonably foresee a future free of slums, when the prospect of gainful employment is realistic, we will see motivation and self-help in abundant enough quantities.

Meanwhile, there is an ironic similarity between the self-help advocated by many liberals and the doctrines of the Black Muslims. Professional sociologists, psychiatrists, and social workers have expressed amazement at the Muslims' success in tranforming prostitutes and dope addicts into respectable citizens. But every prostitute the Muslims convert to a model of Calvinist virtue is replaced by the ghetto with two more. Dedicated as they are to maintenance of the ghetto, the Muslims are powerless to effect substantial moral reform. So too with every other group or program which is not aimed at the destruction of slums, their causes and effects. Self-help efforts, directly or indirectly, must be geared to mobilizing people into power units capable of effecting social change. That is, their goal must be genuine self-help, not merely self-improvement. Obviously, where self-improvement activities succeed in imparting to their participants a feeling of some control over their environment, those involved may find their appetites for change whetted; they may move into the political arena.

III

Let me sum up what I have thus far been trying to say: the civil rights movement is evolving from a protest movement into a full-fledged *social movement*—an evolution calling its very name into question. It is now concerned not merely with removing the barriers to full *opportunity* but with achieving the fact of *equality*. From sit-ins and freedom rides we have gone into rent strikes, boycotts, community organization, and political action. As a consequence of this natural evolution, the Negro today finds himself stymied by obstacles of far greater magnitude than the legal barriers he was attacking before: automation, urban decay, *de facto* school segregation. These are problems which, while conditioned by Jim Crow, do not vanish upon its demise. They are more deeply rooted in our socio-economic order; they are the result of the total society's failure to meet not only the Negro's needs, but human needs generally.

These propositions have won increasing recognition and acceptance, but with a curious twist. They have formed the common premise of two apparently contradictory lines of thought which simultaneously nourish and antagonize each other. On the one hand, there is the reasoning of the New York *Times* moderate who says that the problems are so enormous and complicated that Negro militancy is a futile irritation, and that the need is for "intelligent moderation." Thus, during the first New York school boycott, the *Times* editorialized that Negro demands, while abstractly just, would necessitate massive reforms, the funds for which could not realistically be anticipated; therefore the just demands were also foolish demands and would only antagonize white people. Moderates of this stripe are often correct in perceiving the difficulty or impossibility of racial progress in the context of present social and economic policies. But they accept the context as fixed. They ignore (or perhaps see all too well) the potentialities inherent in linking Negro demands to broader pressures for radical revision of existing policies. They apparently see nothing strange in the fact that in the last twenty-five years we have spent nearly a trillion dollars fighting or preparing for wars, yet throw up our hands before the need for overhauling our schools, clearing the slums, and really abolishing poverty. My quarrel with these moderates is that they do not even envision radical changes; their admonitions of moderation are, for all practical purposes, admonitions to the Negro to adjust to the status quo, and are therefore immoral.

The more effectively the moderates argue their case, the more they convince Negroes that American society will not or cannot be reorganized for full racial equality. Michael Harrington has said that a successful war on poverty might well require the expenditure of a $100 billion. Where, the Negro wonders, are the forces now in motion to compel such a commitment? If the voices of the moderates were raised in an insistence upon a reallocation of national resources at levels that could not be confused with tokenism (that is, if the moderates stopped being moderates), Negroes would have greater grounds for hope. Meanwhile, the Negro movement cannot escape a sense of isolation.

It is precisely this sense of isolation that gives rise to the second line of thought I want to examine—the tendency within the civil rights movement which, despite its militancy, pursues what I call a "no-win" policy. Sharing with many moderates a recognition of the magnitude of the obstacles to freedom, spokesmen for this tendency survey the American scene and find no forces prepared to move toward radical solutions. From this they conclude that the only viable strategy is shock; above all, the hypocrisy of white liberals must be exposed. These spokesmen are often described as the radicals of the movement, but they are really its moralists. They seek to change white hearts—by traumatizing them. Frequently abetted by white self-flagellants, they may gleefully applaud (though not really agreeing with) Malcolm X because, while they admit he has no program, they think he can frighten white people into doing the right thing. To believe this, of course, you must be convinced, even if unconsciously, that at the core of the white man's heart lies a buried affection for Negroes—a proposition one may be permitted to doubt. But in any case, hearts are not relevant to the issue; neither racial affinities nor racial hostilities are rooted there. It is institutions—social, political, and economic institutions—which are the ultimate molders of collective sentiments. Let these institutions be reconstructed *today*, and let the ineluctable gradualism of history govern the formation of a new psychology.

My quarrel with the "no-win" tendency in the civil rights movement (and the reason I have so designated it) parallels my quarrel with the moderates outside the movement. As the latter lack the vision or will for fundamental change, the former lack a realistic strategy for achieving it. For such a strategy they substitute militancy. But militancy is a matter of posture and volume and not of effect.

I believe that the Negro's struggle for equality in America is essentially revolutionary. While most Negroes—in their hearts—unquestionably seek only to enjoy the fruits of American society as it now exists, their quest cannot *objectively* be satisfied within the framework of existing political and economic relations. The young Negro who would demonstrate his way into the labor market may be motivated by a thoroughly bourgeois ambition and thoroughly "capitalist" considerations, but he will end up having to favor a great expansion of the public sector of the economy. At any rate, that is the position the movement will be forced to take as it looks at the number of jobs being generated by the private economy, and if it is to remain true to the masses of Negroes.

The revolutionary character of the Negro's struggle is manifest in the fact that this struggle may have done more to democratize life for whites than for Negroes. Clearly, it was the sit-in movement of young Southern Negroes which, as it galvanized white students, banished the ugliest features of McCarthyism from the American campus and resurrected political debate. It was not until Negroes assaulted *de facto* school segregation in the urban centers that the issue of quality education for *all* children stirred into motion. Finally, it seems reasonably clear that the civil rights movement, directly and through the resurgence of social conscience it kindled, did more to initiate the war on poverty than any other single force.

It will be—it has been—argued that these by-products of the Negro struggle are not revolutionary. But the term revolutionary, as I am using it, does not connote violence; it refers to the qualitative transformation of fundamental institutions, more or less rapidly, to the point where the social and economic structure which they comprised can no longer be said to be the same. The Negro struggle has hardly run its course; and it will not stop moving until it has been utterly defeated or won substantial equality. But I fail to see how the movement can be victorious in the absence of radical programs for full employment, abolition of slums, the reconstruction of our educational system, new definitions of work and leisure. Adding up the cost of such programs, we can only conclude that we are talking about a refashioning of our political economy. It has been estimated, for example, that the price of replacing New York City's slums with public housing would be $17 billion. Again, a multi-billion dollar federal public works program, dwarfing the currently proposed $2 billion program, is required to reabsorb unskilled and semi-skilled workers into the labor market—and this must be done if Negro workers in these categories are to be employed. "Preferential treatment" cannot help them.

I am not trying here to delineate a total program, only to suggest the scope of economic reforms which are most immediately related to the plight of the Negro community. One could speculate on their political implications—whether, for example, they do not indicate the obsolescence of state government and the superiority of regional structures as viable units of planning. Such speculations aside, it is clear that Negro needs cannot be satisfied unless we go beyond what has so far been placed on the agenda. How are these radical objectives to be achieved? The answer is simple, deceptively so: *through political power*.

There is a strong moralistic strain in the civil rights movement which would remind us that power corrupts, forgetting that the absence of power also corrupts. But this is not the view I want to debate here, for it is waning. Our problem is posed by those who accept the need for political power but do not understand the nature of the object and therefore lack sound strategies for achieving it; they tend to confuse political institutions with lunch counters.

A handful of Negroes, acting alone, could integrate a lunch counter by strategically locating their bodies so as *directly* to interrupt the operation of the proprietor's will; their numbers were relatively unimportant. In politics, however, such a confrontation is difficult because the interests involved are merely *represented*. In the execution of a political decision a direct confrontation may ensue (as when federal marshals escorted James Meredith into the University of Mississippi—to turn from an example of non-violent coercion to one of force backed up with the threat of violence). But in arriving at a political decision, numbers and organizations are crucial, especially for the economically disenfranchised. (Needless to say, I am assuming that the forms of political democracy exist in America, however imperfectly, that they are valued, and that elitist or putschist conceptions of exercising power are beyond the pale of discussion for the civil rights movement.)

Neither that movement nor the country's twenty million black people can win political power alone. We need allies. The future of the Negro struggle depends on whether the contradictions of this society can be resolved by a coalition of progressive forces which becomes the *effective* political majority in the United States. I speak of the coalition which staged the March on Washington, passed the Civil Rights Act, and laid the basis for the Johnson landslide—Negroes, trade unionists, liberals, and religious groups.

There are those who argue that a coalition strategy would force the Negro to surrender his political independence to white liberals, that he would be neutralized, deprived of his cutting edge, absorbed into the Establishment. Some who take this position urged last year that votes be withheld from the Johnson-Humphrey ticket as a demonstration of the Negro's political power. Curiously enough, these people who sought to demonstrate power through the non-exercise of it, also point to the Negro "swing vote" in crucial urban areas as the source of the Negro's independent political power. But here they are closer to being right: the urban Negro vote will grow in importance in the coming years. If there is anything positive in the spread of the ghetto, it is the potential political power base thus created, and to realize this potential is one of the most challenging and urgent tasks before the civil rights movement. If the movement can wrest leadership of the ghetto vote from the machines, it will have acquired an organized constituency such as other major groups in our society now have.

But we must also remember that the effectiveness of a swing vote depends solely on "other" votes. It derives its power from them. In that sense, it can never be "independent," but must opt for one candidate or the other, even if by default. Thus coalitions are inescapable, however tentative they may be. And this is the case in all but those few situations in which Negroes running on an independent ticket might conceivably win. "Independence," in other words, is not a value in itself. The issue is which coalition to join and how to make it responsive to your program. Necessarily there will be compromise. But the difference between expediency and morality in politics is the difference between selling out a principle and making smaller concessions to win larger ones. The leader who shrinks from this task reveals not his purity but his lack of political sense.

The task of molding a political movement out of the March on Washington coalition is not simple, but no alternatives have been advanced. We need to choose our allies on the basis of common political objectives. It has become fashionable in some no-win Negro circles to decry the white liberal as the main enemy (his hypocrisy is what sustains racism); by virtue of this reverse recitation of the reactionary's litany (liberalism leads to socialism, which leads to Communism) the Negro is left in majestic isolation, except for a tiny band of fervent white initiates. But the objective fact is that *Eastland and Goldwater* are the main enemies—they and the opponents of civil rights, of the war on poverty, of medicare, of social security, of federal aid to education, of unions, and so forth. The labor movement, despite its obvious faults, has been the largest single organized force in this country pushing for progressive social legislation. And where the Negro-labor-liberal axis is weak, as in the farm belt, it was the religious groups that were most influential in rallying support for the Civil Rights Bill.

The durability of the coalition was interestingly tested during the election. I do not believe that the Johnson landslide proved the "white backlash" to be a myth. It proved, rather, that economic interests are more fundamental than prejudice: the backlashers decided that loss of social security was, after all, too high a price to pay for a slap at the Negro. This lesson was a valuable first step in re-educating such people, and it must be kept alive, for the civil rights movement will be advanced only to the degree that social and economic welfare gets to be inextricably entangled with civil rights.

The 1964 elections marked a turning point in American politics. The Democratic landslide was not merely the result of a negative reaction to Goldwaterism; it was also the expression of a majority liberal consensus. The near unanimity with which Negro voters joined in that expression was, I am convinced, a vindication of the July 25th statement by Negro leaders calling for a strategic turn toward political action and a temporary curtailment of mass demonstrations. Despite the controversy surrounding the statement, the instinctive response it met with in the community is suggested by the fact that demonstrations were down 75 per cent as compared with the same period in 1963. But should so high a percentage of Negro voters have gone to Johnson, or should they have held back to narrow his margin of victory and thus give greater visibility to our swing vote? How has our loyalty changed things? Certainly the Negro vote had higher visibility in 1960, when a switch of only 17 per cent from the Republican column of 1956 elected President Kennedy. But the slimness of Kennedy's victory—of his "mandate"—dictated a go-slow approach on civil rights, at least until the Birmingham upheaval.

Although Johnson's popular majority was so large that he could have won without such overwhelming Negro support, that support was important from several angles. Beyond adding to Johnson's total national margin, it was specifically responsible for his victories in Virginia, Florida, Tennessee, and Arkansas. Goldwater took only those states where fewer than 45 per cent of eligible Negroes were registered. That Johnson would have won those states had Negro voting rights been enforced is a lesson not likely to be lost on a man who would have been happy with a unanimous electoral college. In any case, the 1.6 million Southern Negroes who voted have had a shattering impact on the Southern political party structure, as illustrated in the changed composition of the Southern congressional delegation. The "backlash" gave the Republicans five House seats in Alabama, one in Georgia, and one in Mississippi. But on the Democratic side, seven segregationists were defeated while all nine Southerners who voted for the Civil Rights Act were re-elected. It may be premature to predict a Southern Democratic party of Negroes and white moderates and a Republican Party of refugee racists and economic conservatives, but there certainly is a strong tendency toward such a realignment; and an additional 3.6 million Negroes of voting age in the eleven Southern states are still to be heard from. Even the *tendency* toward disintegration of the Democratic party's racist wing defines a new context for Presidential and liberal strategy in the congressional battles ahead. Thus the Negro vote (North as well as South), while not *decisive* in the Presidential race, was enormously effective. It was a dramatic element of a historic mandate which contains vast possibilities and dangers that will fundamentally affect the future course of the civil rights movement.

The liberal congressional sweep raises hope for an assault on the seniority system, Rule Twenty-two, and other citadels of Dixiecrat-Republican power. The overwhelming of this conservative coalition should also mean progress on much bottlenecked legislation of profound interest to the movement (e.g., bills by Senators Clark and Nelson on planning, manpower, and employment). Moreover, the irrelevance of the South to Johnson's victory gives the President more freedom to act than his predecessor had and more leverage to the movement to pressure for executive action in Mississippi and other racist strongholds.

None of this *guarantees* vigorous executive or legislative action, for the other side of the Johnson landslide is that it has a Gaullist quality. Goldwater's capture of the Republican party forced into the Democratic camp many disparate elements which do not belong there, Big Business being the major example. Johnson, who wants to be President "of all people," may try to keep his new coalition together by sticking close to the political center. But if he decides to do this, it is unlikely that even his political genius will be able to hold together a coalition so inherently unstable and rife with contradictions. It must come apart. Should it do so while Johnson is pursuing a centrist course, then the mandate will have been wastefully dissipated. However, if the mandate is seized upon to set fundamental changes in motion, then the basis can be laid for a new mandate, a new coalition including hitherto inert and dispossessed strata of the population.

Here is where the cutting edge of the civil rights movement can be applied. We must see to it that the reorganization of the "consensus party" proceeds along lines which will make it an effective vehicle for social reconstruction, a role it cannot play so long as it furnishes Southern racism with its national political power. (One of Barry Goldwater's few attractive ideas was that the Dixiecrats belong with him in the same party.) And nowhere has the civil rights movement's political cutting edge been more magnificently demonstrated than at Atlantic City, where the Mississippi Freedom Democratic Party not only secured recognition as a bona fide component of the national party, but in the process routed the representatives of the most rabid racists—the white Mississippi and Alabama delegations. While I still believe that the FDP made a tactical error in spurning the compromise, there is no question that they launched a political revolution whose logic is the displacement of Dixiecrat power. They launched that revolution within a major political institution and as part of a coalitional effort.

The role of the civil rights movement in the reorganization of American political life is programmatic as well as strategic. We are challenged now to broaden our social vision, to develop functional programs with concrete objectives. We need to propose alternatives to technological unemployment, urban decay, and the rest. We need to be calling for public works and training, for national economic planning, for federal aid to education, for attractive public housing—all this on a sufficiently massive scale to make a difference. We need to protest the notion that our integration into American life, so long delayed, must now proceed in an atmosphere of competitive scarcity instead of in the security of abundance which technology makes possible. We cannot claim to have answers to all the complex problems of modern society. That is too much to ask of a movement still battling barbarism in Mississippi. But we can agitate the right questions by probing at the contradictions which still stand in the way of the "Great Society." The questions having been asked, motion must begin in the larger society, for there is a limit to what Negroes can do alone.

IX
The Continuing Effort

The year 1968 saw both advance and defeat in the civil rights movement. The summer riots of 1967 led to the formation of a National Advisory Commission on Civil Disorders (headed by Governor Otto Kerner of Illinois) which, in March 1968, produced a comprehensive report on the causes of urban riots and the manner of preventing them. It may serve as the same guide to action as the President's Committee report of 1947, described earlier. A selection from the summary of the 1968 report appears below.

The tragic assassination of Reverend Martin Luther King, Jr., on April 4, 1968, was a loss not only to the Negro community but to the nation and world as well. Spurred by the killing, Congress acted quickly to pass the civil rights bill pending before it since the Presidential message of May 2, 1966 (see p. 271). Part of the Senate report on the bill, relating to interference with a person's civil rights, and excerpts from the Act itself, signed into law by President Johnson on April 10, 1968, are reproduced also.

Report of the National Advisory Commission on Civil Disorders

SUMMARY OF REPORT

INTRODUCTION

The summer of 1967 again brought racial disorders to American cities, and with them shock, fear and bewilderment to the nation.

The worst came during a two-week period in July, first in Newark and then in Detroit. Each set off a chain reaction in neighboring communities.

On July 28, 1967, the President of the United States established this Commission and directed us to answer three basic questions:

What happened?

Why did it happen?

What can be done to prevent it from happening again?

346

To respond to these questions, we have undertaken a broad range of studies and investigations. We have visited the riot cities; we have heard many witnesses; we have sought the counsel of experts across the country.

This is our basic conclusion: Our nation is moving toward two societies, one black, one white—separate and unequal.

Reaction to last summer's disorders has quickened the movement and deepened the division. Discrimination and segregation have long permeated much of American life; they now threaten the future of every American.

This deepening racial division is not inevitable. The movement apart can be reversed. Choice is still possible. Our principal task is to define that choice and to press for a national resolution.

To pursue our present course will involve the continuing polarization of the American community and, ultimately, the destruction of basic democratic values.

The alternative is not blind repression or capitulation to lawlessness. It is the realization of common opportunities for all within a single society.

This alternative will require a commitment to national action—compassionate, massive and sustained, backed by the resources of the most powerful and the richest nation on this earth. From every American it will require new attitudes, new understanding, and, above all, new will.

The vital needs of the nation must be met; hard choices must be made, and, if necessary, new taxes enacted.

Violence cannot build a better society. Disruption and disorder nourish repression, not justice. They strike at the freedom of every citizen. The community cannot—it will not—tolerate coercion and mob rule.

Violence and destruction must be ended—in the streets of the ghetto and in the lives of people.

Segregation and poverty have created in the racial ghetto a destructive environment totally unknown to most white Americans.

What white Americans have never fully understood—but what the Negro can never forget—is that white society is deeply implicated in the ghetto. White institutions created it, white institutions maintain it, and white society condones it.

It is time now to turn with all the purpose at our command to the major unfinished business of this nation. It is time to adopt strategies for action that will produce quick and visible progress. It is time to make good the promises of American democracy to all citizens—urban and rural, white and black, Spanish-surname, American Indian, and every minority group.

Our recommendations embrace three basic principles:

- To mount programs on a scale equal to the dimensions of the problem.
- To aim these programs for high impact in the immediate future in order to close the gap between promise and performance.
- To undertake new initiatives and experiments that can change the system of failure and frustration that now dominates the ghetto and weakens our society.

These programs will require unprecedented levels of funding and performance, but they neither probe deeper nor demand more than the problems which called them forth. There can be no higher priority for national action and no higher claim on the nation's conscience.

We issue this Report now, four months before the date called for by the President. Much remains that can be learned. Continued study is essential.

As Commissioners we have worked together with a sense of the greatest urgency and have sought to compose whatever differences exist among us. Some differences remain. But the gravity of the problem and the pressing need for action are too clear to allow further delay in the issuance of this Report.

PART I—WHAT HAPPENED?

Chapter 1—Profiles of Disorder

The report contains profiles of a selection of the disorders that took place during the summer of 1967. These profiles are designed to indicate how the disorders happened, who participated in them, and how local officials, police forces, and the National Guard responded. Illustrative excerpts follow:

NEWARK

. . . It was decided to attempt to channel the energies of the people into a nonviolent protest. While Lofton promised the crowd that a full investigation would be made of the Smith incident, the other Negro leaders began urging those on the scene to form a line of march toward the city hall.

Some persons joined the line of march. Others milled about in the narrow street. From the dark grounds of the housing project came a barrage of rocks. Some of them fell among the crowd. Others hit persons in the line of march. Many smashed the windows of the police station. The rock throwing, it was believed, was the work of youngsters; approximately 2,500 children lived in the housing project.

Almost at the same time, an old car was set afire in a parking lot. The line of march began to disintegrate. The police, their heads protected by World War I-type helmets, sallied forth to disperse the crowd. A fire engine, arriving on the scene, was pelted with rocks. As police drove people away from the station, they scattered in all directions.

A few minutes later a nearby liquor store was broken into. Some persons, seeing a caravan of cabs appear at city hall to protest Smith's arrest, interpreted this as evidence that the disturbance had been organized, and generated rumors to that effect.

However, only a few stores were looted. Within a short period of time, the disorder appeared to have run its course.

*   *   *

. . . On Saturday, July 15, [Director of Police Dominick] Spina received a report of snipers in a housing project. When he arrived he saw approximately 100 National Guardsmen and police officers crouching behind vehicles, hiding in corners and lying on the ground around the edge of the courtyard.

Since everything appeared quiet and it was broad daylight, Spina walked directly down the middle of the street. Nothing happened. As he came to the last building of the complex, he heard a shot. All around him the troopers jumped, believing themselves to be under sniper fire. A moment later a young Guardsman ran from behind a building.

The Director of Police went over and asked him if he had fired the shot. The soldier said yes, he had fired to scare a man away from a window; that his orders were to keep everyone away from windows.

Spina said he told the soldier: "Do you know what you just did? You have now created a state of hysteria. Every Guardsman up and down this street and every state policeman and every city policeman that is present thinks that somebody just fired a shot and that it is probably a sniper."

A short time later more "gunshots" were heard. Investigating, Spina came upon a Puerto Rican sitting on a wall. In reply to a question as to whether he knew "where the firing is coming from?" the man said: "That's no firing. That's fireworks. If you look up to the fourth floor, you will see the people who are throwing down these cherry bombs."

By this time four truckloads of National Guardsmen had arrived and troopers and policemen were again crouched everywhere looking for a sniper. The Director of Police remained at the scene for three hours, and the only shot fired was the one by the Guardsman.

Nevertheless, at six o'clock that evening two columns of National Guardsmen and state troopers were directing mass fire at the Hayes Housing Project in response to what they believed were snipers. . . .

DETROIT

. . . A spirit of carefree nihilism was taking hold. To riot and destroy appeared more and more to become ends in themselves. Late Sunday afternoon it appeared to one observer that the young people were "dancing amidst the flames."

A Negro plainclothes officer was standing at an intersection when a man threw a Molotov cocktail into a business establishment at the corner. In the heat of the afternoon, fanned by the 20 to 25 m.p.h. winds of both Sunday and Monday, the fire reached the home next door within minutes. As residents uselessly sprayed the flames with garden hoses, the fire jumped from roof to roof of adjacent two- and three-story buildings. Within the hour the entire block was in flames. The ninth house in the burning row belonged to the arsonist who had thrown the Molotov cocktail. . . .

* * *

. . . Employed as a private guard, 55-year-old Julius L. Dorsey, a Negro, was standing in front of a market when accosted by two Negro men and a woman. They demanded he permit them to loot the market. He ignored their demands. They began to berate him. He asked a neighbor to call the police. As the argument grew more heated, Dorsey fired three shots from his pistol into the air.

The police radio reported: "Looters, they have rifles." A patrol car driven by a police officer and carrying three National Guardsmen arrived. As the looters fled, the law enforcement personnel opened fire. When the firing ceased, one person lay dead.

He was Julius L. Dorsey . . .

* * *

. . . As the riot alternately waxed and waned, one area of the ghetto remained insulated. On the northeast side the residents of some 150 square blocks, inhabited by 21,000 persons had, in 1966, banded together in the Positive Neighborhood Action Committee (PNAC). With professional help from the Institute of Urban Dynamics, they had organized block clubs and made plans for the improvement of the neighborhood. . . .

When the riot broke out, the residents, through the block clubs, were able to organize quickly. Youngsters, agreeing to stay in the neighborhood, participated in detouring traffic. While many persons reportedly sympathized with the idea of a rebellion against the "system," only two small fires were set—one in an empty building.

*   *   *

. . . According to Lt. Gen. Throckmorton and Col. Bolling, the city, at this time, was saturated with fear. The National Guardsmen were afraid, the residents were afraid, and the police were afraid. Numerous persons, the majority of them Negroes, were being injured by gunshots of undetermined origin. The general and his staff felt that the major task of the troops was to reduce the fear and restore an air of normalcy.

In order to accomplish this, every effort was made to establish contact and rapport between the troops and the residents. The soldiers—20 percent of whom were Negro—began helping to clean up the streets, collect garbage, and trace persons who had disappeared in the confusion. Residents in the neighborhoods responded with soup and sandwiches for the troops. In the areas where the National Guard tried to establish rapport with the citizens, there was a similar response.

NEW BRUNSWICK

. . . A short time later, elements of the crowd—an older and rougher one than the night before—appeared in front of the police station. The participants wanted to see the mayor.

Mayor [Patricia] Sheehan went out onto the steps of the station. Using a bullhorn, she talked to the people and asked that she be given an opportunity to correct conditions. The crowd was boisterous. Some persons challenged the mayor. But, finally, the opinion, "She's new! Give her a chance!" prevailed.

A demand was issued by people in the crowd that all persons arrested the previous night be released. Told that this already had been done, the people were suspicious. They asked to be allowed to inspect the jail cells.

It was agreed to permit representatives of the people to look in the cells to satisfy themselves that everyone had been released.

The crowd dispersed. The New Brunswick riot had failed to materialize.

Chapter 2—Patterns of Disorder

The "typical" riot did not take place. The disorders of 1967 were unusual, irregular, complex and unpredictable social processes. Like most human events, they did not unfold in an orderly sequence. However, an analysis of our survey information leads to some conclusions about the riot process.

In general:

- The civil disorders of 1967 involved Negroes acting against local symbols of white American society, authority and property in Negro neighborhoods—rather than against white persons.
- Of 164 disorders reported during the first nine months of 1967, eight (5 percent) were major in terms of violence and damage; 33 (20 percent) were serious but not major; 123 (75 percent) were minor and undoubtedly would not have received national attention as "riots" had the nation not been sensitized by the more serious outbreaks.
- In the 75 disorders studied by a Senate subcommittee, 83 deaths were reported. Eighty-two percent of the deaths and more than half the injuries occurred in Newark and Detroit. About 10 percent of the dead and 38 percent of the injured were public employees, primarily law officers and firemen. The overwhelming majority of the persons killed or injured in all the disorders were Negro civilians.

- Initial damage estimates were greatly exaggerated. In Detroit, newspaper damage estimates at first ranged from $200 million to $500 million; the highest recent estimate is $45 million. In Newark, early estimates ranged from $15 to $25 million. A month later damage was estimated at $10.2 million, over 80 percent in inventory losses.

In the 24 disorders in 23 cities which we surveyed:
- The final incident before the outbreak of disorder, and the initial violence itself, generally took place in the evening or at night at a place in which it was normal for many people to be on the streets.
- Violence usually occurred almost immediately following the occurrence of the final precipitating incident, and then escalated rapidly. With but few exceptions, violence subsided during the day, and flared rapidly again at night. The night-day cycles continued through the early period of the major disorders.
- Disorder generally began with rock and bottle throwing and window breaking. Once store windows were broken, looting usually followed.
- Disorder did not erupt as a result of a single "triggering" or "precipitating" incident. Instead, it was generated out of an increasingly disturbed social atmosphere, in which typically a series of tension-heightening incidents over a period of weeks or months became linked in the minds of many in the Negro community with a reservoir of underlying grievances. At some point in the mounting tension, a further incident—in itself often routine or trivial—became the breaking point and the tension spilled over into violence.
- "Prior" incidents, which increased tensions and ultimately led to violence, were police actions in almost half the cases; police actions were "final" incidents before the outbreak of violence in 12 of the 24 surveyed disorders.
- No particular control tactic was successful in every situation. The varied effectiveness of control techniques emphasizes the need for advance training, planning, adequate intelligence systems, and knowledge of the ghetto community.
- Negotiations between Negroes—including your militants as well as older Negro leaders—and white officials concerning "terms of peace" occurred during virtually all the disorders surveyed. In many cases, these negotiations involved discussion of underlying grievances as well as the handling of the disorder by control authorities.
- The typical rioter was a teenager or young adult, a lifelong resident of the city in which he rioted, a high school dropout; he was, nevertheless, somewhat better educated than his nonrioting Negro neighbor, and was usually underemployed or employed in a menial job. He was proud of his race, extremely hostile to both whites and middle-class Negroes and, although informed about politics, highly distrustful of the political system.
- A Detroit survey revealed that approximately 11 percent of the total residents of two riot areas admitted participation in the rioting, 20 to 25 percent identified themselves as "bystanders," over 16 percent identified themselves as "counter-rioters" who urged rioters to "cool it," and the remaining 48 to 53 percent said they were at home or elsewhere and did not participate. In a survey of Negro males between the ages of 15 and 35 residing in the disturbance area in Newark, about 45 percent identified themselves as rioters, and about 55 percent as "noninvolved."
- Most rioters were young Negro males. Nearly 53 percent of arrestees were between 15 and 24 years of age; nearly 81 percent between 15 and 35.
- In Detroit and Newark about 74 percent of the rioters were brought up in the North. In contrast, of the noninvolved, 36 percent in Detroit and 52 percent in Newark were brought up in the North.
- What the rioters appeared to be seeking was fuller participation in the social order and the material benefits enjoyed by the majority of American

- Little basic change in the conditions underlying the outbreak of disorder has taken place. Actions to ameliorate Negro grievances have been limited and sporadic; with but few exceptions, they have not significantly reduced tensions.
- In several cities, the principal official response has been to train and equip the police with more sophisticated weapons.
- In several cities, increasing polarization is evident, with continuing breakdown of inter-racial communication, and growth of white segregationist or black separatist groups.

Chapter 3—Organized Activity

The President directed the Commission to investigate "to what extent, if any, there has been planning or organization in any of the riots."

To carry out this part of the President's charge, the Commission established a special investigative staff supplementing the field teams that made the general examination of the riots in 23 cities. The unit examined data collected by federal agencies and congressional committees, including thousands of documents supplied by the Federal Bureau of Investigation, gathered and evaluated information from local and state law enforcement agencies and officials, and conducted its own field investigation in selected cities.

On the basis of all the information collected, the Commission concludes that:

The urban disorders of the summer of 1967 were not caused by, nor were they the consequence of, any organized plan or "conspiracy."

Specifically, the Commission has found no evidence that all or any of the disorders or the incidents that led to them were planned or directed by any organization or group, international, national or local.

Militant organizations, local and national, and individual agitators, who repeatedly forecast and called for violence, were active in the spring and summer of 1967. We believe that they sought to encourage violence, and that they helped to create an atmosphere that contributed to the outbreak of disorder.

We recognize that the continuation of disorders and the polarization of the races would provide fertile ground for organized exploitation in the future.

Investigations of organized activity are continuing at all levels of government, including committees of Congress. These investigations relate not only to the disorders of 1967 but also to the actions of groups and individuals, particularly in schools and colleges, during this last fall and winter. The Commission has cooperated in these investigations. They should continue.

PART II—WHY DID IT HAPPEN?

Chapter 4—The Basic Causes

In addressing the question "Why did it happen?" we shift our focus from the local to the national scene, from the particular events of the summer of

1967 to the factors within the society at large that created a mood of violence among many urban Negroes.

These factors are complex and interacting; they vary significantly in their effect from city to city and from year to year; and the consequences of one disorder, generating new grievances and new demands, become the causes of the next. Thus was created the "thicket of tension, conflicting evidence and extreme opinions" cited by the President.

Despite these complexities, certain fundamental matters are clear. Of these, the most fundamental is the racial attitude and behavior of white Americans toward black Americans.

Race prejudice has shaped our history decisively; it now threatens to affect our future.

White racism is essentially responsible for the explosive mixture which has been accumulating in our cities since the end of World War II. Among the ingredients of this mixture are:

- *Pervasive discrimination and segregation* in employment, education and housing, which have resulted in the continuing exclusion of great numbers of Negroes from the benefits of economic progress.
- *Black in-migration and white exodus,* which have produced the massive and growing concentrations of impoverished Negroes in our major cities, creating a growing crisis of deteriorating facilities and services and unmet human needs.
- *The black ghettos* where segregation and poverty converge on the young to destroy opportunity and enforce failure. Crime, drug addiction, dependency on welfare, and bitterness and resentment against society in general and white society in particular are the result.

At the same time, most whites and some Negroes outside the ghetto have prospered to a degree unparalleled in the history of civilization. Through television and other media, this affluence has been flaunted before the eyes of the Negro poor and the jobless ghetto youth.

Yet these facts alone cannot be said to have caused the disorders. Recently, other powerful ingredients have begun to catalyze the mixture:

- *Frustrated hopes* are the residue of the unfulfilled expectations aroused by the great judicial and legislative victories of the Civil Rights Movement and the dramatic struggle for equal rights in the South.
- *A climate that tends toward approval and encouragement of violence* as a form of protest has been created by white terrorism directed against non-violent protest; by the open defiance of law and federal authority by state and local officials resisting desegregation; and by some protest groups engaging in civil disobedience who turn their backs on nonviolence, go beyond the constitutionally protected rights of petition and free assembly, and resort to violence to attempt to compel alteration of laws and policies with which they disagree.
- *The frustrations of powerlessness* have led some Negroes to the conviction that there is no effective alternative to violence as a means of achieving redress of grievances, and of "moving the system." These frustrations are reflected in alienation and hostilty toward the institutions of law and government and the white society which controls them, and in the reach toward racial consciousness and solidarity reflected in the slogan "Black Power."

- Little basic change in the conditions underlying the out
  has taken place. Actions to ameliorate Negro grievances
  and sporadic; with but few exceptions, they have not sig
  tensions.
- In several cities, the principal official response has been to
  the police with more sophisticated weapons.
- In several cities, increasing polarization is evident, with d
  down of inter-racial communication, and growth of white
  black separatist groups.

Chapter 3—Organized Activity

The President directed the Commission to investigate "to
any, there has been planning or organization in any of the

To carry out this part of the President's charge, the Con
lished a special investigative staff supplementing the field tea
the general examination of the riots in 23 cities. The unit
collected by federal agencies and congressional committees, in
sands of documents supplied by the Federal Bureau of Investiga
and evaluated information from local and state law enforcer
and officials, and conducted its own field investigation in selec

On the basis of all the information collected, the Commiss
that:

The urban disorders of the summer of 1967 were not caused
they the consequence of, any organized plan or "conspiracy."

Specifically, the Commission has found no evidence that al
the disorders or the incidents that led to them were planned or
any organization or group, international, national or local.

Militant organizations, local and national, and individual agi
repeatedly forecast and called for violence, were active in the
summer of 1967. We believe that they sought to encourage vic
that they helped to create an atmosphere that contributed to the c
disorder.

We recognize that the continuation of disorders and the pola
the races would provide fertile ground for organized exploitati
future.

Investigations of organized activity are continuing at all levels
ment, including committees of Congress. These investigations relate
to the disorders of 1967 but also to the actions of groups and in
particularly in schools and colleges, during this last fall and wi
Commission has cooperated in these investigations. They should

PART II—WHY DID IT HAPPEN?

Chapter 4—The Basic Causes

In addressing the question "Why did it happen?" we shift our foc
the local to the national scene, from the particular events of the sun

- *A new mood* has sprung up among Negroes, particularly among the young, in which self-esteem and enhanced racial pride are replacing apathy and submission to "the system."
- *The police are not merely a "spark" factor.* To some Negroes police have come to symbolize white power, white racism and white repression. And the fact is that many police do reflect and express these white attitudes. The atmosphere of hostility and cynicism is reinforced by a widespread belief among Negroes in the existence of police brutality and in a "double standard" of justice and protection—one for Negroes and one for whites.

*   *   *

To this point, we have attempted to identify the prime components of the "explosive mixture." In the chapters that follow we seek to analyze them in the perspective of history. Their meaning, however, is clear:

In the summer of 1967, we have seen in our cities a chain reaction of racial violence. If we are heedless, none of us shall escape the consequences.

*   *   *   *   *   *   *   *   *

Chapter 16—The Future of the Cities

By 1985, the Negro population in central cities is expected to increase by 72 percent to approximately 20.8 million. Coupled with the continued exodus of white families to the suburbs, this growth will produce majority Negro populations in many of the nation's largest cities.

The future of these cities, and of their burgeoning Negro populations, is grim. Most new employment opportunites are being created in suburbs and outlying areas. This trend will continue unless important changes in public policy are made.

In prospect, therefore, is further deterioration of already inadequate municipal tax bases in the face of increasing demands for public services, and continuing unemployment and poverty among the urban Negro population:

Three choices are open to the nation:

- We can maintain present policies, continuing both the proportion of the nation's resources now allocated to programs for the unemployed and the disadvantaged, and the inadequate and failing effort to achieve an integrated society.
- We can adopt a policy of "enrichment" aimed at improving dramatically the quality of ghetto life while abandoning integration as a goal.
- We can pursue integration by combining ghetto "enrichment" with policies which will encourage Negro movement out of central city areas.

The first choice, continuance of present policies, has ominous consequences for our society. The share of the nation's resources now allocated to programs for the disadvantaged is insufficient to arrest the deterioration of life in central city ghettos. Under such conditions, a rising proportion of Negroes may come to see in the deprivation and segregation they experience, a justification for violent protest, or for extending support to now isolated extremists who advocate civil disruption. Large-scale and continuing violence could result, followed by white retaliation, and, ultimately, the separation of the two communities in a garrison state.

Even if violence does not occur, the consequences are unacceptable. Development of a racially integrated society, extraordinarily difficult today, will be virtually impossible when the present black ghetto population of 12.5 million has grown to almost 21 million.

To continue present policies is to make permanent the division of our country into two societies; one, largely Negro and poor, located in the central cities; the other predominantly white and affluent, located in the suburbs and in outlying areas.

The second choice, ghetto enrichment coupled with abandonment of integration, is also unacceptable. It is another way of choosing a permanently divided country. Moreover, equality cannot be achieved under conditions of nearly complete separation. In a country where the economy, and particularly the resources of employment, are predominantly white, a policy of separation can only relegate Negroes to a permanently inferior economic status.

We believe that the only possible choice for America is the third—a policy which combines ghetto enrichment with programs designed to encourage integration of substantial numbers of Negroes into the society outside the ghetto.

Enrichment must be an important adjunct to integration, for no matter how ambitious or energetic the program, few Negroes now living in central cities can be quickly integrated. In the meantime, large-scale improvement in the quality of ghetto life is essential.

But this can be no more than an interim strategy. Programs must be developed which will permit substantial Negro movement out of the ghettos. The primary goal must be a single society, in which every citizen will be free to live and work according to his capabilities and desires, not his color.

Chapter 17—Recommendations For National Action

INTRODUCTION

No American—white or black—can escape the consequences of the continuing social and economic decay of our major cities.

Only a commitment to national action on an unprecedented scale can shape a future compatible with the historic ideals of American society.

The great productivity of our economy, and a federal revenue system which is highly responsive to economic growth, can provide the resources.

The major need is to generate new will—the will to tax ourselves to the extent necessary to meet the vital needs of the nation.

We have set forth goals and proposed strategies to reach those goals. We discuss and recommend programs not to commit each of us to specific parts of such programs but to illustrate the type and dimension of action needed.

The major goal is the creation of a true union—a single society and a single American identity. Toward that goal, we propose the following objectives for national action:

- Opening up opportunities to those who are restricted by racial segregation and discrimination, and eliminating all barriers to their choice of jobs, education and housing.

- Removing the frustration of powerlessness among the disadvantaged by providing the means for them to deal with the problems that affect their own lives and by increasing the capacity of our public and private institutions to respond to these problems.
- Increasing communication across racial lines to destroy stereotypes, to halt polarization, end distrust and hostility, and create common ground for efforts toward public order and social justice.

We propose these aims to fulfill our pledge of equality and to meet the fundamental needs of a democratic and civilized society—domestic peace and social justice.

*   *   *   *

CONCLUSION

One of the first witnesses to be invited to appear before this Commission was Dr. Kenenth B. Clark, a distinguished and perceptive scholar. Referring to the reports of earlier riot commissions, he said:

> I read that report . . . of the 1919 riot in Chicago, and it is as if I were reading the report of the investigation committee on the Harlem riot of '35, the report of the investigating committee on the Harlem riot of '43, the report of the McCone Commission on the Watts riot.
> I must again in candor say to you members of this Commission—it is a kind of Alice in Wonderland—with the same moving picture re-shown over and over again, the same analysis, the same recommendations, and the same inaction.

These words come to our minds as we conclude this report.

We have provided an honest beginning. We have learned much. But we have uncovered no startling truths, no unique insights, no simple solutions. The destruction and the bitterness of racial disorder, the harsh polemics of black revolt and white repression have been seen and heard before in this country.

It is time now to end the destruction and the violence, not only in the streets of the ghetto but in the lives of people.

Senate Report on the Civil Rights Act of 1968 (November 2, 1967)

PURPOSE OF THE LEGISLATION AS REPORTED

H.R. 2516, as reported, adds a new section 245 to title 18, United States Code, in the form of a criminal statute designed to deter and punish inter-ference by force or threat of force with activities protected by Federal law or the Constitution and specifically set out in the bill. The purpose of the legislation is to strengthen the capability of the Federal Government to meet the problem of violent interference, for racial or other discriminatory reasons, with a person's free exercise of civil rights. The areas of protected activity are specifically described. They include voting and activities related to voting; enrolling in or attending public schools or public colleges; participating in or enjoying the benefits of services, programs, facilities, or activities of Federal,

State, or local governments; enjoying employment, union membership, or the services of employment agencies; serving on juries; using vehicles, terminals, or facilities of common carriers; participating in programs or activities receiving Federal assistance; and enjoying the facilities of hotels, restaurants, and other public accommodations.

The statute would punish interference or attempts to interfere, by force or threat of force, with any person because of his race, color, religion, or national origin and because such person is or has been engaging or seeking to engage, while acting lawfully, in any of the enumerated activities. H.R. 2516 would also make it a crime to interfere or attempt to interfere (by force or threat of force) with any person to discourage him from participating in such activities. Also punishable would be violence directed against persons not involved in civil rights activity where such persons are selected as victims in order to intimidate others.

The bill would protect persons who urge or aid participation in the protected activities, as well as those who engage in speech or peaceful assembly opposing denial of the opportunity to so participate. Persons who have duties to perform with respect to the protected activities—such as public school officials, restaurant owners, employers, or voter registration officials—would also be protected.

Forcible interference with any of the activities set out in the bill would be prohibited whether committed by persons acting under color of law or by private individuals. Persons acting alone, as well as those acting in concert, would be reached by the bill's prohibitions.

Penalties are graduated in accordance with the seriousness of the results of violations, ranging from misdemeanor penalties to life imprisonment. A similarly graduated penalty structure is provided for in existing criminal civil rights statutes, 18 U.S.C., sections 241 and 242.

THE NEED FOR THE LEGISLATION

The great majority of Americans have either welcomed or peacefully accepted the movement of Negroes toward full enjoyment of equal rights. Unfortunately, however, a small minority of lawbreakers has resorted to violence in an effort to bar Negroes from exercising their lawful rights. Brutal crimes have been committed not only against Negroes exercising Federal rights but also against whites who have tried to help Negroes seeking to exercise these rights. Acts of racial terrorism have sometimes gone unpunished and have too often deterred the free exercise of constitutional and statutory rights.

Such acts of violence have occurred in retaliation against Negroes who have exercised or sought to exercise their civil rights. In some cases, violence has been used against Negroes who have not engaged in any civil rights activities in order generally to intimidate and deter all Negroes in the exercise of their rights. White and Negro civil rights workers have also been victimized.

Under the Federal system, the keeping of the peace is, for the most part, a matter of local and not Federal concern. Racial violence almost invariably involves a violation of State law. Where the administration of justice is colorblind, perpetrators of racial crimes will ordinarily be apprehended by local police and appropriately punished by local courts; and, as a natural consequence, other would-be lawbreakers will be deterred.

In some places, however, local officials either have been unable or unwilling to solve and prosecute crimes of racial violence or to obtain convictions in such cases—even where the facts seemed to warrant. As a result, there is need for Federal action to compensate for the lack of effective protection and prosecution on the local level.

But Federal legislation against racial violence is not required solely because of the sometimes inadequate workings of State or local criminal processes. Too often in recent years, racial violence has been used to deny affirmative Federal rights; this action reflects a purpose to flout the clearly expressed will of the Congress. Thus, when a Negro is assaulted for attending a desegregated school or casting a ballot, it is not only the individual Negro and the peace and dignity of the State that is injured. Such lawless acts are distinctly Federal crimes and it is, therefore, appropriate that responsibility for vindication of the rights infringed should be committed to the Federal courts.

Several criminal and civil statutes designed to reach both private and official interference with Federal rights were enacted by Congress in the 1860's and early 1870's. This legislation included the statutory predecessors of what are now sections 241 and 242 of the Federal Criminal Code. A number of these early provisions, however, were invalidated or greatly restricted in application by the courts; others were repealed by later Congresses.

Only recently the Supreme Court had occasion to interpret two of the still existing criminal provisions—sections 241 and 242. In *United States* v. *Guest,* the Court was faced with a Federal indictment based on the shooting of a Negro educator, Lemuel Penn, while he was driving through the State of Georgia; *United States* v. *Price* involved the 1964 killings of the three civil rights workers in Neshoba County, Miss.

While Supreme Court decisions in these cases clarify some aspects of sections 241 and 242, the opinion of the Court and the separate opinions of Justices Clark and Brennan in the *Guest* case point up a number of serious deficiencies in both statutes and suggest how they might be overcome.

First, the opinions indicate that section 241 may not cover purely private actions which interfere with 14th amendment's rights. At the same time, a majority of the Justices made it clear that Congress could, under section 5 of the 14th amendment, enact a statute reaching private conduct denying such rights. H.R. 2516 is such a statute and would—as six Justices said was constitutionally possible—cover racially motivated acts of violence which do not involve participation on connivance of public officials. (It has long been settled, of course, that Congress may prohibit private interference with those rights which are based on Congress legislative authority under article I, such as the power to regulate commerce.)

Second, the present Federal criminal laws—18 U.S.C., section 241 and 242—while applicable to some racial violence, are inadequate to deal with present problems. Worded in general terms, they apply to a whole range of Federal rights, including—without specification—rights under the 14th amendment. As a result, prosecutions under both statutes have been plagued by serious "vagueness" problems, often requiring protracted litigation.

Such delays seriously undermine enforcement efforts. And because these statutes do not spell out clearly what kinds of conduct are prohibited, they lack the deterrent effect that would result from plainly worded prohibitions. Commenting on the vague language of section 241, Justice Brennan said last year in *United States* v. *Guest, 383 U.S. 745, 786*—

> * * * since the limitation on the statute's effectiveness derives from Congress failure to define—with any measure of specificity—the rights encompassed, the remedy is for Congress to write a law without this defect. To paraphrase my Brother Douglas' observation in *Screws* v. *United States,* 325 U.S. at 105, addressed to a companion statute with the same shortcoming, if Congress desires to give the statute more definite scope, it may find ways of doing so.

H.R. 2516 meets this need by spelling out the kinds of activity to be protected, and the bill provides an effective means of deterring and punishing forcible interference with the exercise of Federal rights. The clear language of the bill would avoid unnecessary litigation concerning coverage and would provide unmistakable warning to lawless elements not to interfere with any of these activities.

Finally, there are two other significant defects in the present laws which H.R. 2516 would remedy. First, section 241 applies only to conspiracies. Thus, even with respect to conduct held to be within the scope of section 241, a prosecution may not be brought for action by a single individual unless in some way another person has been involved. Second, the maximum penalties are inadequate for cases in which bodily injury or death has occurred. Section 241 provides a maximum penalty of a $5,000 fine or a 10-year prison sentence, or both. Under section 242, the maximum penalty is only a $1,000 fine or one year's imprisonment, or both.

H.R. 2516 would prohibit forcible interference with any of the specified activities by individuals acting alone as well as by public officers or other persons acting under color of law.

The penalties prescribed in the bill are graduated in accordance with the seriousness of the results of violations, ranging from misdemeanor penalties when no one is harmed, to $10,000 fines and 10 years imprisonment when there is physical injury, and life imprisonment when death occurs.

CONSTITUTIONALITY

Depending upon the nature of the activity involved, the constitutional basis for the bill varies. It has long been settled that Congress may make it a crime for any person (whether or not an official or acting "under color of law") to interfere with the exercise of rights arising out of the relationship between the citizen and the National Government or rights created by Federal statutes enacted under article I, section 8, of the Constitution. See *Civil Rights cases,* 109 U.S. 3, 18; *Ex Parte Yarbrough,* 110 U.S. 651; *United States* v. *Waddell,* 112 U.S. 76. Specifically, there is no question of the constitutional power of Congress to punish private interference with voting in Federal elections (*Ex Parte Yarbrough, supra*), interstate travel or interstate commerce (*United States* v. *Guest,* 383 U.S. 745). Thus, so far as the bill vindicates rights based on article I, section 8 of the Constitution it is plainly not subject to objection.

Nor does any problem arise because, in a few instances, the scope of protection is greater than that afforded by the substantive statutes defining rights dependent on the commerce clause. Congress is not constitutionally bound by the lines of coverage announced in the Civil Rights Act of 1964, with respect to access to places of public accommodation or equal employment opportunities, nor by its earlier decision to regulate, for some purposes, only interstate carriers and their terminals. In dealing with violent interference with the right to be free from racial discrimination in interstate activities it is reasonable to conclude that effective regulation requires reaching related local activities also.

Indeed, it is all too clear that if racial violence directed against activities closely related to those protected by Federal antidiscrimination legislation is permitted to go unpunished, the exercise of the protected activities will be deterred. A Negro prevented by violence or the threat of violence from seeking employment in a firm of less than 50 employees will likely be too intimidated to seek a job with an employer who is subject to the Civil Rights Act of 1964. Likewise, a Negro violently prevented from using an intrastate bus may be hesitant to assert his right to equal treatment on interstate buses, and a Negro prevented by force from entering a place of public accommodation not covered by that act will fear to claim equal treatment in public accommodations covered by the act. Experience teaches that racial violence has a broadly inhibiting effect upon the exercise by members of the Negro community of their Federal rights to nondiscriminatory treatment. Such violence must, therefore, be broadly prohibited if the enjoyment of those rights is to be secured. Legislation that regulates intrastate commerce in order to assure the effective regulation of interstate commerce is a commonplace, and its constitutionality is beyond serious debate. See especially, *United States* v. *Darby,* 312 U.S. 100, 118-119; *United States* v. *Wrightwood Dairy,* 315 U.S. 110, 119; *Atlanta Motel* v. *United States,* 379 U.S. 241, 258.

H.R. 2516 also vindicates the right to the equal enjoyment, without distinction on account of race, religion, or national origin, of State facilities or activities (such as public schools, municipal parks, public assistance programs, and the State electoral process). This is, of course, a right secured by the 14th and 15th amendments against denial by officials or agents of the States, and there are many decisions upholding the power of Congress to punish criminally State officials who by force deny this right. *E.g., Screws* v. *United States,* 325 U.S. 91; *United States* v. *Price,* 383 U.S. 787.

The present bill reaches private interference as well as interference by State officials. While the 14th and 15th amendments, of their own force, do not forbid private discrimination, they expressly authorize Congress to enact appropriate legislation to "enforce" the substantive guarantees. The scope of this congressional implementing power is broad. *South Carolina* v. *Katzenbach*, 383 U.S. 301, 326-327; *Katzenbach* v. *Morgan*, 384 U.S. 641. It surely comprehends legislation punishing private persons who for racial reasons engage in acts or threats of violence that obstruct access on equal terms to the facilities and benefits which a State provides its citizens, and thereby thwart the attainment of the promise of the 14th and 15th amendments. Any doubt on this score was laid to rest by the opinions of Mr. Justice Clark and Mr. Justice Brennan (speaking together for six of the nine Justices), in the *Guest* case which declare in almost the same words that "there now can be no doubt that the specific language of section 5 [of the 14th amendment] empowers the Congress to enact laws punishing all conspiracies—with or without State action—that interfere with 14th amendment rights." 383 U.S. at 762 (opinion of Justice Clark), 782 (opinion of Justice Brennan).

Nor is the power of Congress limited to the punishment of *conspirators* who attempt to interfere with 14th amendment rights. As Justice Brennan said in the *Guest* case:

> * * * I can find no principle of federalism nor word of the Constitution that denies Congress power to determine that in order adequately to protect the right to equal utilization of State facilities, it is also appropriate to punish other individuals—not State officers themselves and not acting in concert with State officers—who engage in the same brutal conduct for the same misguided purpose (383 U.S. 745, at 784).

*   *   *   *

Civil Rights Act of 1968

TITLE I
INTERFERENCE WITH FEDERALLY PROTECTED ACTIVITIES

Sec. 101. (a) That chapter 13, civil rights, title 18, United States Code, is amended by inserting immediately at the end thereof the following new section, to read as follows:

"§ 245. *Federally protected activities*

"(a)(1) Nothing in this section shall be construed as indicating an intent on the part of Congress to prevent any State, any possession or Commonwealth of the United States, or the District of Columbia, from exercising jurisdiction over any offense over which it would have jurisdiction in the absence of this section, nor shall anything in this section be construed as depriving State and local law enforcement authorities of responsibility for prosecuting acts that may be violations of this section and that are violations of State and local law. No prosecution of any offense described in this section shall be undertaken by the United States except upon the certification in writing of the Attorney General or the Deputy Attorney General that in his judgment a prosecution by the United States is in the public interest and necessary to secure substantial justice, which function of certification may not be delegated.

"(2) Nothing in this subsection shall be construed to limit the authority of Federal officers, or a Federal grand jury, to investigate possible violations of this section.

"(b) Whoever, whether or not acting under color of law, by force or threat of force willfully injures, intimidates or interferes with, or attempts to injure, intimidate or interfere with—

"(1) any person because he is or has been, or in order to intimidate such person or any other person or any class of persons from—

"(A) voting or qualifying to vote, qualifying or campaigning as a candidate for elective office, or qualifying or acting as a poll watcher, or any legally authorized election official, in any primary, special, or general election;

"(B) participating in or enjoying any benefit, service, privilege, program, facility, or activity provided or administered by the United States;

"(C) applying for or enjoying employment, or any perquisite thereof, by any agency of the United States;

"(D) serving, or attending upon any court in connection with possible service, as a grand or petit juror in any court of the United States;

"(E) participating in or enjoying the benefits of any program or activity receiving Federal financial assistance; or

"(2) any person because of his race, color, religion or national origin and because he is or has been—

"(A) enrolling in or attending any public school or public college;

"(B) participating in or enjoying any benefit, service, privilege, program, facility or activity provided or administered by any State or subdivision thereof;

"(C) applying for or enjoying employment, or any perquisite thereof, by any private employer or any agency of any State or subdivision thereof, or joining or using the services or advantages of any labor organization, hiring hall, or employment agency;

"(D) serving, or attending upon any court of any State in connection with possible service, as a grand or petit juror;

"(E) traveling in or using any facility of interstate commerce, or using any vehicle, terminal, or facility of any common carrier by motor, rail, water, or air;

"(F) enjoying the goods, services, facilities, privileges, advantages, or accommodations of any inn, hotel, motel, or other establishment which provides lodging to transient guests, or of any restaurant, cafeteria, lunchroom, lunch counter, soda fountain, or other facility which serves the public and which is principally engaged in selling food or beverages for consumption on the premises, or of any gasoline station, or of any motion picture house, theater, concert hall, sports arena, stadium, or any other place of exhibition or entertainment which serves the public, or of any other establishment which serves the public and (i) which is located within the premises of any of the aforesaid establishments or within the premises of which is physically located any of the aforesaid establishments, and (ii) which holds itself out as serving patrons of such establishments; or

"(3) during or incident to a riot or civil disorder, any person engaged in a business in commerce or affecting commerce, including, but not limited to, any person engaged in a business which sells or offers for sale to interstate travelers a substantial portion of the articles, commodities, or services which it sells or where a substantial portion of the articles or commodities which it sells or offers for sale have moved in commerce; or

"(4) any person because he is or has been, or in order to intimidate such person or any other person or any class of persons from—

"(A) participating, without discrimination on account of race, color, religion or national origin, in any of the benefits or activities described in subparagraphs (1)(A) through (1)(E) or subparagraphs (2)(A) through (2)(F); or

"(B) affording another person or class of persons opportunity or protection to so participate; or

"(5) any citizen because he is or has been, or in order to intimidate such citizen or any other citizen from lawfully aiding or encouraging other persons to participate, without discrimination on account of race, color, religion or national origin, in any of the benefits or activities described in subparagraphs (1)(A) through (1)(E) or subparagraphs (2)(A) through (2)(F), or participating lawfully in speech or peaceful assembly opposing any denial of the opportunity to so participate—

shall be fined not more than $1,000, or imprisoned not more than one year, or both; and if bodily injury results shall be fined not more than $10,000, or imprisoned not more than ten years, or both; and if death results shall be subject to imprisonment for any term of years or for life. As used in this section, the term 'participating lawfully in speech or peaceful assembly' shall not mean the aiding, abetting, or inciting of other persons to riot or to commit any act of physical violence upon any individual or against any real or personal property in furtherance of a riot. Nothing in subparagraph (2)(F) or (4)(A) of this subsection shall apply to the proprietor of any establishment which provides lodging to transient guests, or to any employee acting on behalf of such proprietor, with respect to the enjoyment of the goods, services, facilities, privileges, advantages, or accommodations of such establishment if such establishment is located within a building which contains not more than five rooms for rent or hire and which is actually occupied by the proprietor as his residence.

"(c) Nothing in this section shall be construed so as to deter any law enforcement officer from lawfully carrying out the duties of his office; and no law enforcement officer shall be considered to be in violation of this section for lawfully carrying out the duties of his office or lawfully enforcing ordinances and laws of the United States, the District of Columbia, any of the several States, or any political subdivision of a State. For purposes of the preceding sentence, the term 'law enforcement officer' means any officer of the United States, the District of Columbia, a State, or political subdivision of a State, who is empowered by law to conduct investigations of, or make arrests because of, offenses against the United States, the District of Columbia, a State, or a political subdivision of a State."

(b) Nothing contained in this section shall apply to or affect activities under title VIII of this Act.

(c) The provisions of this section shall not apply to acts or omissions on the part of law enforcement officers, members of the National Guard, as defined in sectin 101 (9) of title 10, United States Code, members of the organized militia of any State or the District of Columbia, not covered by such section 101(9), or members of the Armed Forces of the United States, who are engaged in suppressing a riot or civil disturbance or restoring law and order during a riot or civil disturbance.

Sec. 102. The analysis of chapter 13 of title 18 of the United States Code is amended by adding at the end thereof the following:

"245. *Federally protected activities.*"

Sec. 103. (a) Section 241 of title 18, United States Code, is amended by striking out the final paragraph thereof and substituting the following:

"They shall be fined not more than $10,000 or imprisoned not more than ten years, or both; and if death results, they shall be subject to imprisonment for any term of years or for life."

(b) Section 242 of title 18, United States Code, is amended by striking out the period at the end thereof and adding the following: "; and if death results shall be subject to imprisonment for any term of years or for life."

(c) Subsections (a) and (c) of section 12 of the Voting Rights Act of 1965 (79 Stat. 443, 444) are amended by striking out the words "or (b)" following the words "11(a)".

Sec. 104. (a) Title 18 of the United States Code is amended by inserting immediately after chapter 101 thereof, the following new chapter:

"CHAPTER 102.—RIOTS

"Sec.
"2101. Riots.
"2102. Definitions.

"§ 2101. Riots.

"(a)(1) Whoever travels in interstate or foreign commerce or uses any facility of interstate or foreign commerce, including, but not limited to, the mail, telegraph, telephone, radio, or television, with intent—

"(A) to incite a riot; or

"(B) to organize, promote, encourage, participate in, or carry on a riot; or

"(C) to commit any act of violence in furtherance of a riot; or

"(D) to aid or abet any person in inciting or participating in or carrying on a riot or committing any act of violence in furtherance of a riot;

and who either during the course of any such travel or use or thereafter performs or attempts to perform any other overt act for any purpose specified in subparagraph (A), (B), (C), or (D) of this paragraph—

"Shall be fined not more than $10,000, or imprisoned not more than five years, or both.

"(b) In any prosecution under this section, proof that a defendant engaged or attempted to engage in one or more of the overt acts described in subparagraph (A), (B), (C), or (D) of paragraph (1) of subsection (a) and (1) has traveled in interstate or foreign commerce, or (2) has use of or used any facility of interstate or foreign commerce, including but not limited to, mail, telegraph, telephone, radio, or television, to communicate with or broadcast to any person or group of persons prior to such overt acts, such travel or use shall be admissible proof to establish that such defendant traveled in or used such facility of interstate or foreign commerce.

"(c) A judgment of conviction or acquittal on the merits under the laws of any State shall be a bar to any prosecution hereunder for the same act or acts.

"(d) Whenever, in the opinion of the Attorney General or of the appropriate officer of the Department of Justice charged by law or under the instructions of the Attorney General with authority to act, any person shall have violated this chapter, the Department shall proceed as speedily as possible with a prosecution of such person hereunder and with any appeal which may lie from any decision adverse to the Government resulting from such prosecution; or in the alternative shall report in writing, to the respective Houses of the Congress, the Department's reason for not so proceeding.

"(e) Nothing contained in this section shall be construed to make it unlawful for any person to travel in, or use any facility of, interstate or foreign commerce for the purpose of pursuing the legitimate objectives of organized labor, through orderly and lawful means.

"(f) Nothing in this section shall be construed as indicating an intent on the part of Congress to prevent any State, any possession or Commonwealth of the United States, or the District of Columbia, from exercising jurisdiction over any offense over which it would have jurisdiction in the absence of this section; nor shall anything in this section be construed as depriving State and local law enforcement authorities of responsibility for prosecuting acts that may be violations of this section and that are violations of State and local law.

"§ 2102. Definitions

"(a) As used in this chapter, the term 'riot' means a public disturbance involving (1) an act or acts of violence by one or more persons part of an assemblage of three or more persons, which act or acts shall constitute a clear and present danger of, or shall result in, damage or injury to the property of any other person or to the person of any other individual or (2) a threat or threats of the commission of an act or acts of violence by one or more persons part of an assemblage of three or more persons having, individually or collectively, the ability of immediate execution of such threat or threats, where the performance of the threatened act or acts of violence would constitute a clear and present danger of, or would result in, damage or injury to the property of any other person or to the person of any other individual.

"(b) As used in this chapter, the term 'to incite a riot', or 'to organize, promote, encourage, participate in, or carry on a riot', includes, but is not limited to, urging or instigating other persons to riot, but shall not be deemed to mean the mere oral or written (1) advocacy of ideas or (2) expression of belief, not involving advocacy of any act or acts of violence or assertion of the rightness of, or the right to commit, any such act or acts."

(b) The table of contents to "PART I.—CRIMES" of title 18, United States Code, is amended by inserting after the following chapter reference:
"101. Records and reports _____2071"
a new chapter reference as follows:
"102. Riots _____2101".

*   *   *   *

TITLE VIII
FAIR HOUSING

Sec. 801. It is the policy of the United States to provide, within constitutional limitations, for fair housing throughout the United States.

Definitions

Sec. 802. As used in this title—

(a) "Secretary" means the Secretary of Housing and Urban Development.

(b) "Dwelling" means any building, structure, or portion thereof which is occupied as, or designed or intended for occupancy as, a residence by one or more families, and any vacant land which is offered for sale or lease for the construction or location thereon of any such building, structure, or portion thereof.

(c) "Family" includes a single individual.

(d) "Person" includes one or more individuals, corporations, partnerships, associations, labor organizations, legal representatives, mutual companies, joint-stock companies, trusts, unincorporated organizations, trustees, trustees in bankruptcy, receivers, and fiduciaries.

(e) "To rent" includes to lease, to sublease, to let and otherwise to grant for a consideration the right to occupy premises not owned by the occupant.

(f) "Discriminatory housing practice" means an act that is unlawful under section 804, 805, or 806.

(g) "State" means any of the several States, the District of Columbia, the Commonwealth of Puerto Rico, or any of the territories and possessions of the United States.

Effective Dates of Certain Prohibitions

Sec. 803. (a) Subject to the provisions of subsection (b) and section 807, the prohibitions against discrimination in the sale or rental of housing set forth in section 804 shall apply:

(1) Upon enactment of this title, to—

(A) dwellings owned or operated by the Federal Government;

(B) dwellings provided in whole or in part with the aid of loans, advances, grants, or contributions made by the Federal Government, under agreements entered into after November 20, 1962, unless payment due thereon has been made in full prior to the date of enactment of this title;

(C) dwellings provided in whole or in part by loans insured, guaranteed, or otherwise secured by the credit of the Federal Government, under agreements entered into after November 20, 1962, unless payment thereon has been made in full prior to the date of enactment of this title: *Provided,* That nothing contained in subparagraphs (B) and (C) of this subsection shall be applicable to dwellings solely by virtue of the fact that they are subject to mortgages held by an FDIC or FSLIC institution; and

(D) dwellings provided by the development or the redevelopment of real property purchased, rented, or otherwise obtained from a State or local public agency receiving Federal financial assistance for slum clearance or urban renewal with respect to such real property under loan or grant contracts entered into after November 20, 1962.

(2) After December 31, 1968, to all dwellings covered by paragraph (1) and to all other dwellings except as exempted by subsection (b).

(b) Nothing in section 804 (other than subsection (c)) shall apply to—

(1) any single-family house sold or rented by an owner: *Provided,* That such private individual owner does not own more than three such single-family houses at any one time: *Provided further,* That in the case of the sale of any such single-family house by a private individual owner not residing in such house at the time of such sale or who was not the most recent resident of such house prior to such sale, the exemption granted by this subsection shall apply only with respect to one such sale within any twenty-four month period: *Provided further,* That such bona fide private individual owner does not own any interest in, nor is there owned or reserved on his behalf, under any express or voluntary agreement, title to or any right to all or a portion of the proceeds from the sale or rental of, more than three such single-family houses at any one time: *Provided further,* That after December 31, 1969, the sale or rental of any such single-family house shall be excepted from the application of this title only if such house is sold or rented (A) without the use in any manner of the sales or rental facilities or the sales or rental services of any real estate broker, agent, or salesman, or of such facilities or services of any person in the business of selling or renting dwellings, or of any employee or agent of any such broker, agent, salesman, or person and (B) without the publi-

cation, posting or mailing, after notice, of any advertisement or written notice in violation of section 804(c) of this title; but nothing in this proviso shall prohibit the use of attorneys, escrow agents, abstractors, title companies, and other such professional assistance as necessary to perfect or transfer the title, or

(2) rooms or units in dwellings containing living quarters occupied or intended to be occupied by no more than four families living independently of each other, if the owner actually maintains and occupies one of such living quarters as his residence.

(c) For the purposes of subsection (b), a person shall be deemed to be in the business of selling or renting dwellings if—

(1) he has, within the preceding twelve months, participated as principal in three or more transactions involving the sale or rental of any dwelling or any interest therein, or

(2) he has, within the preceding twelve months, participated as agent, other than in the sale of his own personal residence in providing sales or rental facilities or sales or rental services in two or more transactions involving the sale or rental of any dwelling or any interest therein, or

(3) he is the owner of any dwelling designed or intended for occupancy by, or occupied by, five or more families.

Discrimination in the Sale or Rental of Housing

Sec. 804. As made applicable by section 803 and except as exempted by sections 803(b) and 807, it shall be unlawful—

(a) To refuse to sell or rent after the making of a bona fide offer, or to refuse to negotiate for the sale or rental of, or otherwise make unavailable or deny, a dwelling to any person because of race, color, religion, or national origin.

(b) To discriminate against any person in the terms, conditions, or privileges of sale or rental of a dwelling, or in the provision of services or facilities in connection therewith, because of race, color, religion, or national origin.

(c) To make, print, or publish, or cause to be made, printed, or published any notice, statement, or advertisement, with respect to the sale or rental of a dwelling that indicates any preference, limitation, or discrimination based on race, color, religion, or national origin, or an intention to make any such preference, limitation, or discrimination.

(d) To represent to any person because of race, color, religion, or national origin that any dwelling is not available for inspection, sale, or rental when such dwelling is in fact so available.

(e) For profit, to induce or attempt to induce any person to sell or rent any dwelling by representations regarding the entry or prospective entry into the neighborhood of a person or persons of a particular race, color, religion, or national origin.

Discrimination in the Financing of Housing

Sec. 805. After December 31, 1968, it shall be unlawful for any bank, building and loan association, insurance company or other corporation, association, firm or enterprise whose business consists in whole or in part in the making of commercial real estate loans, to deny a loan or other financial assistance to a person applying therefor for the purpose of purchasing, constructing, improving, repairing, or maintaining, a dwelling, or to discriminate against him in the fixing of the amount, interest rate, duration, or other terms or conditions of such loan or other financial assistance, because of the race, color, religion, or national origin of such person or of any person associated with him in connection with such loan or other financial assistance or the purposes of such loan or other financial assistance, or of the present or prospective owners, lessees, tenants, or occupants of the dwelling or dwellings in relation to which such loan or other financial assistance is to be made or given: *Provided,* That nothing contained in this section shall impair the scope or effectiveness of the exception contained in section 803(b).

Discrimination in the Provision of Brokerage Services

Sec. 806. After December 31, 1968, it shall be unlawful to deny any person access to or membership or participation in any multiple-listing service, real estate brokers' organization or other service, organization, or facility relating to the business of selling or renting dwellings, or to discriminate against him in the terms or conditions of such access, membership, or participation, on account of race, color, religion, or national origin.

Exemption

Sec. 807. Nothing in this title shall prohibit a religious organization, association, or society, or any nonprofit institution or organization operated, supervised or controlled by or in conjunction with a religious organization, association, or society, from limiting the sale, rental or occupancy of dwellings which it owns or operates for other than a commercial purpose to persons of the same religion, or from giving preference to such persons, unless membership in such religion is restricted on account of race, color, or national origin. Nor shall anything in this title prohibit a private club not in fact open to the public, which as an incident to its primary purpose or purposes provides lodgings which it owns or operates for other than a commercial purpose, from limiting the rental or occupancy of such lodgings to its members or from giving preference to its members.

Administration

Sec. 808. (a) The authority and responsibility for administering this Act shall be in the Secretary of Housing and Urban Development.

(b) The Department of Housing and Urban Development shall be provided an additional Assistant Secretary. The Department of Housing and Urban Development Act (Public Law 89-174, 79 Stat. 667) is hereby amended by—

(1) striking the word "four," in section 4(a) of said Act (79 Stat. 668; 5 U.S.C. 624b(a)) and substituting therefor "five,"; and

(2) striking the word "six," in section 7 of said Act (79 Stat. 669; 5 U.S.C. 624(c)) and substituting therefor "seven."

(c) The Secretary may delegate any of his functions, duties, and powers to employees of the Department of Housing and Urban Development or to boards of such employees, including functions, duties, and powers with respect to investigating, conciliating, hearing, determining, ordering, certifying, reporting, or otherwise acting as to any work, business, or matter under this title. The persons to whom such delegations are made with respect to hearing functions, duties, and powers shall be appointed and shall serve in the Department of Housing and Urban Development in compliance with sections 3105, 3344, 5362, and 7521 of title 5 of the United States Code. Insofar as possible, conciliation meetings shall be held in the cities or other localities where the discriminatory housing practices allegedly occurred. The Secretary shall by rule prescribe such rights of appeal from the decisions of his hearing examiners to other hearing examiners or to other officers in the Department, to boards of officers or to himself, as shall be appropriate and in accordance with law.

(d) All executive departments and agencies shall administer their programs and activities relating to housing and urban development in a manner affirmatively to further the purposes of this title and shall cooperate with the Secretary to further such purposes.

(e) The Secretary of Housing and Urban Development shall—

(1) make studies with respect to the nature and extent of discriminatory housing practices in representative communities, urban, suburban, and rural, throughout the United States;

(2) publish and disseminate reports, recommendations, and information derived from such studies;

(3) cooperate with and render technical assistance to Federal, State, local, and other public or private agencies, organizations, and institutions which are formulating or carrying on programs to prevent or eliminate discriminatory housing practices;

(4) cooperate with and render such technical and other assistance to the Community Relations Service as may be appropriate to further its activities in preventing or eliminating discriminatory housing practices; and

(5) administer the programs and activities relating to housing and urban development in a manner affirmatively to further the policies of this title.

Education and Conciliation

Sec. 809. Immediately after the enactment of this title the Secretary shall commence such educational and conciliatory activities as in his judgment will further the purposes of this title. He shall call conferences of persons in the housing industry and other interested parties to acquaint them with the provisions of this title and his suggested means of implementing it, and shall endeavor with their advice to work out programs of voluntary compliance and of enforcement. He may pay per diem, travel, and transportation expenses for persons attending such conferences as provided in section 5703 of title 5 of the United States Code. He shall consult with State and local officials and other interested parties to learn the extent, if any, to which housing discrimination exists in their State or locality, and whether and how State or local enforcemen programs might be utilized to combat such discrimination in connection with or in place of, the Secretary's enforcement of this title. The Secretary shall issue reports on such conferences and consultations as he deems appropriate.

Enforcement

Sec. 810, (a) Any person who claims to have been injured by a discriminatory housing practice or who believes that he will be irrevocably injured by a discriminatory housing practice that is about to occur (hereafter "person aggrieved") may file a complaint with the Secretary. Complaints shall be in writing and shall contain such information and be in such form as the Secretary requires. Upon receipt of such a complaint the Secretary shall furnish a copy of the same to the person or persons who allegedly committed or are about to commit the alleged discriminatory housing practice. Within thirty days after receiving a complaint, or within thirty days after the expiration of any period of reference under subsection (c), the Secretary shall investigate the complaint and give notice in writing to the person aggrieved whether he intends to resolve it. If the Secretary decides to resolve the complaint, he shall proceed to try to eliminate or correct the alleged discriminatory housing practice by informal methods of conference, conciliation, and persuasion. Nothing said or done in the course of such informal endeavors may be made public or used as evidence in a subsequent proceeding under this title without the written consent of the persons concerned. Any employee of the Secretary who shall make public any information in violation of this provision shall be deemed guilty of a misdemeanor and upon conviction thereof shall be fined not more than $1,000 or imprisoned not more than one year.

(b) A complaint under subsection (a) shall be filed within one hundred and eighty days after the alleged discriminatory housing practice occured. Complaints shall be in writing and shall state the facts upon which the allegations of a discriminatory housing practice are based. Complaints may be reasonably and fairly amended at any time. A respondent may file an answer to the complaint against him and with the leave of the Secretary, which shall be granted whenever it would be reasonable and fair to do so, may amend his answer at any time. Both complaints and answers shall be verified.

(c) Wherever a State or local fair housing law provides rights and remedies for alleged discriminatory housing practices which are substantially equivalent to the rights and remedies provided in this title, the Secretary shall notify the appropriate State or local agency of any complaint filed under this title which appears to constitute a violation of such State or local fair housing law, and the Secretary shall take no further action with respect to such complaint if the appropriate State or local law enforcement official has, within thirty days from the date the alleged offense has been brought to his attention, commenced proceedings in the matter, or, having done so, carries forward such proceedings with reasonable promptness. In no event shall the Secretary take further action unless he certifies that in his judgment, under the circumstances of the particular case, the protection of the rights of the parties or the interests of justice require such action.

(d) If within thirty days after a complaint is filed with the Secretary or within thirty days after expiration of any period of reference under subsection (c), the Secretary has been unable to obtain voluntary compliance with this title, the person aggrieved may, within thirty days thereafter, commence a civil action in any appropriate United States district court, against the respondent named in the complaint, to enforce the rights granted or protected by this title, insofar as such rights relate to the subject of the complaint: *Provided,* That no such civil action may be brought in any United States district court if the person aggrieved has a judicial remedy under a State or local fair housing law which provides rights and remedies for alleged discriminatory housing practices which are substantially equivalent to the rights and remedies provided in this title. Such actions may be brought without regard to the amount in controversy in any United States district court for the district in which the discriminatory housing practice is alleged to have occurred or be about to occur or in which the respondent resides or transacts business. If the court finds that a discriminatory housing practice has occurred or is about to occur, the court may, subject to the provisions of section 812, enjoin the respondent from engaging in such practice or order such affirmative action as may be appropriate.

(e) In any proceeding brought pursuant to this section, the burden of proof shall be on the complainant.

(f) Whenever an action filed by an individual, in either Federal or State court, pursuant to this section or section 812, shall come to trial the Secretary shall immediately terminate all efforts to obtain voluntary compliance.

Investigations; Subpenas; Giving of Evidence

Sec. 811. (a) In conducting an investigation the Secretary shall have access at all reasonable times to premises, records, documents, individuals, and other evidence or possible sources of evidence and may examine, record, and copy such materials and take and record the testimony or statements of such persons as are reasonably necessary for the furtherance of the investigation: *Provided, however,* That the Secretary first complies with the provisions of the Fourth Amendment relating to unreasonable searches and seizures. The Secretary may issue subpenas to compel his access to or the production of such materials, or the appearance of such persons, and may issue interrogatories to a respondent, to the same extent and subject to the same limitations as would apply if the subpenas or interrogatories were issued or served in aid of a civil action in the United States district court for the district in which the investigation is taking place. The Secretary may administer oaths.

(b) Upon written application to the Secretary, a respondent shall be entitled to the issuance of a reasonable number of subpenas by and in the name of the Secretary to the same extent and subject to the same limitations as subpenas issued by the Secretary himself. Subpenas issued at the request of a respondent shall show on their face the name and address of such respondent and shall state that they were issued at his request.

(c) Witnesses summoned by subpena of the Secretary shall be entitled to the same witness and mileage fees as are witnesses in proceedings in United States district courts. Fees payable to a witness summoned by a subpena issued at the request of a respondent shall be paid by him.

(d) Within five days after service of a subpena upon any person, such person may petition the Secretary to revoke or modify the subpena. The Secretary shall grant the petition if he finds that the subpena requires appearance or attendance at an unreasonable time or place, that it requires production of evidence which does not relate to any matter under investigation, that it does not describe with sufficient particularity the evidence to be produced, that compliance would be unduly onerous, or for other good reason.

(e) In case of contumacy or refusal to obey a subpena, the Secretary or other person at whose request it was issued may petition for its enforcement in the United States district court for the district in which the person to whom the subpena was addressed resides, was served, or transacts business.

(f) Any person who willfully fails or neglects to attend and testify or to answer any lawful inquiry or to produce records, documents, or other evidence, if in his power to do so in obedience to the subpena or lawful order of the Secretary, shall be fined not more than $1,000 or imprisoned not more than one year, or both. Any person who, with intent thereby to mislead the Secretary, shall make or cause to be made any false entry or statement of fact in any report, account, record, or other document submitted to the Secretary pursuant to his subpena or other order, or shall willfully neglect or fail to make or cause to be made full, true, and correct entries in such reports, accounts, records, or other documents, or shall willfully mutilate, alter, or by any other means falsify any documentary evidence, shall be fined not more than $1,000 or imprisoned not more than one year, or both.

(g) The Attorney General shall conduct all litigation in which the Secretary participates as a party or as amicus pursuant to this Act.

Enforcement By Private Persons

Sec. 812. (a) The rights granted by sections 803, 804, 805, and 806 may be enforced by civil actions in appropriate United States district courts without regard to the amount in controversy and in appropriate State or local courts of general jurisdiction. A civil action shall be commenced within one hundred and eighty days after the alleged discriminatory housing practice occurred: *Provided, however,* That the court shall continue such civil case brought pursuant to this section or section 810(d) from time to time before bringing it to trial if the court believes that the conciliation efforts of the Secretary or a State or local agency are likely to result in satisfactory settlement of the discriminatory housing practice complained of in the complaint made to the Secretary or to the local or State agency and which practice forms the basis for the action in court: *And provided, however,* That any sale, encumbrance, or rental consummated prior to the issuance of any court order issued under the authority of this Act, and involving a bona fide purchaser, encumbrancer, or tenant without actual notice of the existence of the filing of a complaint or civil action under the provisions of this Act shall not be affected.

(b) Upon application by the plaintiff and in such circumstances as the court may deem just, a court of the United States in which a civil action under this section has been brought may appoint an attorney for the plaintiff and may authorize the commencement of a civil action upon proper showing without the payment of fees, costs, or security. A court of a State or subdivision thereof may do likewise to the extent not inconsistent with the law or procedures of the State or subdivision.

(c) The court may grant as relief, as it deems appropriate, any permanent or temporary injunction, temporary restraining order, or other order, and may award to the plaintiff actual damages and not more than $1,000 punitive damages, together with court costs and reasonable attorney fees in the case of a prevailing plaintiff: *Provided,* That the said plaintiff in the opinion of the court is not financially able to assume said attorney's fees.

Enforcement By The Attorney General

Sec. 813. (a) Whenever the Attorney General has reasonable cause to believe that any person or group of persons is engaged in a pattern or practice of resistance to the full enjoyment of any of the rights granted by this title, or that any group of persons has been denied any of the rights granted by this title and such denial raises an issue of general public importance, he may bring a civil action in any appropriate United States district court by filing with it a complaint setting forth the facts and requesting such preventive relief, including an application for a permanent or temporary injunction, restraining order, or other order against the person or persons responsible for such pattern or practice or denial of rights, as he deems necessary to insure the full enjoyment of the rights granted by this title.

Expedition of Proceedings

Sec. 814. Any court in which a proceeding is instituted under section 812 or 813 of this title shall assign the case for hearing at the earliest practicable date and cause the case to be in every way expedited.

Effect on State Laws

Sec. 815. Nothing in this title shall be construed to invalidate or limit any law of a State or political subdivision of a State, or of any other jurisdiction in which this title shall be effective, that grants, guarantees, or protects the same rights as are granted by this title; but any law of a State, a political subdivision, or other such jurisdiction that purports to require or permit any action that would be a discriminatory housing practice under this title shall to that extent be invalid.

Cooperation with State and Local Agencies Administering Fair Housing Laws

Sec. 816. The Secretary may cooperate with State and local agencies charged with the administration of State and local fair housing laws and, with the consent of such agencies, utilize the services of such agencies and their employees and, notwithstanding any other provision of law, may reimburse such agencies and their employees for services rendered to assist him in carrying out this title. In furtherance of such cooperative efforts, the Secretary may enter into written agreements with such State or local agencies. All agreements and terminations thereof shall be published in the Federal Register.

Interference, Coercion, or Intimidation

Sec. 817. It shall be unlawful to coerce, intimidate, threaten, or interfere with any person in the exercise or enjoyment of, or on account of his having exercised or enjoyed, or on account of his having aided or encouraged any other person in the exercise or enjoyment of, any right granted or protected by section 803, 804, 805, or 806. This section may be enforced by appropriate civil action.

Appropriations

Sec. 818. There are hereby authorized to be appropriated such sums as are necessary to carry out the purposes of this title.

Separability of Provisions

Sec. 819. If any provision of this title or the application thereof to any person or circumstances is held invalid, the remainder of the title and the application of the provision to other persons not similarly situated or to other circumstances shall not be affected thereby.

TITLE IX
PREVENTION OF INTIMIDATION IN FAIR HOUSING CASES

Sec. 901. Whoever, whether or not acting under color of law, by force or threat of force willfully injures, intimidates or interferes with, or attempts to injure, intimidate or interfere with—

(a) any person because of his race, color, religion or national origin and because he is or has been selling, purchasing, renting, financing, occupying, or contracting or negotiating for the sale, purchase, rental, financing or occupation of any dwelling, or applying for or participating in any service, organization, or facility relating to the business of selling or renting dwellings; or

(b) any person because he is or has been, or in order to intimidate such person or any other person or any class of persons from—

(1) participating, without discrimination on account of race, color, religion or national origin, in any of the activities, services, organizations or facilities described in subsection 901(a); or

(2) affording another person or class of persons opportunity or protection so to participate; or

(c) any citizen because he is or has been, or in order to discourage such citizen or any other citizen from lawfully aiding or encouraging other persons to participate, without discrimination on account of race, color, religion or national origin, in any of the activities, services, organizations or facilities described in subsection 901(a), or participating lawfully in speech or peaceful assembly opposing any denial of the opportunity to so participate—

shall be fined not more than $1,000, or imprisoned not more than one year, or both; and if bodily injury results shall be fined not more than $10,000, or imprisoned not more than ten years, or both; and if death results shall be subject to imprisonment for any term of years or for life.

TITLE X
CIVIL OBEDIENCE

Short Title

Sec. 1001. This title may be cited as the "Civil Obedience Act of 1968".

Criminal Penalties for Acts Committed in Civil Disorders

Sec. 1002. (a) Title 18, United States Code, is amended by inserting after chaper 11 thereof the following new chapter:

"CHAPTER 12.—CIVIL DISORDERS

"Sec.
"231. Civil disorders.
"232. Definitions.
"233. Preemption.

"§ 231. Civil Disorders

"(a)(1) Whoever teaches or demonstrates to any other person the use, application, or making of any firearm or explosive or incendiary device, or technique capable of causing injury or death to persons, knowing or having reason to know or intending that the same will be unlawfully employed for use in, or in furtherance of, a civil disorder which may in any way or degree obstruct, delay, or adversely affect commerce or the movement of any article or commodity in commerce or the conduct or performance of any federally protected function; or

"(2) Whoever transports or manufactures for transportation in commerce any firearm, or explosive or incendiary device, knowing or having reason to know or intending that the same will be used unlawfully in furtherance of a civil disorder; or

"(3) Whoever commits or attempts to commit any act to obstruct, impede, or interfere with any fireman or law enforcement officer lawfully engaged in the lawful performance of his official duties incident to and during the commission of a civil disorder which in any way or degree obstructs, delays, or adversely affects commerce or the movement of any article or commodity in commerce or the conduct or performance of any federally protected function—

"Shall be fined not more than $10,000 or imprisoned not more than five years, or both.

"(b) Nothing contained in this section shall make unlawful any act of any law enforcement officer which is performed in the lawful performance of his official duties.

"§ 232. Definitions

"For purposes of this chapter:

"(1) The term 'civil disorder' means any public disturbance involving acts of violence by assemblages of three or more persons, which causes an immediate danger of or results in damage or injury to the property or person of any other individual.

"(2) The term 'commerce' means commerce (A) between any State or the District of Columbia and any place outside thereof; (B) between points within any State or the District of Columbia, but through any place outside thereof; or (C) wholly within the District of Columbia.

"(3) The term 'federally protected function' means any function, operation, or action carried out, under the laws of the United States, by any department, agency, or instrumentality of the United States or by an officer or employee thereof; and such term shall specifically include, but not be limited to, the collection and distribution of the United States mails.

"(4) The term 'firearm' means any weapon which is designed to or may readily be converted to expel any projectile by the action of an explosive; or the frame or receiver of any such weapon.

"(5) The term 'explosive or incendiary device' means (A) dynamite and all other forms of high explosives, (B) any explosive bomb, grenade, missile, or similar device, and (C) any incendiary bomb or grenade, fire bomb, or similar device, including any device which (i) consists of or includes a breakable container including a flammable liquid or compound, and a wick composed of any material which, when ignited, is capable of igniting such flammable liquid or compound, and (ii) can be carried or thrown by one individual acting alone.

"(6) The term 'fireman' means any member of a fire department (including a volunteer fire department) of any State, any political subdivision of a State, or the District of Columbia.

"(7) The term 'law enforcement officer' means any officer or employee of the United States, any State, any political subdivision of a State, or the District of Columbia, while engaged in the enforcement or prosecution of any of the criminal laws of the United States, a State, any political subdivision of a State, or the District of Columbia; and such term shall specifically include, but shall not be limited to, members of the National Guard, as defined in section 101 (9) of title 10, United States Code, members of the organized militia of any State, or territory of the United States, the Commonwealth of Puerto Rico, or the District of Columbia, not included within the definition of National Guard as defined by such section 101(9), and members of the Armed Forces of the United States, while engaged in suppressing acts of violence or restoring law and order during a civil disorder.

"§ 233. *Preemption*

"Nothing contained in this chapter shall be construed as indicating an intent on the part of Congress to occupy the field in which any provisions of the chapter operate to the exclusion of State or local laws on the same subject matter, nor shall any provision of this chapter be construed to invalidate any provision of State law unless such provision is inconsistent with any of the purposes of this chapter or any provision thereof."

(b) The table of contents to "PART I.—CRIMES" of title 18, United States Code, is amended by inserting after

"11. Bribery and graft .... 211"

a new chapter reference as follows:

"12. Civil disorders .... 231".

Selected Bibliography

GENERAL READING

Belfrage, Sally. *Freedom Summer.* New York: Viking, 1965.

Brown, Claude. *Manchild in the Promised Land.* New York: Macmillan, 1965.

Carter, Robert L.; Kenyon, Dorothy; Marcuse, Peter and Miller, Loren. *Equality.* New York: Pantheon 1965.

Clark, Kenneth. *Dark Ghetto.* New York: Harper & Row, 1965.

Drake, St. Clair and Cayton, Horace R. *Black Metropolis.* New York: Harcourt Brace, 1945.

Dorman, Michael. *We Shall Overcome.* New York: Delacorte, 1964.

Hentoff, Nat. *The New Equality.* New York: Viking, 1964.

Holt, Len. *The Summer That Would Not End.* New York: Morrow, 1965.

Housing and Home Finance Agency. *Our Nonwhite Population and Its Housing.* July 1963.

Huie, William B. *Three Lives for Mississippi.* New York: Trident, 1965.

Lewis Anthony. *Portrait of a Decade.* New York: Random House, 1965.

Lord, Walter. *The Past That Would Not Die.* New York: Harper & Row, 1965.

Parsons, Talcott, and Clark, Kenneth. *The Negro American.* Boston: Houghton, Mifflin, 1966.

Roche, John P. *Quest For The Dream.* New York: Macmillan, 1963.

Silberman, Charles. *Crisis in Black and White.* New York: Random House 1964.

Silver, James W. *Mississippi: The Closed Society.* New York: Harcourt Brace, 1963.

Smith, Frank. *Congressman From Mississippi.* New York Pantheon, 1965.

United States Commission on Civil Rights Reports, Volumes 1-5, Washington, D.C., 1961.

Woodward, C. Vann. *The Strange Career of Jim Crow.* New York: Oxford, 1955.

EDUCATION

Blaustein, Albert P. and Ferguson, Clarence Clyde, Jr. *Desegregation and the Law.* New Brunswick: Rutgers University Press, 1957. Vintage edition, 1962.

Clark, Kenneth. *Prejudice and Your Child.* Boston: Beacon Press, 1955.

Coles, Robert. *The Desegregation of Southern Schools: A Psychiatric Study.* New York: Anti-defamation League of B'nai B'rith, 1963.

Equality of Educational Opportunity. Office of Education, United States Department of Health, Education, and Welfare, July 1966.

Giles, Harry. *The Integrated Classroom.* New York: Basic Books, 1959.

LAW AND GOVERNMENT

Friedman, Leon, Ed. *Southern Justice.* New York: Pantheon, 1965.

Gosnell, Harold F. *Negro Politicians.* Chicago: University of Chicago, 1965.

Kalven, Harry, Jr. *The Negro and the First Amendment.* Chicago: University of Chicago, 1965.

Kuntsler, William M. *Deep in My Heart.* New York: Morrow, 1966.

Marshall, Burke. *Federalism and Civil Rights.* New York: Columbia, 1964.

Miller, Loren. *The Petitioners: The Story of the Supreme Court and the Negro.* New York: Pantheon, 1965.

Sovern, Michael. *Legal Restraints on Racial Discrimination in Employment.* New York: 20th Century Fund, 1966.

Peltason, J. W. *58 Lonely Men.* New York: Harcourt Brace, 1961.